✦ WEST OF SLAVERY ⤫

⇥ WEST OF ⇤
SLAVERY

The Southern Dream of
a Transcontinental Empire

Kevin Waite

THE UNIVERSITY OF NORTH CAROLINA PRESS

CHAPEL HILL

Manufactured in the United States of America

Designed by April Leidig
Set in Kepler by Copperline Book Services, Inc.

The University of North Carolina Press has been a member
of the Green Press Initiative since 2003.

Cover illustration by Diego Rios

Library of Congress Cataloging-in-Publication Data
Names: Waite, Kevin (Historian), author.
Title: West of slavery : the Southern dream of a
transcontinental empire / Kevin Waite.
Other titles: David J. Weber series in the new borderlands history.
Description: Chapel Hill : University of North Carolina Press, [2021] |
Series: The David J. Weber series in the new borderlands history |
Includes bibliographical references and index.
Identifiers: LCCN 2020044309 | ISBN 9781469663180 (cloth ; alk. paper) |
ISBN 9781469663197 (paperback ; alk. paper) | ISBN 9781469663203 (ebook)
Subjects: LCSH: Slavery—Southwestern States—History—19th century. |
African Americans—Southwestern States—Social conditions—19th century. |
Indians of North America—Southwestern States—Social conditions—19th
century. | Peonage—Southwestern States—History—19th century. |
Southwestern States—Politics and government—19th century. | Southwestern
States—Relations—Southern States. | Southern States—Relations—
Southwestern States. | United States—History—Civil War, 1861–1865.
Classification: LCC E449 .W155 2021 | DDC 306.3/62097909034—dc23
LC record available at https://lccn.loc.gov/2020044309

For Mom and Dad

CONTENTS

PART III

War and Reunion

———————

ILLUSTRATIONS

FIGURES

MAPS

ACKNOWLEDGMENTS

THIS IS A WELL-TRAVELED BOOK. While researching and writing it, I moved from coast to coast and then across the Atlantic, amassing intellectual debts at every stop along the way. Those debts can never be adequately repaid, but they're very gratefully acknowledged.

For as far back as I can remember, I've been guided by great teachers. The late Barbara Sheinkopf convinced a distractible sixth grader that literature could be more fun than kickball. Robert Farrar and Garine Zetlian kindled my love of history, while dozens of other teachers, coaches, and mentors at Poly cheerfully endured my adolescence. At Williams College, I had the great fortune of studying under Charles Dew. Now, as an advisor of undergraduate thesis students myself, I consistently find myself asking, "What would Dew do?" Charles's scholarship, generosity, and kindness place him in a league of his own. My Williams friends and I still speak of our experiences in Steve Fix's English classes in tones of reverential awe. He has the pedagogical ability to make Samuel Johnson thrilling and Thomas Pynchon comprehensible. At Cambridge, Peter Mandler provided direction and encouragement as I muddled through the history of sport and masculinity in Georgian-era English public schools.

The research that culminated in this book began at the University of Pennsylvania, under Steve Hahn's mentorship. More so than anyone else, Steve has shaped the way I approach the past. With humbling intellect and good humor, he guided this project in all the right ways. He encouraged me to read widely, think big, and pursue my intellectual interests as far as they would take me. Others at Penn were almost equally instrumental. I'm especially grateful to Kathy Peiss, Stephanie McCurry, Kathy Brown, and Dan Richter. As director of the McNeil Center and mentor to too many graduate students to count, Dan was unfailingly generous with what he had so little to spare: time. He made the McNeil Center a second home within Philadelphia.

A big family of fellow students at Penn and across Philadelphia ensured that the ups of grad school always outnumbered the downs. That noble list includes Holly Stephens, John Lee, Matthew Kruer, Sam Lacy, Robert Hegwood, Jessie Regunberg, Tommy Richards, Nora Slonimsky,

Jane Dinwoodie, Sarah Rodriguez, Alexis Broderick Neumann, Alexandra Montgomery, Evgenia Shnayder Shoop, Tina Irvine, Camille Suárez, Gloria Young, and Emma Teitelman. From our first seminar together, Roberto Saba has been a true friend and an inspiration. While researching, I spent a productive year at Stanford, thanks to the comradery and insights of Alex Stern, Andy Hamman, and Cameron Blevins.

I'm immensely fortunate to count Sally Gordon as a mentor, coauthor, and dear friend. Our collaborative project on Biddy Mason, a Georgia slave turned Los Angeles philanthropist and real estate entrepreneur, has been a continual source of joy these past two years—and a fitting complement to my work on this book. Thanks go to Lydia Medici and everyone else at the National Endowment for the Humanities for generously supporting our project.

Since 2016, I've had the great fortune to work and teach at Durham University. I still pinch myself. My colleagues' brilliance is matched only by their generosity. From the day I arrived, they made this Southern Californian feel right at home in northern England. There are too many friends to name here, but special mention is due to Jennifer Luff, Richard Huzzey, Eleanor Barraclough, John Henry Clay, Skye Montgomery, Tom Stammers, James Koranyi, Helen Foxhall Forbes, David Minto, Adrian Green, Jo Fox, Christian Liddy, Giles Gasper, Ana Dias, Ludmilla Jordanova, Stephen Taylor, and Matt Johnson (and also my godson, Aidan Johnson, honorary professor of firetruck studies, who's grown too quickly while I've been in London and Oxford on sabbatical). Sarah Davies has been a terrific and terrifically supportive head of department. Academics, of course, are hopelessly dependent on our colleagues in professional support roles. Fortunately for us, we've had the very best in Durham's history department: Imogen Barton, Audrey Bowron, Jasmine Baker-Sones, Lydia Price, Hannah Martin, Kelly Groundwater, and several new colleagues whom I'm just beginning to meet. Joining St. Cuthbert's Society has been one of the best decisions I've made at Durham, not least because it introduced me to the peerless Elizabeth Archibald.

"Peerless" is also a term I regularly apply to my students at Durham. On a daily basis, they astound me with their intellectual curiosity and remind me why teaching is rightfully at the heart of our mission as academics. A shout-out to everyone in my Special Subject, my undergraduate advisees, and my PhD students, Dan Doherty and Mark Markov. Teaching was made even more joyful by the assistance and enthusiasm of Catherine Bateson, Tom Ellis, and Liana Valerio.

As nearly everyone who's worked there can tell you, the Huntington Library is a scholar's paradise. The setting is stunning, of course, but it's the people that make the Huntington such a special place. More than anyone else, Bill Deverell deserves the credit (or the blame) for getting me into the business of history. When a cheeky high school student sauntered into his office with a few questions about the Civil War, Bill had no idea what was in store. A decade and a half later, he remains a tireless mentor, editor, and dear friend. The intellectually omnivorous Steve Hindle has offered crucial advice and support at every turn in my career. Peter Blodgett is the consummate curator. My thanks go also to Juan Gomez, Chris Bronson, and especially Hally Prater. Because of all these people, returning to the Huntington means coming home.

A host of generous, patient scholars greatly improved this manuscript through their close readings and constructive criticism. My deepest thanks are due to Ben Johnson, Andy Graybill, Heather Cox Richardson, Will Cowan, Elizabeth Logan, Andy Wood, Tom Hamilton, Adam Smith, and the two anonymous readers through the University of North Carolina Press. Jennifer Luff, Richard Huzzey, and Ari Kelman merit special mention here, not only for their detailed feedback on the full manuscript but also for their unflagging support over the years. Ari has been a guru to me since my days in graduate school, while Richard and Jennifer helped steer me past the common pitfalls of a new academic career. They are all models of collegiality.

Writing can be a lonely endeavor, but it rarely felt that way, thanks to the dozens of friends I met along the way. From the time this project was little more than a half-baked proposal, Stacey Smith has shared sources, corrected mistakes, and provided support in innumerable ways. Stacey, Elliott West, and I have been engaged in a long-running conversation over the significance of unfree labor in the nineteenth-century American West. We don't always agree, but that's half the fun and yet another reminder of why Elliott is so often regarded as one of the nicest people in the business— not to mention one of the very finest scholars. In addition to Elliott, several others generously shared sneak peeks of their soon-to-be published work for my enlightenment. My thanks go to Megan Kate Nelson, Alice Baumgartner, Cameron Blevins, and Michael Woods. For their insights and guidance, I'm also indebted to Greg Downs, Luke Harlow, Rachel Shelden, Bob Lockhart, Brian DeLay, Nick Guyatt, Rachel St. John, Tommy Richards, Michael Green, Aaron Sheehan-Dean, Gary Gallagher, Joan Waugh, Matt Karp, Sarah Gronningsater, Mike Magliari, Catherine Clinton, Seth Archer, Mary Ann Irwin, Dan Lynch, Jackie Broxton, David Gleeson, David Silkenat, Erik Mathisen, Patty Coleman, Josh Reid, Knute Berger, John Mack Faragher, and Matt Hulbert.

Generous grants from a number of research centers made this work possible. I'm particularly indebted to the librarians and archivists at those institutions: the University of Pennsylvania, the McNeil Center, the Huntington Library, the Bancroft Library, the Virginia Historical Society, the Massachusetts Historical Society, the Boston Athenaeum, the Library Company of Philadelphia, and the Historical Society of Pennsylvania. I finished the manuscript while on a yearlong visiting fellowship at the University of Oxford's Rothermere American Institute in the excellent company of Adam Smith, Raphaël Lambert, Kariann Yakota, Alice Kelly, Sonia Tycko, and Peter Mancall.

The good people at UNC Press took an early interest in the project. A special thanks goes to my editor, Chuck Grench, for his knowledge, direction, and untiring faith in the project. As he rode off into the sunset to enjoy a very well-deserved retirement, he placed me in the care of Debbie Gershenowitz, who skillfully stewarded the manuscript to completion. Dylan White, Mary Carley Caviness, and Cate Hodorowicz offered helpful feedback on matters of presentation and style, while Julie Bush performed meticulous copyediting. Andy Graybill and Ben Johnson are, simply put, the best series editors in the business. I've long admired the books in their David J. Weber Series, and now I understand why: they put a tremendous amount of time, effort, expertise, and humor into their editorial work. Thanks also go to Linda Greb for her beautiful maps, and to my friend Diego Rios for the striking cover illustration.

Portions of this book previously appeared in several articles. Chapters 2 and 3 expand on arguments introduced in "Jefferson Davis and Proslavery Visions of Empire in the Far West," *Journal of the Civil War Era* 6, no. 4 (December 2016), while some ideas in chapter 8 can be found in "The West and Reconstruction after the American Civil War," in *The Oxford Handbook on Reconstruction*, edited by Andrew L. Slap (New York: Oxford University Press, 2021); and "The 'Lost Cause' Goes West: Confederate Culture and Civil War Memory in California," *California History* 97, no. 1 (February 2020). I'm grateful to the publishers for allowing some of this material to be reproduced here.

My greatest debts are, of course, personal. Thelma Hernandez has been a second mother to me since I was three. I've known Pra Chandrasoma and Greg Steinbrecher for almost as long, and they remain the best friends a guy could have. For a lifetime of friendship and support, I thank Dave Spahn, Lyndon and Deborah Dodds, and my beloved Uncle Lee and Aunt Rhonda. With great love and affection, I remember Nana, Pa, Mary Ann Spahn, Karen Hayes, Mark Lanier, and Bruce Stephenson.

My wonderful in-laws, Monolita and Raman Mitra, have shown unconditional love and care for their *jamai*, even though he prompted a transatlantic move for their daughter. My brother-in-law, Rono, beats me in every competition and wager we make, but I still love the guy. I'm also deeply grateful to our grandparents, Khama, Ma, and my study buddy Nana.

Lindsay is the kindest, funniest, most generous, and unwaveringly supportive sister there is. And all she ever asked in return was to occasionally festoon her baby brother in costumes of her choosing. I apologize to my students, whose research presentations I flagrantly ignored as I was awaiting word of my niece's birth that happy Tuesday afternoon. Lindsay's daughter, Gigi, has been a brightly burning light of joy in all our lives.

I've been surrounded by great teachers all my life, but none better than my parents, Nancy and Les. This book is dedicated to them. Throughout my academic career and everything that came before, they have been my cheerleaders and my counselors, my advocates and my motivators. Truth be told, I was a somewhat slow learner as a child, but their encouragement never ceased. And that has made all the difference.

My wife, Rumi, is the source of too many good things and warm feelings to possibly enumerate here. She's been with the book since the beginning, enduring a long period of transatlantic separation with characteristic grace and good cheer. This manuscript was completed amid the scary and surreal months of a global pandemic, and even then—especially then—her humor never faded and her high spirits rarely dimmed. In good times and in bad, she is my companion, my muse, and my heart. Because of her, every day is a new adventure, and life is infinitely sweet.

✦ WEST OF SLAVERY ✦

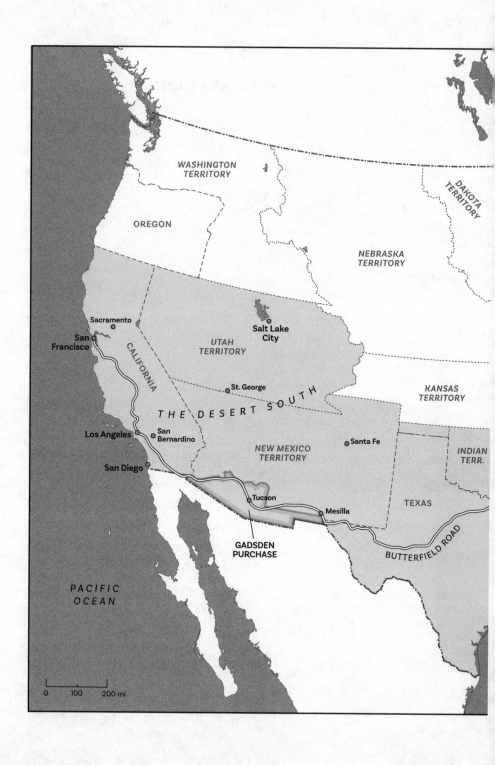

The Continental South

The Continental South

———— ◆◆◆ ————

A S THE NATION CAREENED toward civil war, a pair of curious tunes rang through the streets and saloons of Los Angeles. "We'll Hang Abe Lincoln to a Tree" and "We'll Drive the Bloody Tyrant from Our Dear Native Soil" were not composed in California, but they quickly found favor with the town's rebellious element in the spring of 1861. Through these songs, white Angelenos taunted the region's outnumbered Unionist population and gave voice to their deep-seated southern allegiances. Over the coming years, California's would-be rebels demonstrated their secessionist sympathies through an array of related activities. They paraded Confederate symbols through public spaces across the state; they cheered Jefferson Davis and his generals; they bullied federal soldiers stationed at military outposts; and they conspired, in ways big and small, to turn California against the United States. Hundreds of them aided the rebellion more directly by fleeing the state and enlisting in Confederate armies. Los Angeles furnished the only Confederate militia from a free state, a unit of eighty men commanded by the county's former undersheriff.[1] As one of the region's rare Unionists lamented, "The leading men of the county were for the Jeff Davis government first, last and all the time."[2]

Why did Los Angeles, a frontier town in a free state more than 2,500 miles from the Confederate capital, respond so enthusiastically to a slaveholder's rebellion? The answer to that question requires a long view of western history and the geopolitics of slavery. And it illuminates the surprising ways in which the South and West intersected, interlocked, and overlapped in the mid-nineteenth century, with profound repercussions for national development and, conversely, national dissolution. White Angelenos had no discernible tyrants to drive from their native soil in the spring of 1861, as they claimed in their rebel anthem. But they did express a deep sense of kinship, built over the preceding decade, with the slaveholders of the South.

Los Angeles was not an anomaly within the Far Southwest. Rather, its secessionist movement was an extreme manifestation of a proslavery ethos that had stretched across the entire region prior to the Civil War—from the territory of New Mexico to the shores of the Pacific. This was no historical accident. It was the product of a carefully constructed political coalition, emanating from the slave states and spreading westward after the close of the US-Mexico War in 1848. For the next decade and a half, slaveholders and their allies mobilized federal power to forge this coalition and extend their influence across the continent. They passed slave codes in New Mexico and Utah, sponsored separatist movements in Southern California and Arizona, orchestrated a territorial purchase from Mexico, built roads to facilitate the westward flow of southern migrants, monopolized patronage networks to empower proslavery allies, and even killed antislavery rivals. This was, wrote an observer from New Mexico, "a grand scheme of inter-communication and territorial expansion more vast and complicated than was ever dreamed of by Napoleon Bonaparte in his palmiest days of pride and power."[3]

Collectively, these efforts created what we might call the Continental South. Proslavery partisans transformed the southwest quarter of the nation—California, Arizona, New Mexico, and even parts of Utah—into an appendage of the slave states. Plantation slavery never took root in the region, as some hoped and others feared. But other coercive labor regimes, including the trade in captive Native Americans and the institution of debt peonage, flourished. And African American chattel slavery, while not economically central to the far western economy, was legally protected nonetheless. Not only an outlet for slavery, the Far West also provided southern partisans with a crucial base of support. Westerners—whether congressmen from California or territorial officials in New Mexico—threatened to tip the political scales in the South's favor, upsetting the precarious balancing act between a nation half slave and half free. In the process, they ignited some of the gravest crises of the nineteenth century.

How this transcontinental sphere of proslavery influence was created, how it was destroyed at the end of the Civil War, and how it reemerged from the ashes of that conflict—albeit in a modified and more modest form—is the subject of this book. In describing these developments, *West of Slavery* raises big questions about the violent processes of disunion and reunion in the United States. First, when slaveholders looked west, what did they see? Second, how did they incorporate these visions into an increasingly aggressive political and diplomatic program? And finally, how did that western program shape the causes, conduct, and consequences of the American Civil War?

The answers to these questions unfold across the three main sections of the book. Structurally, they move from South to West and from grand visions of empire to local struggles that gave substance to slaveholders' geopolitical ambitions. The first section faces west from slave country. It explores how southern powerbrokers imagined the far end of the continent and how they schemed, through a series of transportation projects, to bring this distant region into their political and commercial orbit. The second section inverts the perspective to face east from gold country and other far western locales.[4] It explains how residents in California, New Mexico, Arizona, and Utah embraced key parts of the proslavery agenda, triggering a wide-ranging crisis of the Union by 1861. The final section examines how the logic of westward expansion shaped Confederate grand strategy during the war and ultimately sowed the seeds for slavery's destruction. Yet elements of this transcontinental network outlived slavery itself. In the immediate postwar years, political ties between the South and West were reconstituted to fuel a national, rather than merely sectional, revolt against federal Reconstruction.

THE STRUGGLE OVER SLAVERY and its legacies played out on a transcontinental stage. As southerners reached west, they drew a diverse cast of characters—California miners, Mormon polygamists, Hispano lawmakers, Apache warriors, Arizona separatists, and enslaved African Americans—into a conflict over federal authority and the shape of the United States itself. *West of Slavery* reconstructs this sprawling, decades-long contest and thereby reframes the standard narrative of the Civil War era. In the process, it presents new ways of understanding America's slaveholders, the conflicts they unleashed, and the world they made.

These pages reveal an American master class more formidable and far-reaching than previously imagined. Historians, in numerous important works, have tracked slaveholders' expansionist projects in the Atlantic world. We now understand how American southerners, through diplomatic influence, commercial power, and direct assaults on foreign soil, extended their imperial agenda across this swath of the globe.[5] Yet planters' horizons could never be confined to a single ocean basin. While they operated primarily in an Atlantic world, slaveholders lusted after a transpacific dominion. "The Eastern World!" future Louisiana senator Judah Benjamin proclaimed in 1852. "Its commerce makes empires of the countries to which it flows, and when they are deprived of it they are empty bags, useless, valueless."[6] Convinced that the markets of Asia and its 600 million consumers promised a vast new frontier for their plantation economy, slaveholders devised a set of initiatives to harness the Pacific trade. They sought nothing less than a global web of cotton commerce, stretching from the docks of Liverpool in one direction to the trading houses of Canton in the other.

Slaveholders achieved some notable successes within the Pacific world. By the mid-1840s, they had extended the Monroe Doctrine to Hawaii and opened new Asian ports for slave-grown staples, securing cotton's place as the leading US export to China. They also waged a campaign to construct a transcontinental railroad through the Deep South and into California—what abolitionists ominously dubbed the "great slavery road." A Pacific railway, white southerners argued, would funnel their plantation goods across the continent and to the sea lanes beyond. Meanwhile, their political rivals advocated for lines across free soil, sparking a fifteen-year struggle over transcontinental infrastructure and Asian commerce. The Pacific—at least as it was envisioned by northern and southern expansionists—thus became a crucial theater in the sectional conflict. Although rising political tensions prevented either section from constructing a transcontinental railroad during the antebellum period, slaveholders achieved the next closest thing by fixing the nation's major overland mail road along a far southern route.

In pursuit of their Pacific fantasies, slaveholders built a transcontinental complex. The Overland Mail Road accelerated the migration of white southerners, who infiltrated the political and judicial machinery of the Far Southwest. Ironically, the free state of California became the linchpin of the Continental South. There, a southern-born minority seized power by 1850, dominating the state's patronage networks, legislative sessions, and judicial proceedings through the antebellum period. Immediately to the east, in the territory of New Mexico and what would become Arizona, white southern migrants and their allies followed a similar script to achieve local control. They wielded power, not only to legalize black chattel slavery across the territorial Southwest but to defend other forms of labor coercion as well, namely the trade in Native American captives and the institution of debt peonage.

While several important studies chart the proslavery trajectories of individual western states and territories, few scholars have situated these regional developments within the context of a national movement.[7] To understand the struggle over slavery in California, New Mexico, Arizona, or Utah requires such a framework. The slave South and the Far West came together through a far-flung network of agents, often acting in concert across the continent: revolutionaries from Texas, congressmen from California, cabinet secretaries from Mississippi and Tennessee, territorial officeholders in New Mexico, foreign ministers from South Carolina, writers from Louisiana, miners in Arizona, geographers from Virginia, and the list goes on.[8] Like any coalition, this one had its fissures and divergences. But it proved more extensive and durable than historians have yet recognized.[9]

The federal government—and more specifically, the executive branch—was the primary mechanism through which southerners extended their influence over the Far West. From 1853 to 1861, proslavery Democrats controlled the executive. Presidents Franklin Pierce and James Buchanan, although natives of free states, appointed slaveholding partisans to key cabinet positions, a gesture to the southern voters who secured their elections. Armed with the resources of the War Department and the Post Office Department, in particular, slaveholding secretaries directed major projects in the West to the benefit of the South. Democrats also used executive authority to fill the Far West with slaveholders and their allies. The president and his cabinet oversaw the appointment of hundreds of federal agents in California as well as all the major territorial officials within New Mexico and Utah. By the mid-1850s, the San Francisco Customs House was so crowded with southern-born appointees on federal sinecures that it became known as the "Virginia Poorhouse."[10] This tactical use of federal authority explains how white southern migrants in the Far Southwest, despite representing only a fraction of the region's total population, wielded a decisive influence over local policy. The political history of this region—and all the president's men who administered it—is a case study in minority rule.[11]

Slaveholders' western strategies seemingly clashed with their state-rights dogma.[12] For decades, southern ideologues like John C. Calhoun had croaked about the menace of federal power and the primacy of local government. Yet even supposed state-rights champions could make exceptions (often frequently) in the interest of slavery's expansion. An activist federal government, after all, was essential to southerners' transcontinental development projects. The Pacific railroad of their fantasies called for a vast outlay of federal resources, whether in the form of land grants, subsidies, or more direct financing. Even smaller projects, like mail roads across the Southwest, required substantial sums and an activist state. The budget for the Post Office Department ballooned under a slaveholder's watch as the government subsidized these western roads. Infrastructure, slave labor, and federal power—this was the planter prescription for westward expansion. Despite abolitionists' claims that an economy rooted in slavery would wither under its intrinsic inefficiencies, this vision proved remarkably durable and distinctly modern.[13]

What contemporaries called the "Slave Power" operated not just in Washington and through the foreign policy of the United States, as historians have ably demonstrated, but within territorial politics as well.[14] Indeed, it was on the peripheries of the nation that the combination of slaveholding influence and federal power came into stark relief.[15] A vast web of western legislators, jurists, journalists, and presidential appointees advanced the political program of the South, sounding alarm bells among antislavery activists. The "high-road to a slave empire," in the words of Abraham Lincoln, ran through these western territories.[16] The beginnings of that empire had been extended by local officials, who legalized slavery and protected other unfree labor regimes across the Far Southwest. Although Lincoln, among other Republicans, had a tendency to exaggerate planters' power, his underlying concerns were well-founded. Increasingly through the 1850s, the long arm of the South reached west, manipulating federal authority at the edges of the nation to shape the future direction of the United States.[17]

No monolithic conspiracy, however, guided southerners and their western allies. America's slaveholding regions (fifteen states, in addition to Indian Territory and the territories of the Far Southwest) were as diverse as they were expansive. And they contained an eclectic set of leaders, who often pursued conflicting regional agendas and feuded from competing parties: Democrats, Whigs, and Know-Nothings (though almost no Republicans). There were, in short, "many Souths" within the Continental South.[18] These divisions often dashed slaveholders' best laid plans. To an extent, therefore, this book is a study of failure—a catalog of dreams deferred, schemes interrupted, and plans forestalled—as well as an analysis of the overlooked triumphs of the self-described master class. These pages thus stress contingency as a key property of the long Civil War era.[19] Yet while white southerners often argued over tactics, they generally agreed on the overriding strategy: the extension of a proslavery commercial and political orbit.[20] The various projects of the Continental South—the negotiation of treaties, the routing of roads, the importation of enslaved laborers to the Pacific coast, the rewriting of local laws—emerged from this common aim.

The Continental South depended on a broad, if sometimes loose, coalition of allies who shared a commitment to slavery's long-term survival. Those alliances even crossed sectional fault lines. It was two northern-born presidents, after all, who lavished public offices on southern politicos and thus bolstered the proslavery agenda in its many manifestations.[21] And just as some northerners aided the planter class, certain influential southerners sought to block slavery's extension. Yet, as contemporary observers remarked, there was something unique about the way in which white southerners operated in the Far West, as opposed to migrants from other parts of the country. In antebellum accounts of California, for instance, "Southerner" was shorthand for someone with a partisan commitment to the slave states. A proslavery orientation was assumed in any white southern migrant, whether or not that individual owned slaves (and the majority did not).[22] This imprecise terminology reflects an important dynamic: when they moved west, white southerners often banded together to forge powerful political cliques, acting with a collective purpose that antislavery emigrants could rarely match.

These pages destabilize conventional understandings of slavery in the United States. Scholars have traditionally partitioned the history of American slavery into two discrete categories: a huge literature on African American bondage in the US South and, more recently, a growing body of work on the "other slavery," involving Native American captives and peon servants.[23] There are meaningful distinctions, to be sure, between forms of unfreedom in the nineteenth-century South and West. Yet antebellum slaveholders recognized the interdependence of these systems in ways that historians have not fully grasped.[24] The institution of debt peonage, white southerners realized, was the western flank in a vast network of unfree labor that buttressed the property rights of multiple master classes. An assault on one form of human property might erode another. Strip a New Mexican master of his right to discipline indebted mestizo laborers, for instance, and soon a Georgian planter may no longer wield the same degree of control over his enslaved African Americans. Slaveholders and their allies thus fought within Congress and the legislative capitals of the Southwest to preserve unfreedom in its various guises and locales. According to their logic, American slavery was not the "peculiar institution" of the South alone, as some claimed. It was a transcontinental regime.

Slaveholders triggered a multifront challenge to the United States by 1861. Although historians frequently cite the westward expansion of slavery as the driving issue that led to disunion, many fail to look beyond Bleeding Kansas. California's 1850 admission to the Union as a free state, some scholars suggest, effectively banished proslavery intrigue to the east of the Sierra Nevada or even the Rocky Mountains. In the most influential and significant studies of the sectional crisis, the trans-Mississippi West remains a land apart, entering the narrative only briefly, and usually as an abstraction in debates between easterners.[25] But for many antebellum Americans, the West's importance was concrete and immediate—and never more so than during the secession crisis. Separatist movements in Southern California and Arizona, as well as plans for a so-called Pacific republic, drew strength from the insurgency brewing in the slave South. Where one rebellion began and the other ended could be difficult to determine, especially from the perspective of beleaguered US authorities in the Far West. This was a continental crisis of the Union.[26]

Confederate grand strategy evolved from slaveholders' antebellum projects in the West. If the Far West is often absent from historical accounts of the sectional crisis, the same can no longer be said of the literature on the war itself. Thanks to a rich and growing body of work, we now know a great deal about how the Civil War unfolded beyond the major theaters in the eastern half of the country.[27] From the canyons of New Mexico to the shores of the Pacific, scholars have explored a series of far-flung plots and armed engagements.[28] Yet we understand far less about the deep-rooted geopolitical objectives that set western armies in motion.[29] By tracking a decade and a half of political struggles over the fate of the West, this book explains how slaveholders' antebellum visions shaped the conduct of the war itself. The Civil War in the Far West was the continuation, by military means, of a southern campaign to control the far end of the continent, dating to the late 1840s. From this perspective, the Confederate invasions of Arizona and New Mexico cannot be dismissed as errands into the wilderness. They were the bloody, if ultimately failed, climax to a tenacious dream.

It was during these four years of war that the southern dream of transcontinental expansion took its most overtly imperialist form. Yet not all elements of the slaveholding project for the West were themselves imperialist. Southerners' canny exploitation of patronage networks, for instance, were acts of political expansion, but not of empire, properly understood. Furthermore, the concept of the Continental South refers to a sphere of slaveholding influence, rather than a distinct imperial dominion. This book deploys the language of imperialism carefully—defined here as an expansionist action that deliberately infringes upon the sovereignty of another polity.[30] But this work also takes slaveholders at their word when they spoke of their emerging "empire" in the West or in the Pacific, which they did frequently.[31] Mexico, China, numerous Native nations, and eventually the United States itself became targets of this imperial agenda. From the early 1840s through the Civil War, southerners' imperial fantasies shifted in nature and scope—and sometimes competed internally—but nevertheless remained fixated on the promise of the West. Only with the Confederacy's collapse in 1865 would slaveholders' dreams of transcontinental empire finally die.

Yet even in the absence of chattel slavery, elements of the Continental South survived into the postwar period. California was again a safe haven for southerners and their allies within the Democratic fold. By exploiting white voters' anxieties over African Americans and Chinese immigrants, western Democrats revived their recently moribund party. California was the only free state that refused to ratify either of the major civil rights enactments of the Reconstruction era, the Fourteenth and Fifteenth Amendments. Meanwhile, white vigilantes, some of whom identified as western members of the Ku Klux Klan, assaulted Chinese workers in a Californian twist on the racial violence sweeping simultaneously across the South. In neighboring New Mexico, landholders challenged the emancipationist agenda of the Republican Party, retaining control over many of their debt peons for decades after the Thirteenth Amendment outlawed slavery and involuntary servitude. The revolt against federal Reconstruction, like the struggle over slavery that preceded it, stretched from one end of the country to the other.[32]

THE CONCEPT OF the Continental South rests on an apparent contradiction. Traditionally, the antebellum South has been defined as the region encompassing the fifteen slave states of the United States. The South extended as far west as the plains of Texas, according to this common understanding, but never reached across the arid soils of New Mexico, nor made a beachhead on the shores of California. *West of Slavery* blurs the conventional fault lines of America's nineteenth-century geography. By uncovering the Old South in unexpected places, beyond the cotton fields and sugar plantations that exemplify the region, this book brings together histories that are often divorced in the popular mind, with consequences for how we understand politics and race to this day.[33]

The West, as it exists in the American imagination (and even in much historical literature), lies far beyond the shadow of slavery. The most enduring images of the nineteenth-century frontier feature white pioneers and rugged individualists, leaving behind the political schisms that convulsed the eastern half of the country. From Thomas Jefferson, to Frederick Jackson Turner, to popular portrayals today, the West has come to symbolize fresh starts and forward progress. These pioneer tropes obscure the ways in which slavery and its legacies radiated outward from the old plantation districts, instead placing the source of the nation's racial problems squarely in the Southeast. The New Western History and careful studies of unfreedom within particular western locales have challenged many of these frontier fictions.[34] Yet we are in need of a wider optic. To appreciate the full scope of slavery and slaveholding power in nineteenth-century America requires histories that transcend regions, as did slaveholders themselves. How the South shaped the West and how the West empowered the South—this interplay was central to the making, unmaking, and remaking of the United States and its racial politics.

The preposition in this book's title is possessive. In other words, the Far

Southwest was a land *of* slavery and slaveholding influence; it was not free from it. West of the plantation districts, the American landscape faded into what we might call the Desert South. For more than a decade, this region—a vast swath of the map encompassing New Mexico, Arizona, southern Utah, and much of California—gave the South its transcontinental reach. Although the Desert South's arid soils provided poor nourishment for plantation agriculture, its leading residents nevertheless defended chattel bondage, alongside other forms of labor coercion. The view from the Desert South thus highlights slavery's flexibility and range. Aspiring masters adapted unfree labor regimes to a variety of locales and ensnared a diverse population of laborers. Captives—whether African American, Native American, or mestizos of Spanish ancestry—could be found laboring across the length of the continent. Their road to freedom did not run west.[35]

Yet in an era of rising antislavery activism, these labor regimes were vulnerable. Slavery's transcontinental terrain was a landscape of struggle—political, diplomatic, and military. From the Mexican War through the Civil War, the North and South increasingly divided over the shape of the West and its labor order. To check slaveholders' expansionist schemes, antislavery leaders advanced their own program for the region. They sought to overturn territorial slave codes, build a Pacific railroad across free soil, and break the hold of proslavery politicians along the southern corridor of the country. More often than not, they were outmaneuvered by proslavery partisans during the antebellum era. But antislavery northerners refused to relinquish the fight over the region. The two sections struggled over the Far Southwest because they saw in it a cipher for the fate of the nation. At stake was the balance of power in Congress, the future direction of American commerce, and, some would say, the very soul of the United States.

✦ PART I ✦

From Memphis to Canton

—————◆◆◆—————

→ CHAPTER ONE ←

The Southern Dream of a Pacific Empire

———— ◆◆◆ ————

THOMAS JEFFERSON lived in an Atlantic world, but he dreamed of a Pacific gateway. From his term as the nation's first secretary of state (1790–93) to his time as president (1801–9), Jefferson actively promoted transcontinental exploration in order to locate an American outlet to the Pacific trade. In the early 1790s, he placed his hopes in the French botanist and adventurer André Michaux, who was then preparing for an overland exploration of North America. Writing on behalf of fellow patrons, Jefferson instructed Michaux on "the chief objects" of the expedition: "to find the shortest & most convenient route of communication between the US. & the Pacific ocean, within the temperate latitudes."[1] Jefferson's interest in a more direct passageway to the Pacific trade was nothing new under the sun. It had been the fantasy of Columbus as he sailed from Spain in 1492, and the lure of Asian markets continued to propel the early European explorers of North America.[2] But with Jefferson and American independence, the search for a passage to India—or, as it were, China—took fuller form. Although diplomatic complications ultimately scuttled Michaux's mission, it was only a momentary setback in America's advance into the Pacific world.[3]

A decade after writing to Michaux, Jefferson launched another transcontinental enterprise, this time with considerably more success. His agents were Captain Meriwether Lewis and Lieutenant William Clark. Their mission, as Jefferson instructed, was to establish a deeper understanding of the continent's geography, especially its waterways, and to locate "the most direct & practicable communication" to the Pacific slope. While Jefferson had stressed the scientific value of Michaux's mission, his interests were now more commercial and diplomatic. Lewis and Clark were to scout for furs along the Pacific coast and determine whether trade could be conducted along this transcontinental route "more beneficially than by the circumnavigation now practiced." Upon "your arrival on that coast," the president continued, "endeavor to learn if there be any port within your reach."[4] A port, Jefferson recognized, would provide a source of contact with other maritime powers, as well as a future emporium for Asian trade. It was the lure of such outlets that would guide American policy makers through the coming decades.

Scholars have characterized the early eastern Pacific Ocean as something of a Yankee lake. To be sure, it was primarily New England traders who plied the waters off the coast of California in the early nineteenth century, transforming the tallow and hide trade into a lucrative American enterprise. Similarly, America's whaling ships sailed for the Pacific—what Herman Melville called the "tide-beating heart of earth"—almost exclusively from northeastern harbors.[5] Yet historians have been too quick to write slaveholders out of this story.[6] Although some southerners did cleave to strict constructionism and agrarian parochialism to dismiss the search for Pacific commerce, they were out of step with the leading thinkers of their region. Beginning with Jefferson and continuing through the antebellum period, southern statesmen pursued a geopolitical agenda that set the United States on the path toward continental and Pacific empire. America built much of that empire in three great lunges—the Louisiana Purchase, the annexation of Texas, and the seizure of New Mexico and California—each of which was orchestrated by a president from the slave states. Another southern-born executive advanced America's maritime interests by formalizing trade relations with China and protecting US access to the Hawaiian Islands.

Reckoning with southern visions of Pacific empire opens a new window into the worldview of American slaveholders. The caricature of the antebellum planter—as a backward-looking aristocrat clinging to musty copies of Walter Scott's chivalric romances and cloistered from the concerns of the modern world—has been upended by the past generation of historical scholarship. American slaveholders, we now know, looked well beyond the confines of their plantations and chased bold international ambitions, from commercial integration to outright conquest. The Caribbean Basin, scholars argue, was the object of their fantasies. Some slaveholders sought more territory for plantation agriculture by invading Cuba and Nicaragua; others hoped to strengthen slavery at home by protecting it across the Atlantic world.[7]

Yet for many white southerners, the most promising field of opportunity lay in the opposite direction. Asia beckoned. And so they devised a set of commercial initiatives in the belief that hundreds of millions of Chinese consumers would one day clothe themselves in slave-grown cotton products. The fact that few slaveholders understood the dynamics of the Asian markets after which they lusted did little to diminish their zeal for the purported value of the Far East. From the policy makers of the early republic to the thinkers and politicians of the antebellum period, slaveholders played a leading role in America's Pacific agenda.

They did so, at first, as nationalists. Long before regional identities hardened into sectional rivalries, southern statesmen, like their northern counterparts, pursued Pacific commerce in an effort to bolster America's position on the global stage. There was no conspiracy among slaveholders to press into the Pacific world for their exclusive benefit. Southern leaders, such as Thomas Jefferson and Andrew Jackson, may have coveted Pacific frontage for the United States, but neither did so as part of an expressly proslavery agenda. Such a weighty enterprise required the coordinated efforts of leaders from across the country. In 1844, when President John Tyler of Virginia sought to strengthen America's trading position in the Pacific world, and particularly the flow of cotton into China, he turned to Caleb Cushing, a Massachusetts lawyer and politician, to carry out that mission. As Cushing recognized, increased trade would shower benefits on producers and manufacturers across antebellum America's integrated economy. In other words, the mercantile class of New England stood to gain as much from the transpacific outflow of cotton as the planter class of South Carolina did. Tracking their collective efforts helps reorient the Atlantic-centric narrative of the antebellum United States.[8]

Yet, in time, the issue of transpacific trade erupted in sectional controversy. When Congress began debating the first major proposal for a transcontinental railroad in 1845, lawmakers raised a thorny set of questions about the political costs of American development. Most crucially, where would this railroad run: through slave country or across free soil? Partisans understood that whichever section won this national highway would control not only the commerce of the American West but access to the China trade as well. Slaveholding expansionists squabbled among themselves over tactics. But they directed most of their energies against competing plans from the North, in what they viewed as a winner-take-all contest for American and Asian commerce. As a result, the railroad question gave shape to some of the major geopolitical developments of the period, including the US-Mexico War and the rush to California's goldfields. Conflicting visions of Pacific empire were at the heart of an emerging sectional crisis.

From Texas to the Pacific

Thomas Jefferson brought the United States one step closer to the Pacific with the Louisiana Purchase of 1803. But another three decades would pass before Americans advanced concrete schemes for the prized deep-water harbors along California's coast. By the 1830s, dealings with Mexico prompted US leaders to think more expansively about their nation's geography. President Andrew Jackson attempted not only to annex Texas but also to acquire a piece of the Pacific coast. He instructed his minister to Mexico to enter negotiations in order to purchase the region surrounding the harbor of San Francisco. In Jackson's mind, this was "a most desirable place of resort of our numerous vessels engaged in the whaling business in the Pacific, far preferable to any to which they now have access."[9] Again, the Pacific at this time had little connection to the question over slavery's expansion or the South's political future. Whaling, after all, was an industry controlled by New England, and empire-building was a national, rather than sectional, endeavor.

That began to change with the Republic of Texas, which won its independence in 1836 after a successful rebellion against Mexico (with the issue of slavery at the center of that struggle).[10] Conceived in conquest and sustained by military force, Texas made several attempts at territorial expansion—albeit ineffectual—before its annexation to the United States a decade later. Like Jefferson and Jackson before them, several leading Texans set their sights on the Pacific coastline, though they did so under the banner of an independent slaveholding republic. "As a separated Power, the splendid harbours on the South Sea or Pacific Ocean, will be indispensable for us," wrote Memucan Hunt, the republic's minister to the United States, in April 1838. He coveted San Francisco most of all.[11] In his inaugural address a year later, President Mirabeau Lamar similarly looked westward across the new republic's "vast extent of territory, stretching from the Sabine to the Pacific."[12] The new president quickly dispatched a minister to Mexico to negotiate the extension of Texas's national boundary into California.[13] Although the effort failed, Lamar insisted that such a vast (and presumably expanding) republic would be ill-served by incorporation into the United States, which was haunted by the specter of abolitionism from the northern free states.[14] Lamar articulated what was becoming a central tenet of American slaveholders: push slavery's frontier westward, or fall prey to the North's abolitionist faction.

Expansionist Texans knowingly risked collisions with Mexico and the United States, whose leaders also maneuvered to claim outlets like San Francisco. When the Congress of Texas passed a resolution extending its jurisdiction to the California coastline, Daniel Webster warned that the republic "was too grasping and might excite the jealousy of other nations."[15] Still, Texan expansionists would not bow to the foreign policy objectives of the United States or to the legitimate territorial claims of Mexico. On the contrary, some Texan policy makers assumed that they could redraw the North American map at the expense of their much larger neighbor to the south. The republic's leaders organized several invasions of Mexican territory, including the failed 1841 effort to seize New Mexico and the valuable Santa Fe trade. Such defeats hardly dimmed the expansionist ambitions of certain Texans. Even two-time Texas president Sam Houston—who proved less jingoistic and more pro-annexationist than Lamar—entertained flights of imperial fancy up until the final years of the republic. In his farewell message of December 1844, Houston sounded a familiar note. "If we remain an independent nation, our territory will be extensive—unlimited," he proclaimed. "The Pacific alone will bound the mighty march of our race and our empire."[16]

Although such boasts often bordered on self-caricature, especially given Texas's deepening budgetary problems and repeated failures to secure international recognition, they anticipated the visions of continental destiny that would guide slaveholding leaders over the coming decades.[17] Texas expansionists and American southerners alike shared an unwavering faith in the power of cotton in the international marketplace, a hunger for more Mexican territory, and a gnawing fear of abolitionism. They were also among the first to promote the development of transcontinental infrastructure.

Few slaveholding expansionists matched Thomas Jefferson Green for his vision, ambition, and mobility. Green was a proslavery partisan with a transcontinental résumé. Both a soldier and a politician of fortune, he chased various opportunities in a long career that took him westward across North American and back again. Born in North Carolina in 1802, Green first came to international attention in 1836 as a brigadier general in Texas's revolutionary army. Over the next two years, he won seats in both houses of Texas's Congress before attempting to extend the republic's borders through force of arms. In 1842, as second-in-command of the ill-fated Mier expedition into northern Mexico, Green was captured along with more than 200 other Texan invaders. He was confined to a Mexican prison but managed to escape after tunneling through eight feet of volcanic rock over the course of six months. By the time he retired from public life, Green had served in more legislatures—North Carolina, Florida, California, and the Republic of Texas—than perhaps any other figure of his era.[18] (Although he spent as much time drinking as he did legislating, Green earned his place in western history as the first lawmaker to propose the formation of a public university in California.)[19]

Green devoted his energies to two mutually reinforcing projects: the westward extension of slavery and the construction of railroads. In 1836, he helped organize the first chartered railroad in Texas and continued to play a leading part in western transit operations over the next two decades. Back in the United States by 1845, Green published a memoir of his failed invasion of Mexico that doubled as an appeal for continental conquest and commercial integration. He called for the seizure of Mexican California and the establishment of American control across this terrain, "the most desirable portion of this continent." Particularly enticing to Green were the natural harbors that dotted this long coastline: Guaymas, San Diego, San Gabriel, Monterey, and San Francisco, among others. With an eye to America's continued commercial expansion, Green argued that "the port of San Francisco, or some other port in the south, is absolutely necessary."[20] And he rightly noted that Texas occupied a central position to channel this North American and Pacific trade—a natural thoroughfare between the slave states and the ports of California. Soon, Green predicted, a series of railroads and canals would unite the two halves of the continent, via the Lone Star Republic.[21] Here was the slaveholding vision of Pacific empire taking shape. The Deep South, Texas, the Pacific West, and Asia naturally invited commercial integration that, once achieved, would grant America's slave economies a substantial share of global trade.

John C. Calhoun, perhaps the most influential figure in the South at the time, also saw America's future in the ports of the Pacific. In the early 1840s, Senator Calhoun frequently enthused to congressional colleagues about the untapped potential of the California coastline. His reveries left a strong impression on a young slaveholding congressman from Mississippi, William McKendree Gwin. As Gwin recalled in his memoirs, Calhoun predicted that a future city on the bay of San Francisco, which at that point constituted little more than a cluster of ramshackle buildings, "was destined to be the New York of the Pacific Coast." In fact, it would be "more supreme," Calhoun claimed. San Francisco "would have no such rivals as Boston, Philadelphia, and Baltimore." It was only a matter of time before America claimed that territory, he insisted, at which point the United States would control "the direct route of the great commerce of Asia."[22] Calhoun's projections clearly wooed Gwin, who set off for California in 1849, becoming one of the state's first two US senators a year later.

Calhoun remained in Washington and South Carolina, where he used his influence to advocate for a strong American position on the Pacific. In an 1843 debate over American policy in Oregon, which the United States held jointly with Britain, Calhoun again stressed the importance of Pacific harbors. He cited the British victory in the Opium War the year before as evidence that soon Japan's ports would be opened to the West, as had China's per the recently concluded terms of surrender. America and Europe could then bid for the commerce of "the whole of that large portion of Asia, containing nearly half of the population and wealth of the globe," he continued. "No small portion" of this vast Asian commerce "is destined to pass through the ports of the Oregon Territory to the valley of the Mississippi, instead of taking the circuitous and long voyage round Cape Horn."[23] At the same time, Calhoun also clamored for a vast expansion of the nation's naval might. [24]

The Pacific, as Calhoun recognized, was an imperial theater. Britain had made that clear in its recent victory over China. After a string of military defeats, China agreed to cede Hong Kong Island to Britain, pay a large indemnity, and increase the ports open to British trade from one (Canton) to five. American statesmen drew the central lesson: to secure the Pacific gateway of Jefferson's fantasies, and the trade that would inevitably follow, required force. Within the Pacific Basin, Americans would pursue what they often called "commercial empire" and what historians refer to as "informal empire"—one based not on the conquest and control of overseas territories but on the manipulation of foreign governments.[25]

Although many American expansionists disdained overseas invasions, their emerging Pacific empire was anything but pacific. Rather, it depended on immense violence, including a number of continental conquests in the coming years. The US push into the Pacific world would be made possible by diplomatic coercion in Hawaii, China, and Japan, and by the seizure of vast amounts of Mexico's territory. Furthermore, access to the Pacific slope stemmed from the subjugation of numerous Native nations and the control of roads through their homelands. The US imperial presence would be made manifest in the coming decade by roughly 100 military posts located mostly in Indian country, along with thousands of troops to coerce Indigenous populations—albeit often unsuccessfully—and to guard transcontinental thoroughfares. [26] In short, only the force of the American state could forge a Pacific empire. And more often than not, slaveholders held the reins of that state power.[27]

The Tyler Doctrine and the China Trade

John Tyler, a Virginia slaveholder, played perhaps the most decisive role in shaping America's early advance into the Pacific world. While Jackson's successor, Martin Van Buren of New York, did not pursue the diplomatic campaign for California, President Tyler renewed the effort in the early 1840s. His administration proposed a bold bargain to Great Britain, another nation with imperial designs on the Pacific. According to the tripartite proposal, the United States would settle the contested Anglo-American boundary in Oregon by relinquishing all territorial claims north of the

Columbia River. In return, Britain would convince Mexico to cede California to the United States, while the Tyler administration would drop its $2 million claim against the Mexican government. Ultimately, the bargain failed, though not for lack of effort or ingenuity.[28]

But Tyler's vision stretched well beyond the shores of California. In a short but forceful message to Congress in December 1842, the president advocated the extension of American power into the Pacific world. Central to Tyler's commercial ambitions were the Sandwich Islands (known today as Hawaii). The islands served as the way station for most vessels passing between East Asia and the North American mainland, Tyler rightly noted, which made them a geostrategic linchpin in the China trade. Their continued independence and security—meaning independence and security from European imperialism—was a top priority for the Tyler administration. In order to prevent the Sandwich Islands from falling into British hands, Tyler formally recognized the archipelago's independence and warned that any threats to that sovereignty from foreign powers would be met with a "decided remonstrance."[29] The threat was vague, but the underlying message was unmistakable: Tyler had vastly expanded the scope of the 1823 Monroe Doctrine, pushing it 2,500 miles into the Pacific Ocean.[30]

Although Tyler himself promised to protect, rather than seize, the Sandwich Islands, his Pacific policies encouraged others to consider the possibility. American southerners, better known for their interest Cuba, were among the earliest advocates of Hawaiian annexation. "There are other islands beside Cuba in which the United States are interested," Mississippi planter-cum-California-senator William Gwin reminded his colleagues. "There are a set of islands called the Sandwich Islands, which we in California look upon as our summer residence. And when the Senator from Virginia talks about ripe fruit [Cuba], it ought to be known that that fruit [the Sandwich Islands] is ripe also, and ready to fall."[31] Similar musings on Hawaii's value and vulnerability ran through the southern press in the antebellum years.[32]

The islands' agricultural potential and labor order—vast numbers of Native Hawaiian and Asian contract workers under white management on large sugar plantations—enticed proslavery enthusiasts. Elizabeth Parker, wife of an American official in Hawaii, argued that the fertile islands could not afford to maintain free labor. "Whether, eventually, these Islands should be annexed to the United States, or become an independent republic, the introduction of slavery is indispensable to their value," she wrote.[33] Another observer recommended a system of feudalism. In language eerily reminiscent of proslavery polemics, one Dr. Wood suggested that the islanders' "naturally inoffensive natures and child-like docility" and "their disposition to be guided" rendered them fit subjects for a type of ameliorated serfdom. Under such a system, he argued, the rich soils of the islands would finally reach their full potential, yielding stores of coffee, sugar, and cotton.[34] Establishing a slave regime across the entire archipelago was little more than a pipe dream at this point, especially since so few American planters ever settled in Hawaii. But their aspirations underline a central, and often overlooked, point: slaveholders' imagined future embraced both the Atlantic and Pacific worlds. And while American slaveholders never seized Cuba, despite numerous attempts, a southern president paved the way for a US protectorate over Hawaii.

By his own admission, Tyler "had his eye fixed on China."[35] He used the same presidential message in which he recognized the Sandwich Islands to propose, for the first time in US history, a formal commercial relationship with the Qing dynasty. Trade goods had passed between the two nations since the Boston-built ship *Empress of China* docked in the port of Canton in 1784. But from that moment until the early 1840s, US merchants faced a legion of restrictions and lacked an official representative in China. To achieve more favorable conditions for American trade, Tyler embraced a policy of diplomatic coercion, at a time when the Chinese Empire was still reeling from its defeat in the First Opium War. In August 1843, the president authorized an American delegation on a flotilla of four ships, carrying more than 200 guns, to set sail for Chinese waters.[36]

Of all the industries that might benefit from the presence of a US consul in China, Tyler highlighted one in particular: slave-grown cotton. True, Tyler conceded, "the cheapness of labor among the Chinese, [and] their ingenuity in its application," should temper hopes for "the opening of any great and sudden demand" for cotton "fabrics." But trade in American-made goods had doubled in the last decade, Tyler added, and the opening of more Chinese ports would only increase demand.[37] Tyler's faith in the power of cotton was not unfounded. Beginning around 1835, manufactured cotton goods, and to a lesser extent raw cotton, made up the majority of American exports to China.[38] According to Tyler's logic, China's 400 million customers would alleviate "the greatest evil" of "a surplus of production beyond the home demand." This was the language that the commercial imperialists of the late nineteenth century would employ in their search for overseas markets. But their largely unrecognized precursors were antebellum visionaries like Tyler, and some of the major intended beneficiaries were southern slaveholders.[39]

Although Tyler framed negotiations with China as an opportunity for America's cotton interests, he was not guided by purely sectional motives. After all, his agent in the Pacific and the architect of the new US-China policy was the Massachusetts lawyer and statesman Caleb Cushing. As Tyler and Cushing recognized, increased demand for America's cotton goods would benefit southern planters and northern manufacturers alike. Even if that cotton was sent first to the mills of Britain before reaching China, it would still provide a vital lift for the American economy, according to Cushing. In an 1845 speech in Boston, he highlighted cotton, raw and manufactured, as the key to America's future success in China. "Two hundred and fifty millions of people, up to this time, have manufactured their own articles," he claimed. "Now ours will take the places of their own fabrics."[40] That such a champion of the international cotton trade was once an outspoken critic of slavery may seem curious. But Cushing himself saw no contradiction between his earlier aversion to human bondage and his later diplomatic efforts. In any case, he was acting in the best interests of American commerce writ large, not of any sectional constituency.

Although he failed to secure an audience with the emperor, as he had intended, Cushing ultimately got what he came for: a formal commercial agreement with China. The final settlement, known as the Treaty of Wangxia, benefited the cotton planters of the South and, to an even greater extent, the shipping interests of the American Northeast. It opened five ports to American traders, gave them the right to purchase land in these seaside cities, granted the US most-favored nation status, and fixed the tariffs on American trade. This was a treaty without a strong sectional character, which all commercially minded Americans, North and South, could applaud. It was also a treaty that gave the United States more favorable and detailed conditions than rival Britain. And unlike Britain, the Tyler administration did not even need a war to win it.[41]

Yet these inroads into the China market, as promising as they appeared in 1844, brought unforeseen complications. As trade between the United States and China grew, partisans began to consider what America's policies in the Pacific would mean for sectional alignments. The Tyler administration's diplomatic triumph would soon shade into a domestic crisis.

Imagined Railroads and Sectional Conflict

Few issues fueled sectional conflict quite like infrastructure, especially the struggle to determine where America's first transcontinental railroad should run. As early as 1836, the *New Orleans Bee* envisioned a grand contest for transcontinental communication and Asian trade fought between the commercial capitals of the North and South—New York and New Orleans. Within a decade, the *Bee* predicted, a railroad from the Crescent City to California would be constructed, making the Gulf South one of the great trade centers of the world.[42] But aside from the brassy predictions of newspapers like the *Bee* and expansionists like Thomas Jefferson Green, transcontinental transit did not become a major national issue until 1845. Not coincidentally, that year also marked the beginning of a rapid acceleration in the Pacific trade due to the recently concluded Treaty of Wangxia. As Pacific commerce became nearly synonymous with railroad development, American expansionists fractured over the question of slavery.

The New York dry-goods merchant Asa Whitney was the first to bring the railroad to national prominence. Whitney witnessed firsthand the potential of Pacific trade, having amassed a small fortune by exporting tea and spices from Canton in the early 1840s. On his return journey from China in 1844, he drew up plans for the nation's first transcontinental railroad, a line running from the Great Lakes to Puget Sound. Whitney proposed to finance the road himself. According to his plan, Congress would first sell Whitney a sixty-mile-wide strip of land along the route. He would then privately fund the railroad's construction, recouping his costs by selling developed land along the length of the road. Whitney enlisted the aid of a New York congressman, and by January 1845, his memorial for a Pacific railroad reached the House of Representatives. Although Congress tabled the bill several months later, the debate had only just begun.[43]

Southern railroad promoters, editors, and politicians united in opposition to Whitney's proposed northern line. Barren, inaccessible, unfeasible— this was the verdict of most commentators from the slave states. Although every "patriotic and thinking citizen" desires the accomplishment of a Pacific railroad, wrote a contributor to the *Charleston Courier*, Whitney's route from the Great Lakes was simply too northerly to justify the expense. The writer also criticized Whitney's plans to privately finance the road. Such a monumental undertaking, he argued, called for government aid.[44] Out of all major publications from the slave states, only the *Baltimore American* stood by Whitney's plan. The other prominent papers, with varying degrees of paranoia, foresaw the South's financial subordination in any road that linked northern cities to the Pacific trade.[45] Instead of awaiting such a fate, the South must build more of its own lines westward, urged James Gadsden of South Carolina. Through commerce and infrastructure, Gadsden hoped to ally the western states with "the Great Commercial and Agricultural interests" of the South, rather than "the Tax gathering and Monopolizing interests of the North."[46]

White southerners rallied behind this western agenda at Memphis in November 1845. In a frenzy of press coverage and public enthusiasm, 580 delegates from sixteen states, including John C. Calhoun as president, converged on the booming Tennessee town for one of the largest conventions the region had ever seen. The vast majority of attendees hailed from slave states. Indeed, this was a convention of southerners, by southerners, and for southerners. At stake was "commercial empire," according to Gadsden. And while the construction of railway lines from southeastern cities into Memphis was the first order of business, the Charlestonian could not refrain from advocating a route all the way to the shores of California.[47] Others shared his Pacific aspirations. One delegate looked forward to the day when a line would connect Charleston to California, and the "vast trade" of "Golden Carthy [sic] and the Orient Ind" would pour into American harbors.[48] Calhoun, too, predicted that the United States would have a Pacific railroad within the next generation.[49]

The Memphis convention brought southerners together to articulate, as a powerful commercial and political bloc, an alternate vision to Whitney's transcontinental proposal. Still, there was no perfect southern consensus on either the location of the road or the means of funding it. New Orleans merchants viewed the gathering at Memphis as a threat to their stranglehold on southwestern trade, and they continued to favor river transportation over the promises of a transcontinental railway.[50] For their part, the shipping interests of the Atlantic Seaboard preferred ocean routes to western railroads. In short, local interests often precluded a collective strategy for the South's plantation economy. Yet the very presence of almost 600 leaders at Memphis testified to a budding movement of railroad enthusiasts—including planters, journalists, financiers, statesmen, engineers, developers, and boosters—within the slave states. From the Memphis convention and on through the next decade, southern transcontinental promoters proved more systematic and often better organized than their northern counterparts, keeping the prize of western commerce steadily within their sights.[51] That California was a Mexican possession at this point seemed almost irrelevant to men like Gadsden. The horizons of southern railroaders stretched well beyond the borders of the nation.

The Memphis convention also served as the debut for one of the most important new voices in the South, James Dunwoody Brownson (J. D. B.) De Bow. Born into a South Carolina planter family, De Bow later moved to New Orleans, where he began a long, prolific career in journalism. He published the first issue of his *Commercial Review of the South and West* (later, more simply, *De Bow's Review*) in January 1846, which featured detailed reporting on the convention at Memphis.[52] Like others in attendance at that event, De Bow believed railroads would carry westward the commercial and political power of the slave states. Although the periodical struggled financially at first, it would soon become what De Bow's biographer calls "the most recognizable journal in the antebellum South."[53] In monthly installments, De Bow and his corps of contributors articulated the platform of a modernizing South. Here was a periodical that promoted railroad development, urban growth, and industrialization as a bulwark for slave-based agriculture. The Far West and the Pacific occupied a central place in De Bow's vision, and as the sectional crisis intensified, so too did his interest in the commercial expansion of the slave states. In the coming years he would serve as the director of the US Census, the president of a railroad corporation, and one of the most vocal boosters of slavery's westward advance.[54]

By the time De Bow published his first issue, the Pacific railroad debate had been thoroughly sectionalized. As a matter of course, railroaders claimed to work for the national good, rather than for regional gain. But their nationalist appeals generally rang hollow. Promoters and developers, North and South, often held strong local ties and sectional agendas, and their transcontinental plans could enrich only specific parts of the country. Even those with truly national intentions would have been foiled by the state of antebellum American railroads. The railway system simply did not cohere. Railroads at the time ran on more than twenty different gauges, and while the 4-foot-8½-inch gauge accounted for roughly half of the nation's total mileage, most of the South ran on a 5-foot gauge. Anytime a train encountered a difference in track gauge, its freight had to be transported at considerable cost to the next train, sometimes miles away.[55] Thus, cities on the main trunk of a transcontinental railroad would likely receive the lion's share of the commerce, while those linked by connecting branches would have to settle for the scraps. Boosters expected the eastern terminus of the railway to become a vast emporium—or, in the words of one New Orleans writer, the "market of the world"—bringing together goods from Asia and across the United States.[56] The location of the railroad would remain a sticking point for the next decade and beyond.

A War for the Pacific

The Pacific—and to a significant degree, the issue of a transcontinental railroad—was at the heart of America's greatest imperial undertaking to date. The US-Mexican War was, according to one of its combatants, Ulysses S. Grant, "one of the most unjust ever waged by a stronger against a weaker nation." It was a nakedly imperialist venture, according to Grant, in which the United States followed "the bad example of European monarchies, in not considering justice in their desire to acquire additional territory."[57] The United States provoked the conflict with Mexico by annexing

Texas in December 1845 and then sending troops to the contested region between the Nueces River and the Rio Grande several months later. When Mexican forces fired upon the US troops there, President James K. Polk declared war.

From the very outset of the conflict, it was the deepwater harbors of California that most enticed Polk. In fact, even before war started, Polk's secretary of the navy, George Bancroft, instructed the commander of the Pacific Squadron to direct his attention to California's ports. "If you ascertain with certainty that Mexico has declared war against the United States," he wrote, "you will at once possess yourself of the port of San Francisco." That harbor, Bancroft later elaborated, was to be considered "the most important public object."[58] The former US minister to Mexico, Waddy Thompson of South Carolina, placed similar value in San Francisco. "To say nothing of other harbors in California, that of San Francisco is capacious enough for the navies of the world," Thompson wrote in 1846. The acquisition of California would be especially beneficial to the Gulf South, he predicted. Through a series of canals and railroads, the region could be linked to the Pacific more efficiently than could any part of the American Northeast. Once constructed, this transcontinental network would "throw into [New Orleans's] lap the vast commerce of China and India."[59]

Over the next two years, the Polk administration poured nearly 80,000 troops into a war of conquest that claimed the lives of roughly 13,000 Americans and an estimated 25,000 Mexicans, mostly civilians. The conflict culminated with an amphibious landing at Veracruz, followed by a 250-mile march over the Sierra Madre and the capture of Mexico City. With the signing of the Treaty of Guadalupe Hidalgo in 1848, the United States gained more than half a million square miles of territory—including all or parts of present-day California, Nevada, Arizona, Utah, New Mexico, Colorado, and Wyoming—and secured several prized harbors along the Pacific coast. Thus, the Polk administration achieved through military force what previous presidents had unsuccessfully attempted through diplomatic coercion. The United States now had its empire on the Pacific.[60]

During treaty negotiations with Mexico in 1848, the railroad question again came to the fore. Although the United States did not go to war for the express purpose of acquiring a suitable Pacific railroad route, Polk's government made transcontinental transit an important part of the peace process. Unfortunately for southern railroad promoters, even with California secured, the favored route to San Diego still did not pass entirely within US territory. Proslavery railroaders, therefore, lusted after even more territory, or at least a right-of-way through Mexico. With the Mexican military on the ropes, the United States should now push for a southern railway, argued J. D. B. De Bow. Securing rights of passage through Mexican territory should be a *"sine qua non* in our treaty with that republic," he insisted.[61] Meanwhile, Jefferson Davis hoped for more Mexican land in order to "secure the railroad route to San Diego," while even John C. Calhoun, who proved less eager for foreign territory, suggested a similar route.[62] So too did Secretary of State James Buchanan. In a letter to Nicholas Trist, then negotiating in Mexico, Buchanan urged the diplomat to secure the Gila River valley along the thirty-second parallel, which had been deemed prime real estate for railroad construction.[63]

Trist pressed hard for southern railroad interests in his dealings with Mexico. Ultimately the United States would not win quite as much land as Buchanan or Davis had hoped. Nor would Trist secure transit rights across the Isthmus of Tehuantepec, for which he offered $15 million (the same amount that the US government paid for the entire Mexican cession). Still, his negotiations secured a right-of-way for railroad development through northern Mexico. Thus, by the conclusion of treaty negotiations in early 1848, the American map appeared more inviting than ever for southern railroaders. They finally had a viable western terminus along the Pacific coast, as well as potential routes through either the Deep South or the Mexican North.[64]

Slaveholders also had a new champion in Matthew Fontaine Maury, superintendent of the US Naval Observatory. In a series of letters, reprinted widely after the war, Maury brought coherence, visibility, and scientific expertise to the case for a southern transcontinental railroad. The "Pathfinder of the Seas" had been rendered lame and land-bound by a stagecoach accident early in his career. But where the Virginian could not go by sea, he went in his imagination and through his scientific calculations. Perhaps the finest American geographer of his generation, Maury won international acclaim for his work in the related fields of oceanography, astronomy, and meteorology.[65] Across his long and successful career, Maury's writings consistently reinforced one of the central premises of southern railroaders: slavery, science, technology, and economic progress would all march in lockstep.[66]

In an 1848 letter to John C. Calhoun, Maury gave full latitude to his globetrotting fantasies, while positioning the slave South at the heart of international trade currents. He prophesied a glorious future for the United States as the world's undisputed commercial powerhouse—once the Atlantic and Pacific coasts were linked by rail. "Commercially speaking, our country is in the centre of the people of the earth, and occupies a position for trade and traffic with them which no nation that ever existed has held," he exulted. Mustering an impressive array of astronomical measurements to calculate the best route, Maury rebutted Whitney's plan and concluded that the train should run from Monterey, California, to Memphis and branch from there to all parts of the Eastern Seaboard. If this could be accomplished, he imagined, "you might then drink tea made in Charleston within the same month in which the leaf was gathered in China." Given Maury's well-known sectional allegiances, it required only a short leap of the imagination to draw an even more enticing conclusion: one might then buy slave-grown cotton in China within the same season in which the staple was picked from the South Carolina Low Country. Geography had marked the United States, and the slave South in particular, for greatness.[67]

Here was a potential antidote to the South's often cited commercial and political ailments. In newspapers, legislatures, and commercial conventions, white southerners fretted compulsively about their position vis-à-vis the free states. The North's fast-growing edge in industrial development was luring business and immigrants, leading free states to outpace the South not only in economic capacity but also in population, and thereby upsetting the delicate balance of congressional representation. Meanwhile, slaveholders saw their commerce carried away on northern ships, as they themselves were becoming more dependent on Europe and New England for manufactured goods.[68] To stem this tide, southerners placed their hopes in the twin objectives of a transcontinental railroad: to unite South and West and to open a way to the China trade. Such a road would accelerate southern migration into newly acquired western territory, which in time would become states with congressional representatives, beholden to slaveholding interests. It would also secure what De Bow called a "*commercial Empire*" centered in the slave South. "As a Southron, we confess a deep and abiding interest in these schemes to connect the two oceans," he wrote in 1849. "Our own cities must revive under their influence, and commerce visit again and rule in her wonted marts."[69]

Cotton would play a central role. Many southern expansionists believed that Asian consumers clamored for plantation staples, especially slave-grown cotton. The flow of trade from the slave states to the Chinese mainland would become self-perpetuating, they argued, once Chinese consumers developed a dependence on American goods. "By constant and familiar intercourse with our people," Maury wrote, "they will soon learn to want and [be] taught to buy."[70] This was essentially an elaboration of John Tyler's position, sketched out briefly in his 1842 message to Congress. But by the late 1840s, after the Treaty of Wangxia and the territorial gains of the recent war with Mexico, southern visions for Asian commerce came into clearer focus.

For Congressman Thomas Butler King, cotton was the key to the China market and America's prosperity more generally. King, a Georgia planter, would soon embark for California and run for one of the state's new senate seats. But before he did, he made a name for himself as one of the South's keenest Pacific expansionists. From his position on the House Committee on Naval Affairs, he authored a frequently cited 1848 report on cotton and the US-China trade. King argued that, while America's share of trade in China still lagged far behind Great Britain, its major rival in the Far East, the United States was slowly closing the gap. This was largely due to the quality of American cotton. Together, raw and manufactured cotton accounted for well over half of American imports to China, according to King's data, and those figures were "gradually and surely increasing." Britain also exported a substantial amount of cotton goods to China—fabrics spun from the American staple and from raw cotton grown in British India. But its Indian product was "very inferior to American cotton," King claimed. Considering that China contained hundreds of millions of consumers—many of whom were clothed in this lesser Indian cotton—the market appeared ripe for a vast expansion of American exports. In short, King argued, "the great field for American enterprise and skill, in our intercourse with China, lies in the adaptation of our cotton fabrics to the wants and tastes of the Chinese."[71]

To bolster their great expectations, slaveholding expansionists could look to the quickening pace of trade throughout the Pacific. In 1845 alone, the United States exported $2 million in cotton to China.[72] From there, the numbers climbed steadily. Between 1845 and 1860, the annual Sino-American trade grew from $9.5 million to $22.5 million. Although the trade balance still favored the Chinese, the value of American exports had quadrupled over that same period, to well over $8 million by 1860.[73] Cotton, raw and manufactured, remained America's leading export.

That American cotton goods could eventually supplant homespun Asian products in China's market was not a wild-eyed fantasy. In the last several decades, the South's plantation economy had undergone a phenomenal expansion, a testament to the power of slave-grown cotton in the international marketplace. Until the late eighteenth century, China and India produced far more cotton textiles and raw cotton than did Europe and North America. But within just several decades, the balance swung dramatically in America's favor. Whereas the United States produced a mere 1.5 million pounds of cotton in 1790, that figured multiplied more than a hundredfold over the next forty years. To meet the soaring global demand for cotton, American slaveholders forcibly transported 1 million African American bondpeople from the Atlantic states to the southern interior—a process historians call the "Second Middle Passage." The rich calcareous soils of central Alabama and Mississippi and the alluvial bottoms of the lower Mississippi and Red River valleys fueled the further growth of slave-grown cotton.[74] Between 1815 and 1860, cotton comprised more than half of all US exports.[75]

Even so, planters could expect no sudden revolution in trade with Asia. America's Pacific shipping was still dominated by northern firms and represented only a fraction of the nation's total global trade. At nearly $250 million in 1860, for instance, American exports to Europe dwarfed the value of goods shipped to China.[76] Furthermore, Britain's far larger share of China's market rested on its control of Indian opium, a supply that American traders could never match. The outbreak of the Taiping Rebellion in 1851, led by the Christian millenarian Hong Xiuquan, convinced some traders and policy makers that the toppling of the Qing dynasty would bring about more favorable relations with the United States. But as the war dragged on, ultimately claiming an estimated 20 to 70 million lives, it became increasingly clear that there would be no sea change in trade relations.[77] The joint British and French operation against the Qing dynasty from 1857 to 1860, known as the Second Opium War, further destabilized the region. In short, this was a tumultuous era in China, over which American slaveholders, in particular, had little control. But no amount of bloodshed seemed to dim their outlook on Asian trade.

The view from the Pacific vastly expands the geography of what one group of historians calls the "Old South's modern worlds."[78] Antebellum planters sought commercial networks and diplomatic influence on a global scale, not least in the Pacific Basin. They clung to neither strict constructionism nor rural seclusion. Instead, slaveholders lobbied for a massive mobilization of state power and looked westward to a new field of opportunity. Although their visions for Pacific ascendency often lacked concrete detail—for instance, who would control which components of this growing trade—they possessed the essential ingredients for their so-called commercial empire: soaring international demand for slave-grown staples, an activist federal government, a new treaty with China, and deepwater ports along the California coast. Cotton was king in the Atlantic world; the railroad, these expansionists predicted, would bring its dominion to the Pacific as well.

From Slave Country to Gold Country

The conquest of the Mexican Northwest fired the global imaginations of expansionists like Matthew Fontaine Maury, but it also touched off vigorous debates about the future of American slavery. Through Representative David Wilmot's eponymous proviso, a group of congressmen attempted, at three separate points during the war, to bar human bondage from all lands taken from Mexico. Southerners in the Senate parried these efforts, safeguarding the possibility of slavery's expansion into what would become the US Southwest. America's advance to the Pacific had divided Congress into warring camps.[79]

Some of the most influential politicians of the day insisted that slavery was naturally confined to the southeastern portion of the United States, that the West's aridity would render the institution unprofitable and unsustainable. "What more do you want?" Henry Clay asked in early 1850. "You have got what is worth more than a thousand Wilmot provisos. You have nature on your side—facts upon your side—and thus truth staring you in the face, that there is no slavery in those territories."[80] Daniel Webster famously reiterated this point. "Now, as to California and New Mexico, I hold slavery to be excluded from those territories by a law even superior to that which admits and sanctions it in Texas," he argued in the Senate. "I mean the law of nature—of physical geography—the law of the formation of the earth."[81] Even President Polk dismissed the likelihood that slavery could take root in the territories that his war had won.[82]

Other observers were justifiably skeptical of this natural limits thesis—what the *New York Daily Times* later dubbed a "clap-trap" argument, drummed up merely to defeat the Wilmot Proviso.[83] David Wilmot himself noted that black chattel slavery had found its way into New Mexico as early as 1847.[84] Few were more critical of the natural limits argument than Horace Mann, a Whig congressman and educational reformer from Massachusetts. In a series of publicly circulated letters, Mann scolded Webster for his shortsighted acquiescence to the westward expansion of slavery. The institution would not obey the dictates of a "thermometer," Mann warned. "Slavery depends, not upon Climate, but upon Conscience," he wrote in 1850. "Wherever the wicked passions of the human heart can go, there slavery can go." Even if plantation agriculture proved unprofitable, the households of the Southwest would soon call for 100,000 domestic slaves, he predicted. Furthermore, who was to say that substantial quantities of gold would not be found in New Mexico, as it had been in California a year earlier? "This is the very kind of labor on which slaves, in all time, have been so extensively employed," Mann argued.[85] Indeed, unfree Natives Americans, as well as coerced African and Asian laborers, had helped pull nearly 100 million pounds of silver from the mines of Mexico over the preceding centuries, turning the metal into the first global currency.[86] Unless checked by some external power, Mann wrote, slavery would roll inexorably westward.

In an exceedingly rare occurrence, Jefferson Davis of Mississippi found himself agreeing with the antislavery New Englander Horace Mann. There was no reason, Davis argued, to assume that slavery would not be profitable and adaptable in the Mexican cession. Most abolitionists clearly did not subscribe to the natural limits thesis themselves, he noted. Otherwise, why go to such lengths to restrict slavery in the new territories with controversial stratagems like the Wilmot Proviso? Rather than natural limits, Davis suggested, there were natural incentives for the expansion of slavery. Reports from hunters indicated that the lower Colorado River boasted "widespread and fruitful valleys." And there was always the prospect of further gold discoveries, especially in the valleys around the Gila River.[87] Like Mann, Davis believed that slaves would soon be used profitably in mining operations in New Mexico. The Mississippi senator solicited reports on the mineral opportunities in the Gila River valley from the ongoing US-Mexico joint boundary commission. The news he received from the commissioner indicated that the area around the Gila possessed a "richness ... as a mineral region unsurpassed in New Mexico, both in Gold Silver & Copper."[88] Although much of this terrain remained terra incognita to white Americans, it beckoned to slaveholding expansionists like Davis.

As politicians in Washington debated the adaptability of slave labor to the Far West, emigrants to the region field-tested these theories. In January 1848, prospectors discovered gold at Sutter's Mill near Sacramento, California, setting off a mad scramble for the Pacific coast later that year. Among the tens of thousands of emigrants from China, Chile, Mexico, Hawaii, Australia, Europe, the American East, and elsewhere came a smaller, but by no means insignificant, population of enslaved blacks. Historians estimate that southern slaveholders forcibly transported between 500 and 600 bondpeople to California during the gold rush, though more recent evidence has suggested that as many as 1,500 African American slaves may have reached the Pacific coast by the early 1850s.[89]

Slavery had taken root in California well before the arrival of these white southerners and their African American bondpeople. When the Spanish Empire began colonizing California in the late eighteenth century, Franciscan missionaries imposed a system of captive labor over the Indigenous people of the Pacific coast. The Spanish confined California Indians to fortified missions, forcing them to work church lands or face severe beatings.[90] Mexico won independence from Spain in 1821 and outlawed slavery across its possessions, including California, eight years later. But the forced servitude of California Indians continued. In the 1830s and 1840s, Hispano and Anglo landholders created vast ranchos with coerced Indigenous labor. As many as 4,000 California Indians worked the land in conditions ranging from nominal wage labor to debt servitude to captive slavery.[91] American observers routinely commented on the exploitation of Indian labor in California. "They are certainly in a most miserable condition," wrote a Virginia slaveholder in 1846, "worse by far than [the] worst treated slaves in the United States."[92] California Indians, according to another writer, lived in "a state of absolute vassalage."[93]

The gold rush brought even more Indigenous people into coercive labor relationships. Beginning in 1848, thousands of California Indians moved to mines on the Sierra Nevada's western slopes—sometimes of their volition, but often not. John Sutter alone, on whose land gold was first discovered, brought some 100 Indians to the Central Mines. In search of valuable labor, slave hunters raided Native communities and carted their captives to the gold diggings. There, miners bought, sold, beat, and killed Indigenous people with impunity. Murder, in fact, was often profitable. By killing Indians, other miners reduced competition in the diggings and seized the claims of their victims. The gold rush marked the beginning of what historians rightly regard as a genocide of California's Indigenous people.[94]

Those who carried African American slaves into frontier California, whether traveling by sea or by land, engaged in a risky undertaking.[95] Given that an able-bodied bondperson could fetch up to $1,000 at auction, slaveholders had to be confident of high returns to hazard such a journey. Perhaps no slaveholder was as optimistic about the prospects for bonded labor in California as the former minister to Brazil and future Virginia governor Henry A. Wise. He insisted that the Far West would be a lucrative market for the surplus slave population of the Upper South. According to Wise's calculations, if the Missouri Compromise line was extended to the Pacific and slavery legally protected in gold country, Virginia alone would gain more than $1 billion through the sale of bondpeople to California.[96]

Wise's figure may have bordered on the farcical, but masters demonstrated that they could indeed reap tidy sums from slave labor in mining regions. Decades before the discovery of gold in California, slaveholders had forced African Americans into the placer mines of North Carolina.[97] When in the goldfields of California, North Carolinian slaveholders often replicated time-tested mining techniques, organizing bondpeople into gangs under the direction of overseers. Isaac Thomas Avery, whose family owned a mine in Burke County, North Carolina, sent at least five enslaved African Americans to California along with a trusted associate to supervise their labor. Although his slaves were often ill, they returned healthy profits for Avery, including one shipment of $1,450.[98] Even while living thousands of miles from his human property—a relatively common practice, especially for wealthier slaveholders—Avery expressed few misgivings about the venture. He trusted in his overseer's watchfulness and assurances that "we have nothing to apprehend from abolitionists."[99] For absentee masters like Avery, California slavery proved secure and profitable.

Most slaveholding gold seekers, however, traveled with fewer slaves—generally one or two—and worked alongside their chattel on more modest claims. Even these smaller operations could be lucrative. One South Carolinian, for instance, was offered $300 per month for the hire of his slave Scipio. He refused, believing that Scipio would be more valuable by his side.[100] That was a wise decision, if Scipio proved anywhere near as lucky or skilled as the two slaves of a Mississippi emigrant, who reportedly earned their master $5,000 in two months.[101] Within the space of three weeks, one North Carolinian argonaut made an estimated $1,500 to $1,800 off the labor of his several bondmen.[102] According to reports received by a Mississippi paper, slaves could fetch as much as $3,000 to $4,000 on the San Francisco market.[103] As in the South, enslaved laborers in California could also be used as collateral, or even as stakes in a game of cards. According to one California observer, a slave by the name of Harry "changed owners about every Saturday night" as the prize in a weekly game of freeze-out poker.[104]

The correspondence of George McKinley Murrell illustrates the many advantages that masters derived from slave labor in California. Setting out from his family's plantation in Bowling Green, Kentucky, in the spring of 1849, Murrell traveled with Reuben, one of his father's twenty-seven slaves.[105] By September, the two had reached Sacramento and commenced a modest mining venture.[106] Although Reuben had some success in the diggings that fall, Murrell soon began renting his bondman to the owner of the boardinghouse at which they lodged. In fact, it seems unlikely that Murrell would have been able to cover his expenses without the profits he accrued from Reuben's work, which "more than pays my board although that is $4.00 per day."[107] Months later, it was still the profits from Reuben's labor that secured a roof over his master's head. Working as a cook for $10 a day, Reuben generated a steady source of income in a country that could be notoriously inhospitable to unlucky miners like Murrell. "I have Rheubin hired out at $10.00 a day and foolish I was that I did not have him hired out all the time," Murrell wrote. "I might have been a great deal better off. $10.00 a day is big wages & but few hands can get it now."[108] The versatile Reuben even learned to bake, which enabled Murrell to profit from bread sales, "as the miners don't love to cook."[109]

But if the profits from slave labor in gold country were steady, the risks could be substantial. Not only were overworked bondpeople subject to illness and death, but they might also attempt to break for freedom on the California frontier. Murrell, like other white masters, was alert to a

White southerners transported an estimated 500–1,500 enslaved African Americans into gold rush California. Here, an interracial party mines for gold in Spanish Flat, El Dorado County, in 1852. Although the status of these black men is unknown, they were likely enslaved, as El Dorado County had one of the highest concentrations of slaveholders in the state at this time. Joseph Blaney Starkweather, *Spanish Flat, 1852*, California History Room, California State Library, Sacramento.

perceived abolitionist threat in the diggings. According to Murrell, he and Reuben resided "in the midst of the most fanatical of the abolition party," although he professed an abiding faith in his bondman. "I do not think that their contaminating & poisoning principles has in the least weakened his fidelity & devotedness to me," he added.[110] In contrast, a Louisiana slaveholder, Jesse Holcomb Chaney, watched the workings of antislavery forces in California with great unease. "The abolitionist[s] will go and sit by him [his enslaved worker] while at work and beg him to leave me," he noted.[111] Hinton Rowan Helper also fretted over the "meddling abolitionists" who attempted to "entice away" enslaved blacks in California's goldfields. Helper—who would later scandalize the planter class with his influential critique *The Impending Crisis of the South* (1857)—sympathized with the transplanted slaveholders of the West and took comfort in the fact that few bondpeople actually made good on abolitionists' offers, due to "their attachment to their masters."[112]

A sense of fidelity may have deterred many enslaved people from seeking their freedom in California, but it was a different sort of fidelity from the one Murrell and Helper had in mind. In gold country, slaves were thousands of miles from their homes, their friends, and their families. Escape on the California frontier may have promised freedom, but it also threatened life-long separation from loved ones in the South. This was the dilemma that an enslaved man named Prince faced when he was carried into the goldfields and away from his family in Buncombe County, North Carolina. "State to me whether you would reather I would send you what gold dust I make between now and next winter or if you reather I would sell the gold and bring you the money," he dutifully wrote to his absentee master.[113] If he hoped to see his family again, he had no other choice. Reuben, too, was separated from his kin and friends on the plantation in Bowling Green and regularly expressed his desire to return to them. "There is no country like home," Reuben dictated to Murrell, "if I can just only live to get back."[114] Such a reunion, however, was not to be. Two years after his departure from Kentucky, Reuben was swept up in a current while helping a traveler cross a river.[115] Reuben lost his life and Murrell lost his steadiest source of income.

Even if their bondpeople did not run away, white southern argonauts had to adjust to a new master-slave dialectic. Enslaved people themselves recognized the new opportunities available to them in an open frontier, and they exploited their masters' anxieties to renegotiate the conditions of their bondage. In a number of instances, slaves reached agreements with their masters to work in California for a set period of time, usually several years, in exchange for their freedom.[116] In other cases, enslaved workers secured for themselves what was known as a Sunday claim: the right to keep the earnings from their mining on what would have otherwise been a day of rest. It was likely an arrangement of this nature that enabled an enslaved man named Albert to send his wife $200, along with $950 for his absentee master in North Carolina.[117] The payoff from such arrangements could be even more sizable. A group of four black bondmen from North Carolina amassed a collective total of over $1,100, with one of them, "Big Jim," bringing in $486 himself.[118]

With these earnings, black people in California occasionally purchased their own freedom, as well as the freedom of their family members in the South.[119] Scholars estimate that hundreds of slaves emancipated themselves and their family members through these means, collectively spending as much as $750,000 in the process.[120] Sensing the possibility of freedom, enslaved people were eager to claim a share of California's wealth, with or without the blessings of their masters. A Tennessee slaveholder who had settled in a small gulch with his three bondmen faced open rebellion when he attempted to claim the gold dust that they had recently washed out. As he approached the gold, the three men warned him to take his hands off their earnings. He was welcome to work with them on shares, they explained, but they would dig no more as slaves.[121] White masters now had to negotiate rather than merely command.

To guard against rebellion, slaveholders often journeyed and settled with kin and close friends, those they could trust to oversee their chattel. They were mindful of the fact that California's placers were "so hidden and retired" that escaped slaves "could not in many instances be recaptured," as one southern gold seeker put it.[122] Thus masters did all in their power to maintain surveillance and to cloister their human property from interference. Slaveholding miners often organized informal posses to discipline and police bondpeople, thereby bringing to California an analogue to the slave patrols of the plantation South. Generally settling in the Southern Mines (east of San Francisco near the end of the southern overland trail), slaveholders concentrated in Mariposa, Tuolumne, and Calaveras counties.[123] In essence, these slaveholding argonauts carved out miniature Souths across the western landscape.

Prominent among them was the settlement of Colonel Thomas Thorn. Having organized a caravan of 200 wagons from Texas to California, Thorn settled in the goldfields of Mariposa with a community of southern whites along with thirty slaves. He attempted to instill discipline through severe beatings, although like other slaveholders in California, his command was far from absolute. His slaves proved susceptible to the influence of antislavery forces in the area and to the lure of freedom along the sparsely policed frontier. Several successfully escaped, while at least one other man eventually purchased his freedom.[124] Settling among fellow slaveholders may have provided some security, but it was hardly a failsafe strategy, and California masters felt their vulnerability keenly.

Like Thorn, Thomas Jefferson Green sought to recreate a slaveholding community within California. And also like Thorn, Green discovered the limits of his mastery. Since his days in the Republic of Texas, Green had been an advocate of slaveholding expansion to the Pacific. Now in charge of his own mining company and armed with the patent for a so-called compound action gold extractor, he sought to make good on his vision for the American West.[125] Along with a dozen or so fellow Texans and their fifteen slaves, Green settled in the mining colony of Rose's Bar in the summer of 1849. But because his company made claims not only in the Texans' own names but also in the names of their bondmen—a common practice among slave-owning miners to maximize the extent of their holdings—Green's company soon attracted unwanted attention from non-slaveholders in the region.

A committee of white miners approached Green but was quickly rebuffed by the Texans. In response, another committee formed and passed a resolution "that no slaves or negroes should own claims or even work in the mines," according to the memoir of one of the committee members, Edwin Sherman.[126] This committee then approached Green a second time and again received threats of violent resistance. But Sherman and the free miners held their ground. "If you want to keep your slaves, you will have to go back to Texas or Arkansas," Sherman threatened, "or by tomorrow morning you will not have one slave left, for the miners will run them out and you will never get them back." The threat was apparently real enough for Green and his company, who moved off their claim, with their slaves, the next day.[127]

Some scholars have mistakenly marked this confrontation as "California's standard free-soil creation story," according to historian Stacey Smith.[128] A victory for the nonslaveholding miners of Rose's Bar, Green's flight has been seen as the last gasp of a brief southern experiment in gold rush California. Yet this was a turf war, not an abolitionist movement. Like many white miners in California, Sherman's group opposed slave labor only insofar as it encroached on their own claims. Because "slaves were not citizens," Sherman and his allies argued, "their owners could not take up pre-emption claims for them."[129] Morally ambivalent on the issue of slavery and unconcerned with the plight of African Americans in general, supporters of a free California sought simply to secure the region for white labor. They would score some victories, notably at Rose's Bar and, later, in the state's constitution. But such success did not amount to a complete repudiation of California's proslavery politics.

Just as gold rush California proved a lucrative field for many slaveholders, it would continue to attract southerners and their proslavery political culture in the coming years. As Green himself would demonstrate, southern dreams of westward expansion and Pacific empire had not been extinguished. In fact, 1849 marked only the beginning of a new phase in the campaign.

Conclusion

Well before gangs of celebrated yet ill-fated filibusters attempted to carve up the Caribbean Basin for American slavery, a group of influential southerners, along with well-placed northern allies, set their sights on more distant shores. They sought the markets of China and its hundreds of millions of potential customers for slave-grown cotton. The Treaty of Wangxia, signed in 1844, brought them one step closer to their Pacific fantasies. And with some justification, the *New Orleans Bee* could proclaim later that year the advent of "a new and highly favorable era not only for the commerce and manufactures of the United States but particularly to the cotton planting interest of the South."[130] Of course, America's profits from the Pacific trade never matched the lofty expectations of these antebellum expansionists. Sheer distance, political turmoil in Asia, and China's disinterest in most western imports put a ceiling on just how much could be reaped from this commerce. Yet cotton, as planters and merchants alike recognized, had provided an important wedge in the China market, and trade figures were on the rise in the aftermath of Wangxia.

By the mid-1840s, the Pacific world—at least as it existed in the American imagination—had become yet another theater in the controversy over slavery. The question of the transcontinental railroad catalyzed this debate. Whichever section secured that railroad would control the most important commercial artery in North America and, in the process, tip the balance of power inexorably in its favor. For partisans of this railroad struggle, the coordinated efforts of a Massachusetts lawyer and a Virginia slaveholder to advance America's presence in the Pacific world would have seemed a distant memory. Once Asa Whitney's railroad memorial came before Congress, it forever altered the calculus of transpacific trade and sectionalized the debate. The war with Mexico, followed by the discovery of gold in California, only raised the stakes and deepened the controversy over the Pacific. The transcontinental railroad, a great national project designed to bind together the American East and West, had triggered a rupture between North and South.

→ **CHAPTER TWO** ←

The Great Slavery Road

———◆●◆———

HIS HUMAN PROPERTY may have been driven from California's goldfields in 1849, but five years later, Thomas Jefferson Green still saw a bright future for the slave South in the Far West. In the summer of 1854, Green traveled to East Texas to celebrate the Atlantic and Pacific Railroad Company as it broke ground on its transcontinental undertaking. "This road is emphatically the Southern, yea, what the abolitionist truly calls the '*great slavery road*,'" he exulted. To Green, this marked a particularly promising chapter in the campaign to extend the South's labor system and political influence across the western half of the continent. After nearly a decade of lobbying, slaveholding railroaders had made real headway in their plans for a Pacific connection. Most notably, they had orchestrated the purchase of roughly 30,000 square miles of Mexican territory to facilitate construction of a railroad along a far southern route. With such a railway, built "by Southern labor both white and black," Green predicted, slavery would spill westward and cement the South's political power at the national level.[1]

By the early 1850s, slaveholders' continental visions had come into focus. Whereas earlier railroad schemers directed their gaze across the Pacific and toward the consumer markets of China, expansionists of the new decade oriented their efforts primarily toward the Far West. That California, the proposed terminus of this southern route, had outlawed slavery by 1850 did not deter them. If anything, a free-soil California lent new urgency to plans for the great slavery road. With iron ribbons connecting the Pacific coast to the Deep South, slaveholders argued, California would be greeted by an influx of southern-born migrants and their plantation goods. "When the road is finally completed to the Pacific," the *Arkansas State Gazette and Democrat* projected in 1853, "the State of California, and the States which will intervene between that and Texas, being so intimately identified with us, in their commercial relations, will . . . join with our division of the country, as a common community, contending for common rights."[2] Politics, in other words, would follow commerce along the line of the railroad. Residents at opposite ends of the continent would then read the same news, buy the same goods, and ultimately share a political outlook. Here was the blueprint for the Continental South. As slaveholding statesmen seized control of several federal projects in the West by the early 1850s, what had once seemed a distant dream had suddenly become an attainable reality.

Through their railroad boosterism, slaveholders articulated some of the most ambitious and forward-thinking objectives of the era. They pursued a project that would subdue and settle the West, tap the burgeoning markets of the Pacific coast, extend cotton's dominion into China, boost the commercial capacity of the slave states, and unite the southern half of the continent along what was destined to become America's great commercial highway. What would make all of this possible, white southerners argued, was slave labor. According to slaveholding orthodoxy, African American bondpeople in the South and, possibly, unfree Indigenous workers in the West would build this railroad faster, cheaper, and better than wage laborers along any free-soil route. Slavery was to be the handmaiden of a modernizing, industrializing South. While historians of capitalism have carefully studied slavery's role in the making of the Atlantic world, they have largely missed southerners' struggles for the Pacific West and what those struggles reveal about the scope and scale of slaveholding power.[3] The American West spurred a clash between competing visions of modernity—a contest over which labor order, slave or free, could harness technology and federal power to build America's gateway to the future.

The great slavery road was no mere pipe dream, as northern statesmen understood all too well. Whereas proslavery filibusters have more effectively captured the historical imagination, southern railroaders presented a graver threat to the free-soil agenda. In contrast to would-be conquistadors like William Walker in Nicaragua, slaveholding railway advocates largely controlled the levers of power in Washington. From the executive branch, in particular, they overcame their numerical disadvantages to dictate policy for the West in the early 1850s. Northern leaders scrambled to block these proslavery initiatives and advance competing visions of their own.[4] The result was one of the longest-lived political controversies of the period, which lay at the root of sectional flashpoints like the Gadsden Purchase and Bleeding Kansas. Railroad debates also fueled a rising separatist impulse in the South, as partisans considered ways to construct a great slavery road free from northern oversight. The story of the sectional crisis is largely one of unbuilt railroads and the dreams they inspired.

The California Terminus

By late 1849, as emigrants rushed to California's goldfields, the political struggle over the Pacific railroad intensified. A transcontinental railway, once considered an extravagant fantasy by some, now seemed a necessity. The billowing population of the Pacific coast called for speedier transit options in order to shuttle migrants, mail, gold, and goods from coast to coast. The overland wagon roads and circuitous sea routes to California were deemed insufficient for this growing demand. Furthermore, a railroad could protect the Pacific coast from the imperial intrigues of America's favorite bogeyman, Great Britain. Although Britain never manifested the interest in California that some Americans suspected, expansionists like Jefferson Davis insisted that a Pacific railway was necessary to maintain military and political control over such an extensive territorial domain.[5] Citing these imperatives, a flurry of memorials poured into Congress in 1849, nominating various cities as the railroad's eastern terminus: Milwaukee, Chicago, St. Louis, and Memphis.

The debate spilled beyond the halls of Congress, as commercial conventions and newspapers across the country joined the fray. As in 1845, Memphis was again a hothouse for railroaders. While St. Louis attracted the largest gathering that year with roughly 1,000 delegates in attendance, the 400 representatives at Memphis put together, by all accounts, a less fractious and more successful convention (that is, after a cholera outbreak in the city pushed the event from July to November). Again, the organizers of the convention looked toward Asia and its "six hundred millions of people" and touted the far southern route as shorter and more temperate than its northern competitors. "We shall do what Christopher Columbus was attempting when he discovered a new world," the corresponding committee boasted, "find a direct passage to the East Indies by going west." Especially heartening to the committee was a growing network of railroads in the South, thus ensuring that a route from Memphis would have speedy access to the slave states of the Southeast as well as to the new markets of the Far West.[6] In attendance were men from fifteen different states—including Asa Whitney himself, who received a respectful hearing—though, again, southerners controlled the agenda. Most delegates strongly favored the construction of a route from Memphis to San Diego, not least among them the convention's president, Matthew Fontaine Maury.[7]

The political tide was beginning to turn in the South's favor. Prior to the California gold rush, Whitney's far northern route had dominated the debate on transcontinental communication, garnering endorsements from eighteen state legislatures and favorable reports from select committees in both houses of Congress in 1848.[8] But just a year later, the focus drifted southward. Published that year, a report and accompanying series of maps drew authoritatively on recent explorations of the American West to mount the evidence in favor of a far southern line.[9] Thanks to the organizational abilities and sectional fervor of southern railroaders, the so-called Gila route along the thirty-second parallel and into San Diego was fast becoming a major contender to Whitney's proposal. Whitney, who had never ceased campaigning for his northern line, sensed the shift in opinion and struck a defensive posture in his 1849 pamphlet, *A Project for a Railroad to the Pacific*. He devoted a substantial portion of the work to an attack on the Gila route, now his major rival. The land along the thirty-second parallel, he argued, was barren, underpopulated, and lacked the resources necessary to support railroad construction.[10] In the years to come, other opponents of the southern route would reiterate these objections, their chorus a gauge of how popular the thirty-second parallel had become.

Yet just as southern hopes were soaring to new heights, a blow came from California. With its swelling population and pressing land claims, California's elites assembled a constitutional convention in September 1849 in order to hurry the transition to statehood. The question of slavery occupied a central place in the proceedings of the convention at Monterey. To the shock of some and the relief of many, the assembled delegates resolved to bar the institution from California.[11] "What surprised us perhaps more than anything else was the unanimity with which the clause prohibiting slavery was passed," one former delegate recalled. "We had expected very considerable opposition from the Southern element."[12] White southerners were indeed well-represented at Monterey. But they fell in line behind northern-born and Hispano delegates, despite grumblings from prominent slaveholding émigrés beyond the convention's walls.[13] With the passage of this provision, California's constitution would read, "Neither slavery, nor involuntary servitude, unless for the punishment of crimes, shall ever be tolerated in this State."[14]

As with the earlier confrontation between Thomas Jefferson Green and the free-soil miners at Rose's Bar, the prohibition on slavery in California was not a moral crusade against human bondage. If anything, it was a crusade against African Americans. A number of delegates sought to bar not only slavery from California but also black laborers more generally. Although their efforts ultimately failed—primarily because the convention recognized that such restrictions would endanger California's chances at congressionally recognized statehood—they engendered a lively debate within the convention. One Kentucky-born delegate worried that unless California also banned African American immigration, slaveholders would circumvent the state's antislavery constitution. Masters would bring slaves by the hundreds into California as indentured laborers, he argued, only to set them free after they had worked a set term in the gold mines. The fact that a number of California slaveholders already employed this practice in the diggings gave some credence to these arguments.[15] The president of the convention, Robert Semple of Kentucky, predicted that a well-known Louisiana planter would, alone, transport 1,000 slaves into California in this manner.[16] Although such estimates stretched credulity, delegates were right to suspect the slipperiness of slaveholders, who would continue to devise various stratagems in order to dodge the restrictions on human bondage in California. As time would show, not even a constitutional ban on slavery could extinguish unfree labor within the state.

The southern delegates at Monterey did not abdicate their proslavery aspirations for the West; they simply recalibrated their strategy. A decisive influence on the antislavery measure came from what may seem an unlikely source: William McKendree Gwin. Born in Tennessee, educated in Kentucky, and groomed politically in Mississippi, Gwin still owned a large plantation in Natchez and some 200 slaves. Before coming to California, he had represented Mississippi in Congress, where he was mentored by John C. Calhoun, a fellow enthusiast for an American empire on the Pacific. An "ultra pro-slavery man," Gwin nevertheless urged his peers to adopt the antislavery clause to the constitution.[17] He did so in a shrewd gambit for power. According to fellow delegate John Sutter, on whose land the gold rush began, "When the question of slavery came up men from the south kept very quiet, as they wanted offices."[18] While others streamed toward California's gold, Gwin had come to California in 1849 for a different kind of prize: a seat in the US Senate.

Gwin knew that waging unwinnable battles at this early juncture was no way to endear himself to the future legislators who would elect him. The institution of chattel slavery was unpopular with thousands of Hispanos within California, many of whom had witnessed the passage of Mexico's 1829 antislavery law. Eight Hispanos, alongside a larger number of delegates from the free states, held a majority of the convention's seats and could, if necessary, block any slavery measure to the constitution.[19] Gwin did the electoral math, read the mood of the Monterey assembly, and opted to save his political capital for more promising contests.[20]

The convention's delegates finished their deliberations by October 1849, crafting a final document that outlawed slavery but not black immigration. Submitted for a popular vote in November, the constitution passed overwhelmingly, 12,061 in favor and 811 against; 66 of those negative votes came from Mariposa County, where gold-seeking southerners wanted a constitution without restrictions on slavery.[21] But they represented an extreme minority in a population that sought to avoid any sectional issues that would delay statehood.

Those within the South were not as willing to cede California to free labor. Slaveholders in Jackson, Mississippi, hatched a scheme to overrule the antislavery constitution through the power of immigration. They planned to raise a force of 5,000 white settlers and 10,000 slaves to colonize the mining and agricultural regions of California. According to one northern observer, by March 1850 there were already "a few stray specimens" of this would-be colony in California. Ultimately, this mass migration never materialized. As even the most petulant slaveholding expansionists could have recognized, such an undertaking would raise legal problems for masters in a free state and hazard millions of dollars in human property.[22]

The fiercest struggle over California's fate took place in Congress. In the debates that ultimately yielded the Compromise of 1850, southerners battled to secure at least a portion of California for slaveholding settlement. Jefferson Davis, a relatively junior senator at the time, distinguished himself by opposing the antislavery agenda for the West, what he called the "robber's law."[23] Davis pledged to "avail ourselves of every means . . . to prevent the admission of California as a State unless her southern boundary be reduced to 36 deg. 30 min."[24] His main ally in this struggle was the other senator from Mississippi, Henry Foote. Foote introduced a bill to extend the Missouri Compromise line to the Pacific and break off the southern section of California as the slaveholding territory of Colorado. The bill failed in the Senate by a vote of thirty-three to twenty-three.[25] But it would not be the last proslavery attempt to carve out a piece of the Pacific coast, as prominent residents continued to agitate for a division of California.[26]

What slaveholding statesmen feared most from free-soil California was not the loss of property rights in the Far West but the loss of power in Washington. Invoking a familiar trope, James Henry Hammond of South Carolina predicted that the South would be transformed into Haiti, the independent black republic whose enslaved population had violently overthrown their former masters by 1804.[27] Henry A. Wise of Virginia, who had once imagined a mass exodus of slaveholders to gold country, considered the loss of California a "military usurpation" by the North.[28] New Mexico and California belonged to the South by right of conquest, Jefferson Davis insisted, as the slave states had sacrificed a disproportionate amount of blood and treasure to wrest that land from Mexico.[29] Upon the passage of the statehood bill, Davis considered seizing the document from the leader of the Senate and shredding it.[30] Davis's desperation was seasoned by a belief that he and his fellow slaveholders would soon represent a political rump in Congress. According to his logic, a free California, with its two Senate and two House seats, would erode southern power and threaten slaveholding interests throughout the country.

That was the central theme of what would be John C. Calhoun's final speech. Worn down by age and illness, a dying Calhoun shuffled onto the Senate floor on March 4, 1850, to issue a dire warning of disunion unless sectional balance could be restored. Too weak to read his own speech, Calhoun delegated the task to James Mason of Virginia. He opened with a straightforward diagnosis of the Union's major ailment: "The equilibrium between the two sections . . . has been destroyed." According to Calhoun, the free states were outpacing the South in aggregate population, and soon enough, the North would hold a decisive share of Senate seats as well. The real problem for the South, he continued, lay in the West. There, the North would add to its majority by turning the territories of Oregon and Minnesota into free states, as well as the recent Mexican cession: Utah, New Mexico, and California. "What was once a constitutional federal republic," he continued, "is now converted, in reality, into one as absolute as that of the Autocrat of Russia, and as despotic in its tendency as any absolute government that ever existed."[31] Illness had not diminished Calhoun's talent for hyperbole. That only California had been slated for statehood was of little consequence to the ailing South Carolinian. He could read the proverbial writing on the wall, or so he claimed, and it spelled doom for slavery and the South. Several weeks later, Calhoun was dead.

Some scholars, perhaps swayed by the alarmist tone of their subjects, have represented the Compromise of 1850 as a breaking point in the history of slaveholders' western ambitions.[32] To be sure, the compromise dealt a serious blow to southerners on certain issues. It banned the slave trade in the District of Columbia, surrendered Texas's claim to the territory of New Mexico, and, most crucially, admitted California to the Union as a free state. In return, southerners gained a more stringent Fugitive Slave Law, while the fate of slavery in the territories of Utah and New Mexico was left to popular sovereignty, rather than simply outlawed. This, many southerners argued, was a raw deal.[33]

But the calamity that Calhoun had prophesied for the South and its master class would not come to pass. Despite their hysterical rhetoric, white southerners rallied from the loss of California and redirected their political energies toward more favorable contests. Whereas Calhoun saw disaster in the Far West, particularly the Mexican cession, the slaveholding statesmen who followed in his wake saw a railroad thoroughfare. They may have occupied a shrinking share of seats within the House of Representatives, as Calhoun complained, but this did not confine them to a subordinate position in national affairs. In the contest over the Pacific railroad, slaveholders consistently punched above their demographic weight, bending state power to their ends.

William Gwin personified the South's recovery from the Compromise of 1850. After a contested vote within the California statehouse in late 1849, Gwin won a seat in the US Senate, along with the western military celebrity John C. Frémont. The Mississippi transplant managed to convince a sufficient number of legislators that the election of a southern-born senator was a necessary counterbalance to Frémont and essential to California's chances at statehood. "I was induced to vote for him as U.S. Senator because he was known as an extreme Southern man," one legislator recalled. "If another northern man had been selected it would have been so palpable a cut or insult to the South that the State never would have had a chance of admission."[34]

Although he went to Washington as a representative from a free state, Gwin's political loyalty lay with the slave South. His sectional allegiance shone through in the debates over the transcontinental railroad. Gwin persistently claimed to work in the interests of the Union, rather than for the aggrandizement of a particular section, but he called for a railroad that ran almost entirely through slave country, with only branch lines radiating into the North. In this plan, Gwin followed in the footsteps of the proslavery expansionists of the preceding decade. Like John C. Calhoun, J. D. B. De Bow, and Matthew Fontaine Maury, Gwin saw in transcontinental transit the formula for southern revival. If slavery was to be barred from California, the Pacific could still be tethered to the South, Gwin and others rightly reasoned, by a bond of iron.

The Great Slavery Road at High Tide

While railroad promoters focused primarily on regional development during the two years after the Compromise of 1850, transcontinental plans again took center stage beginning in early 1853. That year, Congress devoted more time and attention to Pacific railroad proposals than to any other subject, as the transcontinental debate reached "fever heat," according to the *American Railroad Journal*.[35] Southerners approached the issue with particular fervor and focus. Between 1852 and 1859, large southern commercial conventions met once a year or more, and in at least three of these meetings, the Pacific railroad was the main agenda item. Northern industrialists, while committed to railroad development as much as if not more than their slaveholding counterparts, nevertheless lacked the sectional fire that animated commercial conventions south of the Mason-Dixon Line.[36]

Gwin reinvigorated the debate within the Senate. His campaign began in 1851, when he read to his congressional colleagues California's resolutions for a federally funded transcontinental railway, though Gwin would not launch headlong into railroad promotion until two years later. In January 1853, he pitched one of the most ambitious proposals to date: a plan for a transcontinental network with multiple branches. Starting from San Francisco, the line would sweep down the valley of California and begin radiating through the Southwest. Although he urged his colleagues to lay aside "sectarian principles" and scorn "all sectionality," Gwin's own sympathies were unmistakable. His proposed railway would run primarily through slave country—Arkansas, Missouri, Tennessee, Louisiana, and Texas—with additional lines into Puget Sound in the Pacific Northwest and Dubuque, Iowa. These were small concessions to the North for a railroad that otherwise resembled many southern expansionists' fantasies.[37]

The ensuing debate accentuated the central issues over the railroad question—location, financing, and the remit of the federal government. Gwin's plan would have set loose one of the largest state-sponsored operations in American history. To pay for the road, the government would need to issue nearly 100 million acres of land along 5,000 miles of track, supplemented by a subsidy of $12,000 per mile across Texas, where Congress owned no land. A later amendment called for contractors to carry out the construction, whose work would be financed by land grants and up to $20 million in government bonds. Such vast government expenditures riled several strict constructionist Democrats, including a Virginia senator who dubbed the plan a "rape of the Constitution." But state-rights purists were in the minority. Most agreed that only with substantial federal aid—whether in the form of bonds, subsidies, or land grants—could a transcontinental railroad break ground. The sticking point was location. An amendment to Gwin's original bill, put forward by Senator Thomas Jefferson Rusk of Texas, attempted to circumvent the issue by empowering the president to determine the road's route. Still, the tactic did not calm sectional jealousies, as congressmen speculated about President-elect Franklin Pierce's proclivities and accused one another of angling for regional advantage. Several amendments later, the bill died.[38]

Slaveholding expansionists had more leverage through the executive branch than they did in Congress. Beginning in 1853, planters found a comfortable home in Pierce's presidential administration. Although a native of New Hampshire, Pierce owed his victory to large Democratic majorities in the slave states. In tribute, he packed his cabinet and key diplomatic posts with globally minded southerners: Secretary of War Jefferson Davis (Mississippi), Secretary of the Navy James Dobbin (North Carolina), Assistant Secretary of State Ambrose Dudley Mann (Virginia), minister to France John Y. Mason (Virginia), and minister to Spain Pierre Soule (Louisiana).[39] As Pierce's most trusted advisor, Jefferson Davis shaped much of the executive agenda. He lent his powers to western development projects, in particular, and most of all to the southern transcontinental railroad.[40] Even as their proportional representation was waning in the House of Representatives, slaveholders and their allies retained control of the executive branch through the rest of the decade.

After Gwin's railroad bill died in Congress, the Pierce administration turned national attention to the Mexican border. There, land disputes around the Mesilla Valley reopened an opportunity for proslavery expansionists. Since the signing of the Treaty of Guadalupe Hidalgo in 1848, white southerners had been agitating for more land along the Mexican border, which was necessary so that their great slavery road could steer around a series of desert mountains currently blocking its proposed path. In 1850, the proslavery journalist and foreign minister Duff Green attempted to negotiate a large purchase of territory "extending the whole length of the northern boundary of Mexico, with the right of occupation and of making a railroad."[41] Green's negotiations failed, but the Pierce administration revived the plan, reentering talks with Mexico in 1853. Encouraged by Davis, the president sought a dusty stretch of land in what is now southern New Mexico and Arizona—uncultivable terrain, according to some. The only crop in mind, however, were iron rails bound for the Pacific.

To carry out this mission, Pierce appointed the proslavery partisan James Gadsden of South Carolina. Over the past three decades, Gadsden had steadily built his reputation on two interlinked endeavors: clearing land for slaveholding settlers and promoting the development of southern railroads. A veteran of the War of 1812 and of later conflicts with Native Americans in the Southeast, Gadsden helped oversee the expulsion of the Seminole people from their homelands in Florida and southern Georgia in 1823. That year, a county in Florida was named in his honor. Gadsden himself owned a slave plantation in the territory. In 1840, he was made president of the South Carolina Railroad Company, which had once owned the longest railroad in the world. Gadsden soon emerged as one of the most influential advocates of a deep southern railroad along the Gila trail, what he considered the "most practicable, easiest ... cheapest of construction, and shortest of distance."[42] He had become, according to J. D. B. De Bow in 1847, "the life of all these [western railroad] movements, and their pioneer."[43] After California was ostensibly lost to free labor, Gadsden headed a group of planters who petitioned the California assembly to form a slaveholding colony in the southern part of the state, with plans to bring 2,000 bondpeople into the breakaway territory. His California-bound slaveholders would be preceded by a mounted corps and a team of engineers to survey the route to the Pacific, which could be used as a stagecoach line and later a railway. "Open such a way, and the Railroad follows," Gadsden declared, thus wedding his plans for a Pacific slave colony with his railroad promotion.[44]

Gadsden's mission to Mexico was a fitting sequel to these earlier efforts. Before departing, he sought the counsel of his unofficial sponsor, Jefferson Davis. "I should be pleased to hear from you, and to receive any suggestions of importance relative to the mission," he wrote in May 1853. "I shall need the countenance & encouragement of my Southern Friends, as my appointment to Mexico is said to have been induced by my being a Southern Man." As if there was any doubt, Gadsden pledged to "uphold & apply" the "principles of the South" in his forthcoming negotiations.[45] Although Gadsden disguised his proslavery motives in his public correspondence and statements, few observers were under any illusions. He went to Mexico as Davis's handpicked man, an agent of the South, and a champion of the great slavery road. Indeed, "the sole object" of the mission, as Secretary of State William L. Marcy wrote in his official instructions, was to create "an eligible route for a rail-road."[46]

When Gadsden returned to Washington in late December 1853 with a treaty calling for $15 million in exchange for nearly 40,000 square miles of Mexican territory, critics came out in force. This was the same amount, after all, that the United States paid for all of New Mexico and California just five years earlier. "The friends of the Southern Pacific Railroad are the only *bona fide* supporters of the treaty," a correspondent to the *Philadelphia Public Ledger* complained, "and it might just as well be called a 'purchase of the right of way for a railroad to the Pacific,' as by any other name." That such an important diplomatic mission had been entrusted to a proslavery schemer was a serious breach of political etiquette, the correspondent added.[47] According to the *National Era,* Gadsden's negotiations had not only opened the way for a Pacific railroad "favored by Southern Nullifiers" but also handed the present "Slaveholding Administration" an opportunity to create two or three additional slaves states from the new territory.[48] During deliberations in the House of Representatives, hotheaded Thomas Hart Benton of Missouri deemed the treaty a monumental waste of money. A longtime supporter of a central transcontinental route, Benton ridiculed the prospects for railroad construction through this new territory, "a country so utterly desolate, desert, and God-forsaken, that . . . a wolf could not make his living upon it." He accused the treaty's architects of orchestrating a vast conspiracy to push a Pacific railroad through barren borderlands and into New San Diego, a yet-to-be-built city where slaveholding speculators would make untold fortunes.[49]

In the spring of 1854, the treaty passed over the strenuous objections of congressmen like Benton, although the Senate shaved 9,000 square miles and $5 million off the initial agreement.[50] Gadsden griped about the scaled-down version of his original deal, but his negotiations had resulted in a decisive victory for proslavery expansionists: the final strip of land, measuring about 30,000 square miles, provided crucial real estate for a southern railroad. Furthermore, it signaled that southern expansionists possessed the political capital necessary to advance their designs in the West at a time when sectional compromise was proving increasingly elusive. The last major territorial acquisition of the era, the Gadsden Purchase moved Jefferson Davis and his allies one step closer toward their transcontinental ambitions.

As Congress wrangled over Gadsden's treaty, Albert Pike of Arkansas delivered perhaps the most ambitious plan yet for a southern railroad. A teacher, poet, newspaper editor, soldier, and lawyer, Pike's career had carried him across much of the continent before he settled into railroad boosterism by the early 1850s.[51] At the Charleston commercial convention of 1854, Pike blasted the federal government for its inaction and its alleged northern bias. He proposed the formation of a Pacific Railroad Company, jointly owned by a confederation of southern states, to build a line along the Gila route. This company, Pike elaborated, would negotiate with Mexico and Indian peoples for a right-of-way, a necessary measure should the Gadsden Treaty fail in Congress.[52] If southerners wished to prevent their section from sliding even further behind the North, he demanded, they would have to take matters into their own hands. "Who ever heard of a Northern man giving another an advantage in a matter of trade!" he added to great applause. A railroad built by Congress would be a railroad along a northern line, and the South would be stuck with the bill, he argued. Only by building the railroad themselves could southerners prevent the North from capturing the Pacific.[53]

Pike's audacity invited some pushback from fellow delegates at Charleston, but he ultimately carried the day. Matthew Fontaine Maury deemed it "unlawful," while others insisted that only the federal government had the right to negotiate with foreign powers. The scheme, they argued, was impractical at best and probably even unconstitutional. Furthermore, the federal government had proved a better friend to southern railroad schemes than Pike cared to admit. But other prominent railroaders, most

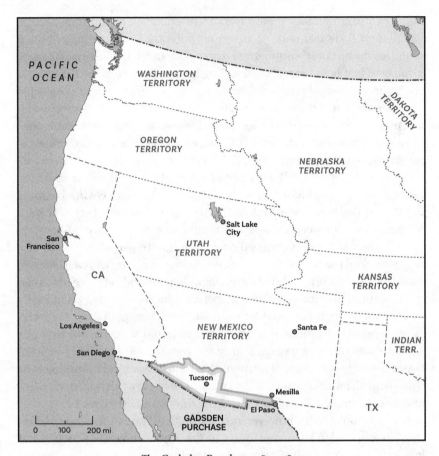

The Gadsden Purchase, 1853–1854

notably James Gadsden, sided with Pike's plan. Pike followed with a bombastic appeal for "a sort of declaration of independence on the part of the South."[54] Interrupted frequently by loud ovations, Pike promised action and a southern railroad at long last. "For my own part, I would rather go and buy the right of way, than walk into the halls of Congress and ask them to give," he roared to immense applause.[55] Voting by states, the convention adopted his resolution unanimously, determined "to secure to the South, so far as may be in their power, the exclusive benefits and advantages of the commerce of the Pacific." The convention agreed to invite California to join the proposed organization.[56]

Outside the convention's halls, interest in Pike's resolution proved less enthusiastic. Although the Louisiana legislature eventually granted a charter in 1855, no company was ever organized under its auspices.[57] Nevertheless,

Pike's campaign underscored slaveholders' enduring commitment to the Pacific and their readiness to drum up potentially dangerous sectional impulses on behalf of commercial expansion. Indeed, Pike's resolution is a gauge of just how far sectional feeling had progressed since the start of the transcontinental railroad debates and just how important the Pacific had become to many slaveholders. Pike and his numerous allies were willing, perhaps even eager, to risk secession for greater commercial autonomy. Here was a southern declaration of independence—rhetorically, at least— roughly seven years before the real thing.

Meanwhile, Jefferson Davis opened yet another front in the southern railroad campaign. Passed in March 1853 with William Gwin's backing, the Pacific Railroad Survey bill authorized Davis, as secretary of war, to assemble teams to carry out a reconnaissance of the trans-Mississippi West.[58] The work was to proceed over a ten-month period, although surveys stretched into late 1854. The act was born out of a belief that scientific objectivity could break the congressional logjam and settle the railroad question once and for all. Whereas sectional motives guided the nation's statesmen, its engineers could presumably put aside politics in the interest of topological precision. Under great national scrutiny, six federally appointed engineers surveyed four major routes: a far northern route between the forty-seventh and forty-ninth parallels, a central route along the thirty-eighth parallel, a south-central route along the thirty-fifth parallel, and an extreme southern route along the thirty-second parallel.[59]

Scientific objectivity, however, met its limits in Davis. Feigning indifference, he channeled the opportunity to the South's advantage, a fact not lost on political rivals like Thomas Hart Benton.[60] To maintain the appearance of impartiality, Davis appointed mostly northern surveyors. In his detailed summary of their work, though, Davis let his sectional bias shine. Starting with the northernmost survey, he argued that every route except that along the thirty-second parallel faced severe obstacles: cost, length, climate, or a combination of all three. He then dismissed, as mere trifles, serious impediments to the far southern route, such as a lack of water and timber. "A comparison of the results," Davis stated, "conclusively shows that the route of the 32nd parallel is, of those surveyed, 'the most practicable and economical route for a railroad from the Mississippi river to the Pacific ocean.'"[61] For him, this was a foregone conclusion. But for many others, his summary was further proof of southern intrigue and slaveholders' determination to drive the railroad through their section at any cost.

Construction did not proceed from these surveys as Davis and his allies had hoped. Despite the effort and expense—launching four separate expeditions (five including a shorter survey of California's terrain) and

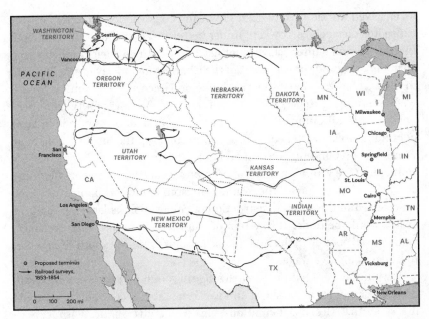

Routes of the Pacific Railroad Surveys, 1853–1854

publishing their findings in a twelve-volume government report—the entire operation brought no clear resolution to an increasingly fraught and sectionalized debate.[62] Yet the surveys, together with the Gadsden Purchase, did provide southern expansionists with an important template for further action. Despite Albert Pike's grumblings, recent experience demonstrated that the federal government, and namely the executive branch, was a powerful avenue through which to pursue a sectional agenda. Furthermore, the Davis report itself enjoyed an afterlife in debates over the Pacific. White southerners routinely cited Davis's work to argue that the government had already given its imprimatur to the great slavery road. By the end of the decade, another proslavery cabinet minister would deploy it, as we shall see, to legitimate the most significant transcontinental project of the antebellum era.

Railroad Bound

When advocating for their preferred route, proslavery railroaders boasted of a number of advantages: flatter terrain, warmer climate, shorter distances. But perhaps the most compelling advantage the South possessed lay in its massive unfree labor force. As southern railroad boosters regularly noted, an enslaved workforce kept costs down and construction on schedule. "Because it is cheaper, can be kept under better discipline" and "worked both in summer and winter," slave labor gave the South an edge in railway construction, bragged the president of the Charleston and Savannah Railroad in 1855.[63] One year later, Thomas Jefferson Green made a similar appeal when attempting to negotiate the purchase of 300 slaves for the Southern Pacific Railroad Company. "The experience of the entire south is in favor of building roads with negro labor as the cheapest the most reliable in all works of road building, the best and not liable to strikes and riots," he proclaimed.[64] One Virginian railroad promoter quantified such benefits. With an enslaved labor force, "the grading, masonry, and mechanical work on railroads, and the entire construction of canals, will be less than half the cost it would be under the system of contracts," he estimated. Contracts worked well enough in the free states, he argued, but the South should play to its peculiar advantages.[65]

The numbers are telling. At an average of roughly $30,000 per mile, railroad construction in northern and western states cost double what it did in the South.[66] Green's calculations, based on conversations with "experienced southern rail road builders," indicated that a Pacific railroad through the Deep South might be constructed at less than $12,000 per mile.[67] According to the ledger books of the Richmond, Fredericksburg and Potomac Railroad, a railroad corporation could own an enslaved person's labor for a year at roughly $120, compared to the weekly wages of about $7 to $10 for free white workers.[68] In addition to the expense of their weekly wages, white workers in the South—often of Irish or German origin—brought with them the specter of labor strife. Rather than risk purported wage strikes, walk-offs, drinking binges, and European ethnic rivalries, southern railroad companies generally opted for cheaper, more regulated slave labor.[69]

These preferences led to massive concentrations of enslaved laborers on southern railroad works. For instance, the Virginia and Tennessee Railroad employed 435 slaves (out of a total labor force of 643 people) on its projects in 1856. The overall number of enslaved people working in southern railroad construction climbed in the following years. The most careful student of the subject found that in 1860, thirty-seven southern companies each used at least 100 enslaved laborers in railroad construction. The Atlantic & Gulf line in southern Georgia oversaw a workforce of 1,200 slaves, a larger population of bonded laborers than could be found on any single plantation in the South. Such companies generally hired slaves from nearby planters on an annual basis, rather than buying them outright, due to the high cost of able-bodied enslaved men, who were considered most suitable for railroad work. According to recent estimates, southern railroads collectively employed an average of 10,000 slaves per year at the end of the antebellum period. But some scholars suggest that number may have been as high as 20,000 by the eve of the Civil War.[70]

Slave labor was essential in the laying of thousands of miles of track across the South. Frederick Nims, a civil engineer from Massachusetts, discovered this when he moved south to work for the Georgia State Railroad in the 1830s. Nims claimed to be an antislavery man, fretting to his brother, "I know not as I should escape the linch-laws were even my sentiments known on slavery." Yet those views proved flexible enough on the railroad works of Georgia. Nims's theoretical opposition to slavery gave way to a practical adoption of the institution, with a gang of six bondmen under his control by 1837. He consoled himself that "those with us are treated well, I have seen but a few cases of ill treatment."[71] Yet no amount of self-assurance could disguise the fact that the South's railroads had converted this Massachusetts engineer into a Georgia slave driver. In later years, Nims would write to his brother, detailing his attempts to recruit scores of slaves in order to press forward with his production schedule.[72]

Such labor practices may have suited the needs of corporations and engineers in the Southeast, but how would railroad construction adjust to the vaster spaces and sparser populations of the American Southwest? Here was a pressing question for anyone who seriously contemplated a Pacific railroad. The Virginian surveyor Andrew Belcher Gray, who knew the region as well as any white American, suggested two possibilities. "The Papigos and Pimas Indians, by proper management, might be made very useful, in working upon the road where there is not much rock excavation," he argued. What "proper management" might entail, Gray did not elaborate, although he might have contemplated the use of Indian slaves, who circulated widely throughout the region. He also pointed to the possibilities of cheap Mexican peon labor. Because they were "regularly acclimated" and accustomed to hard labor, peons "might be very useful," Gray suggested. "I have seen some good stone work done by these peons in Chihuahua and Sonora," he added.[73] Between the black slaves of the Southeast and the Mexican peons and Native Americans of the Southwest, expansionists like Gray could imagine an entire continent of unfree labor, ready to serve the needs of their Pacific railroad.

Much like agricultural plantations, southern railroad corporations extracted as much labor for as little cost as possible. Enslaved African Americans often worked in regimented gangs from sunup to sundown, even in the blistering heat of the southern summer, driven by overseers with strict construction quotas. As one contractor near Columbia, South Carolina, boasted, "I go out there about half past five and get the niggers to work—

stay till seven then come up to breakfast—back at eight work till half past twelve then turn out for dinner. Commence again at two and work till sun down."[74] Because railroads generally rented rather than owned slaves, overseers were advised against beating black laborers under their watch. Yet that did not militate against mistreatment. Status as a rented slave seemed to invite especially harsh floggings from managers on the Hamburg and Charleston Rail Road. "There they were, cutting and slashing all the time," a formerly enslaved man recalled of the overseers on the railroad line. "After we were whipped we had to go straight back to our work. They did not care whether we got well or not, because we were other people's niggers."[75] No wonder, then, that some masters took out life insurance policies for the slaves they rented to railroad companies.[76] And no wonder that some enslaved people protested against mistreatment by running away, including eighty-four bondpeople on the Montgomery and West Point Railroad between the years 1845 and 1850.[77] But for those who stayed, and for those who were caught and returned, the possibility of maiming or even death was ever-present. "There was hardly a day that some of the slaves did not get crippled or killed," a former slave on the Hamburg and Charleston line recalled. "There were more killed there than at any other place I ever worked at."[78]

Even in the absence of whippings, railroad work was backbreaking. From clearing brush, chopping down trees, and removing boulders, to excavating cuts, leveling terrain, and laying track, enslaved railroad laborers conducted their work almost entirely by hand. Some railroad companies allowed bondpeople to work on Sundays and holidays for pay, but in general, the enslaved were provided only a meager allowance of food and clothing, along with shoddy accommodations.[79] The Montgomery and West Point Railroad spent twice as much per year to feed a horse or mule as it did a slave.[80] Railroad work was particularly devastating for enslaved families. Although some companies rented enslaved women for jobs like washing and cooking, construction sites were a largely male world. Husbands were separated from wives, sons from parents, and fathers from children whenever railroad contractors visited the plantation for recruitment. "Poor fellows!" an abolitionist journalist lamented. "In that God-forsaken section of the earth they seldom see a woman from Christmas to Christmas."[81]

Slaves not only worked the railroads, they also rode them—though very rarely of their own free will.[82] Between 1800 and 1860, roughly 1 million enslaved people were transported from the coastal states to the southern interior. Railways facilitated much of this human traffic. Some corporations incentivized this commerce by shipping bonded children for free and by offering discounted rates for enslaved adults. On James Gadsden's South

Carolina Railroad, for instance, slaves and dogs traveled for the same price.[83] For Jacob Stroyer and many other African Americans, railroad depots were the sites of tragic human spectacles, to which bondpeople were driven "like so many cattle" and packed onto cars for sale. Decades later, he was still haunted by the memory of such a station, where a group of black people from his plantation, including his sisters, had been loaded onto train cars. As the cars began to pull away "the colored people cried out with one voice as though the heavens and earth were coming together," Stroyer recalled. "We heard the weeping and wailing from the slaves as far as human voice could be heard."[84]

For Stroyer and thousands of African Americans this was tragedy; for southern planters and businessmen it was a lucrative commerce. Railroad development helped fuel a steep rise in slave prices during the 1850s. By connecting plantation districts to major markets and by increasing the demand for bondpeople on construction projects, railway expansion placed a premium on slave labor.[85] This was a self-perpetuating cycle. As lines were extended into the southern hinterland, more acreage came under the cultivation of slave labor, which in turn made more bonded workers available for hire by railroad corporations.[86] It did not take a particularly fanciful imagination to foresee this cycle repeating itself across the Far West with the construction of a Pacific railroad. Indeed, Thomas Butler King of Georgia pointed to the mutual relationship between slavery and railway construction in promoting his new transcontinental enterprise, the Southern Pacific Railroad Company. With a reliable rail connection, Texas would become a planter's paradise, Butler argued, drawing slaveholding emigrants from the worn-out soils of the East into the untapped cotton frontier of the West.[87] An empire of slavery and plantation commerce would march in step with the railroad.

Recent trends buoyed slaveholders' hopes. Southerners had been early and eager adopters of the railway. At 136 miles, the line from Charleston to Hamburg, South Carolina, completed in 1833, was the longest railroad in the world at the time.[88] But it was not until the 1850s that southern railroad construction—what one upcountry planter called the "ruling Mania of the day"—accelerated rapidly on the backs of enslaved laborers.[89] That decade, the slave states laid down more than 8,300 miles of track, as well as a staggering number of junctions, depots, and terminal points, thereby providing their white citizens with better railroad facilities and infrastructure than could be found in many parts of the North. This in spite of the South's relatively low demand for consumer goods, which made railroads such a lucrative enterprise in the more densely populated free states.[90] Every slaveholding state more than doubled its total rail mileage in the 1850s. Only the northwestern states of Ohio, Illinois, Indiana, Michigan, and Iowa matched this rate of growth.[91] Furthermore, the slave states vastly outspent free states in railroad investment. State and local governments in the South provided 57 percent of the capital for railroads within their borders, compared to just 15 to 21 percent for the free states, which relied primarily on private investment.[92] By the end of the decade, the slave states contained more track mileage than any European nation.[93]

While prominent northeasterners, like writer Ralph Waldo Emerson, disparaged slavery's relationship to the railroad and the modern world in general, the southern expansionists of the 1850s were anything but backward-looking.[94] Indeed, American slaveholders pursued the most advanced technologies and promoted the most extensive public works on the continent and perhaps even the globe. Had the South won independence, it would have ranked among the top six most industrially advanced nations in the world and among the top four in total wealth.[95] Nothing showcased slaveholders' commercial savvy or modernizing impulses quite like their commitment to railroad development. That southerners advanced slave labor to achieve this end does not signify that they had turned their backs on the modern age. In fact, midcentury southerners had good reason to believe that liberalism was on the wane, unfreedom was on the rise, and a political economy built on plantation agriculture was the surest path to international ascendency. As cotton boomed and slave prices soared in the United States, abolitionist Britain began importing indentured Asian laborers—so-called coolies—to its West Indian sugar colonies, an implicit concession that slave emancipation had proved bad for business.[96] Slaveholders may have lamented their dependence on northern industry and shipping, but recent developments seemed to indicate that the way forward—and ultimately the road to the Pacific—would be blazed by slave rather than free labor.

If slaveholders embraced economic modernization and global integration, can we call them capitalists? This question has been at the center of a growing body of literature, which traces the financial networks, management techniques, and enterprising spirit of slaveholding Americans. A group of historians have illustrated how global capitalism fed off the slave-grown staples of the American South. And they have shown how slaveholders, in turn, participated in an international market and integrated financial systems that made them among the richest individuals on the continent.[97] Thanks to these studies, we can no longer view slaveholders as willfully isolated agrarians or quasi-feudal holdovers from a bygone era. Like northern industrialists and western entrepreneurs, southern slaveholders moved in sync with many of the economic trends of the modern age. This has led some scholars to suggest that the traditional geographic boundaries "that organize so much nineteenth-century American scholarship" have outlived their usefulness. When following slavery's commodities and capital, these old geographies "begin to crumble," they argue, "rendering an unclear line of demarcation between a capitalist North and a slave South, with consequences for how we understand North and South as discrete economies—and whether we should do so in the first place."[98]

Such works sit uncomfortably beside—and sometimes directly challenge—a related body of scholarship: the vast literature on the sectional crisis and the Civil War. While one group of scholars emphasizes the interconnectedness of North and South, the other group of historians pushes in the opposite direction. The free-labor political economy of the North and the plantation system of the South increasingly drifted apart, many Civil War scholars argue, until the two reached a point of no return by 1861. How to reconcile these two interpretations? In other words, can we explain the road to the Civil War while still acknowledging the dynamism of the plantation South and the capitalist world order to which it was bound?[99]

In following global connections, we should not lose sight of regional distinctions. Whereas the capital that slavery generated may have transcended borders, the political economy upon which it rested was not nearly as portable. A study of proslavery railroading illustrates this point. Southern railway enthusiasts were among the most commercially savvy and globally minded leaders of their age, but their economic vision served to heighten, rather than diminish, sectional rivalry. Expansionists like Albert Pike framed the railroad campaign as a direct challenge to northern commercial power, as something of a proto-nationalist project to liberate the southern economy from what he considered a Yankee yoke. White southerners often defined themselves and their political economy in stark contradistinction to what they believed existed in the North, and their dependence on chattel slavery created an ideological worldview—while relentlessly profit-oriented—at odds with that of their northern counterparts.[100] The rush to the Pacific only deepened these divisions.

Conclusion

If optimism could roll iron and lay track, southerners would have driven their railroad into California before the ink dried on the Gadsden Treaty. Yet the *Texas State Gazette* was not just whistling Dixie when it reported, "The prize is within her reach—she will not fail to grasp it."[101] By 1854, the prospect of a southern-oriented "commercial empire" stretching into the Pacific had never seemed closer at hand. Gadsden had negotiated a favorable purchase of land from Mexico. Davis was in control of the railroad surveys. Arkansas and Texas were poised to extend their railway networks and link them with other burgeoning southern lines. Slave labor had proved cost-effective on major railroad works throughout the South. And President Pierce remained sympathetic to planters' expansionist aims.[102] Furthermore, slaveholders could count on a powerful body of Southern Californians to support a rail line through slave country. In the summer of 1853, delegates at a San Diego convention resolved to promote the route along the Gila River into their city and dispatched Colonel John B. Magruder to press their case in Washington.[103] The winds of history, it would seem, were blowing in a distinctly southerly direction.[104]

Yet for clear-eyed slaveholders, every silver lining still had its storm cloud. While southern leaders had successfully leveraged executive power to make way for their preferred road, they nevertheless lacked the votes in Congress to authorize and fund construction. The debate over William Gwin's 1853 Pacific railroad bill was a cautionary tale. A combination of sectional hostility and more local jealousies had killed one of the most promising railroad proposals yet. Unless slaveholders and their allies could cobble together a larger coalition, a free-soil road might supplant the Gila route as the odds-on favorite. Or perhaps the entire enterprise would collapse under the weight of congressional indecision and sectional rivalry. Southern expansionists and their political opponents were attempting a precarious balancing act: how to push a divisive measure without irredeemably dividing the nation?

→ CHAPTER THREE ←

The Lesser Slavery Road

◆◆

"**W**E DO NOT RIDE on the railroad," lamented Henry David Thoreau from his cabin on Walden Pond; "it rides upon us."[1] Thoreau had retreated into the wilderness in 1845 to escape the rattle and clank of America's iron horse, among other modern disturbances. By the late 1850s, even railroad enthusiasts in Washington were coming to share his cynical outlook. Senator William Gwin may have dealt primarily in imagined railways, but his frustrations were real. As chair of the select committee on the Pacific railroad bill, Gwin had seen his hobbyhorse fall from the priorities of Congress. While debate on the transcontinental railroad had consumed the congressional agenda in the early years of the decade, by 1858 a weary Gwin could not even count on his own committee to exert much effort on behalf of the project. As Gwin bitterly recalled in his memoirs, the Pacific railroad bill "lay dead on the files of the Senate, only being called up occasionally," a victim of the legislative logjam caused by rising sectional tensions.[2] Plans for the "great slavery road," which appeared so promising a few years earlier, had been thrown off track.

Although neither section would concede defeat in the contest over the Pacific railroad, by mid-decade southern railroad partisans had shifted some of their energies toward new but related fields of opportunity.[3] Jefferson Davis again set the agenda for western transit. While simultaneously lobbying for a far southern railroad, Davis hatched one of the oddest experiments of the antebellum era: the importation of dozens of camels for use in military transport across the Far Southwest. In the mind of Davis, these camels could serve as a corollary, or perhaps a precursor, to the great slavery road. They would help soldiers quell Indian resistance in the region, facilitate westward migration, and open the way for greater infrastructural development, thus strengthening America's grip on the lower half of the country. Davis's camels never became a mainstay of the US military presence in the West, with many of the animals auctioned off or simply set loose by the end of the Civil War.[4] But the experiment confirmed, for both Davis's allies and his critics, the lengths that certain slaveholders were willing to go in order to extend their influence across the continent.

Slaveholders achieved a stunning geopolitical victory with another project in the region—what one might call the "lesser slavery road." Overriding northern opposition, southern statesmen won a large federal subsidy for the nation's major overland mail road in 1857. When the road was completed a year later, what became known as the Butterfield Overland Mail Company (or more simply, the "Overland") followed the far southern route that many had proposed for a Pacific railway. Perhaps due to its short life, truncated by the outbreak of the Civil War, the Overland has largely fallen out of the narrative of the sectional conflict. Yet during the final years of the decade, the road—which inspired the much more famous Pony Express—was a flashpoint in the sectional struggle for the Far Southwest. On one side of the divide it met with exultation, and on the other, with outrage. According to the *Chicago Tribune*, the Overland amounted to "one of the greatest swindles ever perpetrated upon the country by the slave holders."[5] Such indignation is understandable only when one considers the vast hopes that antebellum Americans vested in transcontinental transportation, and in this road in particular. Partisans on both sides of the debate expected that iron rails would eventually follow wagon ruts and that the Overland would therefore blaze the trail for the Pacific railway.

While southern transportation schemes were assailed by northern rivals in Washington, another formidable group of adversaries asserted themselves far from the halls of Congress. Any serious transcontinental promoter ignored Native Americans—especially the powerful Comanche, Apache, Navajo, and Ute peoples of the Southwest—at their own peril. Jefferson Davis, one of the era's most active secretaries of war, recognized this fact in almost everything he wrote about the West. He may have failed to understand their political economies and cultures, but he never underestimated the strength of the "numerous and warlike bands of Indians" between the Rocky Mountains and the Sierra Nevada. "With an army three times as great as ours," Davis concluded, "it would be impracticable . . . to guard all points of our extended frontier as entirely to prevent Indian depredations."[6] For instance, with a combined population of more than 40,000, the Navajos and Apaches controlled much of New Mexico Territory prior to the Civil War. By that point, the entire US Army contained only 15,000 men, concentrated in a series of fortifications across a vast western borderland.[7] Complete pacification was Davis's endgame, but for

the foreseeable future, the US military would act more like a frontier police force than an army of conquest. Thus, all proposed transcontinental
thoroughfares across the West would have to balance both political and
military considerations and make practical concessions to the people who
claimed these lands. Native Americans would not readily acquiesce to a
road that threatened their existence.

Perhaps the most surprising aspect of this history is not that slaveholders
failed to construct the railroad of their fantasies but that, given the odds,
they came as close as they did. The Butterfield Overland Road was merely
the latest in a string of interlinked proslavery victories across the Far West.
The Gadsden Purchase, the Pacific railroad surveys, the US Camel Corps,
and finally the Overland—each one of these operations was designed, in
part, to extend the slave South's control across the continent. Not all southern statesmen prioritized or even supported such initiatives. In advancing a
far western agenda, slaveholders like Davis had to overcome not only fierce
northern opposition and Indian resistance but also substantial pushback
from within the southern Democratic fold. Once completed, the Overland
became one of the signal geopolitical victories of this generation of slaveholders, a tribute to their political dexterity, influence, and willingness to
deploy federal power. And, however briefly, it also stood as a powerful symbol on the American landscape—a monument to the Continental South.

Rival Lines

Proslavery victories appear even more remarkable when considering the
strength of northern opposition and the depth of intra-regional competition. The expansionists of the Deep South had to contend with a vast field of
political rivals, from the well-organized railroad promoters of the North, to
the strict constructionists of the Democratic Party, to numerous competing projects across the slave states themselves. Many of the greatest challenges that proslavery expansionists faced came from within their own
section. The geographic region that contemporaries and historians have
labeled the "South" in truth contained several subregions and conflicting
constituencies that repeatedly confounded the efforts of statesmen like
John C. Calhoun to impose a collective identity or unified political mission
on the slave states.[8] Despite numerous attempts to close ranks against the
perceived threat of Yankee encroachment, southerners persistently suc-
cumbed to internal divisions. The potential spoils of railroad development
exacerbated these rivalries.

From Asa Whitney's first petition in 1845 to the outbreak of the Civil War,
northerners agitated for several different routes across free soil. During the

1850s, voting on Pacific railroad bills increasingly followed sectional lines, and antislavery forces proved eager to divert attention from the popular thirty-second-parallel route. For well over half a decade, Whitney kept up his campaign for a railroad into the Pacific Northwest, although he eventually discontinued the fight by the early 1850s.[9] Others picked up the torch. A free-soil possibility gained greater visibility with the work of Theodore Judah, a Yankee engineer and surveyor, whose efforts, years later, would pave the way for the construction of the Central Pacific Railroad between California and Utah. Initially, however, he was derided as "Crazy Judah" for his suggestion that a railroad might cross California's Sierra Nevada, then thought to be an insurmountable range.[10] By the end of the decade, the soldier, explorer, and expansionist William Gilpin imagined a line through Denver to the mouth of the Columbia, shifting America's empire toward the Pacific "to disinfect ourselves of inane nepotism to Europe."[11]

The most dogged opponent of the Gila River route came from within the South itself. Democrat Thomas Hart Benton of Missouri rarely missed an opportunity to scold proslavery congressmen for their sectional bias. Recall that Benton lambasted the Gadsden Purchase and the far southern railroad it was designed to facilitate, as well as the railway surveys under Secretary of War Jefferson Davis. Instead, he put forward, again and again, a route that would begin at St. Louis and follow a more central path to San Francisco.[12] Fellow Missourians, like US representative and future governor John S. Phelps, also criticized the far southern road as too distant from the main arteries of American commerce.[13] Due to the persistence of Benton, Phelps, and others within Missouri, St. Louis would become the primary competitor to Memphis as the preferred eastern terminus within the South. Their efforts underline the fact that not all expansionists from the slave states had slaveholding interests in mind when pressing for western infrastructure.

Yet railroaders from the Deep South ultimately had the last laugh. Benton's hostility to the westward extension of slavery earned him powerful enemies within his state. The Missouri legislature denied him a sixth Senate term in 1851. By 1855, his opposition to the Kansas-Nebraska Act ultimately drove him out of the House (to which he had been elected in 1853) after a single term. Benton's removal from Congress cleared a major hurdle to the great slavery road.

The advocates of the thirty-second-parallel route also had to contend with rivals farther south. Over the course of the decade, private American companies, often with the backing of the US government, attempted to construct railroads over several different isthmuses in Central America. These routes required far fewer miles of track than any railroad across the

United States, although none of them passed over US territory and each required steamship lines from both Atlantic and Pacific ports. Despite the logistical and diplomatic obstacles, by 1860 ministers of the United States successfully negotiated treaties with four Latin American states for transit rights across their territory. To make these routes pay, though, required a rare combination of entrepreneurial foresight, engineering skill, and historical accident.

The route over the Isthmus of Tehuantepec—the narrow waist of Mexico—attracted a powerful body of backers, concentrated primarily in New Orleans. Shipping interests in the Crescent City rightfully viewed the Memphis movement as a threat to their grip on western trade and remained less committed to transcontinental railroad construction so long as they controlled southern river transportation. Although he later became a strong American railroad advocate, J. D. B. De Bow, who operated his *Review* out of New Orleans, was among the most prominent early defenders of a route across Tehuantepec.[14] Over the course of the decade, several New Orleans–based partnerships purchased transit rights across Mexico in order to preserve the commercial power of their city. The US government also saw the utility of the isthmus. The finalized Gadsden Treaty of 1854, for instance, included a clause to guarantee a right-of-way across Tehuantepec. By 1859, the Louisiana Tehuantepec Company, led by prominent proslavery expansionists Judah Benjamin, Emile La Sére, and John Slidell, broke ground on a railroad. Future Mexican president Porfirio Díaz, then but a caudillo-in-training, looked on admiringly.[15] Escalating civil war in Mexico, which broke out in 1858, and an enduring mistrust of all things American forestalled further construction. A railroad across the Mexican isthmus was not constructed until 1894, during the three-decade presidency of Díaz.[16]

Other Central American isthmian projects proved more successful—albeit only after substantial investments. After five years, $8 million, and the deaths of thousands of workers, the New York–based firm of William Aspinwall finally succeeded in constructing a railroad across the Isthmus of Panama by 1855. Until Cornelius Vanderbilt slashed prices for his competing enterprise across Nicaragua, the Panama route ruled the shipping business that carried goods and emigrants to California and back again. The company netted $6 million in profits in its first seven years of operation and at one point commanded the highest price, per share, of any stock traded on the New York Stock Exchange. The proslavery push for a transcontinental railroad was, in some ways, an attempt to cut into the profits of these private shipping businesses and to demonstrate that southerners could also compete in large-scale transportation enterprises. Jefferson Davis, in particular, criticized isthmian connections "as temporary

expedients only" that would distract the government from the more important projects to link both halves of the North American continent.[17]

The major competitor to the Pacific Mail Steamship Company operating
across Panama was Vanderbilt's Nicaragua route, which presented a more
convenient bridge between the Atlantic and the Pacific. In 1849, the United
States signed a treaty with Nicaragua, securing the exclusive right to build
and operate a canal across the country. That same year, the government
granted Vanderbilt the construction contract. Due to a combination of
factors—civil war in Nicaragua, lack of financing from British banks, and
American filibusters—the canal was never built. But Vanderbilt's company
nevertheless managed to ferry travelers across Nicaragua for several years,
undercutting his Panama rival in the process. The lucrative venture would
have likely continued were it not for a certain "grey-eyed man of destiny":
the filibuster and momentary Nicaraguan dictator William Walker. The
architect of an abortive invasion of Sonora, Mexico, in 1853, Walker seized
power in Nicaragua three years later. But when he revoked the charter and
confiscated the property of Vanderbilt's Accessory Transit Company, then
sold that property to Vanderbilt's rivals, Walker made a serious strategic
miscalculation. Vanderbilt closed his Atlantic steamships to Walker's
potential recruits in the United States, depriving the filibuster of much-
needed manpower and effectively dooming his brief and bloody reign.[18]

By the fall of 1859, Vanderbilt and the directors of the Pacific Mail Steamship Company reached an agreement by which each organization would
operate service in only one ocean—the Atlantic for Vanderbilt, the Pacific
for his erstwhile competitors. Such an arrangement only sharpened the
long-running criticism that steamship service to the Pacific coast was
monopolistic and inefficient.[19] Meanwhile, in Washington, most congressmen could agree on at least one point regarding Pacific communication:
isthmian options might reasonably serve as a complement to overland
routes but never a substitute.

Kansas and the Limits of Southern Railroading

Among Democratic railroad promoters, in particular, the issue of funding
presented a potential sticking point. Who should pay for the railroad—
the federal government, the states across which it passed, individual corporations? And how should it be financed—land grants, federal bonds, subsidies to states, the initiative of private capitalists, or some combination
of these means? Furthermore, was such a sweeping national undertaking,
which even the most conservative estimates placed at over $100 million,

compatible with the state-rights position so many southern politicians claimed to represent?[20]

As William Gwin grumbled in his memoirs, it was often these strict constructionists along with "extremists, north and south," who stymied railroad bills.[21] The Democratic senator Lewis Cass of Michigan, for instance, helped scuttle Gwin's 1853 Pacific railroad bill when he dismissed it as "entirely too magnificent."[22] Gwin's fellow southerners could be equally obstructionist. "Government was instituted for the protection of its citizens against foreign invasion and domestic insurrection," Representative Zedekiah Kidwell of Virginia declared in a minority report on an 1856 Pacific railroad bill, "and not to enter into the freighting business, or into railroad building, for the benefit of the trading and travelling classes." Even if it could be built, he argued, such a railroad would require "a sum of money greater, probably, than is yearly earned by all the shipping of all the oceans of the world!"[23] Of course, southern Democrats like Kidwell did not have a monopoly on strict constructionism. The abolitionist and New York congressman Gerrit Smith opposed a Pacific railroad for similar reasons, as he outlined in an 1854 speech, published as *Keep Government within Its Limits.* "Let Government build this road," he claimed, "and there will be no assignable limits to its future departure from its own province, and to its future invasion of the province of the people."[24]

Slaveholders who opposed federal action on such a massive scale could have found a suitable alternative in the private railroad enterprise of Robert Walker and Thomas Butler King. Chartered in 1852 and capitalized at $100 million, their Atlantic and Pacific Railroad was to follow the line favored by the Deep South's expansionists. This was the project that Thomas Jefferson Green praised as the "great slavery road." Yet like so many proslavery enterprises of this ilk, it soon attracted the criticism of the northern press. The editor of the *New-York Examiner* dismissed Walker as a "flibberty-gibbet" who was heading a team of "Southern slaveholders" in the process of committing "a gross fraud on the stockholders of the Company."[25] Ultimately Walker and King failed to secure a charter to construct a line through Texas, and thus the Atlantic and Pacific Railroad Company folded. But the board members did not concede defeat so easily. They reorganized and renamed the operation, not once but twice, and continued fighting for transit rights through Texas.[26]

Although they never constructed their great slavery road, Walker and King made their mark on the West by bankrolling Andrew Belcher Gray's extensive survey of the region. A more seasoned surveyor or keener advocate for the far southern route could hardly have been found anywhere in the country. Gray had served as the chief surveyor of the US-Mexican boundary commission in the early 1850s, and his report was used to justify the $10 million congressional allocation for the Gadsden Treaty. His subsequent expedition, under Walker and King's renamed Texas Western Railroad Company, reinforced his earlier claims about the feasibility of a railroad through the Far Southwest. To carry out the task, he enlisted a team of fellow southerners. His twenty-six men hailed almost exclusively from Texas, except for one Kentuckian and Gray himself, a Virginian. Together, they surveyed roughly 2,200 miles over the course of five months and revealed new insights into what, for many Americans, appeared a distant and inhospitable landscape. So convinced was Gray about the richness of the region that he later settled in Tucson, Arizona, a community populated largely by fellow migrants from the slave states.[27]

Published in 1856, Gray's report advanced the most exhaustive argument to date for a far southern railroad. He stressed the practicality of construction and detailed the riches, agricultural and mineral, that could be found across this route. For a total cost of $45 million, Gray predicted, the South could secure a highway for the transport of "cotton, tobacco, wheat, corn, hemp and wool" across the West, in the process transforming "the whole valley of the Rio Grande, from Santa Fe to the Presidio del Norte, the extensive interior of Sonora, Chihuahua, New Mexico, and Texas," into a tributary for plantation commerce. The road would ultimately terminate in the port of San Diego, where Gray had invested personally. To complete the task, Gray recommended the labor of Mexican peons and Native Americans—under "proper management," of course.[28]

Even as they cheered such private enterprises (which still depended on various forms of public support), a majority of proslavery leaders agreed on the necessity of federal aid for the Pacific railroad.[29] The buccaneering spirit of individual politicians explains much of this logic. After all, railroading was big business, and slaveholders were just as eager to snatch the financial fruits of internal improvements as their Yankee counterparts. Southern railroad advocates had been reaping the rewards of federal largesse since at least 1850, when Congress began offering free land to railway corporations in order to incentivize settlement and development. The land was distributed in a checkerboard pattern, with alternating plots either available for sale to the public or given gratis to railroad companies. Southern politicians were particularly adept at bending railroad legislation to their own ends. Led by Senator David Rice Atchison of Missouri, a clique of proslavery congressmen claimed much of this free federal land for themselves and for their friends. Atchison and his allies scuttled bills that would have benefited railroad construction in the North while directing most land grants toward the slave states.[30]

Southern Democrats could easily shelve their state-rights scruples when properly enticed by the financial windfall of a transcontinental railroad through their region. Even John C. Calhoun, the patron saint of limited government and nullification, favored federal land grants in order to finance railway construction.[31] Centralization at the national level, which so many planters decried from the early republic onward, was considered a menace only when it threatened slavery and southern economic interests. Strict constructionism generally took a back seat to expansionist imperatives. Slaveholders relinquished their state-rights doctrine when presented with the opportunity to acquire Louisiana from France in 1803. They embraced federal power when, in the 1830s, the government cleared valuable plantation real estate by forcibly relocating Indians from the Southeast. They cheered the annexation of Texas and the conquest of New Mexico and California, again made possible only through overwhelming federal force. They cried foul when several northern legislatures turned state rights to their own advantage by passing so-called Personal Liberty Laws in opposition to the Fugitive Slave Act of 1850. And they endorsed the federal judiciary when it handed down its proslavery ruling in the *Dred Scott* case. As the long history of proslavery politicking makes clear, the only consistent element of the southern state-rights mantra was its inconsistency. State rights was a banner to be unfurled whenever politically and economically expedient, then quietly stashed when the full force of the federal government was needed.[32]

Slaveholding expansionists achieved a pyrrhic victory by mid-decade. Bleeding Kansas is remembered today as the tipping point in the nation's spiral toward civil war. At the time, however, it was seen largely as the by-product of the intractable Pacific railroad feud. Indeed, the Kansas-Nebraska Act of 1854 had its roots in opposition to the great slavery road.[33] As observers noted, railroad construction would have to be accompanied by white settlement along its path, and Nebraska, prime terrain for a central railway, had been guaranteed to Native populations, including the Shawnee, Delaware, Omaha, Kickapoo, Otoe, Missouri, Miami, Kaskaskia, and Peoria. So long as Indian Country remained closed to white settlers, the odds on a northern route winning a Pacific railroad were slim. On the other hand, the thirty-second-parallel route ran through lands, though occupied by formidable Indigenous nations, technically open to white settlement. When it appeared as if the southern route had become the favorite, political rivals mobilized.

Thomas Hart Benton took an early lead in the campaign for a railroad from St. Louis and the organization of Nebraska. Soon thereafter Willard Hall of Missouri and William Richardson of Illinois spearheaded a bill in the House. Just as the Senate was debating William Gwin's southern-oriented Pacific railroad proposal of 1853, Hall made a plea for a more northerly route, accompanied by the opening of Nebraska. "Why, everybody is talking about a railroad to the Pacific ocean," he complained. "In the name of God, how is the railroad to be made if you will *never* let people live on the lands through which the road passes?" Without the organization of Nebraska, he reasoned, Congress would likely be forced to settle on some point in Texas as the road's eastern terminus. Overwhelming opposition from southerners in the Senate, including William Gwin, effectively killed Hall and Richardson's bill.[34]

Illinois Democrat Stephen Douglas revived the Nebraska question the next year, but this time with the support of the South. To gain these crucial votes, he made what many northerners regarded as a Faustian bargain: his bill repealed the Missouri Compromise line, split the western territory into two halves—Nebraska and Kansas—and left the slavery question to the dictates of popular sovereignty. The southern congressmen who lent their support to Douglas's bill were willing to take the gamble of supporting a rival railroad plan so long as they might introduce slavery into these new western territories. And if these territories became slave states, Douglas's preferred railroad route through Kansas would no longer run across free soil.[35]

Ironically, a bill designed to facilitate another transcontinental route ultimately derailed the Pacific railroad debate. Almost immediately, antislavery Jayhawkers and proslavery Border Ruffians poured into Kansas to stamp their preferred labor order on the territory. The conflict between these forces, known as Bleeding Kansas, cost the lives of more than 100 settlers. By pushing sectional tensions to a near breaking point, Kansas effectively foreclosed the possibility of compromise over a transcontinental railroad by the mid-1850s. Northerners would not countenance a southern route, while southerners closed ranks against a northern line. Congressmen would continue to agitate for various Pacific railroad routes but with increasing jadedness and diminishing expectations.[36]

Jefferson Davis's Camels

And yet, slaveholders' western dreams did not die on the bloodied soil of Kansas. As railroad bills languished in a factionalized Congress, southern statesmen turned their attention to corollary projects. Jefferson Davis opened an international front in the struggle over the Far West when he designed an elaborate plan to import camels from Africa and Asia. Framed as a nationalist project to extend US interests, the scheme nevertheless betrayed Davis's sectional prejudices. After all, this was an enterprise that would benefit the southern corridor of the country more than any other, facilitating travel between the slave states and the Far West.

When Davis first introduced his plan for an American camel corps in 1851, he was almost laughed out of the Senate. But when his colleagues finally stopped snickering, they had to take stock of a serious proposal. Beginning with a modest appropriation of $30,000 for the importation of thirty Bactrian camels (two humps) and twenty dromedaries (one hump), Davis expected to eventually revolutionize transportation in the American Southwest. He argued that the camels, being naturally suited to arid conditions, would help overcome the region's powerful Indian peoples and provide protection for settlers and mail routes. Davis praised the camel as the "ship of the desert," destined to become "the greatest stroke of economy which has ever been made in regard to transportation."[37]

After years of lobbying, he finally won his camel appropriation by 1855. To acquire the animals, Davis appointed the Mexican War veteran Major Henry C. Wayne of Georgia, who had been an outspoken advocate of camel labor and Davis's confidant since the late 1840s. Wayne set off on a world tour, with visits to Tunis, Constantinople, Cairo, and Smyrna, where he acquired thirty-four camels and five Arab and Turkish handlers. The exotic caravan reached Indianola, Texas, by April 1856. Nine months later, a further forty-one camels arrived in the United States.[38]

Davis's camel scheme was of a less patently proslavery nature than his railroad campaigning, although it still had a decidedly southern flavor to it. After all, these camels were bound for the Southwest, across terrain that Davis and others hoped would soon host a southern transcontinental line. As Davis recognized, railways and overland roads would not build themselves. They had to be carved out of Indian country and guarded against Native peoples. Furthermore, almost 2,000 miles separated the Pacific coast from the Mississippi valley, with no major intervening rivers crossing east to west. Camels, Davis reasoned, would help subdue this region and expedite travel for westward-bound settlers. Safer transit across this corridor would facilitate the expansion of proslavery interests. "If we had a good railroad and other roads making it convenient to go through Texas into New Mexico, and through New Mexico into Southern California," Davis mused to a friend in 1855, "our people with their servants, their horses and their cows would gradually pass westward over fertile lands into mining districts . . . [where] the advantage of their *associated labor* would impress itself upon others about them."[39] By this logic, infrastructural development would serve as the handmaiden of slaveholding expansion. And camels could play a vital part.

In pursuing his vision for the American West, Davis drew from the military playbook of Europe's empires. As his enthusiastic collaborator Henry Wayne noted, Napoleon Bonaparte had created an effective dromedary corps for operations against the "marauding Arabs" in his Egyptian campaign. Wayne and Davis saw no reason why an American analogue would not give the US military a similar edge in "controlling the Indians by checking and promptly punishing their aggressions."[40] The parallels between northern Africa and western North America—with their arid landscapes, vast unmapped terrain, and populations of powerful mounted peoples— were not lost on Wayne, Davis, or the US military establishment more generally. Davis himself translated a French account of camels' military use in North Africa and encouraged Wayne to seek out several high-ranking French officers who could share further insights into the deployment of camel forces.[41] Following in the footsteps—or hoofprints, as it were—of Europe's imperial armies, Secretary of War Davis made the subjugation of vast stretches of territory one of his principal aims, however prolonged and difficult that work proved to be. To this end, he oversaw the largest peacetime expansion of the US military since the War of 1812. Davis increased the size of the army by nearly 50 percent: from under 11,000 to nearly 16,000 active troops, most of whom were concentrated in the West. By 1859, military expenditures consumed more than half of the total US budget.[42]

If these camels did not revolutionize transport in the Southwest, they nevertheless proved effective (and eye-catching) in their initial operations. While overseeing the first shipment of camels in East and Central Texas, Wayne packed one of the animals with over 1,200 pounds of hay, astounding the spectators who had gathered to observe the test.[43] Further positive reports came from Lieutenant Edward Fitzgerald Beale, who employed dozens of camels in several high-profile expeditions across the Southwest between 1857 and 1859. Crowds regularly gathered to watch Beale's camel corps pass, while newspapers across the country reported on his progress.[44] Beale himself enthused about the capacities of the camels, whom he compared favorably to mules.[45] Camels, as observers noted, boasted several advantages in desert travel: they could survive without water for long stretches of time, manage heavy loads, travel more than thirty miles per day, and do so while consuming less food than horses and mules. "A greater boon to the 'Dry Plains' of the Southwest could scarcely be imagined," wrote one observer in the South.[46]

Jefferson Davis's successor in the War Department, John B. Floyd of

Thanks to the efforts of Jefferson Davis and several private shippers, roughly 200 camels were brought to the United States in the 1850s. For decades thereafter, they could be found in zoos and circuses and lumbering across the American Southwest. Here, a camel train travels through Nevada in 1877. *Harper's Weekly,* June 30, 1877.

Virginia, was also impressed and accordingly urged further appropriations for the camel experiment.[47] Joining Davis, Floyd, Wayne, and Beale in the growing ranks of camel supporters was the temporary commander of the Department of Texas, Robert E. Lee. Incidentally, Lee ordered what was to be the last long-range camel expedition of the era—a reconnaissance of the country between Camp Hudson and Fort Davis in West Texas in 1860—before the project, and his US military career, was ended by the Civil War.[48]

Despite its successes and its supporters, the camel corps never became a significant presence in the West. When it came to his animals, Davis was often on the defensive, guarding against accusations that the project was a thinly veiled proslavery plot.[49] He had always been careful to maintain a nationalist rather than a sectional posture whenever discussing his camels, yet criticism persisted.[50] Amid rising sectional tensions, Congress refused to appropriate funds for the animals in 1858, 1859, and again in 1860. By then more than eighty camels were scattered across forts in California and Texas, but popular support for the experiment had waned. According to one historian, the public could never quite look beyond the camel's "personal habits of regurgitating on passersby or blowing a bloody bladder out of its mouth when frightened, its acute halitosis and general bad odor, its fierceness during rutting season, its voluminous sneeze, its shedding of large clumps of hair until it looked perfectly hideous, and its awkward appearance."[51] Camels, in short, did not endear themselves to American travelers.

They did, however, endear themselves to slave traders. Davis certainly did not foresee camels being used as a smokescreen to sneak in shiploads of captive Africans to the North American mainland. But by the late 1850s, the camel experiment was largely beyond his control, as federal funding dried up and private shippers and individual buyers entered the game.

Henry Wayne was again a central, albeit unwitting, player in this drama. In November 1858, his letter to the *National Intelligencer* sparked a new interest in camels: not as agents of the US military but as beasts of burden on southern plantations. Reprinted by newspapers and periodicals across the country, Wayne's letter praised the utility of camels in agricultural tasks, including their ability to transport heavy loads, such as baled cotton, "to and from the railway or market." As a self-proclaimed "Southern man" as well as Davis's hand-picked camel importer, Wayne was well-positioned to comment on the animals' adaptability to plantation labor. "So far as the negro is concerned," he wrote, "I am satisfied, from a knowledge of the nature and habits of both, that no animal is better suited to him in all respects than the camel."[52]

Many onlookers were convinced. "I want one of the '*critters*,'" one correspondent wrote to the *Southern Cultivator*, "and must beg you to tell me how I can get one, transported or shipped to Macon, Geo." In the same issue, another correspondent advocated for the dual importation of camels and African slaves. "Let 'Cuffy' come and his appropriate co-laborers the Camel," he pleaded.[53] As if heeding these calls, a shipment of twenty-one camels arrived in Mobile within weeks. Several months earlier, the largest camel cargo of the era had docked in Galveston—a payload of eighty-nine animals—bringing the total number of camels in the slave states to over one hundred.

At least ten of those were sent to Benjamin Woolsey, an enterprising planter and railroad promoter in Dallas County, Alabama, who put them to a series of tests in plowing and transporting heavy burdens.[54] Not only did they perform well, according to Woolsey, but they were also cheap to maintain and "will eat almost anything that the goat does not refuse."[55] More tests followed in other parts of the South, including a successful competition against mules, drawing large crowds and hearty endorsements from the southern press.[56] In one such "trial of strength," two bales of cotton with a combined weight of 1,100 pounds were tied to a camel's back, "with which he marched off apparently as unconcerned as though they were not there," reported one observer.[57]

Although no records exist to prove it, these camels almost certainly arrived on the American mainland with African slaves. Several pieces of evidence strongly suggest that camels were a cover, albeit a lucrative one, for the more valuable traffic in humans. The main importer of these animals was John A. Machado, a well-known slave trader. More incriminating still, the *Thomas Watson*, the same vessel that he used to import eighty-nine camels to Galveston in October 1858, had previously been seized by a British steamship off the coast of Africa after a naked human captive had escaped from its hold. But because maritime law prohibited the search of American ships, the *Thomas Watson* was spared. Camels provided an ideal alibi for slavers like Machado. Slave ships were generally recognizable by their substantial food supplies, large water tanks, and the stench of excrement. Yet any ship carrying a large number of camels also required an abundance of supplies and gave off similarly strong smells of waste. With camels aboard, Machado could explain away these telltale signs, so often associated with slavers, and then secure an extra layer of security by flying the American flag. Machado had an additional decoy in his beguiling business partner and mistress, Mary Jane Watson, who acted as the primary promoter and salesperson of his camels once they were unloaded. Unable to resist the odd traveling partners—beautiful woman with hairy animal companions—the press followed her throughout the South, never suspecting (or at least never reporting on) Machado's illicit payload.[58]

Machado often left chaos in his wake. The British consul at Galveston saw through the slaver's ruse and urged the US attorney stationed there to inspect the vessel. Although agreeing that the camels were likely a cover for African captives, the official refused to search the vessel without direct evidence of illicit activity. Machado thus escaped detection, and the *Thomas Watson* continued to sail in the service of slavery, becoming the first ship to raise a Confederate flag in Liverpool, England, shortly after the outbreak of the war. The ship's career ended ingloriously several months later, however, when it ran aground while attempting to break through the Union blockade of Charleston in October 1861. One year later, Mary Jane Watson drank herself to death in Madrid.[59] The fate of the slaves who arrived with Machado's camels is unknown.

Over the coming years, the camels that once elicited such interest fell out of favor and slipped from the historical record. Despite Wayne's earlier claims, they proved ill-suited to the demands of intensive agricultural labor. The soft soil of the cotton belt slowed their movement, while mules

generally performed better in the light and fast tasks upon which plantations depended. As military beasts of burden, the camels' record was similarly unremarkable. They made cameo appearances in both Union and
Confederate units during the Civil War yet were not widely adopted. By the
end of the conflict, many of the animals were either auctioned off or simply
set loose. Some found their way into zoos and circuses—five went to the
Ringling Brothers—while others disappeared into the wild. For decades to
come, astonished travelers in the Southwest reported sightings of strange
beasts moving across the desert landscape. As late as 1901, camels were
spotted in Arizona and Sonora, Mexico—the last relics of a bygone era.[60]

Quixotic and comical though this project may seem in hindsight, the
camel experiment was more than a curiosity. It was, however briefly, a key
component of Jefferson Davis's transcontinental vision. The project underscores his commitment to southwestern development and his versatility
in bringing such dreams to fruition. Davis sought international solutions
in order to master America's geography, enduring the initial derision of
Congress and drawing directly on European imperial models to make his
case. The feral camels that continued to roam the Southwest for decades
thereafter were reminders of the limitations of this vision. But they were
also a peculiar testament to the ingenuity of slaveholders—from the secretary of war down to individual planters and slave traders—in the global
pursuit of their aims.

The Overland

More so than the camel corps, the campaign for an overland mail route
revived slaveholders' western fantasies. Nearly forgotten today, what contemporaries called the Overland Mail, or simply the Overland, was a cause
célèbre of the late antebellum era and one of the slave South's greatest
coups. The project did not begin as a sectional affair, however. In March
1857, Congress passed a $600,000 annual appropriation for the operation
of a mail road from an undetermined point in the Mississippi Valley to
San Francisco. The price was high but the payoff, many congressmen reasoned, would be substantial. Not only would this new road provide faster,
more regular mail service to the Pacific coast, but it would also offer a
safe overland trail for westering emigrants. This route was also expected to
become the precursor to the long-awaited Pacific railroad. According to a
common theory, iron rails would follow this emigrants' trail, and East and
West would finally be connected along a well-traveled, federally financed
thoroughfare. To avoid the sort of sectional standoff that had so frequently

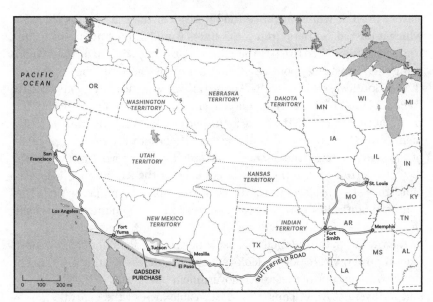

The Butterfield Overland Mail Road, 1858–1861

stymied Pacific railroad bills, the route's location was left to contractors, who began submitting bids in the summer of 1857.

There was just one problem: Aaron V. Brown, the US postmaster general. Brown—a former congressman, governor of Tennessee, champion of Texas annexation, and law partner of James K. Polk—had established his credentials as a "strong Southern man," according to *Harper's Weekly*.[61] He was appointed postmaster general by James Buchanan in 1857, as a favor to the southern voters who secured the president's election. Several months later, Brown repaid the favor to this proslavery base by striking down all nine routes proposed by the bidders for the overland contract, likely because none passed south of Albuquerque. Instead, he took it upon himself to designate a new route and forced all contractors to conform to his geographic strictures. In direct violation of the congressional act establishing the service, Brown stipulated a bifurcated route with eastern termini at St. Louis and Memphis (his hometown). The two routes would then converge at Little Rock, Arkansas (later changed to Fort Smith), before passing through Texas to El Paso, then move along the southern part of New Mexico to Fort Yuma and Los Angeles, and finally shoot up the Central Valley of California to San Francisco. In total, his route added 600 miles to the longest alternative bid.[62]

Although this road would not necessarily serve the expansion of chattel slavery itself, it would advance the interests of the slave states through which it passed. Settlers from these states would fan out along the route. And even if they failed to carry their human property with them, they would bring their proslavery politics, strengthening ties between the South and the Far Southwest. Because the Pacific railway was ultimately expected to trace this mail route, Brown's maneuver also marked a signal victory for the great slavery road. "The route for a Southern railroad and the establishment of the Great Overland Mail line upon that route, are considered parts of the same system," the *Sacramento Daily Union* reported in December 1857. "Undertaken with the view of connecting the Atlantic with the Pacific," these two projects were "devised" to enable "a population from the Southern States [to] naturally take possession of the country over which the railroad and mail line will pass."[63]

The view from the antebellum Post Office Department underscores how federal power, strategically deployed, could buttress southern interests. Brown oversaw one of the largest government operations in the country—and for average Americans, the most visible arm of the central state—which dwarfed its European counterparts in manpower and scope. By 1831, the post office employed 8,700 people, more than the US Army. Not until the corporate consolidation of the Gilded Age would an American enterprise—the Pennsylvania Railroad—surpass the post office's employee rolls. Through the antebellum era, the Post Office Department grew rapidly to keep pace with the vastly expanded borders of the United States. By the end of Brown's tenure, the nation boasted some 240,000 miles of post roads and roughly 28,000 post offices. Those offices were staffed by local officials appointed by the postmaster general. Thus, with the possible exception of the US president, no other American figure at the time administered a larger and more dispersed network of agents than Brown.[64]

Brown's political compass pointed true south, and he did little to disguise his partisanship in his official report. Like Davis before him, he dismissed more northerly routes as excessively cold and inaccessible. Along a northern path, he insisted, the mail would not reach the Pacific coast in the twenty-five-day window stipulated by Congress's act. In addition to these delays, Brown argued, travelers would also be imperiled. He imagined passengers along an Albuquerque route, "benumbed by the cold for more than a week, overcome by the loss of sleep." Such a route, "under circumstances of so much severe exposure, would, in a few years, mark every station with the fresh graves of its victims."[65] He rightly argued that the southernmost route was flatter and warmer, while implausibly claiming that it also boasted more water than the alternatives. He invited northern opposition when he bragged that his mail route would link up with a vast southern transportation network, feeding off "all the great railroads of Virginia, South Carolina, Georgia, Alabama, Tennessee, and Kentucky . . . and New Orleans and Texas." Trains would soon follow stagecoaches, making his mail road the "pioneer route for the first great railroad . . . to the Pacific."[66]

Brown struck an imperialist note in the final part of his report. This road would contribute to southern transportation fortunes, help populate western territories, and bind the eastern United States to the Pacific. It would also facilitate America's empire along the border with Mexico, serving as a springboard for future conquests. "In time of peace it will shed its blessings on both nations," he argued, "whilst in time of war it will furnish a highway for troops and munitions of war, which might enable us to vindicate our rights, and preserve untarnished our national honor."[67] Again, western infrastructure and American imperialism fit hand-in-glove.

Brown drew on another western expansionist to justify his work. He cited Jefferson Davis as the ultimate authority, "who collected a larger amount of reliable information on this subject than any other person" while overseeing the Pacific railroad surveys—and who also happened to favor this southernmost route.[68] Indeed, Brown's arguments for a southern overland mail route and Davis's earlier arguments for a southern transcontinental railroad were largely indistinguishable. And just as Davis pursued the lodestar of southern expansion at the expense of national interests, Brown trampled congressional mandates to advance a proslavery agenda for the West. Although Davis's report never resulted in the railroad of his fantasies, it enjoyed a productive afterlife through Brown's maneuverings.

The slave states applauded their newest champion. The *Alexandria Gazette* called Brown's report "clear, simple, and comprehensive," while the *Memphis Daily Appeal* cheered him as "able and masterly."[69] Brown had become a hometown hero in Memphis. "The citizens of Memphis, especially, should thank and remember him for the strong stand he has taken for their city as a terminus," the *Appeal* reported, "and for the unanswerable arguments he has so successfully brought to bear to sustain it."[70] President Buchanan, a southern sympathizer despite his Pennsylvania origins, was jubilant. "It is a glorious triumph for civilization and the Union," he announced. "Settlements will soon follow the course of the road, and the East and the West will be bound together by a chain of living Americans, which can never be broken."[71]

Northern indignation was proportional to the audacity of Brown's act. The *Ohio State Journal* dubbed it "a shameful outrage" and a "*revolution of law.*" The road would enrich not only the slave states, the *Journal* complained, but Brown himself, who purportedly owned real estate across the route he selected.[72] "The South demanded the sacrifice of the public convenience upon the altar of Slavery propagandism," protested the *National Era*, "and the South must be gratified at every cost."[73] The San Francisco press echoed many of these complaints, noting that all mail and passengers would have to be routed through Los Angeles, a proslavery bastion, before ultimately reaching the much more populous areas around the San Francisco Bay. "Under the miserably short-sighted policy of the Executive," the *San Francisco Bulletin* complained, "California is made to suffer, and the public Treasury is robbed"—and all for a route that passed too far south to attract a critical mass of passenger traffic.[74] Part of the Overland Mail Road followed the San Antonio–San Diego line, what critics called a route "from no place through nothing to nowhere."[75]

Brown also drew abuse from members of Congress, who linked his road to a longer history of proslavery scheming in the Far Southwest. In a lengthy and impassioned speech, Republican representative Francis Blair connected the dots between the Gadsden Purchase, Davis's Pacific railroad surveys, the camel corps, and now the Overland Mail. "Why was it that an appropriation of $10,000,000 to purchase Arizona, appropriations to import camels, to bore artesian wells . . . could be made during the dominancy of the so-called Democracy, and no effort whatever made to find a line for the central route?" Blair, an antislavery Missourian, demanded. The answer was simple. The "southern faction" forced the hand of both the executive and Congress to "dictate absolutely its policy." The newest outrage, Brown's Overland Mail Road, was yet another example of proslavery expansionists sacrificing national interests and considerable capital to advance their sectional agenda, Blair added.[76] In later debates in the Senate, other critics piled on. Lyman Trumbull of Illinois slammed the postmaster general for overriding the congressional will to build a road "as crooked as an ox-bow" and a good deal longer than originally advertised.[77] To Henry Wilson of Massachusetts, the new road passed along a "desert route, now and hereafter to be known, I trust, as the disunion route."[78] As these congressmen recognized, the stakes were high in the contest for western transportation, and slaveholders again held the winning hand.

It was not only the Overland Mail Road that made Brown a darling of the South and a nemesis of the North. In his brief but productive tenure as postmaster general, Brown oversaw six mail lines to the Pacific coast, whereas only two had existed when he first took office (a central overland route and a steamship route, via Panama). Brown therefore ranks as perhaps the most active postmaster general of the antebellum era, which places him high on the list of most active postmasters general in American history. He was also one of the most partisan. Of the four additional lines that he established, three of those—the Overland Mail, a road from San Antonio to San Diego, and a route from New Orleans across the Isthmus of Tehuantepec and into San Francisco—benefited southern commercial interests above all others. True, he did establish a line from Kansas City to Stockton, California, and he tightened connections over the central route from St. Joseph, Missouri, to Placerville, California. But he granted those operations smaller contracts and less frequent service than their southern competitors.[79]

Brown thus transformed the US Post Office Department into a southern-oriented, continental system—and an expensive one at that. The federal subsidies that funded the six routes to the Pacific coast cost the government nearly $2.2 million in 1859 alone. With annual receipts of just under $340,000, the sprawling system generated a shortfall of $1,845,000.[80] Yet these were all worthy investments, William Gwin argued. He praised Brown as a hero of California and called his postal routes "one of the most important policies ever adopted by this Government."[81] Like Gwin, Brown was yet another southern Democrat who could embrace federal power and dispense with state-rights orthodoxy when it suited his purposes. His tenure in the Post Office Department therefore reinforces a recurring theme: the Continental South was the product of federal largesse, dispensed strategically by well-positioned slaveholders.

Brown formalized his most consequential and controversial act in September 1857, when he awarded the contract for the Overland Mail to John Butterfield, a New York expressman and personal friend of President Buchanan. Under the terms of the contract, twice-weekly mail service was to begin one year later, a formidable task even with a $600,000 annual federal subsidy. Butterfield had to operate a road that ran over roughly 2,800 miles of terrain that, for much of its expanse, was sparsely populated, rugged, and short on water. To make travel possible, his team dug a series of wells along the route, constructed reservoirs, and ran relays over the driest sections to fetch additional water. Butterfield also constructed roughly 200 stations across the Far Southwest, spaced at intervals of eight to twenty-five miles. These stations, along with military forts, remain the oldest American-made structures in the region. For the work ahead, the line purchased 100 coaches, 1,000 horses, and 500 mules and recruited nearly 800 men.[82]

In addition to the imposing landscape, there was also the imposing presence of Native peoples, especially the Comanches and Apaches in West Texas and New Mexico. The Overland Mail passed through both Comanchería and Apachería, the extensive and well-defended domains of these polities. For hundreds of years, Indigenous peoples had held the balance of power across the western borderlands of North America. Northern Mexico, in particular, suffered repeated attacks by Comanche and Apache raiding parties. Native warriors effectively transformed northern Mexican settlements into their supply depots, carrying off livestock, horses, trade goods, and human captives. By the time northern Sonora—what became southern Arizona and New Mexico—passed into US hands by the terms of the Gadsden Treaty in 1854, large portions of this land had been abandoned by Mexican settlers. Assailed by the powerful Chiracahua band of Apaches, the once-thriving mining community of Tubac, situated on the new border between the United States and Mexico, had become a ghost town.[83]

Vastly outnumbered Anglo-American arrivals to the region had to tread carefully. Jefferson Davis and other antebellum leaders had bold imperial ambitions but lacked the military might to wrest control of the Far Southwest from formidable Native peoples. Accommodation, rather than conquest, became the US strategy within its southwestern borderlands. The US Army provided a degree of security—deterrence more than anything else—when it established a new post just south of Tubac by mid-decade. But individual settlers in southern New Mexico found that the surest means of protection came by negotiating directly with local Indigenous leaders. By the terms of ad hoc arrangements, known as *calico* treaties, Apaches received trade goods and gifts from Anglo-Americans in return for peace. US settlers also agreed not to interfere with Apache raiding into northern Mexico. Far better, these Anglo-Americans reasoned, to deflect violence onto their southern neighbors than contend with Apache warriors themselves. It did not take a particularly shrewd white settler to recognize the military advantages that the Apaches possessed: manpower, unparalleled horsemanship, long martial traditions, knowledge of the landscape, and the ability to slip across a national border.[84]

Like the Europeans and Americans who came before him, Butterfield relied on gift-giving to maintain peace with Indigenous peoples in the Southwest borderlands. He distributed more than $10,000 annually to American Indians in the region, essentially for a right-of-way through their lands. The Overland Mail Company also maintained a small private army in case of emergency. Many of Butterfield's stations doubled as fortresses, which were manned by four to five soldiers equipped with Sharps rifles and Colt revolvers. But these interlopers were always outnumbered. As one student of the Overland Mail has argued, Native American raiders could have easily obliterated Butterfield's operations in the Southwest, yet they held back.[85] They only occasionally struck a station, generally to retaliate for Anglo-American aggressions. For the time being at least, Native peoples preferred Butterfield's payments to open warfare.

Aside from the US military, the Overland Mail Company was the largest federally supported operation in the Far West. By 1860, the line was carrying more letters than the US steamship service, which had dominated the mail to the Pacific since the arrival of the first gold seekers in 1849.[86] Yet the combined challenges of the enterprise—diplomacy with American Indians, the forbidding landscape, and the daily costs of the service—took its toll on the Butterfield business. Even with the $600,000 annual contract, expenses quickly mounted. In March 1860, Butterfield was forced out of his own firm for failing to cover debts to Wells Fargo, his major creditor, which then assumed control of the entire operation.[87]

By providing safe passage for settlers, the Overland Mail Road accelerated population growth in the Far Southwest. Chief towns along the route nearly doubled in size, while smaller settlements also sprang up along its path, constructed around the local Overland stations.[88] Spurred by rumors of gold, thousands of American and Mexican miners poured into southern New Mexico in 1860, many of them traveling along the Butterfield route.[89] The Overland Mail Road functioned as something of a far southern complement to the Santa Fe Trail, which had funneled migrants and trade goods between Missouri and New Mexico for generations. Others were drawn west by opportunities to profit from the Overland operation. Merchants were needed to supply travelers and local communities, freighters to haul goods, contractors to stock roughly 200 stations, ranchers to provide livestock, drivers to guide wagons and carry the mail, and soldiers to guard against Indian attacks. Although the central route from Independence, Missouri, remained the most popular emigrant trail, the Overland was steadily bringing together South and Southwest.

Westerners were especially grateful for the service. The road "was working wonders in this region," one observer from New Mexico reported, "opening the country, and inducing the enterprising to venture from home and to try their fortunes in a new land."[90] For Californians, the Overland proved a more reliable method of sending and receiving mail than via steamships. "We are kept in news altogether from that source now," wrote one Maryland transplant living in San Francisco, "and I will be pleased if they bestow *all* the patronage of Government upon the Overland and do away with steamers entirely."[91] Even the *San Francisco Bulletin*, a critic of the road because of its sectional orientation, had to concede by June 1859, "The Overland is the most popular institution of the Far West."[92]

Although a monumental undertaking, the Overland Mail has been eclipsed in historical memory by its short-lived competitor, the Pony Express. A fixture in American lore and a favorite subject of mythmakers like "Buffalo Bill" Cody (who was employed for a time as a messenger), the Pony Express traces its origins to the sectional struggle over western mail

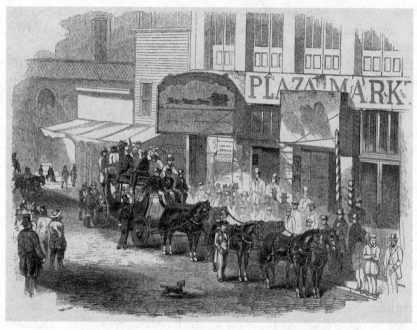

A crowd gathers as a Butterfield stagecoach prepares to depart from San Francisco. The *San Francisco Bulletin* called the Overland Mail "the most popular institution of the Far West." *Harper's Weekly*, December 11, 1858.

roads.[93] It was conceived in 1860 as a rival to the Butterfield line, a publicity stunt to demonstrate the feasibility of the central route it followed and to attract a lucrative federal contract for the mail road from Independence to California's gold country. Ironically, the slaveholding William Gwin threw his support behind the Pony Express. In this case, Gwin's desire for better mail routes to his adopted hometown of San Francisco—a top priority for his constituents—trumped his sectional allegiances.[94]

The privately funded enterprise that resulted was an elaborate relay network of mounted mailmen, who could be resupplied at 150 stations across roughly 1,900 miles of rugged terrain. In April 1860, these riders went through seventy-five ponies in ten and a half days to complete the first run of the Pony Express from St. Joseph, Missouri, to San Francisco. The spectacle of human endurance overshadowed the extravagant rates of the service (the equivalent of $140 per letter today).[95] The riders attracted fulsome praise from the press and generated enough literary treatments—including a poetic passage in Mark Twain's famed travel narrative *Roughing It*—to cement the place of the Pony Express in American mythology.[96]

Yet when congressional champions of the central route attempted to divert funding from the Overland Mail in the spring of 1860—the stated purpose behind the Pony Express—their attempts once again foundered on the shoals of sectional opposition. And when the overland telegraph was completed in October 1861, it effectively rendered obsolete the Pony Express mail service. The enterprise was thus discontinued after its nineteen-month run. The frontier riders of the Pony Express may be the stuff of legend, but they could not outmaneuver partisans in Congress or outpace electricity.[97] Meanwhile, the old Butterfield road, although it had lost federal funding by this point, continued to funnel travelers, migrants, and eventually Confederate soldiers between the slave South and Far West.

Conclusion

In the long-running sectional struggle over western infrastructure, slaveholders built an impressive record: the Gadsden Purchase, the Pacific railroad surveys, Jefferson Davis's camel corps, and finally the Overland Mail. Slaveholding partisans passed all these measures over the fierce resistance of northern and even some southern statesmen—a tribute to their political agility and the long reach of the so-called Slave Power.[98] Although the controversy regarding Kansas created a legislative impasse over the railroad question by mid-decade, slaveholders continued to outflank their adversaries and dictate policy for the West. They did so through the power of the federal government and their influence within it. If Postmaster General A. V. Brown was troubled by congressional opposition or state-rights dogma, he did not show it when routing western mail roads through slave country and amassing federal deficits. He had the long-term future of slavery in mind as he advanced the probable precursor to a far southern railroad.

With the advantage of hindsight, it may be tempting to dismiss plans for the great slavery road as a monumental non-event. Despite the bold projections and soaring rhetoric it inspired, a Pacific railway was never constructed during the antebellum period. Yet western infrastructure projects produced several positive outcomes for slaveholders. Davis's camels, for instance, provided a smokescreen for slavers, as they smuggled African captives into the United States. Meanwhile, the Overland Mail Road accelerated the migration and commercial exchange that had been conducted between the slave states and the western borderlands for decades. In a highly visible and even dramatic fashion, it symbolized the bonds connecting South and Southwest. More broadly, the feud over the Pacific railroad directed the southern gaze westward and focused slaveholders' attention on the political and commercial value of this distant region. While some slaveholders lobbied within Washington for transcontinental transit, others began building coalitions within the Far Southwest itself. By the end of the decade, they had co-opted the political machinery of California, New Mexico, and what would become Arizona. It was through these local networks, as the next section illustrates, that the Continental South was made.

⇥ PART II ⇤

Making the South Continental

———◆◈◆———

CHAPTER FOUR

The Southernization of Antebellum California

WHEN CALIFORNIA was admitted to the Union as a free state in 1850, its troubles with slavery had only just begun. The very next year, James Gadsden started a national movement to settle a colony of 2,000 bondpeople and their white owners on the Pacific coast.[1] As unfeasible and unconstitutional as his scheme may appear in hindsight, Gadsden had good company at the time. His plan was an opening gambit in a decade of proslavery operations on the ostensibly free soil of California. While black slave labor never became a cornerstone of the state's economy, the ideology upon which it rested would achieve a prominent position in California politics. Disproportionally represented in the legislature, courtrooms, and California's congressional delegation, white southern emigrants bent the state's political path toward a proslavery end. They marginalized antislavery politicians and ensured that the slave South and the Far West were separated by a thin, and at times imperceptible, line.

Such a turn in fortune was inconceivable to a previous generation of slaveholders. In what would be his final Senate speech, John C. Calhoun had prophesied a dark future for slavery once California fell to free labor, thereby dooming the South to perpetual political subordination.[2] He went to his grave with this grim vision before his eyes. But had Calhoun lived a few more years, he would have seen that the politics of slavery could survive and even flourish on free soil. Slavery was becoming an increasingly national institution. With the enforcement of the Fugitive Slave Act of 1850, runaways could expect no refuge, even thousands of miles from the cotton belt. Meanwhile, masters roamed the streets of northern cities and sojourned throughout the federal territories with their slave property—practices that received a blessing from the Supreme Court in the 1857 *Dred Scott* decision.[3] And from California, local leaders effectively overrode the state's antislavery constitution and redrew the political map in the South's favor.

White southern partisans transformed antebellum California into a grand laboratory for proslavery experimentation. Their initiatives typically took one of three often overlapping forms. There were those who, like Jefferson Davis, sought to construct transportation networks across the southern corridor of the country, creating a commercial and political bond between California and the slave states. Then there were those who, like James Gadsden, sought to overturn California's free-soil constitution and reintroduce chattel slavery to the Pacific coast. Finally, there were those who, like William Gwin, sought political control and dictated a proslavery policy agenda for the state through a vast patronage network.

These three strategies did not necessarily cohere into a synchronized conspiracy. Plenty of proslavery political operatives, for instance, pursued careers in the Democratic machine of California with no intention of smuggling enslaved African Americans into the state. Yet white southerners could and did pursue multiple projects simultaneously, with dovetailing outcomes, as the schemes of Davis, Gadsden, and Gwin illustrate. Greater political leverage enhanced the prospects for infrastructural development, which could, in turn, spur the importation of enslaved African Americans to the Pacific coast.

California's proslavery political culture was not a strictly local creation; it was the outgrowth of white southerners' expansionist agendas. To turn the Pacific coast into a client of the slave states required coordination from leaders on both sides of the country, as Jefferson Davis understood as well as anyone. His correspondence with supporters and supplicants in the Far West testifies to the scope of this proslavery coalition. From the West and South, partisans advanced a program to pull the regions together and preserve slaveholders' power on a national level. One of Davis's many California correspondents, Lewis Sanders, drew the link between southern expansion and western politics when he wrote of the need for transcontinental transportation. "Of all things most desired here is a national road or high way" along a southern route, he reminded Davis. By encouraging migration from the slave states, he continued, such a road would give southern interests "a controlling influence in the country and thereby put a check to mad fanaticism."[4] Politics, in other words, followed railroads and migrant's trails.

Sanders need not have worried about what he called the "pestilence" of New England inundating California.[5] Slaveholders may have fallen short in their grand plans for a Pacific railway, but nonetheless they achieved one of the route's major objectives: to politically link the South and the Far West. With planters like William Gwin at the helm, California became, in a sense, the west coast of Kentucky.[6] Its legislators opened legal loopholes to benefit California's emigrant slaveholders. Its jurists upheld the property rights of this master class and imperiled the liberties of African Americans in the West. And its congressional delegation lent the South a valuable ally in the national debate over slavery. In their fealty to proslavery doctrine, Californians gave shape and substance to southerners' western fantasies.

Thomas Jefferson Green's California

From its inception, California's legislature made clear that an antislavery agenda would not follow from its free-soil constitution. This was the same legislature that had elected William Gwin to the US Senate, after all (and that body's other choice, John C. Frémont, was at this point hardly a committed abolitionist). It was also the legislature that placed brazen slaveholding expansionists, like Thomas Jefferson Green, in senior positions within the statehouse. The same year that California was admitted to the Union as a free state, the southern clique within the state senate spoke out against any future congressional action on the slavery question. "Any attempt by Congress to interfere with the institution of slavery in any of the territories of the United States," they resolved, "would create just grounds of alarm in many of the States of the Union."[7]

How did a minority of white southern emigrants set the political agenda for early California? The San Francisco abolitionist John Bachelder Peirce speculated that the state's political profile had formed in such a way because "the Northern men are engaged in business leaving Political affairs to those who have nothing else to do."[8] Peirce's dismissive attitude toward southern-born opportunists belied his deep anxiety about the fate of the West. At its height, the population of California residents originating from slave states stood at 33 percent, yet southerners prevailed in election after election.[9] They did so through a combination of strategies. More effectively than their political rivals, white southerners manipulated California's patronage network, exploited antiblack and anti-Chinese racism, enforced strict party discipline, and collaborated with allies beyond the state.

Thomas Jefferson Green deserves credit for much of their early success. Green quickly recovered from his humiliation at Rose's Bar in 1849, when he and his company's fifteen enslaved laborers were chased out by free-soil miners. Within a year, he found a comfortable position as a state senator and chairman of the new legislature's Finance Committee. Dismissed by a fellow senator as "unsuitable a man as could be" who "made nonsense of everything that was done," Green nevertheless wielded a powerful influence within the statehouse. His Finance Committee set the course for the state's economic program, putting forth ambitious plans for a new tax structure, the issuing of state bonds, and the sale of public lands.[10] What became known as the "legislature of a thousand drinks" earned its sobriquet from Green's frequent invitations to imbibe from his massive whiskey supply just outside the main hall.[11] Such liberality, along with his personal fortune and military reputation, gave Green a stature that few in that body could match. That six fellow Texans also sat in this first legislature only reinforced his authority.[12] As numerous white southerners sought positions within the new state government, they routinely turned to Green to ease their way to plum posts.[13] In the first year of statehood, California's patronage network was already slipping into the hands of slaveholders.

Early legislators served their white constituents to the exclusion of all others. With Green's backing, the legislature passed a foreign miners' tax to discourage international immigration into California and reduce competition for white prospectors in the gold diggings. This was a characteristic measure from Green, who had once insisted that he could "maintain a better stomach killing a Mexican" than killing a louse.[14] The same legislature also barred blacks, "mulattoes," and Indians from testifying against whites in criminal cases. (The testimony ban was extended to civil cases in 1851 and later applied to Chinese immigrants as well.) Meanwhile, California's leaders introduced bills to bar African Americans from the state and to require the deportation of all manumitted slaves. Governor Peter Burnett—a former slaveholder from Missouri who had helped pass a ban on black migration into the territory of Oregon—was the leading advocate for these bills. The California prohibition on black migration ultimately failed, but the message remained clear: this was to be a white man's state.[15]

Southern-born lawmakers did not have a monopoly on racism. A wide seam of antiblack prejudice ran through the free-soil agenda in the West, and California was no exception. The miners who drove Green's men and their slaves from the gold diggings in 1849 did so to reduce competition with whites, not to defend the liberties of African Americans. The same California Constitutional Convention that had outlawed slavery also nearly barred black migration into the state. And while some antislavery legislators opposed the foreign miners' tax and the ban on nonwhite testimony, enough of them supported these measures to enable their passage. The frontier *against* slavery in the West was also a frontier *for* white supremacy.[16]

The proslavery wing of California's Democratic machine, however, more skillfully weaponized racism than its free-soil adversaries did. It was the Democratic record on racial politics that helped give that party its undisputed legislative majority—aside from a brief Know-Nothing insurgency—through the antebellum period. California's Democrats, Whigs, and later

Republicans agreed on some of the major issues of the day, especially the need for federal spending on western infrastructure. On an annual basis, the state's various parties all adopted Pacific railroad platforms, for instance. But Democrats—the proslavery faction of the party, at least—distinguished themselves by branding their political adversaries as racial egalitarians and abolitionist subversives. In short, southern-born Democrats within California cast themselves as the only leaders capable of preserving white rule.[17]

This was an effective tactic in a state that harbored a large white working-class electorate, jealous of its political prerogatives and troubled by black, Chinese, and Mexican immigration. Roughly 15,000 emigrants from Mexico had entered California during the early years of the gold rush. A majority of them, however, would be driven out of the state by the end of 1850, through a combination of the foreign miners' tax and violent intimidation. Hispanos born in California (Californios) still retained some of their social and political clout, even as they saw their land titles stripped away by Anglo-Americans. Unlike African Americans and Chinese immigrants, Californios were recognized as US citizens and eligible to vote. They were also legally defined as "white." Some Californios, namely the Hispano elites of Southern California, intermarried with Anglo-American immigrants and wielded substantial influence within the Democratic Party, at least on a local level. But they proved an exception, not the rule, to California's position on interracial mixing. Although African Americans constituted less than 1 percent of the state's total population (around 100,000 by 1850), they occupied an outsized space in the fevered imaginations of white voters and politicians. An even greater threat, according to many Anglo-Americans, came from China. California's Chinese population was still relatively small in 1850 but soon began to climb rapidly, until some 35,000 Chinese immigrants lived in the state by the end of the decade.[18]

California's southern clique entrenched its position by toppling the congressional career of the state's most prominent antislavery leader. John C. Frémont, who had been appointed to the US Senate in late 1849, served less than a year in office before he came up for reelection. Although he attempted to position himself as a sound southern man—having been born in South Carolina—in order to curry favor with powerful proslavery legislators like Thomas Jefferson Green, Frémont's pitch proved unconvincing.[19] One San Francisco abolitionist saw little hope for Frémont, due to his free-soil leanings. "I am fearful we shall send a pro Slavery man," he wrote in December 1850. "For the active Politicians here are Southern men."[20]

No amount of celebrity could help the Pathfinder overcome the base of proslavery legislators who threw their weight behind two candidates from the Deep South. Solomon Heydenfeldt of South Carolina, a fire-eater in the mold of John C. Calhoun, was the preferred candidate of the most radical group of southerners in the legislature. Also on the ballot was the Whig Thomas Butler King, the Georgia planter who had championed the cotton trade to China and would later cofound the Atlantic and Pacific Railroad Company—the endeavor hailed as the "great slavery road." In this crowded field, Frémont came nowhere near enough votes for reelection, even after a dizzying 142 ballots. But because King and Heydenfeldt split most of the votes, neither was able to secure the necessary support to claim the Senate seat. The legislature postponed the election until January 1852.[21]

With the backing of William Gwin, Democrat John B. Weller triumphed in that election. Gwin antagonized some of the most zealous members of California's proslavery faction in supporting Weller over the radical Heydenfeldt. But Weller, as Gwin reasoned, would make a more effective legislator than the fire-eating South Carolinian while nevertheless maintaining California's fidelity to the South. Although born in Ohio, Weller had married the daughter of a slaveholding Virginia congressman, and his political allegiances reflected his nuptial connections. He opposed the Wilmot Proviso and spoke in favor of slavery's further expansion. In time, Weller would become California's leading doughface, a proslavery Democrat from the North in the mold of James Buchanan.[22] With such representation, one California pioneer could write—albeit with a touch of hyperbole—that "the State of California was as much under the control of the Southern wing of the Democratic party as South Carolina, and voted in Congress for Southern interests to all intents and purposes." It was a place, he continued, "as intensely Southern as Mississippi or any other of the fire-eating States."[23]

It was also a place that nurtured the slaveholding fantasies of James Gadsden. Several years before negotiating the treaty with Mexico that bore his name, Gadsden began conspiring with Thomas Jefferson Green and others to plant a slave colony on California's technically free soil. In December 1851, Gadsden wrote to Green to outline his vision for a slaveholding territory, somewhere near the San Joaquin River in Central California, that would marry southern-style plantation agriculture with western-style mining operations. Along with the continued exploitation of California's mineral resources, Gadsden insisted, "We must introduce rice and cotton and sugar."[24] The colony might also lead the way for the great slavery road. Writing to another political ally, Gadsden explained how his settlers would blaze a trail across the Far West and mark out a suitable path for future railway development. With federal protection, "you will see us with some 500 to 800 domestics with 200 to 300 axes, opening the highway to the cultivation and civilization of the shores of the Pacific."[25]

In early 1852, Gadsden rallied more than 1,200 prospective settlers from South Carolina and Florida and petitioned the California government to enable them to settle in the state with their 2,000 bondpeople. He then tapped California's powerful proslavery faction to push his bill through the state legislature. In addition to Thomas Jefferson Green, Gadsden enlisted the aid of Isaac Edward Holmes, a former US representative from South Carolina, and Archibald Peachy, originally of Virginia and now chair of the state Judiciary Committee.[26] It was Peachy who introduced Gadsden's petition to the California legislature, which then sent it to the Committee on Federal Relations.[27]

There, however, the petition finally died. Much like the stillborn 1850 Mississippi plan for a California slave colony, Gadsden's scheme never moved far beyond the realm of imagination. Yet if Gadsden failed to build a planter's paradise in California, his memorial nevertheless pointed to a promising future for southern ambitions in the West. That the memorial even received a hearing in the legislature, in outright defiance of the state constitution, speaks volumes about the political currents sweeping through California's governing body. His scheme also reflected the depth and breadth of support for slavery in the West. A schemer from South Carolina, settlers from Florida, and politicians in California had come together in a common cause. Here was the Continental South in action.[28]

Gadsden himself carried no slaves into California, but a handful of fellow southerners continued to move their human property westward in defiance of state law, stirring alarm within antislavery circles in the Northeast.[29] Particularly concerning were the reports coming from South Carolina in 1852. According to the Charleston press, the steamship *Isabell* made at least two journeys with California-bound slaveholders and their chattel property, carrying first thirty-nine and then fifty-five enslaved laborers in these two trips. "It would seem that this slave emigration is not an accident, or a spontaneous movement," the *National Era* fretted, "but that it is part of a system of measures concerted between Slavery-Propagandists on the Atlantic and Pacific seaboards." California had technically outlawed slavery, the paper continued, but the state continued to harbor black slaves and their masters in isolated mining communities "where the only law is that of force." Under such conditions, "how are [slaves] to know their rights, and who is there to assert them?"[30]

Here was the rub. Their presence on free soil did not automatically bring freedom to African American bondpeople in California. Slave emancipation required enforcement by antislavery activists, and such individuals were few and far between, especially in the Southern Mines, where slaveholders often clustered. "As to your fears about my taking too active a part in the anti slavery affairs here—I don't do anything," John Bachelder Peirce wrote to his wife in the summer of 1851. "I can't for there is nobody to co-operate with scarcely. We have no organized society here and nothing to act on but now and then a slave case."[31] Robert Givens, the son of a Kentucky slaveholder, saw no need to worry, therefore, over the security of his human chattel in California's gold country. In 1852, he urged his father to send west one of the family's slaves. "I don't consider there is any risk in bringing Patrick alone . . . as no one will put themselves to the trouble of investigating the matter," he wrote. "When he gets in, I should like to see any one get him out."[32]

Legalizing Slavery in a Free State

California slaveholders had the law—or at least the agents of the law—on their side. Even when abolitionists brought freedom suits to trial, they generally faced unsympathetic judges and juries. True, activists like Peirce could point to the state constitution and the Compromise of 1850 to argue that slavery was illegal within the state. But slaveholders and their allies opened legal loopholes, which southern-born jurists readily exploited in several influential rulings through the decade.

Western abolitionists suffered a major setback with the passage of California's Fugitive Slave Act. According to contemporary estimates, hundreds of enslaved African Americans labored in the mining regions in the early 1850s.[33] Many of them had been transported to California before the ban on slavery went into effect. Their legal status—whether enslaved laborers or free workers illegally bound—remained undefined until 1852. That year, a bill drafted by state senator and Tennessee migrant Henry Crabb clarified matters in a distinctly proslavery manner.[34]

The measure stipulated that any bondperson carried into California before statehood would remain enslaved, so long as they were eventually taken back to the South. The state's antislavery constitution, in other words, did not confer freedom on African Americans. Much like the national Fugitive Slave Law, Crabb's measure also mandated state aid for the recapture of fugitive bondpeople in California, while those guilty of aiding escaped slaves or obstructing their recapture were subject to fines and imprisonment. The bill sailed through the state assembly, forty-two to eleven, and passed in the senate, fourteen to nine, with aid from James Estell of Kentucky, who had himself carried fourteen enslaved African Americans into California.[35] As it was initially framed, the act gave masters one year in which to return to the South with their human chattel, but proslavery legislators extended the law until 1855.[36]

The act had dramatic consequences for California's 2,000 resident African Americans, free and enslaved. As historian Stacey Smith argues, Crabb's bill amounted to a "three-year suspension of the antislavery constitution" and exposed California's blacks to fraud and kidnapping. Because African Americans could not testify against whites in California's courts, they could be labeled fugitives and re-enslaved, regardless of their previous condition. With the Fugitive Slave Law in hand and African Americans legally muzzled, California's jurists ruled in defense of slaveholders. In dozens of cases between 1852 and 1855, they rejected the freedom claims of black Americans and remanded them to their owners.[37] While other free states contested the national Fugitive Slave Act with the passage of so-called Personal Liberty Laws, California continued to protect slaveholders' dubious claims to property.

The composition of California's courts ensured unfavorable rulings for African Americans. White southerners occupied a disproportionate share of seats in California's highest judicial body. Five of the seven justices who sat on the state supreme court between 1852 and 1857 hailed from the slave South, while one of the two northerners on the that court, a doughface from New York, had supported John C. Calhoun's presidential bid in in 1844. Chief Justice Hugh C. Murray, a native of Missouri, gave a violently proslavery character to the court until his death in 1857. On multiple occasions, Murray assaulted antislavery opponents, drawing a bowie knife on a future US senator in a barroom in 1853 and bludgeoning an abolitionist in Sacramento in 1856. Murray's successor, David S. Terry, a former Texas Ranger, would commit even more violent acts in defense of slavery.[38]

In an influential 1852 ruling, the Murray supreme court gave judicial sanction to California's Fugitive Slave Law, passed earlier that year. The case, *In re Perkins*, involved three previously liberated African Americans: Robert Perkins, Carter Perkins, and Sandy Jones. The men had been carried to California during the gold rush, only to be emancipated in 1851, shortly before their former master returned alone to Mississippi. But in the spring of 1852, a group of armed whites kidnapped the three men and hauled them to Sacramento, where a justice of the peace proclaimed them fugitives from slavery. When their case came before the state supreme court, the two presiding judges, both southern-born Democrats, ruled in favor of their kidnappers, legally re-enslaving the three African Americans. In his majority opinion, Chief Justice Murray reaffirmed that any enslaved person brought into the state "does not become ipso facto free, [nor is] his status changed."[39] The ruling prefigured the *Dred Scott* decision of 1857 by sustaining slaveholders' rights to carry their human property across free soil without risk.[40]

African Americans remained in bondage for years after California technically outlawed slavery. Thomas Gilman, for instance, was compelled to pay $1,000 to secure his freedom in 1853 rather than trust his fate to the inhospitable legal system of the state.[41] Meanwhile, Robert M. Smith continued to live unobstructed with fourteen enslaved women and children in San Bernardino, making him the largest slaveholder in California by mid-decade. Only when he attempted to move to Texas with his human chattel in early 1856 did he run afoul of the law. Smith's enslaved workers finally won their freedom in a Los Angeles courtroom that January. One of these African Americans, Biddy Mason, later became a wealthy real estate entrepreneur, philanthropist, and founding member of Los Angeles's black community. Hers was a rare success story within a legal and political system that, more often than not, sided with slaveholders and against the enslaved.[42]

California's master class devised stratagems to preserve human bondage under other guises as well. Slaveholders, for instance, forged agreements with the enslaved in order to bind their labor for a fixed term. Taken into California as presumed slaves, African Americans would win their freedom, per these agreements, only after working for a set number of years or after earning a certain amount of money. In this way, the contract—a hallmark of free labor ideology—became a tool for the perpetuation of bondage.[43] For many African Americans, this meant that they would not win freedom until years after the passage of California's antislavery constitution. It took Peter Green until 1855 before a justice of the peace certified that his "obligation has been complied with" and that he was "legally discharged."[44] In other cases, aspiring masters secured the unpaid labor of African Americans by claiming legal guardianship over them. John Rowland, a wealthy Southern California rancher, went to court in order to adopt a black child named Rose, maintaining that her mother was unable to provide adequate care and thus Rose should be relocated to a white home.[45] Framed as an act of charity, Rowland's intention was to bind Rose as an unfree domestic laborer.

Thanks to the statehouse and the courts, slaveholders in California enjoyed a degree of security that they could have found in no other free state at the time. Their letters are telling in this regard. Conspicuously missing from their surviving antebellum correspondence is any real concern over the state's free-soil constitution. Slaveholders did fret over what they perceived as an abolitionist influence in gold country. But what they most feared was enterprising individuals, not the state itself.[46]

Antislavery activists did what little they could within a hostile legal landscape. The Perkins case, in particular, galvanized the small abolitionist

Biddy Mason was forcibly transported to California as a slave
in 1851. She finally won her freedom five years later, along with
thirteen other women and children, in one of the few court rulings
that went against a slaveholder in the state. Mason then launched a
prosperous career as a healer, midwife, philanthropist, and
real estate entrepreneur in postbellum Los Angeles. Undated
and unsigned photograph, Security Pacific National
Bank Collection, Los Angeles Public Library, CA.

community in California, which would continue to press freedom suits for
the enslaved and to lobby against the ban on black testimony.[47] But in such
a proslavery state and with limited resources, theirs was an uphill battle.
Abolitionists as far away as Britain lamented that the United States had
effectively "extended the legalization of the traffic to California"—a reference, most likely, to the security that masters enjoyed under the state's
Fugitive Slave Law.[48]

Looking upon developments in the Far West, Martin Delany, a leading black abolitionist, saw little reason for optimism. "California by three

successive acts of the legislature, has granted to slave-holders the right to take their slaves into the State, for and during the term of three consecutive years," he lamented in an 1855 speech in Pittsburgh. "And now [California] seriously contemplates its permanent establishment, which doubtless will be consummated during the next year."[49] The wholesale reintroduction of slavery to the Pacific coast never came to pass, but southerners would continue to wield an outsized influence in the legislature and in courtrooms across California. They pressed their advantages as the state divided against itself. Half a decade after the passage of its antislavery constitution, California was less free than ever.

Slavery and Unfreedom in Southern California

Southern California—Los Angeles County in particular—was slavery's heartland in the Far West. Geography partly explains the region's sectional orientation. The second-most heavily traveled overland route to California, the Gila River Trail, terminated in Southern California. At the height of the gold rush in 1849, roughly 6,000 Anglo-Americans, a majority of whom came from Texas, traveled over this route. Although most would continue northward to the goldfields near Sacramento, a number of these argonauts eventually settled in the Los Angeles area.[50] The population of Los Angeles, one resident wrote in 1853, resembled "such as you find on the frontiers of Missouri."[51] By 1860, 52 percent of Los Angeles County's US-born settlers still hailed from the slave states. To be sure, this represented only a slim majority of the Anglo-American population. But at a time when only about 39 percent of the nation as a whole had been born south of the Mason-Dixon Line, Los Angeles could indeed be considered a comparatively southern place.[52]

What made Southern California hospitable to proslavery interests was not necessarily the numerical advantage that white southerners in the region enjoyed but rather the political culture they created. As they did within the state capital, white southern migrants in Los Angeles wielded influence well beyond their numbers, amplifying their power through strict party discipline. While William Gwin pulled the strings of the proslavery Democratic machine from his Senate seat in Washington, his friend Joseph Lancaster Brent, a Maryland native and future Confederate general, reigned as the party boss of Los Angeles. Brent installed white southerners in prominent positions and turned the town's governing bodies into proslavery bastions. As a fellow southern-born legislator noted, Brent carried Los Angeles in "his vest pocket." By mid-decade, Brent had become "so decidedly the leader in Los Angeles politics," as he himself recalled, "that

. . . no one could be elected whom I did not support, and no one defeated whom I befriended."[53] Antislavery politicians hit a professional dead end in Brent's Los Angeles.

Brent cultivated allies beyond his narrow circle of fellow southerners. Outnumbered by Hispano residents—who made up more than 55 percent of the county's total population—Anglo-American office seekers had no choice but to appeal to this demographic or face political oblivion. Brent himself represented numerous Californios through his legal practice, cementing his influence within the community.[54] Under Brent's leadership, white southern migrants joined forces with the region's Hispano elite to forge a nearly invincible coalition.

Although proponents of racial slavery and the mixed-race rancheros of Southern California made for unlikely bedfellows, their alliance was rooted in more than mere political expediency. White southerners and Hispano elites shared a cultural vocabulary, the product of their seigneurial social orders. Presiding over large estates, Californio rancheros and southern planters modeled themselves in the image of Europe's landed aristocracy. Leisure pursuits—horse riding, gambling, socializing, shooting—occupied much of their time and created common ground between the two groups.[55] Hispanos and white southerners also adhered to similar masculine codes, which valorized the violent defense of male honor.[56]

What made much of this lifestyle possible and created these affinities was the exploitation of unfree labor. White southerners and Californios alike relied on vast labor forces, whether enslaved blacks or bound Natives, to work their landholdings and tend to their homes. Although the Mexican government had outlawed chattel slavery in California by 1829, it preserved various forms of Native American servitude, dating to the Spanish era.[57] Thus, when white southerners moved west, they did not have to abandon their membership in the master class. They could simply trade one type of unfree labor for another.

California's southern-dominated legislature strengthened the hand of aspiring masters with the passage of the disingenuously titled "Act for the Government and Protection of Indians" in 1850. The measure, spearheaded by a Tennessee transplant, licensed a range of unfree labor practices, including debt peonage, convict leasing, and child servitude. Under the act, employers could secure the labor of Native American convicts—often imprisoned on baseless vagrancy charges—by paying their jail fines or simply by bidding on them. Only after working for a set term without pay—up to four months, in some cases—were Indian convicts released. The act also enabled Californians to claim Indian children's labor, until age fifteen for girls and eighteen for boys. Simply by appearing in court with the child's parents or "friends" to demonstrate the voluntary nature of the transaction, California masters bound Native wards to their households. To justify the measure, lawmakers invoked the language of white paternalism and Native redemption. But few could deny that this was merely another means to undermine the state's antislavery constitution and empower elites, whether Anglo or Hispano.[58]

In many instances, kidnappers did not even bother with legal recourses. They murdered Native American parents and auctioned their orphans to the highest bidders. Because California Indians were prohibited from testifying against whites, attacks on their communities went unpunished by the courts. Nor did the federal government intervene. When California's superintendent of Indian Affairs appealed to Secretary of War Jefferson Davis to license US soldiers stationed within the state to arrest slave raiders, Davis demurred. That responsibility, Davis claimed, rested with civil rather than military officials.[59] News of these practices finally made it to the US Senate in 1860. "Indians are hunted down in some portions of the State of California," Republican senator Henry Wilson of Massachusetts lamented. The Indian men, he continued, "are killed, and the children taken and disposed of, and in certain cases sold as slaves."[60] Wilson, a vocal critic of slavery as it existed in both the South and the West, never mustered the support necessary to defend California's Indians. Slave raiding continued well into the next decade.

Neither white southerners nor Californios cornered the market on unfree labor. Numerous northern-born migrants also exploited the unpaid work of Indigenous people across California. White migrants from the free states predominated in the northern parts of California, for instance, where coerced Indian laborers were commonly found. According to one local source, a quarter of all white households in northwestern California held kidnapped Indian children in bondage. Between 1850 and 1863, an estimated 20,000 California Indians labored in various forms of servitude.[61]

But, through previous experience, labor coercion came more naturally to many white southerners and Hispano landholders. Cave Couts transitioned easily from southern slaveholder to western master when he moved from Tennessee to Southern California in 1849. On his ranch outside San Diego, Couts amassed a large unfree workforce of Indian debt peons, bound apprentices, and convict laborers—all legal categories of labor under the "Act for the Government and Protection of Indians."[62] According to contemporary observers, his California ranch bore striking resemblance to a southern plantation, with unfree Indians taking the place of enslaved blacks. Those parallels were not lost on one of Couts's more observant guests, historian Hubert Howe Bancroft, who noted that, even after the

Civil War, "everything about Guajorne [Couts's property] had the air of the home of a wealthy southern planter."[63]

Indian servitude could be adapted to more urban settings as well, as the residents of Los Angeles discovered. What one observer called an Indian "slave mart" provided a steady supply of labor and municipal revenue. Every Saturday, after the long work week, several hundred Native Americans customarily gathered near Los Angeles's Calle de los Negros to drink, gamble, and fight. Local authorities would wait until these Indians were drunk by sundown on Sunday and then drive the most incapacitated into an open-air corral. On Monday morning, they would be auctioned off to the highest bidders for a week of labor. If they were paid at all, it was often in alcohol, ensuring the whole process could begin again the next weekend. By the 1850s, this Indian auction had become one of the most important sources of municipal revenue, second only to the licensing fees imposed on Los Angeles's drinking and gambling venues. The practice continued into the early 1870s.[64] Due in part to these coercive labor practices, the Indian population of Los Angeles plummeted from roughly 3,700 in 1850 to 219 just twenty years later.[65]

Southern California hosted one of the state's largest concentrations of enslaved African Americans as well. In 1851, Utah's governor and Latter-day Saints church president Brigham Young dispatched some 500 Mormon settlers to establish a new colony in California's inland valley. What resulted was the town of San Bernardino. By mid-decade, San Bernardino rivaled neighboring Los Angeles in both prosperity and size, with a population of roughly 3,000. While Young had encouraged his migrants to experiment with plantation crops like sugar and cotton, settlers found that the region was better suited to grains. At its height, San Bernardino outstripped the field production of Los Angeles, San Diego, and Santa Barbara Counties combined.[66]

That prosperity was built, in part, on the backs of dozens of enslaved African Americans, as well as an untold number of captive Native Americans, who labored within the colony. Many of San Bernardino's migrants came by way of the slave states, some of whom traveled with their bond-people, first to Utah and then to Southern California. One of the colony's co-founders, as well as its bishop and at least one high counselor owned black slaves. Visitors to the settlement commented on the presence of enslaved workers, but for five years authorities in California took no active steps to enforce the state's ban on slavery there.[67] Internal divisions within San Bernardino, rather than any latent abolitionism, finally doomed the slaveholding experiment. A combination of factors—political grievances, disputed land claims, and Brigham Young's waning interest in California—eroded support for the colony. In 1856, Young recalled the Mormon faithful to Utah, and within a year, roughly 1,400 abandoned California.[68] Until its decline, San Bernardino had produced, on a more modest scale, what James Gadsden attempted to create with his colony of would-be settlers from Florida and South Carolina. Here was a transplanted slice of the slave South with a western twist.

Angelenos' sectional leanings and affinity for unfree labor drove one of the boldest proslavery gambits in the Far West: the attempt to divide California and establish an independent territory in its southern half. Proponents of state division cited a litany of reasons in favor of the measure, including the sheer size of the state, the distance separating southern residents from their capital, the regional imbalance in legislative representation, and a tax system that placed disproportionate levies on Southern California's rancheros. During the 1850s, the state legislature fielded petitions for state division on a nearly annual basis.[69] In all these petitions, one issue remained conspicuously unstated: slavery. Yet few observers were blind to the sectional implications of this campaign. If the southern counties could be split from California, this new territory might jettison the antislavery constitution of 1849 and become a magnet for westering masters and their human chattel. This was the poorly kept secret behind the state division campaign.

The movement attracted support from a who's who of proslavery expansionists, including Thomas Jefferson Green, William Gwin, Joseph Lancaster Brent, and James Gadsden. As many of them had argued since the 1840s, Southern California was ideal terrain for the extension of chattel slavery. Numerous observers predicted that if California were to be split, the southern section would eventually become a slave state. Southern California "is settled almost entirely by Southerners," one slaveholding miner wrote, "and they will exert themselves to the utmost extent to carry the day."[70] The new territory would also boost slaveholders' power at the national level. "Upon the subject of the division of California and making one or both of them slave states I and others are quite alive," one correspondent wrote to James Gadsden in 1852. Such a move would help "reinstat[e] the balance of slave power in the U.S. Senate," he continued, which was currently being preserved "through the sweat and blood of senators Gwin & [Stephen] Douglass [of Illinois]."[71] This congressional balance of power is precisely what Mississippi's two senators, Henry Foote and Jefferson Davis, had in mind when, during the debates of 1850, they attempted to extend the Missouri Compromise line to the Pacific coast.[72]

The legislature made a cunning play for state division in 1852. Spearheaded by Henry Crabb, who simultaneously crafted the state's new Fugitive Slave Law, a group of lawmakers agitated for a new constitutional convention in order to remedy, they argued, certain points on taxation and public expenditures. Their true intention, however, was likely to legalize slavery in the Far West by splitting off the southern part of the state as a separate territory. Their call for a new convention passed the state assembly but narrowly failed in the senate, due to the efforts of David Broderick, the most persistent opponent of California's southern faction.[73] Yet plans for state division had been thwarted only momentarily. The campaign would continue to the eve of the Civil War.

A former Illinois congressman named Abraham Lincoln saw the far-reaching consequences of the California state division movement. In a list of resolutions that he drafted in January 1855 but never delivered, Lincoln addressed a number of proslavery initiatives, including the reopening of the African slave trade, the Kansas-Nebraska controversy, and California's territorial campaign. He urged congressmen "to resist, to their utmost, the now threatened attempt to divide California, in order to erect one portion thereof into a slave-state."[74] Here was the Slave Power at work, Lincoln suggested, from the sea lanes of the Atlantic to the shores of the Pacific.

William Gwin's California

Perhaps the most remarkable feature of California's early political history is the degree of control that proslavery southerners maintained despite their numerical disadvantages. They owed much of their success to William Gwin, the Mississippi-planter-cum-California-kingpin. Beginning with the state's first senatorial election in late 1849, Gwin kept a firm grip on political affairs in California, even though he spent much of his time legislating in Washington.[75] He monitored the state's shifting political factions, called in favors from allies, and consistently outmaneuvered his opponents. In the process, Gwin built an extensive network of proslavery Democrats, giving shape to the political faction known as the "Chivalry." Although its etymology is obscure, the term originated in the early 1850s as a pejorative for the proslavery wing of California's dominant Democratic Party—most likely as a play on the feudal sensibilities of antebellum southerners like Gwin himself.[76] Through the decade, Gwin served as the de facto leader of this faction, weathering the vagaries and violence of California politics to steer the ship of state in a consistently southern direction.

When not lobbying for a Pacific railroad, Gwin was often packing California's plum posts with his political favorites. As the state's ranking senator through most of the decade, Gwin effectively wielded veto power over any federal appointment in California. Even during his two years out of office, from 1855 to 1857, he spent much of his time in Washington as a presidential confidant. Gwin had himself created many of these positions through his efforts in the Senate. His bills established both a US mint and a customs house in San Francisco, major operations with dozens of federal positions for Gwin to distribute in return for political fealty. The customs house and the mint sat within the Treasury Department in California, with a payroll of roughly 150 employees, all patronage appointments. In addition to those jobs, California required a legion of appointees to staff its US district courts, the postal service, the Indian Office, the land office, and a number of lesser posts. While California's mines yielded diminishing returns, federal jobs continued to pay, and to pay well, throughout the decade. The head customs collector alone received an annual salary of $7,900 (equivalent to roughly $250,000 in 2020).[77]

In allocating these offices, Gwin was transparently sectional. He "proved treacherous to his northern friends and always favored the south," a former state senator recalled. "No northern man, no friend at the north who was known to be strongly against slavery ever received anything at his hands. Every thing he did was in favor of Southern interests."[78] The San Francisco Customs House came to be known as the Virginia Poorhouse, "from the number of scions of the first families of Virginia that were stowed away there on fat salaries," according to another contemporary observer.[79]

But if Gwin's allies were legion, so too were his enemies. By elevating his southern friends, often with little regard for their professional capacities, Gwin antagonized erstwhile allies from the free states. John Bigler, a doughface from Pennsylvania—who once claimed that those who opposed the spread of slavery were "governed by a spirit of disaffection towards the Union"—had been an important cog in the Chivalry machine before 1852. But he soon discovered a Yankee's political loyalty counted for little in Gwin's California. As governor from 1852 to 1856, Bigler found himself outflanked in the contest for spoils. Writing to his brother, then serving as governor of Pennsylvania, Bigler complained that the administration of President Franklin Pierce "listens to Gwin" and that "we are not heard or consulted."[80] The result, he lamented, was that southerners gobbled up lucrative federal posts within California to the exclusion of everyone else. With nowhere else to turn, Bigler rushed into the arms of Gwin's major Democratic rival, David Broderick.[81]

Broderick was one of the few California politicians with the courage and the backing to challenge Gwin's control of the state. A bare-knuckle boxer from New York City, Broderick won a reputation as a fierce, and often dirty, political fighter. Arriving in gold rush California in 1849, he amassed a small fortune by counterfeiting currency with diluted quantities of precious metal. Broderick then won a senate seat in Thomas Jefferson Green's "legislature of a thousand drinks" later that year. While Gwin headed the Chivalry, Broderick marshaled what became known as the Shovelry, a Democratic faction of moderately antislavery northerners who sought to check the pro-southern agenda that prevailed within California. Broderick, an acolyte of New York's hierarchical Tammany machine, inspired and demanded strong demonstrations of loyalty from his allies. He was "implacable as an enemy, but unswervingly true to his principles and his friendships," one Californian recalled. "The idol of the rougher classes, [Broderick] . . . controlled them to his iron will by a supremacy that brooked no question."[82] The Shovelry—a play on the working-class roots of leaders like Broderick, the son of a stonemason—ensured that the biggest threat to Gwin's power would come from within the Democratic Party itself.

The leaders of the Chivalry and Shovelry factions were natural counterpoints. Broderick, the progeny of the rough-and-tumble ward politics of New York's working-class communities, resented the aristocratic hauteur of Gwin, a wealthy planter. Like Bigler and others in his coalition, Broderick saw condescending southern schemers everywhere he looked. Members of the Chivalry, in turn, dismissed Broderick as "a Bullying rowdy fireman" who had "kept a three cent groggery" during his New York days.[83] Despite their vastly different backgrounds and constituencies, both leaders employed similar tactics to gain an edge in the unforgiving political climate of antebellum California. The Chivalry and the Shovelry alike resorted to bullying, ballot stuffing, and outright violence to win votes. It was rumored, for instance, that Bigler's two gubernatorial victories were the products of fraud.[84]

Broderick was by no means an abolitionist, but the brazenness of Chivalry statesmen drew him into the controversy over slavery and black rights. As early as 1850, Broderick, then in the state senate, helped defeat an act to exclude African American migrants from California. His opposition to Gwin intensified in 1852 after the Chivalry leader blocked Broderick's bid for the open US Senate seat and instead secured the appointment of the doughface John B. Weller. That same year, Broderick led the opposition, albeit unsuccessfully, against Henry Crabb's fugitive slave bill. Broderick had more luck in another contest against Crabb, when he derailed the Tennessean's attempts to call a new constitutional convention, intended to create an independent territory in Southern California.[85] With each successive struggle, the gulf widened between the two factions of the Democratic Party.

A breaking point came in 1854 with the national controversy over the Kansas-Nebraska Act. Overriding the objections of Broderick and other antislavery moderates, the Chivalry men in the statehouse passed a joint resolution approving Stephen Douglas's bill. California thus became the only free state aside from Douglas's Illinois to endorse the legislation that overturned the Missouri Compromise and permitted the introduction of slavery into a northern territory.[86] Perhaps California's Chivalry faction saw in Kansas the first domino in a chain that would push slavery permanently into the Far West. This is certainly what Senator David Rice Atchison of Missouri had in mind when he wrote, "If Kansas is abolitionized, Missouri ceases to be a slave State, and New Mexico becomes a free State; California remains a free State." But, he continued, "If we secure Kansas as a slave State, Missouri is secure; New Mexico and Southern California, if not all of it, become a slave State."[87] California's free-soil constitution, Atchison recognized, was impermanent. Indeed, the same California legislature that endorsed the Kansas-Nebraska Act would continue to give protection to slaveholders by passing an extension of the state's Fugitive Slave Act with three-to-one support in the senate.[88]

The issue of slavery became, at times, a fighting matter in California. Duels between sectional antagonists, often provoked by southerners' prickly sense of honor, were an annual fixture in antebellum California's political calendar. In 1852, Broderick faced Caleb Smith, the son of a former Virginia governor. In 1853, Gwin fought Joseph McCorkle, a native of New York. In 1854, Benjamin Franklin Washington, the scion of a Virginia planter family, exchanged fire with the *San Francisco Herald* editor C. A. Washburn. Although Broderick was wounded in his duel, all combatants escaped with their lives. (The only fatality between these three duels was a donkey, struck by a mortal rifle shot half a mile from Gwin and McCorkle's field of honor.)[89] Violence broke out within the statehouse as well. In April 1854, a proslavery state senator attacked one of his free-soil colleagues with a cane, anticipating by two years Preston Brooks's infamous assault on Charles Sumner on the US Senate floor. The California assailant struck his rival legislator with "several blows . . . over the head," according to one report, after a dispute over the state's Fugitive Slave Act.[90]

The Chivalry and Shovelry threatened mutual annihilation in the run-up to the elections of September 1854. That July, there was little sanctity in Sacramento's largest Baptist church, where 600 delegates from the two factions gathered for the Democratic Party's nominating convention. While feuding over their preferred candidates, a Chivalry delegate drew a cocked pistol and aimed it at Broderick's head. The sharp report of a gunshot then echoed through the church, as delegates dove for cover behind pews and scrambled out of open windows. Screaming that he had been shot, another delegate was carried from the scene amid the pandemonium. Upon closer inspection, however, it was discovered that the warm substance spreading down his trousers was not, in fact, blood. Almost immediately, murderous rage gave way to uncontrollable laughter.[91] Although the hilarity of the episode cooled tempers and helped avert bloodshed, the two factions shortly broke into separate delegations, running on separate platforms. The rifts among California Democrats reflected divisions within the party's national leadership as well, exposed by the Kansas-Nebraska controversy.

Broderick may have avoided assassination (and micturition) at the convention, but his faction was crippled in the ensuing election. Gwin's platform once again hewed to the southern line by reaffirming support for the Kansas-Nebraska Act, endorsing Robert Walker's "great slavery road," and nominating for Congress Philemon Herbert of Alabama and James W. Denver of Virginia. [92] While the Chivalry-Shovelry split allowed the Whigs to pick up seats in the legislature, Democrats still retained a majority of sixty-nine to forty-two. Particularly encouraging to Gwin was the fact that Broderick's coalition shrunk to less than a fifth the size of his own. With such limited support in the statehouse, Broderick was again denied California's open US Senate seat. It was still a Chivalry state, and Gwin's two candidates for Congress were now headed to Washington.[93] "California is politically with the South," Thomas Butler King wrote to Thomas Jefferson Green several months later. "No antislavery man can be elected to any prominent office in the State or to Congress."[94]

The divisions between the two wings of the Democracy proved a greater liability in 1855. That fall, the newly formed Know-Nothing Party upended the old balance of power by winning the governorship, as well as majorities in the assembly and state senate.[95] Although the defeat dislodged many of the Chivalry faithful, it was not a deathblow to proslavery interests in California. Some of the most prominent Know-Nothing leaders, like David Terry of Texas and Henry Foote of Mississippi, advocated for slavery's expansion. Terry supported the reopening of the African slave trade, while Foote cheered the movement to divide California.[96] In any case, the Know-Nothing insurgency was short-lived. Democrats blocked Foote's bid for the open US Senate seat in 1856, and by the winter of that year, politicos could predict that the Chivalry would "rout them [Know-Nothings] horse and foal next fall."[97] True to such forecasts, the Know-Nothings were driven from power in September 1856. The Chivalry regained its dominant position within the statehouse.

Gwin's resilience mirrored that of his faction as a whole. Although persistent divisions within the Democratic Party had denied him reelection to the US Senate—leaving the position unoccupied for two years—he continued to exert his political influence during the lull, before reclaiming his seat in 1857.[98] Like Gwin himself, the Chivalry faction weathered numerous threats to its power, beating back a Know-Nothing insurgency and continuing to check the opposition of Broderick's Shovelry. Through California's Fugitive Slave Act, the election of Chivalry representatives to Congress, the endorsement of the Kansas-Nebraska bill, and hundreds of patronage appointments, the state's leaders made their loyalties clear. California had been southernized.

The Dismal Career of California Republicanism

There was no greater testament to the strength of proslavery politics in California than the chronic troubles of the state's early Republican Party. In most other free states, the divisiveness of the Kansas-Nebraska Act opened a wedge for Republicans and profoundly weakened Democratic machines after 1854. Not so in California. Aside from the brief Know-Nothing interlude, Democrats swept every election within the state and dealt the Republican Party a string of humiliating defeats, up until 1860. Free soil, free labor, free men—this rallying cry fell on deaf ears, by and large, in antebellum California.

By the time California's Republican Party formed in the spring of 1856, antislavery politicians had already founded chapters in most every other free state of the Union. Slow to organize, the state's Republican machine was also small in numbers. "No record, I venture to say, can be found of a political organization starting out with fewer adherents," recalled Cornelius Cole, a founding member. Aside from a few wealthy friends, including the merchants Collis Huntington, Mark Hopkins, Leland Stanford, and the Crocker brothers, the entire early membership "could be counted on one's fingers," Cole wrote.[99] The first state convention in April 1856 attracted delegates from only thirteen of California's forty-two counties, with over half coming from either San Francisco or Sacramento. Unlike their seasoned Democratic adversaries, most of these early adherents to Republicanism were political novices.[100]

The 1856 presidential campaign of John C. Frémont threw hard light on these organizational weaknesses. Frémont carried eleven of sixteen free states, with majorities as large as 78, 64, and 61 percent in parts of the Northeast. Yet in California he captured barely 19 percent of the vote, his weakest showing in any state outside the South. Frémont, one might suspect, could have counted on greater support from the state that had made him one of its first US senators and where he had earned early celebrity as the leader of the Bear Flag rebellion. But a controversy over Frémont's floating land grant in Mariposa antagonized voters in California's mining districts, and Chivalry opponents made the most of his disputed claims. Still, the land issue only partly explains his electoral rout. In the state elections of September 1856, the Republican Party fared even worse than Frémont himself, polling just 18 percent across California.[101]

To speak openly against slavery in antebellum California was to court danger. Among the southern-born majority of Sonoma County, for instance, "the name of 'black Republicans' stunk in their nostrils worse than that of a horse-thief," according to one observer.[102] While Democrats and Know-Nothings ran their party rallies without incident, the threat of violence loomed over every Republican gathering during these early years. A mob interrupted the state's first Republican meeting in April 1856, hounding the speaker and overturning his platform. Matters hardly improved from there. Throughout the 1856 campaign, anti-abolitionist zealots regularly disrupted meetings, pelted speakers with rotten food, and even yanked a Republican candidate from his speaking stand. If a man "was known to have any free-soil sentiments," recalled one Californian, "he was spotted at the ballot-box, and likewise socially."[103] Such threats took on a dire aspect with the appearance, in May 1856, of a handbill titled *TO ARMS!* It called for the lynching of all Republican leaders "and as many of the Attaches of said traitors as may be deemed necessary to restore the public quiet and put a stop to such treasonable practices."[104]

In their tactics of violent intimidation, these anti-Republican obstructionists bore some resemblance to the proslavery squatters then operating in Kansas. They likewise earned the epithet "Border Ruffians" from California's beleaguered free-soilers. Vigilantes in Kansas and California alike resorted to violent force, intimidation, and race-baiting to silence the antislavery opposition and achieve political power disproportionate to their numbers. As a prominent California jurist recalled, these thugs guaranteed that "to be an abolitionist or a freesoiler was certain destruction to the aspirations of any person for political preferment."[105] Antebellum California's political landscape was a battlefield, and proslavery partisans mustered in superior force to sustain their electoral edge.

While white Republicans floundered, California's black leaders organized. In 1855, 1856, and again in 1857, they hosted so-called Colored Conventions, giving California more meetings of this sort than any state other than Ohio. The movement's leaders, including Jeremiah B. Sanderson, Frederick Barbadoes, Mifflin Wistar Gibbs, Peter Lester, and David Ruggles, had been prominent abolitionists in the East before coming to California. They targeted California's racist testimony laws, in particular, which had enabled the kidnapping of dozens of free blacks—not to mention countless Native Americans. The delegates of the 1856 convention adopted Gibbs's

Mirror of the Times, California's first black newspaper, as "the State Organ of the colored people of California."[106]

Yet California's African Americans made little headway against the prevailing antiblack sentiment within the legislature, whose members only accelerated their racial attacks. These were the same lawmakers who regularly derided Republicans as "nigger worshippers," "Black Republicans," "fanatics," "abolitionists," "wooly heads," "negrophilists," and "white niggers."[107] Southern California's preeminent orator, E. J. C. Kewen, blasted Republicans for forming "a party 'conceived in sin, and brought forth in iniquity,'" and for unfurling "their black, piratical ensign" in defense of "traitorous principles."[108]

Facing this avalanche of derision, violence, and electoral defeat, California Republicans quickly moderated their positions. To counter the frequent claims—mostly false—that they harbored racially egalitarian views, California Republicans distanced themselves from the stigma of abolitionism. While the state party platform in 1856 had opposed the expansion of slavery into the territories, Republicans thereafter abandoned this plank in favor of popular sovereignty. Meanwhile, the few Republicans within the statehouse proved regressive on racial issues. They voted for a Chinese exclusion bill, a homestead law denying rights to blacks and Chinese, and a bill to legally void all marriages between whites and "negroes, mulattoes or Mongolians."[109]

In the 1857 state election, the machine's leaders took an unusual, perhaps even singular, step in the history of the Republican Party: they nominated a slaveholder for governor. Although he had voted for the admission of California as a free state while representing North Carolina in Congress in 1850, Edward Stanly still owned one bondperson in his native state at the time of his gubernatorial nomination seven years later. During the campaign, Stanly endeavored to show "that the Republican party was not an Abolition party." He cited his past congressional record, highlighting his opposition to the abolition of slavery in the District of Columbia and to the Wilmot Proviso. "A declaration by Congress that the South should never have any more slave States, I could not support," Stanly reassured a Sacramento audience during his campaign. When it came to slavery, there was "only . . . one evil," and that was the "degradation of labor."[110] At the polls, Stanly and the recalibrated platform on which he ran fared slightly better than Republican candidates the previous year, capturing 22.5 percent of the vote.[111] But compared to the Republican Party's recent returns in other states—which helped to propel antislavery stalwart Nathaniel P. Banks to Speaker of the House by 1856—the outcome amounted to a drubbing.

Republicans scored a victory by proxy, however, in the election of the antislavery Democrat David Broderick to the US Senate. Since 1852, Broderick had been vying for the seat, but the party's proslavery faction consistently checked his ambitions. Finally, the New Yorker mustered the necessary backing within the legislature in the 1857 contest, while three Chivalry candidates cannibalized one another's support.[112] More promising, Broderick's politicking had seemingly secured California's share of federal patronage for the Shovelry. In what some called "the corrupt bargain"—a repurposing of an old Jacksonian slander against John Quincy Adams—Broderick threw his support behind his nemesis, sealing Gwin's election for the second Senate seat. In return, Gwin agreed to surrender the distribution of federal patronage to Broderick's discretion. A day after Gwin's election, news leaked that he had signed and sealed a document to this end, which became known as the "scarlet letter." Both Chivalry and Shovelry leaders were soon embroiled in scandal.[113] But no amount of controversy could sour Broderick's hard-won victory. At long last, it looked as if there might be a chance for California's moderate antislavery forces to exert influence at the national level.

The Chivalry at High Tide

Broderick would not have long to savor his triumph. If he had expected support from President Buchanan, whose campaign he backed in 1856, he was to be disappointed. The president's administration was stuffed with southerners as well as doughface northerners, like Buchanan himself. Thus Broderick won himself few friends with his opposition to the westward expansion of slavery, which Buchanan's official organ, the *Washington Union*, had endorsed. And while Gwin initially remained aloof from the internecine struggles of Washington, the two representatives from California, Charles L. Scott and Joseph McKibbin, joined forces against Broderick.[114]

When he finally secured a meeting with Buchanan, the president was notably cold. And when Broderick pushed to have his friend John Bigler installed as Collector of the Port of San Francisco—one of the juiciest plums in the state—Buchanan instead handed the position to the Chivalry favorite and proslavery extremist Benjamin Franklin Washington. "Broderick is defeated, & is now in open hostility" to the Buchanan administration, gloated Charles Scott in April 1857.[115] Gwin exulted as the humiliated Broderick rushed back to California "in a great rage" after less than a month in Washington, hoping to secure the governorship for Joseph McCorkle, Gwin's nemesis from their 1853 duel.[116] But Broderick was again checkmated by the

Chivalry, which succeeded in electing the doughface Weller. Chivalry politicians also tightened their control over the legislature by picking off several seats once held by Broderick's rapidly disintegrating faction. Embittered and impotent, Broderick lashed out against the Buchanan administration and the Chivalry, further alienating himself from his party.[117]

The sectional struggles of California's Democrats had become well known to those outside the state. Slaveholders like Jefferson Davis took a lively interest in western politics. As one of the South's keenest continental expansionists, Davis sought to strengthen the bonds between the slave states and the Far West. By 1853, if not earlier, Davis had been warned of the "miserable New York tacticians" in California and the Broderick faction, in particular, who "are at heart against the South, against state rights, and favor all schemes of speculation, by legislation or otherwise." Yet Davis could take heart from the fact that politicians would be denied office in California if they did not demonstrate sufficient opposition to "free soil and abolition tendencies."[118] Watching these political developments in the West, Davis concluded that "the country on the Pacific is in many respects adapted to slave labor, and many of the citizens desire its introduction." If only the South could secure a favorable railroad route, he continued, slavery could expand westward and "future acquisitions to the South would insure to our benefit." The result, he concluded, would be greater congressional power for slaveholding interests.[119]

The relationship between proslavery forces in the South and West, as Davis's correspondence illustrates, was symbiotic. Davis coveted California's support in order to bolster southern influence within Congress; Californians, in turn, looked to leaders like Davis to ensure that the state's antislavery forces would not prevail in Washington. Davis's influence became indispensable upon Broderick's election to the US Senate. As one western correspondent wrote, "Southern men here begin to look to you as their champion in the future Congresses to stave off the stealing land and other bills that will be introduced by Broderick, an uneducated low brute as he is." He implored Davis to block Broderick's patronage recommendations. "You have many personal friends as well as admirers in this state," he wrote, "and every man friendly to the South & her institutions here, do not wish traitor politicians to ride over this community."[120] California was not an island unto itself. Southerners had forged a transcontinental network with shared political interests and common enemies. As Broderick's political career crumbled, the Continental South reveled.

Meanwhile, slavery's allies in the Midwest went on the offensive. In September 1857 Kansas's territorial legislature, dominated by slaveholders, met in Lecompton to draft a constitution. Their document overrode the proposed free-soil Topeka Constitution of 1855 and formally legalized human bondage. The territory's free-state majority boycotted the ensuing vote for the Lecompton Constitution, and even Robert J. Walker, the proslavery territorial governor (and spearhead for the "great slavery road"), resigned his office rather than implement a constitution that clearly lacked popular support. Nevertheless, Buchanan gave Lecompton his executive endorsement, igniting an intraparty struggle along sectional lines. Stephen Douglas and many fellow northern Democrats broke with the president and his mostly southern base of support. California's congressional delegation replicated that rift, with Gwin and Scott supporting Lecompton and Broderick and McKibbin, a native Pennsylvanian, opposing it.[121]

As Buchanan's support waned and the Democratic Party fragmented, one might have expected California's proslavery leaders to moderate their position. Instead, they redoubled their efforts and brought the Far West even deeper into the slave South's political fold. While the Lecompton controversy invigorated antislavery politics throughout much of the country, it had the opposite effect in California. The state legislature endorsed the proslavery constitution for Kansas, while the Chivalry press campaigned against free-soilers, blasting opponents of the Buchanan administration as "freedom shriekers," "abolitionists," and "Black Republicans."[122] Meanwhile, Gwin, as chair of the Senate Caucus Committee, punished the Democratic mutiny by booting Broderick from the Committee on Public Lands and removing Douglas from his chair on the Committee on Territories. Gwin would later justify his action by citing Douglas's position on popular sovereignty. Douglas was not fit for the office because he believed, in Gwin's words, that "a Territorial Legislature could *lawfully* by non-action or hostile legislation exclude slavery from such Territory." Gwin, on the other hand, argued that slaveholding rights in the territories were inviolable, regardless of what local voters may decide.[123]

The US Supreme Court agreed. In March 1857, Chief Justice Roger Taney rendered one of the most consequential rulings in US history when his court, in a 7–2 decision, struck down Dred Scott's suit for freedom. Scott, an enslaved African American, had been transported in the 1830s from the slave state of Missouri to Illinois and Wisconsin Territory, where slavery was outlawed. His lawyers argued that his habitation on free soil liberated Scott. Taney, however, ruled that no black person, whether slave or free, qualified for US citizenship or—in a now infamous phrase—possessed any "rights which the white man was bound to respect." Scott's case, therefore, had no standing in a federal court. Not content to discard Scott's suit alone, the chief justice declared unconstitutional the entire Missouri Compromise of 1820. Congress, Taney argued, lacked the constitutional authority to bar slavery from US territories. Like Gwin, Taney's court held that slave-holding rights in the western territories were inviolate.[124]

California's jurists took this logic one step further in February 1858. While the US Supreme Court had protected slaveholding rights in free *territories*, California's highest court extended those rights to a free *state*. The case featured Archy Lee, an African American who had been forcibly transported to Sacramento in October 1857 by Charles Stovall of Mississippi. Once on California's free soil, Lee escaped, only to be recaptured by Stovall and dragged before two separate courts in order to defend his right of ownership. When both courts ruled against Stovall, he took his case to the state supreme court, which, to the shock and outrage of California's antislavery population, overturned the previous rulings and remanded Lee to slavery. That the state's Fugitive Slave Act had lapsed roughly three years earlier did not sway Justice Peter Burnett or Chief Justice David S. Terry, both southern by birth and advocates for slaveholding rights in the West. In what one historian calls a "judicial absurdity," the justices ruled that Stovall's poor health and unfamiliarity with California law merited an exception to the state's free-soil constitution. They granted him permission to return to Mississippi with his human property.[125]

Galvanized by this miscarriage of justice, a group of abolitionists intercepted Stovall before he could return to Mississippi and secured a final hearing for Lee before a federal court, the US District in San Francisco. There, Lee finally won his freedom. But the efforts of California's African American community exacted a heavy toll. Black activists poured a fortune into Lee's legal fees. Consequently, their newspaper, the *Mirror of the Times*, folded. Shortly after the final verdict, California's pro-Lecompton faction proposed a new fugitive slave law and a bill to ban black immigration into the state, which passed the assembly before failing in the senate.[126]

Unable to express their grievances at the polls, California's African Americans instead voted with their feet. In April 1858, more than 200 black people, including Archy Lee, left California for Victoria, British Columbia. "Many of the collored [*sic*] people of California will select their future houses in the British possessions," a former state senator wrote. "They are pleased with the idea of being allowed to vote, to testify in courts & to sit on juries."[127] An estimated 400 to 800 African Americans from California settled in Victoria before the war, one of the largest movements of free blacks prior to the Great Migration of the twentieth century. The discovery of gold in British Columbia enticed prospective migrants, as did the possibility of escape from the discriminatory political and legal culture of California.[128] "Other parts of the world are unpolluted by the pestilential presence of the negro-hater," reported *Frederick Douglass' Paper*, in an article that urged California's blacks to seek the mineral riches and enlightened policies of British Canada. "Here can the black American go as a man."[129]

As the sectional controversy intensified in 1859, white Californians and white southerners continued to operate in tandem. That summer, the Chivalry leader Philip Roach wrote a series of letters to Jefferson Davis, strategizing over the upcoming state elections and affirming California's commitment to slaveholding rights. In a June letter, Roach enclosed the Chivalry platform with a list of candidates for twelve top offices, noting that "we have many fire-eating men as you will note by their places of nativity." Indeed, every candidate, with the exception of a single Pennsylvania doughface, was either southern-born or had come to California after prolonged residence in the South.[130] Much like Davis's other western correspondents, Roach wrote as if California formed part of the Mississippi senator's constituency. He praised Davis for past efforts and urged him to continue his advocacy for both a Pacific railroad and the Overland Mail. "When this question arises in Congress [of increased funding for the Overland]," Roach wrote, "I hope that you will merit our gratitude by its earnest advocacy."[131] In turn, he assured Davis that he would do his utmost to prevent a particular rival from securing a congressional nomination.[132]

Proslavery loyalists carried the state in the 1859 elections, just as Roach had predicted. In the three-way gubernatorial race, the Chivalry candidate, Milton S. Latham, won in a landslide, capturing nearly 62 percent of the vote. Leland Stanford, the Republican candidate, finished with less than 10 percent, the most dismal showing from his party in a decade punctuated by electoral disappointment. Republicans also lost their former toehold in San Francisco to Lecompton Democrats. The stigma of Republicanism was so potent that even the party's most seasoned candidate, Edward Baker—an electrifying orator, former congressman from Illinois, defense attorney to Archy Lee, and longtime ally of Abraham Lincoln—fell far short of securing the necessary votes for one of California's two seats in the House. Those seats went instead to a pair of fire-eating Democrats, Charles L. Scott of Virginia and John C. Burch of Missouri. In an election that can be seen as a referendum on the Lecompton Constitution and the status of slavery in the territories, California stood with the South.[133]

In addition to their electoral victories, proslavery Democrats filled California's federal positions with southern-born men. Virginians now served as the Collector of the Port of San Francisco and as navy agent; Missourians held the San Francisco surveyorship as well as the superintendency of the mint; two Georgians ran the state's Indian agency; and a Texan headed the office of appraiser general. The only non-southerner in a major federal post was James W. Mandeville, a longtime Gwin ally from New York.[134] Senator Broderick was never able to reward his Shovelry friends, as he had once promised.

California's antislavery forces suffered their gravest loss that fall not at the polls but on a remote field near Lake Merced. Aside from the Hamilton-Burr affair, no duel in American history had such far-reaching political consequences as the one between David Broderick and David Terry in September 1859.

Broderick was no stranger to the field of honor, having dueled the son of a former Virginia governor in 1852. He might have died in that encounter, if not for a providentially placed pocket watch, which deflected a shot to his stomach and prevented serious damage.[135] That Broderick, with his hair-trigger temper and penchant for dirty political tricks, found himself in another violent feud surprised few political observers. This was the politician who once disguised a crony in blackface to masquerade as an African American waiter at a Sacramento hotel, hoping to catch gossip from political adversaries who customarily gathered there. Broderick ran a particularly vicious campaign in 1859 as his flailing faction attempted, unsuccessfully, to avert a Chivalry landslide. Newspapers and commentators whispered of a likely duel between Broderick and Gwin.[136]

Instead, Broderick faced David Terry. The senator had a legion of political adversaries, but few as hot-blooded or deadly as Terry, a former Texas Ranger. The son of a Mississippi planter, Terry spent his formative years in Texas before migrating to California with a company of fellow southerners and five slaves. In his decade in California, Terry built an impressive proslavery résumé: he advocated for overturning the free-soil constitution; supported a measure for state division and the formation of a slaveholding Southern California; and, as chief justice on the state supreme court, rendered the decision that remanded Archy Lee to slavery. As a colleague on the supreme court recalled, "Mr. Terry had the virtues and prejudices of men of the extreme South in those days." He aired those prejudices freely, whether on the bench of California's highest court or in public diatribes.[137] When Terry, at the pro-Lecompton Democratic Convention of 1859, accused Broderick of "sail[ing] under the banner of the Black [Frederick] Douglass," he set in motion a series of recriminations that soon led to the duel.[138]

On September 12, Terry resigned his seat on California's supreme court in order to participate in the duel and set out to meet Broderick. Their first attempt at a duel that afternoon ended in their arrest, though they were released almost immediately. Broderick and Terry reconvened the next day, along with their seconds and a crowd of roughly eighty spectators.[139] The two men faced one another at ten paces, armed with French dueling pistols; Broderick was visibly agitated. Before the count of three, his hair-trigger pistol prematurely discharged, leaving the skilled marksman Terry with a clean shot. He steadied his hand, took aim, and delivered the mortal blow. Broderick died three days later, the only US senator to be killed outside a war zone until Huey Long in 1935 and Robert F. Kennedy in 1968.[140]

Broderick's body was still warm when antislavery Californians began to cry foul. Chivalry opponents claimed that Broderick's gun was designed to misfire, while Terry had practiced extensively with hair-trigger pistols.[141] The conspiracy ran deeper than that, according to others. They argued that Broderick's death was part of a long-standing plan to remove from office the most powerful threat to a Chivalry political monopoly. "It became apparent before the election that a settled & fixed determination had been agreed upon by the southern chivalry to kill of [sic] Broderick & thereby create a vacancy in the senate to be filled by one of their own kind," a former state senator wrote. Broderick had become merely "another victim to gratify the sectional malice of southern politicians."[142] Outraged Californians connected the dots between Broderick's death and another dueling fatality one year earlier. In August 1858, a Kentucky-born politician gunned down William I. Ferguson, the former US commissioner who had recently ruled in Archy Lee's favor, finally granting his freedom. Ironically, Ferguson was the author of the state's anti-dueling law.[143] Chivalry politicians amplified accusations of conspiracy when they quickly filled Broderick's seat with Henry P. Haun, a moderately proslavery Democrat from Kentucky.[144]

California's antislavery leaders now wielded a cudgel with which to bludgeon their Chivalry adversaries. Although Broderick had remained a Democrat to his dying day, beleaguered Republicans seized the mantle of the West's antislavery martyr. Edward Baker, the failed Republican candidate for Congress, delivered the eulogy at Broderick's funeral—"the largest and most imposing that had been seen up to that time in San Francisco," according to one observer.[145] Baker reiterated rumors of a Chivalry conspiracy by quoting Broderick's supposed last words: "'They have killed me because I was opposed to the extension of slavery and a corrupt Administration.'" In eulogizing Broderick, Baker hoped to bury Gwin. He harped on proslavery malfeasance. "Never in the history of political warfare has any man been so pursued," Baker claimed. "It has been a system tending to one end, *and the end is here.*" The result, he lamented, was a state without direction, caught in the grasp of the Slave Power. His eulogy ended on a note of despair: "Who now can speak for California?"[146]

Conclusion

The answer was not at all heartening. True, charges of conspiracy had struck a chord with California's voters and badly damaged the reputation of the Chivalry machine. But with a congressional delegation monopolized by proslavery partisans and a statehouse controlled by Lecompton Democrats, California had probably never seemed further from its free-soil origins than it did during the fall of 1859.[147] From the perspective of California's ailing antislavery faction, there was no clear end in sight to the long reign of southerners in state politics. Lecompton Democrats shrugged off the moral outrage that followed in the wake of Broderick's death. "It is astonishing how virtuous men become after they are dead," a southern-born observer wrote from San Francisco. "Obituary addresses are lies, barefaced lies."[148] Meanwhile the abolitionist press looked to political developments in the Far West with increasing disquiet. Reporting on the fallout from Broderick's death, which had created "a sensation in the Federal metropolis," the Washington correspondent to the *National Anti-Slavery Standard* painted a gloomy picture. "California is perhaps the most hopeless State in the Union," he wrote. "She is overrun by Southern lawyers and bankrupt slaveholders. It will take twenty years to give California an anti-slavery sentiment."[149]

Not only powerful, the state's proslavery partisans were also resilient. Southerners did not fold their tents after the passage of a free-soil constitution in 1849, nor did they surrender their political claims when slaveholders like Thomas Jefferson Green were driven from the goldfields. They consolidated their power in a political machine that exercised a virtual monopoly on federal patronage, preserving the spoils of the state for southern-born loyalists. Through the legislature and the judiciary, they crafted laws that gave enormous protection to slaveholders and imperiled the liberties of the state's black population. Finally, they tapped deep-rooted currents of anti-black racism in the West to marginalize a Republican Party that had otherwise been surging across the free states of the Union. With such a deeply entrenched proslavery elite, the state's free-soil constitution was always at risk, whether from conspirators like James Gadsden or justices like David Terry. California never became a slave state, but it certainly voted like one through much of the antebellum period.

→ CHAPTER FIVE ←

Slavery in the Desert South

———— ◆◆◆ ————

B Y THE SPRING OF 1859, Horace Greeley had discovered a new
bête noire. Greeley, who targeted a wide variety of social and political ills through the pages of his *New York Daily Tribune*, now
turned his acid pen on New Mexico's lawmakers. They had recently passed
a "most inhuman and piratical Slave-Code," Greeley lamented, opening a
vast portion of the American map to the South's peculiar institution. With
thirty-one sections, "An Act to Provide for the Protection of Property in
Slaves in This Territory" was far and away the longest bill passed by the
New Mexico legislature during the 1858–59 session. It detailed a litany of
punishable offenses for disobedient slaves and a number of protections for
their masters while outlawing manumission within the borders of the territory. True, Greeley conceded, few black slaves currently lived in New Mexico. But the new act would soon entice a mass migration of southerners. He
envisioned a region overrun by the nation's most unsavory elements: "zealous proslavery Propagandists" filling federal offices, slaveholding army officers monopolizing western military posts, "platoons" of "Border Ruffians"
moving west from Kansas, and "the scum of Southern rascaldom" heading
east from California. In New Mexico, Greeley despaired, "Slavery rules all."[1]

The *Tribune's* editor had a penchant for hyperbole. New Mexico would
not witness the influx of proslavery southerners that he prophesied, while
the population of enslaved blacks in the territory never rose much higher
than a few dozen at any given time. But Greeley's broader anxieties were
warranted. Seven years before the passage of New Mexico's slave code,
Utah had legalized human bondage within its borders. Meanwhile, legislators and jurists in California continued to undermine the state's antislavery constitution and to pack its federal posts with southern-born
partisans. Plans for a great slavery road, too, drew support from the Far
Southwest's political elite, who lobbied for a route through New Mexico

and into Southern California. By the late 1850s, antislavery observers could link these developments and fear for the worst.

No revolution in labor relations or legal doctrine was needed to transform the Far Southwest into a slaveholders' haven. It was slave country already. For centuries, enslaved Natives and their mestizo offspring had been working the mines, the fields, and within the domestic spaces of the western borderlands. When white southerners began moving into the region in the mid-nineteenth century, they showed no inclination to disrupt Indigenous forms of labor coercion. One type of unfreedom, they discovered, could buttress another. Both factions within Congress drew a similar conclusion as they feuded over the fate of debt peonage in New Mexico during the late 1840s and 1850s. At stake was not merely the legal status of coerced laborers in a single territory; it was a contest over the scope of federal power and the government's right to interfere with slave property more generally. Congressional southerners' successful defense of peonage expressed their continental vision: various types of bondage—whether chattel slavery, Native American captivity, or debt servitude—formed parts of an interlocking and mutually dependent system.

Through their continental defense of unfreedom, slaveholders created what we might call the Desert South—a sphere of influence stretching from New Mexico, across parts of Utah, and into Southern California. As a concept, the Desert South can be added to a range of recognized subregions across the lower half of the country. The Deep South, the Upper South, the Gulf South, the Cotton South—these categories help us understand the regional diversity of the slave states as well as the ways in which political and economic interest groups often clustered. The various "Souths" did not always act collectively, as the internecine struggles over the Pacific railroad make clear. Nevertheless, by the late antebellum era, these subregions shared several distinguishing features: a commitment to proslavery lawmaking, Democratic majorities, a strong preference for a transcontinental railroad along a southern route, violent opposition to abolitionism, and economic regimes that relied, to varying degrees, on unfree labor. For all these reasons, slaveholding expansionists like Robert Barnwell Rhett expected Utah, New Mexico, and California to one day join the plantation states in the bid for independence.[2]

The view from the Desert South underscores the insidious reach of America's planter class and exposes a proslavery coalition that was both nimbler and more expansive than scholars have previously recognized.[3] Although plantation slavery never took root there, white southerners wielded a disproportionate influence over the region. The legislators of Santa Fe, for instance, took their political cues from Missouri and South Carolina, and not from the antislavery statesmen of the Northeast. By the time New Mexico passed its slave code in 1859, the territory's political affairs were largely controlled by a clique of southerners and their accomplices: peripatetic politicians like Alexander Jackson of Mississippi, who drafted much of the slave law as territorial secretary. Jackson did so not to satisfy specific labor needs in New Mexico but rather to claim a conquest for his native section. As he boasted to his friend and fellow Mississippian Jefferson Davis, the territorial slave code "perfected the title of the South to New Mexico."[4]

The view from the Desert South also throws new light on the so-called Slave Power, illuminating how it operated thousands of miles from the nation's capital. With growing alarm, Republicans warned that a slaveholding minority had co-opted the machinery of the federal government to advance a sectional agenda. To be sure, the Slave Power often proved more menacing in the imagination of free-soil politicians than it ever did in the affairs of the nation.[5] Even the significant proslavery victories across the Far Southwest cannot be considered the product of a carefully choreographed or fine-tuned conspiracy. Utah, for instance, maintained a greater political distance from slaveholding influence than either Southern California or New Mexico. Yet Republican warnings of a slaveholding expansionist scheme, if sometimes exaggerated, were well-founded.[6] A small clique of territorial lawmakers had vastly extended the terrain of unfreedom, with almost no resistance from other legislators in the Southwest. And as Horace Greeley lamented, it all pointed to something even bigger and more sinister: slaveholders were consolidating a political dominion, from one coast to the other.

Slavery among the Saints

Slavery traveled across the continent through a range of agents, perhaps none more peculiar than members of the Church of Jesus Christ of Latter-day Saints. Little in the Mormon church's early history presaged the eventual turn to proslavery politicking. Founded by Joseph Smith in 1830 in upstate New York—a hub of antislavery activity—the LDS Church welcomed all comers, regardless of race. "All are alike unto God," the *Book of Mormon* reads, "black and white, bond and free, male and female."[7] Touring America in the early 1830s, an English abolitionist praised the followers of this new religious tradition, who "maintain the natural equality of mankind, without excepting the native Indians or the African race."[8]

But the Mormon position on race and slavery would prove malleable. The politics of the church followed from the fundamental desire for security and continued growth. When converts began assembling in Jackson

County, Missouri, in the early 1830s, they ran headlong into the controversy over slavery. A mob of white Missourians (falsely) accused Mormon residents of "tampering with our slaves" and threatening to "corrupt our blacks and instigate them to bloodsheds."[9] To assuage these fears, the Mormon newspaper of record, the *Evening and the Morning Star*, embraced the anti-abolitionist orthodoxy of the white South. "We often lament the situation of our sister states in the south," the editor wrote in 1833, "and we fear . . . the blacks should rise and spill innocent blood." The editorial concluded with a firm declaration: "We are opposed to have free people of color admitted into the state; and we say, that none will be admitted into the church."[10]

The church leadership reinforced this message with a defense of human bondage, parroting some of the proslavery doctrine pouring from southern pulpits (and even some northern ones) that same decade. Mormon leaders and southern preachers alike cited scriptural justifications for slavery, which ran through both the Old Testament and the New.[11] "The fact is uncontrovertable [sic]," Joseph Smith wrote in 1836, "that the first mention we have of slavery is found in the holy bible, pronounced by a man who was perfect in his generation and walked with God." The African race was divinely destined for slavery by the curse of Canaan, he suggested, which condemned Canaan and his supposedly dark-skinned offspring to perpetual servitude as punishment for the sins of Canaan's father, Ham.[12] Smith also quoted the Apostle Paul—a favorite among southern slaveholders—who urged slaves to show obedience to their masters. What God had fixed, Smith argued, abolitionists had no right to undo.[13]

Other Saints followed their prophet's lead. The 1836 issue of the *Messenger and Advocate* that included Smith's letter contained corroborating viewpoints, stressing both the biblical and the constitutional basis for slavery. Abolition, one editorial suggested, would unleash "a reckless mass of human beings, uncultivated, untaught and unaccustomed to provide for themselves the necessaries of life—endangering the chastity of every female who might by chance be found in our streets."[14] A southern preacher could not have said it better himself.[15]

Yet Smith's own position evolved again just a few years later. After his followers' expulsion from Missouri in the wake of the Mormon War of 1838, the prophet abandoned his attempts to gratify slaveholders. He suggested that any Mormon who held property in other humans should free them before joining the new LDS community in Nauvoo, Illinois.[16] He welcomed into his household Jane Manning, a free black woman who had traveled 1,000 miles to settle in Nauvoo among her fellow believers.[17] During his quixotic campaign for the US presidency in 1844, Smith attacked the institution of slavery and called for the emancipation of all bondpeople—albeit with compensation for their owners—by the year 1850.[18]

This, however, was as close as any prominent Saint would come to preaching abolition for the next twenty years. After Smith's assassination and the Mormon exodus to the West, church leaders returned to earlier arguments in defense of slavery. Although slaveholding would never become economically central to the Mormon community, it was politically and theologically accepted nonetheless.

Dozens of enslaved people were forcibly transported westward during the Mormon migration to what would become Utah Territory. That process began in 1847, when roughly 150 of the faithful, along with a handful of enslaved African Americans, followed Brigham Young on the dust-choked overland journey. Still standing in central Salt Lake City, the Brigham Young monument bears testimony to this history. The monument, which records the names of Utah's first white male inhabitants, also includes three enslaved pioneers: Green Flake, Hark Lay, and Oscar Crosby. (At least two other slaves in that first party of emigrants died along the trail.)[19] Due to shaky census data and inconsistent reporting, the exact number of black bondpeople in early Utah is difficult to ascertain. The census of 1850 lists twenty-six slaves and twenty-four free African Americans, although the total figures were undoubtedly higher.[20] Estimates suggest that more than seventy enslaved African Americans had been taken to the territory by the early 1850s.[21]

The most prominent Mormon slaveholders came from a group known as the Mississippi Saints. Many of them had been converted in the early 1840s by a charismatic young missionary named John Brown (no relation to the abolitionist of Harpers Ferry fame). With twenty-five cents in his pocket and the *Book of Mormon* in his pack, Brown began a journey across several slave states, eventually drawing hundreds of white southerners into the LDS fold. He found his ripest fields in northwest Alabama and northeast Mississippi, where he organized several branches of the church.[22] Although nonslaveholding farmers made up the majority of Brown's converts, it was slaveholders, such as William Crosby of Mississippi, who occupied the top positions within these southern branches. When Crosby traveled west to Utah in 1848, his family's inventory included twenty-two enslaved people. He and several other slaveholding Saints settled in Cottonwood Canyon, an isolated stretch of terrain roughly ten miles from the main LDS gathering place at Salt Lake City. Like slaveholding miners in gold rush California, the Mississippi Saints clustered together in order to more effectively monitor their human chattel. They sought to re-create Mississippi in miniature within the Great Basin.[23]

The Brigham Young Monument, with the Salt Lake Temple in the background, circa 1894. The monument was unveiled at the Chicago World's Fair in 1893 and then installed in downtown Salt Lake City. It records the names of the Mormon pioneers who settled what would become Utah. Among the names listed are those of three enslaved black men: Green Flake, Hark Lay, and Oscar Crosby. Photograph by Charles R. Savage, Church History Collections, The Church of Jesus Christ of Latter-day Saints and Intellectual Reserve, Inc., Salt Lake City.

Although the majority of the church's early converts came from the free states and Europe, LDS theology had a special appeal for hundreds of white southern men. The church's patriarchal structure and values explain much of this appeal. White men in the antebellum South embraced an ethos of mastery, which extended over all their dependents—women, children, and slaves. Even yeoman farmers were "masters of small worlds," in the words of historian Stephanie McCurry.[24] Mormon doctrine—with its "unremitting emphasis on male dominance," as one scholar puts it—accommodated and even reinforced the authority of southern men. Joseph Smith built his church around an all-male hierarchy, and admitted all men (but only men) into the lay priesthood. When Mormon women spoke of divine revelation, Smith dismissed their visions. "A woman," he declared in 1841, "has no right to found or organize a church."[25] His successor, Brigham Young, issued a litany of commands about patriarchal authority, touching on everything from plural marriage to the washing of dishes (strictly the duty of women). Mormon patriarchs and southern slaveholders alike cited the same Old Testament commandment (the tenth), which listed the wife alongside servants and livestock as a man's property.[26]

While the movements of the Mississippi Saints drew worried reports from the antislavery press in the East, the LDS church did little to refute its associations with slavery.[27] "The laws of the land recognize slavery," the apostle Orson Hyde wrote in 1851. "If there is a sin in selling a slave, let the individual who sells him bear that sin, and not the church." Anyway, he added, "All the slaves that are there appear to be perfectly contented and satisfied."[28]

Testimony from former slaves themselves tells a different story, however. Along with a party of several other bondpeople, Alex Bankhead was forcibly transported to Utah from Alabama in 1847. In the late 1890s, Bankhead provided his reminiscences of slavery among the Saints for Salt Lake City's black newspaper, the *Broad Ax*. He recalled a small community of fellow enslaved people who would congregate in a large room on State Street to "discuss their condition." Together they would "gaze in wonderment at the lofty mountains, which reared their snowy peaks heavenward, and completely forbade them from ascertaining how they could make their escape back to the South, or to more congenial climes." Their condition in Utah "was far from being happy," according to Bankhead, and "many of them were subjected to the same treatment that was accorded the plantation negroes of the South."[29] Although African Americans could and did join the LDS church, they were barred from the priesthood in Utah (a right enjoyed only by white male Saints).[30] Utah may have represented the promised land for white Mormon migrants, but it was nothing of the sort for their en-slaved black laborers.

Brigham Young, a native of the Northeast, held an ambiguous position on slavery but one largely consistent with earlier Mormon defenses of the institution. In his governor's message of January 1852, he addressed Indian and African slavery at length. "Servitude may and should exist, and that too upon those who are naturally designed to occupy the position of 'ser-vant of servants' [that is, Africans, the descendants of Ham]," Young pro-claimed. "Yet we should not fall into the other extreme, and make them as beasts of the field." He called for the humane treatment of those relegated to "servitude," which, he believed, may eventually ameliorate the condition of "the poor, forlorn, destitute, ignorant savage, or African, as the case may be."[31] Young took a position compatible with the proslavery paternalism of the South, which alleged that bondage would prove a blessing to bond-people themselves. When Horace Greeley questioned Young on these views several years later, the Mormon leader was more explicit. Slavery, accord-ing to Young, was a "divine institution, and not to be abolished until the curse pronounced on Ham shall have been removed from his descendants." Nevertheless, Young did not believe that chattel slavery could flourish in Utah, which, he predicted, would come into the Union as a free state.[32]

Until that time, though, Utah would be a slave territory. With Gover-nor Young's support, the Mormon-controlled legislature legalized slav-ery in February 1852. Compared with southern slave codes, Utah's "Act in Relation to Service" provided far more protections for the enslaved and imposed more restrictions on their enslavers. If a slaveholder was proven guilty of "cruelty or abuse, or neglect to feed, clothe, or shelter his servants in a proper manner," the so-called contract between master and slave could be rendered void. Furthermore, a slaveholder's human property would be forfeited to the "commonwealth" if he was found guilty of "carnal inter-course" with the enslaved—a measure presumably designed to safeguard Utah from the endemic culture of racialized sexual violence that existed in the South. Masters were also obligated to send their slaves to school for "not less than eighteen months, between the ages of six, and twenty years," and were subjected to fines or imprisonment if they transported slaves out of the territory against their will.[33] What constituted the will of the en-slaved, however, was unclear.

Despite these measures, much of Utah's proslavery statute would have been familiar to southern migrants. As was the case across the slave South, white people found guilty of sexual intercourse with free blacks were sub-ject to heavy fines.[34] Furthermore, the act gave Utah's white inhabitants full license to buy and sell slaves. Budgets and bills of sale bear testimony to a limited slave trade within the territory and indicate that bondpeople continued to fetch high prices—as much as $800 to $1,000—throughout the decade.[35] Although the act technically applied brakes on the inherent cruelty of the institution, slaveholders within frontier Utah faced little oversight and therefore few checks on their power.

The passage of "An Act in Relation to Service"—the first legislative measure to formally protect slavery in a far western territory—was not driven by economics. At the time, Utah harbored roughly a dozen slaveholders and perhaps fewer than fifty enslaved black people. To borrow historian Ira Berlin's formulation, Utah was a "society with slaves," not a "slave society."[36] As such, the territory's development did not depend on human bondage. However, those twelve slaveholders hailed from Utah's elite circles: a member of the Council of Twelve Apostles, the first mayor of Salt Lake City, and Utah's territorial representative in Congress.[37] The slave code, therefore, can be read as a concession to an elite minority of slaveholders within the Great Basin, as well as a spur to aspiring migrants from southern states. With the act, the Mormon legislature effectively rolled out the welcome mat for slaveholding southerners, even as Young hoped to curb some of the worst abuses of the chattel system.

In defending slavery, the issue foremost in the minds of Mormon leaders was not southern immigration, however. Their most pressing concern was the maintenance of another peculiar institution: polygamy. The same year that Utah's legislature passed "An Act in Relation to Service," the church establishment took its official stand on plural marriage. Slavery and polygamy were thus legalized and linked by Mormons themselves. Southern slaveholders and Mormon polygamists alike could point to the same chapter in Genesis to lend biblical credence to their respective institutions, both rooted firmly in a patriarchal social order. Their shared Old Testament authority was the patriarch Abraham, a practitioner of plural marriage and an owner of slaves.[38] The *Millennial Star*, one of the two major Mormon publications, connected the proslavery and pro-polygamy defense as early as 1853. "The State laws of the North have nothing to do with the domestic relations of the South," the *Millennial Star* argued. "So it is in regard to Utah; she asks not the interference of any state of this Union to dictate to her what kind of policy she must adopt in her legislative enactments."[39]

When Republican campaigners branded slavery and polygamy the "twin relics of barbarism" during the 1856 presidential election, they drove the Great Basin toward the South.[40] The *Deseret News*, the territory's newspaper and Mormon mouthpiece, left little doubt as to where its loyalties lay. "African slavery in South Carolina is a legalized domestic institution," the paper argued in 1857, "while white slavery, adultery, whoredom and

other gross abominations ... are nevertheless extensively practiced and se-
curely domesticated [in Massachusetts]."[41] The *Dred Scott* decision of 1857
marked a joint victory for slaveholders and polygamists, according to the
Deseret News. "Those 'twin relics of barbarism' can now flourish wherever
the people will it in any of the Territories of the United States," the paper
exulted.[42] In response to Republican attacks on polygamy, the LDS church
establishment urged support for the Democratic Party: "The Democratic
party is the instrument, in God's hand, by which is to be effected our recognition as a sovereign State, with the domestic institutions of Slavery and
Polygamy, as established by the patriarchs, and prophets of old."[43]

Proslavery feeling ran strong in the southern part of the territory, a region tellingly dubbed "Utah's Dixie."[44] In 1852, Brigham Young began dispatching Mormon missionaries to this remote edge of the territory in a bid
for self-sufficiency with a southern twist: settlers were to plant cotton for
local and national markets. They first established an agricultural settlement at Harmony, in a region once controlled by the Southern Paiutes,
where Mormon migrants experimented with cotton and other semitropi-
cal crops. In the next six years, Mormon settlers founded two additional
colonies where they, too, managed to raise modest cotton crops.[45] During
this time, fifty families migrated to the region from the Mormon colony
of San Bernardino in Southern California. With the secession of eleven
southern states in 1861, Utah's leaders stepped up their commitment to cotton cultivation, dispatching another 300 families to what would become
Dixie's central settlement of St. George.[46] That year, they raised roughly
100,000 pounds of seed cotton. By the early 1870s, some 4,000 Mormons
were living along Utah's cotton frontier, with healthy yields continuing
into the next decade.[47]

As its name would imply, Utah's Dixie attracted a disproportionate
number of American southerners, at least initially.[48] To train the arid soils
of Washington County, after all, required those with cotton-growing experience. "The old settlers of Washington were all southerners and southern
sympathizers," wrote the northern-born cotton missionary George Armstrong Hicks, albeit with a touch of hyperbole. The bishop of Washington
and his first councillor both hailed from Mississippi cotton-planting families, while the second councillor had migrated from Texas and the probate
judge from Tennessee. The Mississippians were particularly outspoken in
their support for slavery. According to Hicks, the first councillor would
"entertain" fellow settlers "by narrating acts of cruelty which he had committed in whipping slaves while on plantations in the South." With obvious relish, he recited lurid tales of sexually abusing and raping enslaved

women.[49] As the sectional crisis deepened, the proslavery enthusiasts of southern Utah would provide a vocal base of support for disunion.[50]

While white southerners applauded elements of the LDS agenda, these transregional affinities never translated into legislative support for Mormon Utah. "As a Southern man, my sympathies are with the Mormons," one slavery apologist wrote to the Richmond *South* in 1857. "The same measure that is dealt out to them for their polygamy, would be dealt out to us for our slaveholding."[51] Yet the Democratic Party, despite its proslavery orientation, proved no more sympathetic to Mormonism than did Republicans. Democrats like Stephen Douglas feared that the Mormon defense of polygamy and local rule would endanger the policy of popular sovereignty. Douglas even advocated for the repeal of the organic act that had created Utah Territory, while Congress opposed Utah's several bids for statehood. Reviled by Republicans and soon attacked by a Democratic administration, Mormons had few friends in either major party.

In 1857, President Buchanan mobilized the US Army against Brigham Young's semi-theocratic regime. What became known as the Utah War was a contest over the reach of the federal government. The conflict began when several federal officials fled the territory earlier that year, claiming that they had been subject to harassment by Mormons. Buchanan interpreted these actions as a direct challenge to US authority. He installed a new territorial governor in place of LDS church president Brigham Young and sent a force of 2,500 US troops into the Great Basin. Young, in response, mustered the Mormon militia, known as the Nauvoo Legion—the first independent military command to take up arms against the US government in American history.[52]

During the long military standoff, some of these militiamen—led by John D. Lee, a central figure from Utah's Dixie—attacked a civilian wagon company bound for California, slaughtering roughly 120 would-be migrants. The Mountain Meadows Massacre brought the death toll of the Utah War to roughly the same level as Bleeding Kansas. Mormon militiamen and US troops, on the other hand, avoided any major confrontation. In April 1858, Buchanan pardoned all Mormons for their "seditions and treasons" under the condition that they "aid and assist" all federally appointed officers in the territory.[53] Thus ended the most expensive American military operation of the decade. The upshot was an uneasy truce between the US government and LDS church leaders.[54]

Despite running afoul of a proslavery administration, prominent Mormon commentators never fully relinquished their proslavery sympathies. In a June 1859 editorial, the *Deseret News* defended the international slave trade, a position then in vogue with some of the most zealous fire-eaters of the South. After rehashing the standard theological justifications for the institution, the paper outlined the benefits of the traffic in captive Africans. That individual bondpeople were occasionally subject to inhumane treatment "furnishes no just grounds for reprobating the system," the *Deseret News* argued. Rather, by decriminalizing the international slave trade, Congress would present an olive branch to the South and thereby prevent a threat to the Union. Not only could political disaster be averted, but the enslaved themselves might benefit from such a trade, the paper speculated. "Is it not evident that, when brought to this country and placed under the careful supervision of the humane southern planter, the condition of the native African will be at least in some degree improved?"[55] From the mouthpiece of a frontier territory, populated mostly by northern white families, came many of the hallmarks of the proslavery defense: biblical justifications for human bondage, political sympathy for the South, and paternalistic assurance that enslavement would ameliorate the condition of Africans.

Utah occupied a fringe position within the Desert South. While some Saints cheered slavery's advance, others proved much more ambivalent. Brigham Young, for instance, continued to steer a middle course, distancing himself from northern abolitionists and southern fire-eaters alike.[56] He knew that Utah's bid for statehood would require the support of moderate politicians from both sides of the sectional divide. Accordingly, the slave code that he endorsed in 1852 softened some of the most brutal aspects of American chattel bondage. Yet in many ways, southerners and Saints made natural bedfellows. Both had peculiar institutions to defend from federal interference, both vocally repudiated the abolitionist political agenda, and both had given legal sanction to human bondage. If nothing else, the Republican campaign against the "twin relics of barbarism" had created common cause between the white residents of these two regions. Most tellingly, Utah still felt all too southern for dozens of enslaved African Americans. Many of them had trekked more than 1,000 miles from the cotton fields of Mississippi, yet seemingly not a step closer to freedom.[57]

The Politics of Slavery in New Mexico

When New Mexico became a US territory in 1850, there was little to suggest that it would fall under the South's sway. Only several hundred migrants from the slave states lived in the territory at that point, compared to some 60,000 Hispano and Native American inhabitants.[58] With memories of Texas invasion and US annexation still raw, many Hispano New Mexicans nurtured a deep mistrust of all things Anglo-American, especially when connected to the slavery question. Although Indigenous bondpeople had labored in the region for hundreds of years, New Mexico's potential for southern-style plantation slavery was untested and, many argued, unpromising. Yet by the end of the decade, a southern-born minority had seized control of the territory's affairs and transformed New Mexico into a political client of the slave states. A case study in political intrigue, New Mexico's antebellum history helps explain how a slaveholding minority enacted its transcontinental vision.

Commerce bound large parts of New Mexico to the slave states of the South. Since 1821, the main commercial artery through the region, the Santa Fe Trail, had connected New Mexico's capital with Independence, Missouri. According to the Georgia planter and former congressman Thomas Butler King, trade between Missouri and New Mexico was worth $5 million annually, a compelling reason, he argued, to accelerate this commerce with a Pacific railroad through the region.[59] Commercial prospects brightened further with the arrival of the Butterfield Overland Mail Road in 1858, which ran through slave country and across the Far Southwest. Meanwhile, territorial leaders lobbied for the construction of a far southern transcontinental railroad via New Mexico.[60] From the perspective of New Mexico's commercial elite, most roads ran to the slave South.

Proslavery schemes were brewing in New Mexico by 1850, according to the territory's first congressional delegate, Hugh N. Smith. To Smith, an antislavery partisan, the threat lay less in the expansion of chattel slavery than in the more insidious spread of southern political influence across the Far West. "The cement of this strength in the South is not so much the interest in slave property, but the political power dependent on it," he wrote. Here was the secret to slavery's survival, according to Smith: gain enough new congressional votes in the West, especially Senate seats, to counterbalance the South's declining share of the overall US population.[61] New Mexico would provide two of these Senate seats once the territory became a state—so long as slaveholders exerted sufficient control over its political leadership. To check the western spread of the Slave Power, activists established several abolitionist leagues in New Mexico in the early 1850s. Organized in 1851, the Free Territory League sought to establish and support antislavery newspapers while also financing legal counsel in Santa Fe. Meanwhile, the agent of another abolitionist league was sent to the territory to assume the editorship of the *Santa Fe Gazette*.[62] New Mexico had become a sectional battleground.

These early antislavery activities produced more political backlash than abolitionist zeal. Although New Mexico's northern-born delegates helped draft an antislavery constitution in 1850, Congress never seriously considered the document, and the territory soon abandoned its free-soil position.[63] By 1851 the antislavery Smith was replaced as congressional delegate by R. H. Weightman, a native of Missouri and future Confederate officer. Meanwhile, Santa Fe's *Gazette* remained in the hands of its antislavery editors briefly before taking on distinctly Democratic leanings by 1853.[64] Just as Smith feared, New Mexico was slipping into the hands of southerners.

The territory's political orientation shone through the pages of the *Gazette*, New Mexico's most influential publication. The paper trumpeted its allegiances—"a friend of the south" and a fierce opponent of "the fanatics and disunionists of the North."[65] During the Kansas controversy, the *Gazette*'s Virginia-born editor heaped scorn on "Black Republicans" and endorsed the proslavery Lecompton Constitution.[66] Like the *Deseret News*, the *Gazette* also criticized American attempts to police the international slave trade. When a Georgia planter offered to purchase some 200 to 300 slaves from a captured slave ship rather than return the human cargo to Africa, the *Gazette* waxed paternalistic. "These savage negroes . . . under the discipline and tuition of kind and humane masters, would in a few years have become civilized and Christianized," the paper argued, while "their condition morally, physically, and intellectually, would be improved."[67]

New Mexico's territorial leadership joined Utah's by legalizing black slavery, passing a robust slave code in early 1859. Like Utah, New Mexico possessed an economically and numerically marginal population of enslaved African Americans—somewhere between ten and fifty, by one recent estimate.[68] But as in Utah, a narrow elite controlled the political machinery of New Mexico. The antislavery views of the territory's majority Hispano population mattered little to powerbrokers in Santa Fe. They coveted southern support for several initiatives in the territory, particularly transportation projects, and proved eager to demonstrate their loyalty to the slave states.

The backdoor politicking that led to the passage of "An Act to Provide for the Protection of Property in Slaves in This Territory" showcased the long reach of the South in western territorial affairs. That process began with New Mexico's congressional delegate, Miguel Otero, whose Spanish surname belied his deep southern connections. Born into a prominent political family in Nuevo México, Otero practiced law in Missouri and married a South Carolinian with a proud southern pedigree. That marriage entrenched him in elite slaveholding circles and, later, entangled his territorial mission in sectional politics. Otero recognized that New Mexico required federal favors in order to promote its economic development, finance its territorial government, and provide protection from Indian attacks. He also recognized that his personal connections, along with his territory's southern leanings, made New Mexico a natural ally of proslavery politicians. A slave code, as his southern associates had assured him, would help "attract greater . . . political attentions from the States" and also "elevate our own class of free laborers."[69] At the urging of his friends in Congress, Otero tapped his network of southern-born legislators within New Mexico's territorial system to request the drafting and passage of a slave code.[70]

The biracial channels through which Otero operated mirrored those in neighboring Southern California. In both places, a seemingly unlikely alliance between elite Hispanos and Anglo southerners fueled a proslavery agenda. Although many Hispano lawmakers had little interest in—and sometimes an aversion to—African American chattel slavery, they turned to southern slaveholders for political favors and leverage. In Los Angeles County, Chivalry powerbrokers installed their Hispano friends in local offices and rallied votes for state division, which many Californios had long favored. Meanwhile southern slaveholders won support from New Mexico's Hispano lawmakers by promising to route major infrastructure projects through the Far Southwest. The alliance in both places rested on political expediency, more so than a shared commitment to chattel slavery. Yet whatever the underlying motivations, these dovetailing objectives gave proslavery legislators a decisive influence in local affairs and helped make the Desert South.[71]

In California and New Mexico alike, Democratic patronage had stacked the deck heavily in slaveholders' favor. As residents of a territory, New Mexican voters did not elect their own executives or federal district judges. Rather, candidates for those positions—including governor, secretary, and the judges who made up the territorial supreme court—were nominated by the US president and then confirmed by the Senate. President James Buchanan, northern-born but beholden to a predominantly southern constituency, rewarded his allies with New Mexico's posts: a Mississippian for territorial secretary, a South Carolinian (and Otero's brother-in-law) for one of the seats on the supreme court, and a North Carolinian for governor. The secretary, Alexander Jackson, proved a particularly devoted southern partisan, crafting much of the slave code himself. Together with the publisher of the *Santa Fe Gazette* (a Missourian) and a handful of influential southerners within the territorial legislature, these leaders wed New Mexico's fortunes to the slave states. In early 1859, they jammed the slave bill through the legislative process, bypassing a roll call in the house and thereby preventing members from registering a negative vote.[72]

By February, Governor Abraham Rencher had signed "An Act to Provide for the Protection of Property in Slaves in This Territory," giving New Mexico a more draconian slave statute than the one passed in Utah some seven years earlier. Compared to Utah's proslavery law, the New Mexican act provided fewer protections for the enslaved and stipulated harsher punishments for those interfering with slave property. There were stiff fines and prison terms for enabling slaves to escape, for stealing slaves, for furnishing slaves with free papers, for enticing slaves to absent themselves from service, for inciting slave rebellion, and for arming slaves. Slaves could be whipped for disorderly conduct or for "insolent language, or signs, to any free white person." They were also prohibited from testifying in court against whites (a category that included Hispanos). Like the Utah code, New Mexico's closely policed the color line, outlawing intermarriage between whites and blacks and sentencing to death any black person, free or enslaved, found guilty of raping a white woman. In line with the southern states, New Mexico's bill made slavery a perpetual institution, in that it "totally prohibited" the emancipation of slaves within its borders.[73] According to Senator John J. Crittenden of Kentucky, "The law is as complete on the subject as the law of any State that I know of."[74]

One could dismiss this slave code as needlessly detailed for a territory that harbored so few owners of enslaved African Americans. But as Secretary Alexander Jackson recognized, it marked a crucial victory for the slave South. Slaveholders had recently failed to pass the Lecompton Constitution in Kansas, meaning free labor would likely prevail there. The slave code in New Mexico, then, enabled southerners to save face and flex their political muscle elsewhere in the West. It might also lure potential migrants from the slave states, including neighboring Texas. Although the act's passage did not prompt a sudden mass migration of slaveholders to the territory, it did signal that the peculiar systems of law in the South would now hold sway in yet another territory.

And who could say what would happen over time? The region's aridity and its shared border with Mexico, where chattel bondage had been illegal since 1829, may have deterred some slaveholders from migrating.[75] But those familiar with New Mexico's landscape could locate several areas in which this slave code would eventually pay dividends, beginning with the region's well-documented richness in mineral resources. The deposits of southern New Mexico's mines had been known to American travelers and expansionists since at least the 1840s. Jefferson Davis emphasized this fact when waging his campaign against the Wilmot Proviso.[76] Eventually, the region would attract thousands of European, Asian, and Mexican workers to meet the extensive labor needs of silver mining.[77] If not for the Civil War and emancipation, enslaved African Americans might have satisfied some of this labor demand.

Various investigations had revealed a potentially even more valuable resource: cotton. The Virginian surveyor Andrew Belcher Gray mused on the future career of cotton in the Far Southwest in an 1856 report, following his exploration of the region for Robert Walker's Pacific railroad project.[78] His encounters with the Pima and Maricopa Indians convinced Gray of the agricultural fertility of the region, especially along the Gila River. In their villages he found wheat, corn, tobacco, and cotton. The Indian product contained "an exceedingly soft and silky" fiber, according to Gray, prompting a comparison to the "celebrated" cotton of South Carolina's Sea Islands. "Large tracts of land on the Gila and in other portions of this district, appear to possess the same properties of soil," he concluded, "and where, I have no doubt the finest cotton will soon be extensively raised and brought to its highest state of perfection by proper cultivation."[79]

While Gray speculated, James Gadsden experimented and collaborated. Upon receiving a handful of cotton seeds from a friend at Fort Yuma on the California–New Mexico border, Gadsden grew a small crop in his native South Carolina. The results were promising, he reported to fellow expansionist Matthew Fontaine Maury. Shortly thereafter, the *Washington States* obtained a sample of Gadsden's crop and concluded, "If Arizona [part of southern New Mexico] is to furnish us with cotton-fields capable of producing such a material as this, it will be an additional inducement to Southern people to occupy it."[80] The Gadsden Purchase lands, as Gadsden himself now recognized, were even more valuable than previously imagined. The Gila River valley seemed a natural extension of the southern plantation ecosystem. After all, southern New Mexico—and Southern California for that matter—rested at the same latitude as Gadsden's South Carolina.[81] In time, Gadsden would be vindicated. With improved transportation infrastructure and irrigation methods, America's cotton belt shifted westward during the twentieth century, eventually transforming the Far Southwest into the nation's leading producer of the fabric. Today, Texas, New Mexico, Arizona, and California furnish the largest American cotton crops annually.

Not only a spur to the cotton industry, New Mexico's slave code was also a potential stepping stone toward greater conquests. As Otero had intended, the legislation revived national interest in railroads to link South and West. Now, a transcontinental railway between the two regions could utilize "the most efficient and the most reliable" labor force (that is, enslaved African Americans), as a New Mexican correspondent wrote to the

Memphis Daily Appeal.[82] From New Mexico, slaveholders eyed adjacent territories as well. "Not only does slavery thus secure a firm foothold in the Territory of New Mexico—almost an empire in itself," according to the proslavery *Washington States*, "but the position affords the South every facility of expansion in the very direction most inviting to its institutions." The paper predicted that soon Arizona and Nevada—which had yet to be organized as territories—along with parts of Mexico would fall under slaveholders' control.[83]

Unwilling to cede the West to the South, antislavery writers and statesmen counterattacked. From his office at the *New York Daily Tribune*, Horace Greeley raged for well over a year against New Mexico's proslavery legislation. The Hispano majority, generally unsympathetic to US slaveholders, was an insufficient hedge against southern influence, he argued. "A few cunning, intriguing men manage their politics," Greeley wrote, "the masses being mere counters in the game." While some observers, like the *New York Daily Times*, had assumed that New Mexico's slave code would not dramatically increase the westward flow of enslaved African Americans, Greeley dismissed this line of thinking as dangerously shortsighted. "True, it would have few slaves, but what of that?" Greeley wrote. "Our objection is to widening the base of the Slave Power. Delaware has few slaves; but slavery rules and uses her as thoroughly as though she had twenty times as many."[84] More clearly than perhaps anyone else at the time, Greeley foresaw the broader implications of New Mexico's slave code. Plantation agriculture was not a precondition for the Slave Power's westward expansion.

Antislavery politicians in Santa Fe and Washington organized campaigns to repeal the territorial slave law. In early 1859, New Mexico's Speaker of the House made the first attempt at a repeal. But, after branding him an abolitionist and a black Republican, opponents stripped him of his speakership and then rejected his effort.[85] In May 1860, Ohio representative John Bingham—future coauthor of the Fourteenth Amendment—took the fight to Washington with a federal bill to "disapprove and declare null and void" New Mexico's slave code, as well as its legislation regarding the punishment of bound peon laborers.[86] Although those in Santa Fe had held firm against any repeal efforts, Bingham and his Republican allies reasoned that, under the 1850 law establishing New Mexico as a territory, Congress retained the power to override any gratuitous act of the territorial legislature.

This was not primarily a struggle over the small number of bondpeople currently residing in New Mexico. At stake were pressing constitutional issues over the national position of slavery and the power of the federal government to legislate in western territories. Miles Taylor of Louisiana made that clear in his minority report to the Bingham bill, a thirty-one-page document that rehearsed many of the proslavery arguments about the limits of congressional power. He argued that Congress had the authority to nullify only territorial laws that directly contravened provisions in the US Constitution. Furthermore, American citizens retained the right to carry their property, whether human or otherwise, into any federal territories, a right reaffirmed by the *Dred Scott* decision of 1857. Bingham's bill was the most recent outrage in "the war now waged" against the South, Taylor complained. "And if it should be carried into an act, it would be a palpable usurpation of power by Congress." The repeal effort, he insisted, was nothing short of "a blow aimed at slavery itself."[87]

Bingham's repeal bill passed narrowly in the House along sectional lines, ninety-seven to ninety, but then failed in the Senate, the old proslavery bulwark.[88] Yet up until the eve of the Civil War, Bingham continued to agitate against the slave code—legislation that, in his words, "would bring blushes to the check [*sic*] of Caligula."[89] He never mustered the necessary support, however, and New Mexico's law remained on the books through the remainder of the antebellum period.[90]

The Other Slavery in the Desert South

The greatest impediment to the expansion of chattel slavery in the Desert South was not a regional aversion to unfree labor. It was, ironically, a surfeit of it. Landowners in antebellum California, Utah, and especially New Mexico had far cheaper and more accessible alternatives to enslaved African Americans. They could barter for Native American captives, ensnare peons in lifelong debt bondage, or "adopt" Indian wards as domestic laborers. Although southern slaveholders and their human chattel continued to trickle into the region, the most successful masters in the Southwest were those who harnessed the plentiful local supply of unfree workers. Some proprietors created sprawling agricultural complexes that would have been the envy of southern planters, while others worked their slaves in humbler household settings. Wherever or however they exploited their laborers, southwest masters proved that unfreedom knew no natural limits.

The "other slavery," in the words of historian Andrés Reséndez, long predated the arrival of Americans in the region—or even the Spanish, for that matter.[91] European colonization simply accelerated the trade in captives. By the late eighteenth century, the proportions of enslaved people in the United States and Spanish New Mexico were roughly equivalent, at 15 and 12 percent, respectively.[92] Of course, chattel slavery in the American South expanded rapidly after the cotton revolution of the early nineteenth century, soon dwarfing southwestern systems of bondage in scale and profitability. Yet the arrival of the Santa Fe Trail in 1821 brought New Mexico into the American market economy and boosted the economic potential of the other slavery as well. After the United States formally took control of the region in 1848, a growing population of American migrants embraced Indigenous servitude and the profits it generated.[93]

The political economy of what became the American Southwest thrived on cycles of raiding and captive trading, with Native Americans, Hispanos, and Euro-Americans all engaged in the commerce. "The trading in captives has been so long tolerated in this territory, that it has ceased to be regarded as a wrong," according to James S. Calhoun, New Mexico's Indian Agent and subsequently the territory's first US governor.[94] Under article 11 of the Treaty of Guadalupe Hidalgo, Calhoun was responsible for repatriating Mexican captives taken by Native American raiding parties—which likely only incentivized further raiding by Apaches in search of ransom payments from the United States. Although the Gadsden Purchase of 1853 abrogated article 11, the powerful mounted peoples of the Southwest continued to seize captives and horses from the poorly defended borderlands of Mexico.[95] New Mexican trading parties, in turn, ranged across the territory and into Utah and California in search of Indian captives. The result was a steady supply of unfree laborers circulating across the Far Southwest.

Captive slaves brought handsome returns on the borderlands market. Due to their value as domestic workers and their sexual vulnerability, Native girls were the most highly prized captives in the region. While boys could be sold for roughly $100 or exchanged for a horse, girls generally fetched twice as much. Slavers often killed adult male captives rather than sell them, considering grown men more difficult to control and coerce.[96] As a result of this commerce, some Paiute communities, a preferred target of New Mexican and Ute slavers alike, lost up to half of their women and children.[97]

Although Utah's lawmakers ostensibly outlawed the trade in captives in 1852, they simultaneously created a new, legal way of obtaining unfree workers. "An Act for the Further Relief of Indian Slaves and Prisoners" allowed Utah's white residents to purchase Indian children for adoption into their households for up to twenty years.[98] Native children worked to pay off the price of their purchase in exchange for food, clothing, and religious instruction. According to the Book of Mormon, North American Indians belonged to a fallen branch of Israel called the Laminates. Mormon leaders argued that, through education and assimilation, the Saints could remove the Indians' mark—that is, their dark skin—and transform them into a "white and delightsome people."[99] Adoption was to facilitate this salvation of Native Americans—what Brigham Young euphemistically called "purchasing them into freedom"—while also providing frontier households with much-needed sources of labor.[100]

The policy of adoption encouraged the sort of captive raiding that Young hoped to curb—and that had plagued Native communities across the Southwest and into California. One of the most infamous episodes of the kind occurred during the Black Hawk War in 1866 at Circleville, Utah, where LDS settlers herded some thirty Paiutes into a church meetinghouse. The next day, they executed all the Paiute adults while deliberately sparing the children. One boy was later sold for a horse and a bushel of wheat. Southern Utah, home of the cotton mission, became a crossroads in this commerce in Native children. There, John D. Lee, the lead perpetrator of the Mountain Meadows Massacre, bought at least five Native children.[101] According to one recent estimate, more than 400 Indian children were purchased into white households in Utah between 1847 and 1900.[102]

Despite the veneer of altruism that surrounded this policy, the fate of Indian adoptees was predictably grim. Utah law required schooling for Native children living in Mormon households, but, according to census data, more than half of these Indians had yet to receive formal education by 1860. Some 60 percent of adopted Natives died in their early twenties. Those who survived generally found themselves strangers in their own lands, full members of neither their original tribes nor the white communities in which they were raised. A combination of disease, warfare, displacement, and slavery exacted a horrific toll on Utah's Indigenous people. The Native population was roughly 12,000 when the first white settlers arrived in 1847. By 1900, that figure had fallen to just 2,623.[103]

In addition to the adoption of Indian wards and the purchase of captives, western masters had another recourse available: the institution of debt peonage. The boundaries between slavery and indebted peonage in the Far Southwest could be difficult, and often impossible, to discern. For instance, many of those who were bought as enslaved captives were then made to repay their "debt"—that is, the cost of their own purchase.[104] Debt peonage and captive slavery thus became synonymous. Often, debt peons were the children of captive slaves. Yet in other cases, masters and servants entered into contractual relationships (albeit generally unwritten). Rather than purchasing a slave outright, proprietors could secure their peon workers by trapping them in unescapable cycles of debt.

That process began when an indebted peasant, generally of mixed Hispano and Indian ancestry, agreed to bind himself or herself to a landowner. In exchange, men would receive roughly five dollars or less in monthly wages while women got between fifty cents and two dollars—an income "hardly sufficient to keep them in the coarsest clothing and pay their contingent expenses," according to one observer.[105] Any additional goods had to be purchased at inflated prices from a local store, generally controlled by one's master, thus deepening a peon's debt obligations. The end result was a lifetime of debt and therefore a lifetime of servitude. And because that debt could be transferred to a peon's offspring, servitude became heritable and perpetual, not unlike the chattel slavery of the American South.[106]

Like their southeastern counterparts, southwestern masters faced few limits on their power. Also like southeastern slaveholders, they controlled their laborers with the support of local government and law enforcement. New Mexico's peonage statute of 1851 obligated local prefects to assist in recapturing escaped servants, an echo of the federal Fugitive Slave Act passed the previous year.[107] A more robust peonage statute, passed the same year as New Mexico's slave code, gave masters carte blanche in the punishment of their indebted workers, so long as they did not resort to clubs or whips. "No court of this Territory shall have jurisdiction, nor shall take cognizance of any cause for the correction that masters may give their servants for neglect of their duties as servants," the code read, "for they are considered as domestic servants to their masters, and they should correct their neglect and faults."[108]

Travelers, politicians, and local residents regularly compared peonage to plantation slavery in the American South. The difference between the two institutions, observed James S. Calhoun, was mostly semantic. "*Peons*, you are aware, is but another name for *slaves*, as that term is understood in our Southern States," wrote Calhoun, a native of Georgia.[109] Others concluded that peons suffered a far crueler fate. "Peonage is a state of servitude a thousand times worse than our slavery," a writer for *Harper's Weekly* claimed, albeit with a skewed sense of proportion.[110] W. W. H. Davis, a longtime resident of New Mexico, was more measured but nevertheless critical in his assessment: "Peonism is but a more charming name for a species of slavery as abject and oppressive as any found upon the American continent."[111]

Because they were cheap to maintain and easy to discard, peons provided southwestern landholders with the ideal labor supply. Proprietors had no obligation to provide for peons in sickness or in old age. "When he becomes too old to work any longer, like an old horse who is turned out to die, he can be cast adrift to provide for himself," according to Davis.[112] An 1853 New Mexican law gave masters the right to sell servants at auction if they no longer wished to support them.[113] There was no need for masters to risk capital investments by importing expensive chattel slaves from the American South, even though New Mexican law allowed it. "If, therefore, any slaveholder had occasion to go to New Mexico, to embark in agricultural or other business," a US senator from Connecticut argued, "he would find it greatly to his advantage to sell his slaves, and to employ the native labor of that country."[114]

That Native labor supply allowed southwestern masters to profitably maintain large agricultural complexes and lucrative mining ventures. Concentrations of peons could be found in the gold mines to the southeast of Santa Fe and, more conspicuously, on major landholdings dotting the region's river valleys. A majority of these were run by Hispano elites. Yet the archetypal southwestern master and one of the largest landowners in mid-nineteenth-century America was a transplanted midwesterner, Lucien B. Maxwell, who operated a sprawling agricultural complex with hundreds of indebted peons. While a retinue of domestic servants oversaw the needs of his household, an estimated 500 male peons cultivated his fields—mostly barley, oats, and corn—and tended to his 10,000 cattle and 40,000 sheep. Surrounded by his peon laborers, Maxwell lived, according to one observer, "in a sort of barbaric splendor, akin to that of the nobles of England at the time of the Norman conquest."[115] Few planters in the American South controlled such a large number of unfree workers.

Over the past few decades, scholars have unearthed the once-hidden history of Native American and mestizo slavery in the Southwest, documenting how this labor functioned and how legal systems within the region gave cover for proprietors. Surprisingly little is known, however, about how the world's wealthiest and most powerful slaveholders—those in the plantation South—viewed these systems of labor coercion at the other end of the country. As a result, plantation slavery in the South and the so-called other slavery of the Southwest appear in the scholarship as discrete systems, operating independently of one another. Yet southern planters themselves did not draw a fixed line between various types of unfreedom. The South's masters carefully tracked developments beyond their plantations, especially across western lands they hoped to control. They often saw unfree labor through a continental and indeed a hemispheric lens and guarded against antislavery attacks, no matter how distant from their own cotton fields.

When pressed on the issue, American southerners embraced a seemingly paradoxical position that was simultaneously critical and defensive of the West's labor order. They regularly presented peonage as a foil to plantation slavery. According to John C. Calhoun, these southwestern bondpeople "are as much slaves as our negroes, and are less intelligent and well treated."[116] Similarly, Jefferson Davis argued that the practice of peonage was "far more harsh and repulsive to my mind than our domestic slavery" and lacked "the controlling restraint which interest and the relation of permanent dependence creates in the case of the slave."[117] The treatment of peons drew criticism from the slaveholding stalwart and future California legislator Thomas Jefferson Green as well. "I cannot err in saying that, if the owner of negroes in the United States were to permit such an instrument of torture [the pillory] upon his plantation," Green wrote, "public reproba- tion, universal and overwhelming, would cause him to abandon the neigh- borhood thus outraged."[118] Whether or not there was any truth to these statements, slaveholders like Calhoun, Davis, Green, and others agreed: the western labor order was a pale imitation of what they considered their superior and more humane system of mastery.

The southern critique of peonage was, however, only rhetorical. These criticisms functioned as thinly veiled apologias for plantation slavery rather than as calls for reform. When northern congressmen tried to take action against unfreedom in the region—as they did at several points—southern statesmen closed rank. As early as 1848, the fate of peonage became entan- gled in the debates over the legal status of slavery in newly acquired west- ern territories. Antislavery politicians in the House of Representatives and the Senate called for a ban on peonage within the Mexican Cession. Ameri- can southerners, in turn, recognized that an attack on one type of bondage could easily extend to the other. They therefore devised a counterargument: because slavery already existed within the Southwest in the form of debt peonage, the introduction of more slaves—albeit African American chattel rather than Hispano and Indian debtors—presented no legal problems.[119] Plantation slavery and southwestern peonage were now linked.

The debate resurfaced two years later in the sectional standoff that eventually led to the Compromise of 1850. When Senator Isaac P. Walker of Wisconsin introduced a bill to abolish the system of debt peonage in New Mexico, southern statesmen again presented a united front, trotting out familiar arguments on behalf of unfree labor and local sovereignty. "I do not see, then, how we can destroy this system," Robert M. T. Hunter of Virginia argued, "without at least running the risk of destroying what is regarded as a relation between master and servant in all other countries in the world." An attack on peonage was an attack on the property rights of New Mexicans, according to Jefferson Davis, and therefore a violation of the Treaty of Guadalupe Hidalgo. Thomas Jefferson Rusk of Texas argued that the federal government had no place in the debate. "Every city, every town, every municipality," he insisted, "has a right to make regulations about their peons or servants." These arguments ultimately carried the day in a final vote of twenty to thirty-two against Walker's bill.[120] Thus, while they technically lost California to free labor during the debates of 1850, slaveholding senators had at least preserved peonage in New Mexico.

From the perspective of southern slaveholders, this victory for unfreedom in the Far Southwest coincided with heartening developments elsewhere in the world. While New Mexican traders purchased Indian slaves and trapped peasants in cycles of debt, European empires were importing a growing supply of indentured Asian workers to their overseas colonies. Slaveholders read this as proof that British emancipation had failed and that agriculture in places like Jamaica could not be sustained by free workers.[121] American slaveholders viewed these two phenomena—the growth of "coolie" labor and the maintenance of debt peonage—in notably similar ways. They denounced the abuses of both systems as lacking the purported paternalism that guided the treatment of their own enslaved workforce. At the same time, the mere existence of such labor regimes amounted to an ideological victory for American southerners and a confirmation of their worldview. Whether they faced west to the ranchos of New Mexico or southeast to the plantations of the Caribbean, slaveholders could assure themselves that they were on the winning side of history. Coercion, rather than wages, would continue to drive the workforce of the world.

They fought to keep it this way. Antebellum southern statesmen sought to preserve unfree labor regimes around the world, a political calculus that historian Matthew Karp has termed the "foreign policy of slavery." The health of their plantation system depended, in part, on the continued success of slavery on a hemispheric scale, whether in Texas, Spanish Cuba, or the Empire of Brazil. And they defended these regimes using the full force of the American state.[122] As the congressional debates over peonage make clear, American southerners took a similarly protective approach to the "other slavery" in the Southwest. Recognizing attacks on peonage as indirect assaults on their own coercive institution, southerners sustained the rights of masters, whether in South Carolina or New Mexico, to manage labor as they saw fit. Planters and their allies protected peonage, knowing that peonage, in turn, would protect chattel slavery. By this logic, then, the unfree regimes of the Southwest represented the western flank of a continental slave system. Despite the best efforts of Republican lawmakers, that flank held.

Conclusion

By 1860, slaveholding prospects in the Far West had never appeared brighter. The nation's major overland road now connected the slave states of the East to the Pacific coast. The US Supreme Court had sanctioned the right of slaveholders to carry their human chattel into western territories. Chivalry Democrats had eliminated David Broderick, the main threat to their political hegemony in California. Both Utah and New Mexico had legalized slavery within their territorial borders, while southern politicians suppressed all Republican attempts to overturn these codes. Slaveholding congressmen had also thwarted multiple efforts to outlaw debt peonage within the Southwest. The last of these anti-peonage bills failed in June 1860, when Senator Henry Wilson of Massachusetts took aim at a new law in New Mexico that enhanced the power of masters over their peons—what he and others provocatively dubbed a "white slave code." Like the congressional bills that preceded it, this one collapsed quickly after a vote primarily along sectional lines.[123]

Yet the political tides could shift quickly, especially with the upcoming presidential election. For the better part of the past decade, Democratic presidents and their congressional allies had installed a legion of proslavery appointees in federal positions across the Far West. Much of William Gwin's California machine and New Mexico's territorial leadership had been built through these patronage networks, which could crumble instantly with a Republican victory in the fall. Nevertheless, Democratic appointees and proslavery operatives in the region had good reason for their optimism at the start of the new decade. Whereas the Republican Party continued to grow quickly in the Northeast and the Old Northwest, it was virtually nonexistent in both the slave South and the Far Southwest. Meanwhile, the Republican congressional campaign to curtail the westward extension of slavery had repeatedly failed. Republicans could say what they wished about "Freedom National," yet this slogan would remain precisely that—a slogan, if not a pipe dream—until they managed to achieve some success within the Desert South. As any political observer from the region could have confirmed: freedom remained sectional, while slavery, in various shades and forms, was transcontinental.

→ **CHAPTER SIX** ←

The Continental Crisis of the Union

◆●◆

W
HEN SOUTH CAROLINA'S fire-eaters adopted secessionist ordinances and broke from the Union in December 1860, they triggered a chain reaction that quickly rippled west. By March 1861, the insurrection had reached southern New Mexico, a region known as Arizona. White settlers there gathered at three separate conventions—first at Piños Altos, then Mesilla, and finally Tucson—to air their grievances against the US government and to formally attach themselves to the insurgent slave states. Although they lived roughly 2,000 miles from the rebellion's heartland, in a place settled by relatively few slaveholders, these westerners belonged to the South.

This was the central theme of one of Mesilla's fieriest orators, General W. Claude Jones, a veritable spokesman for the Continental South. "Our destiny is linked with the South," he argued. "Her memory of the past, her principles, her interests, her present glory, her hopes of the future, are ours." The choice for Jones and his compatriots was simple. "Northward, insult, wrong and oppression are frowning upon us," he thundered. "Southward a brilliant and glorious pathway of hope, leads to the star of empire smiling over a constellation of free and sovereign States."[1] Like those at Piños Altos, delegates at Mesilla overwhelmingly voted to break from the Union and throw their allegiances behind the rebel states. One week later, a convention at Tucson passed another set of secessionist resolutions, making Arizona's position triply clear. At the time, only six other slave states had followed South Carolina out of the Union. Arizona found itself at the leading edge of a national rebellion.

Arizona's secession was the most decisive rupture in the Far West during this period. But it was not the only one. Over the preceding decade, the region had given rise to several separatist movements, which, to varying degrees, drew on support from slaveholders to challenge local and national authority. White leaders in Arizona had been lobbying for years to create a separate territory from the southernmost county of New Mexico. Congressmen from the Deep South endorsed the measure, expecting an additional slave state to emerge from this territory. A similar movement unfolded concurrently in Southern California, where settlers from the slave states constituted a majority of the Anglo-American population. California's legislature passed a measure for the formation of a separate territory in 1859, although the bill ultimately foundered in Congress, whose members were preoccupied with the far larger schism of southern secession. Meanwhile, others in California contemplated the creation of a separate Pacific republic. If the Union were to disintegrate, they would harness these centrifugal forces to forge a new nation from the Far West's states and territories. As they saw it, there was no reason why national dissolution should occur strictly along a north-south axis.

With their gaze fixed on the East, scholars of antebellum American politics have largely missed this set of parallel movements in the West. The major narratives of the secession crisis touch only lightly on events beyond the 100th meridian.[2] There is, of course, good reason for this eastern orientation. Given their wealth, population, and military potential, the rebel states of the Southeast constituted, far and away, the greatest threat to the United States. Abraham Lincoln and his government recognized as much and threw their energies into preventing additional southern states from spinning out of the Union. But US officials, with growing alarm, tracked separatist movements in the West as well. They diverted resources to shore up support in the region and quarantine the rebellion to the southeastern part of the country. As they understood, Confederate secession was a powder keg with a potentially transcontinental blast radius. Stretching from the Charleston harbor to the Los Angeles coastline, America's national crisis was far greater than the standard historical narrative allows.

A handful of historians have pushed beyond traditional geographic boundaries and incorporated political actors often deemed peripheral to the Civil War era.[3] Their works skillfully illustrate how partisans in New Mexico, Utah, California, and even the Pacific Northwest responded to the Confederate rebellion. Together, they make clear that, at the outset of the crisis, a spirit of insurrection reached well beyond the slave states.[4] Yet most of these studies focus on a single state or territory; few explore the far-reaching and deep-rooted political affinities that bound together South and West as the Union disintegrated.[5] We have yet to appreciate the full extent of these interlocking rebellions and the expansive political calculus that set them in motion.

The crisis of 1860–61, as it manifested in the Desert South, was the culmination of a long history of separatism in the region. The territorial campaign in Arizona, state division in California, the plot for an independent Pacific republic, and various Confederate schemes across the Southwest— all of these movements drew on deep reservoirs of proslavery enthusiasm and local republicanism. Not every scheme was identical in its aims or sources of support. Many of those advocating for a slaveholding territory in Southern California, for instance, remained neutral or even loyal to the United States when civil war broke out several years later. But western separatists, even those who did not directly aid the Confederacy, nevertheless sustained the broad principle behind the southern rebellion. Each of their operations attempted to redraw the American map in the interests of slavery. And together, they constituted a continental crisis of the Union.

The Southernization of Arizona

To the Americans who first lusted after it, Arizona was merely a place between two points, not a destination in itself. Much of the land that residents called either "Arizona" or "Arizonia" had been carved from Mexico in 1854 through a treaty negotiated by James Gadsden, the Gadsden Purchase. The treaty's aim was to secure a suitable stretch of terrain across which the "great slavery road" could pass. Settlement of the region was an afterthought. Yet as Pacific railroad bills languished in Congress, the Gadsden Purchase paid dividends for proslavery expansionists in ways unforeseen by its original architects. Derided by some as an arid and undesirable corner of the country, Arizona soon attracted American migrants, primarily those from neighboring Texas. When, by the end of the decade, these residents began demanding separate territorial status, they transformed Arizona into another theater in the sectional controversy.

Southern migrants congregated primarily in the Mesilla River valley. Numbering between 2,500 and 3,000 residents, the town of Mesilla was strategically situated in a rich agricultural region along the route linking Texas to California. Mesilla was also proximate to gold, silver, and copper mines—the sort of repositories that Jefferson Davis hoped, and Horace Mann feared, would be operated by slave labor.[6] Many Texan prospectors congregated in the large mining camp of Piños Altos, while another group of white southerners settled in Tucson. In these early years, few migrants carried their African American slaves into Arizona. But they did bring their sectional loyalties, illustrating again that the long arm of the South could reach westward in the absence of chattel slavery itself. By the late 1850s, Arizona had become a satellite of the slave states, a vital link in the Continental South.[7]

Southern migrants took the lead in Arizona's early territorial movement. The Gadsden Purchase lands had been attached to New Mexico in 1854, but residents of the territory's southernmost towns soon began to nurture a sense of separate identity. They complained that they were underrepresented in New Mexico's territorial legislature and received inadequate provision for their defense. They were particularly vulnerable to Chiricahua Apaches, who looked upon recent American arrivals as invaders of their homelands.[8] In January 1855, James A. Lucas, a migrant from Texas and member of New Mexico's legislature, introduced a bill to create a separate territory from Doña Ana County, which included the towns of Mesilla, Tucson, and Piños Altos. The legislature tabled Lucas's measure, but he organized another campaign in the summer of 1856. In August that year, a convention from Tucson petitioned Congress with a memorial signed by 260 residents. Mesilla held its own territorial convention in September 1858 and another in June 1859. By then, Arizona's territorial agenda was generating national consideration.[9]

Partisans on both sides of the Mason-Dixon Line understood that the creation of a new territory in such a proslavery region would amount to a major coup for the South. Northern politicians, therefore, came out in force against Arizona's territorial bid, while southern leaders rallied in support. With J. D. B. De Bow as its president, the 1857 commercial convention at Knoxville endorsed Arizona's territorial campaign.[10] That same year, President Buchanan gave his executive blessing to Arizona. He would continue to recommend separate territorial status for Arizona, even after failing in his other western initiative regarding Kansas's proslavery Lecompton Constitution.[11] A group of slaveholding senators, including Thomas Jefferson Rusk of Texas, William Gwin of California, and Jefferson Davis of Mississippi, also formally supported Arizona's organization as a territory.[12] Davis's Mississippi senate colleague, Albert Gallatin Brown, was more explicit when, in December 1860, he called for the extension of New Mexico's slave code to the separate territory of Arizona. To guard against Representative John Bingham's ongoing crusade against southwestern slavery, Brown stipulated that the slave code "shall not be repealed during the territorial existence of said Territory."[13]

Not all slaveholders, however, were eager for the prompt organization of Arizona, despite its potential. James Gadsden adopted a surprisingly guarded and nuanced position. In a letter to the *Charleston Courier*, Gadsden warned that premature action might revive "the agitations of Kansas on the soil of Arizona, and . . . rob the South of its inheritance before it was prepared to take possession."[14] Like many slaveholding expansionists, Gadsden viewed Arizona as an extension of the South. But he also worried that territorial organization might galvanize abolitionist crusaders. They might then invade the region and establish another antislavery government, as they were attempting in Kansas at that very moment. Gadsden envisioned Arizona as another Bleeding Kansas, with sectional adversaries migrating west to the next available theater. Past experience, he reasoned, indicated long odds for the South.

By 1858, abolitionists and proslavery partisans braced for a new fight in Arizona. According to an antislavery agent in Lawrence, Kansas, "A great many Free State men have stated their determination to go [to Arizona] . . . to help the cause of free institutions there."[15] That same spring, the *Texas State Gazette* fretted over reports of well-drilled companies of New England men who planned on "abolitionizing Arizona by force of arms." By planting antislavery forces in a "Southern clime" (that is, Arizona), abolitionists would cut off slavery's escape valve, blocking the "acquisition of new slave States at the Southwest, where alone we can look for expansion," the *Gazette* moaned.[16] Even more sanguine observers, like De Bow, anticipated "an angry struggle" over the region, given Arizona's importance to southern railroaders.[17]

Slaveholders and their allies rallied in defense. From Georgia came reports of a militia commander who had begun recruitment efforts across several southern cities to "collect emigrants for Arizona." His mission, according to the *Columbus Times* of Georgia, was to colonize "that territory with southern men, with the ultimate purpose of impressing the institutions of the South upon the political fortunes of that country."[18] The *Alexandria Gazette* cheered an upswing in migration from the slave states to Arizona, "the Mecca of aspiring speculators."[19] Other southern papers anticipated a further influx of proslavery migrants in the coming years. Given its mineral wealth and fertility, especially with regard to cotton cultivation, Arizona presented a more enticing prospect to slaveholders than Kansas, over which much blood had already been spilled. As the *Baltimore Sun* projected, "There is a better chance for the establishment of slavery in the latter [Arizona] than there ever was in the former Territory [Kansas]."[20]

Ultimately, it was the steady accumulation of migrants from the slave states, rather than a bloody confrontation, that secured Arizona for the South. By 1860, Arizona's population had swelled to roughly 10,000, with many of the new arrivals hailing from below the Mason-Dixon Line. To disseminate their sectional views, a pair of migrants from Kentucky and Missouri established Arizona's first newspaper, the *Mesilla Times*, in 1860. The Hispano population still outnumbered these Anglo-American southerners, but the two groups found common cause in Arizona's territorial movement. And while some migrants from the free states achieved local prominence, they did so by embracing the proslavery orthodoxy of the region. Take, for instance, the Tucson merchant and politician Sylvester Mowry. A Rhode Islander by birth, Mowry espoused a set of political views largely indistinguishable from his Texan colleagues, who spearheaded the territorial movement. By the end of the decade, Mowry had become one of Arizona's most prominent advocates for a deep southern railroad and the westward expansion of chattel slavery.[21]

Mowry brought greater visibility to Arizona's territorial bid through a series of lectures and publications, which highlighted his region's links with the slave South. He presented Arizona as an outgrowth of the plantation districts, which would support "all the fruits known to a Southern clime."[22] Staples like "rice, sugar and cotton are best adapted to the soil of the Colorado bottom," he claimed in an 1859 address. As for the laborers required to cultivate these crops, "the extreme heat of the climate in the summer months will prevent white labor from agricultural pursuits to any great extent."[23] The only solution, he implied, was unfree African American or Native American labor. Mowry also defended the great slavery road as "not only the most practicable, but probably the only practicable route."[24] He appended to this address a lengthy excerpt from Jefferson Davis's January 1859 speech on the transcontinental railroad. For his fidelity to southern orthodoxy, Mowry was elected Arizona's unofficial delegate to Congress three times over.

With no decisive action coming from a gridlocked Congress on the territorial issue, Arizona's Anglo-American residents took matters into their own hands. In April 1860, a convention of thirty-one delegates met in Tucson to draft a territorial constitution. Although the delegates sidestepped direct mention of slavery during the proceedings, their actions and endorsements betrayed their sectional leanings. Not only did Arizona's delegates approve "the pure, wise, and patriotic administration of our venerable President James Buchanan," they also created a new county in honor of southern partisan and future Confederate general Richard S. Ewell, who had been stationed at nearby Fort Buchanan.[25] The convention elected as provisional governor Lewis S. Owings, a Texan, who then selected his fellow Texan James A. Lucas as territorial secretary. The territorial constitution, drafted by the convention, made no explicit reference to slavery, as the authors likely realized that any outright endorsement of the institution would only enflame sectional discord and potentially scuttle their hopes for territorial recognition. But, crucially, it did recognize the laws of New Mexico "to be in full force and effect in this, the Territory of Arizona."[26] New Mexico's slave code thus became Arizona's slave code. Congress, however, refused to recognize the document, and Arizona remained attached to New Mexico Territory.

By the end of the decade, Arizona had produced more smoke than fire. For all of their conventions and petitions, Arizona separatists failed to establish an independent territory. Furthermore, Bleeding Arizona, the anticipated clash between abolitionists and proslavery migrants, never materialized. Yet these non-events had a powerful influence on the region's politics nonetheless. The repeated refusals of northern congressmen to address territorial petitions hardened white Arizonians against the federal government and against Republican politicians in particular. And the persistent fear of an abolitionist influx spurred some southerners westward while also deepening residents' suspicions of antislavery interference in territorial affairs. Meanwhile, statesmen from the Deep South, including Jefferson Davis and Thomas Jefferson Rusk, won western allies by advocating for separate political status for Arizona. With a divisive national election looming, there was no mistaking where Arizona's loyalties lay. As the two major sections of the nation drifted apart, the Continental South drew closer together.

A State Divided against Itself

While southern New Mexicans battled for separate territorial status, a similar movement was intensifying directly to the west. For nearly a decade, a prominent assortment of Californians—many of them of the proslavery stripe—had advocated for state division. They repeated, on an annual basis, a familiar set of grievances: unfair taxation, their physical distance from the capital of Sacramento, and their underrepresentation in the legislature. The only equitable solution, they argued, was to split the state just south of San Luis Obispo and convert the lower section into an independent territory. Although several historians have studied this state division movement, none of them place developments within California alongside the campaign unfolding concurrently in Arizona.[27] Taken together, these territorial initiatives constituted an integral, if ultimately unsuccessful, component of the southern expansionist project. They were also harbingers of a more violent brand of disunionism that would soon convulse the region. By redrawing the American map, southern partisans hoped to bolster their waning representation in Congress and to strengthen their political grip across the lower corridor of the country.

At first glance, the sponsor of the movement, Andrés Pico, did not fit the description of a proslavery conspirator. A landowner of mixed African,

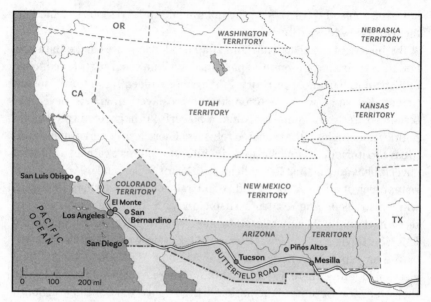

The proposed division of California and New Mexico

Native American, and European ancestry, Pico belonged to the wealthy class of Californios who had ruled the region during the Mexican era. After serving valiantly for Mexico during the US invasion of California in 1846–48, Pico managed to retain much of his wealth and political influence under American sovereignty. He first threw his support behind David Broderick in the early 1850s. But when William Gwin appointed him to the lucrative post of state tax collector for the district of Southern California, Pico's allegiances shifted. He soon became one of the leading members of the Californio-Chivalry alliance that reigned in his hometown of Los Angeles, as well as an intimate friend of party boss Joseph Lancaster Brent. When Brent left California several years later to join the Confederate rebellion in the South, Pico assumed the guardianship of Brent's daughter.[28]

Pico, as a member of the California assembly, put forward his measure for state division in early 1859. His bill called for the division of California just below San Luis Obispo and the creation of the territory of Colorado from the state's southern counties.[29] (Present-day Colorado was not organized as a separate territory until 1861, when it was carved from western Kansas.) The land mass reserved for this Southern California territory mapped almost perfectly onto Senator Henry Foote's proposal nine years before. Pico did not even bother to change the name.

Supporters of the bill attempted to disguise their sectional motives, studiously avoiding direct mention of slavery. Even Chivalry partisans preferred to tread carefully in such a charged political atmosphere, lest they imperil the bill. This was, after all, a year that would witness John Brown's raid on Harpers Ferry, the passage of New Mexico's slave code, Senator David Broderick's death at the hands of a Chivalry rival, and open talk of southern secession. Yet few were fooled by the Pico party line on state division, which presented it as a measure to provide tax relief for Southern California's landowners. Such grievances could have been addressed through an amendment to the tax code rather than by splitting the state in two.[30] The Pico bill may have carried a Spanish rather than an American southerner's surname, but the proslavery undercurrents to the state division movement were unmistakable.

California's antislavery papers, the *Sacramento Daily Union* in particular, linked the state division movement to grander schemes for slaveholding expansion. "Southern empire on the shores of the Pacific is what the leaders of the ultra slavery party in Congress have long coveted above all things," warned the *Daily Union* in late March 1859. In this bid for a western dominion, slaveholders would not stop at the division of California and its "inevitable" conversion to slave territory. "To connect the South with her domain on the Pacific, and bind the intermediate Territories of Arizona and New Mexico, a Pacific Railroad terminating at San Diego will be of the first necessity."[31] According to the *Union,* the proposed territory of Colorado was not merely a protest movement of aggrieved local landholders; it was a crucial component in the South's transcontinental campaign.

Southern expansionists, in turn, cheered the state division movement and mapped these developments onto their larger geopolitical fantasies. Speaking at a Vicksburg convention in the summer of 1859, Henry Foote chided the large body of secessionists there by arguing that slavery could be best preserved, and even extended, within the Union. Just look westward, he urged his audience. He assured the crowd that "in less than two years from this time, if we are wise, we will have a slave State in Southern California. The State has been divided . . . for that purpose."[32] The *Baltimore Sun* linked the separatist movements in Southern California and southern New Mexico, predicting the creation of a vast new slave state from the two would-be territories. "This would seem to be the best prospect that is now offered in any quarter for the early admission of any new slaveholding States," the *Sun* added.[33] Others anticipated a boom in cotton, tobacco, and sugar cultivation in the new Southern California territory.[34]

The Pico bill had to clear three major votes: by legislators in the assembly and the state senate and then by voters in a popular referendum in Southern California. With crucial (though not unanimous) support from Chivalry lawmakers, including all members from Southern California, the measure passed by tallies of thirty-three to twenty-five and fifteen to twelve in the lower and upper houses of the legislature, respectively.[35] From there, the bill traveled to Governor John B. Weller's desk, who signed his support. Finally, in September, the measure came before a popular referendum in Southern California. Voters approved state division by a three-to-one margin.[36]

The Pico bill faced one final obstacle before Southern Californians could be granted separate territorial status: the Thirty-Sixth Congress, where Republicans held a plurality of House seats. Southerners could at least find some solace in the fact that Governor Milton S. Latham would communicate the bill to Washington. Although born in Ohio, Latham had spent several years in Alabama before coming to California and had established his bona fides as a Lecompton Democrat. A proponent of "proper subjugation" for African Americans and the right of slaveholders to carry their human property into the territories, Latham enjoyed the backing of California's Chivalry faction.[37]

But if slaveholders expected the governor to stand firmly on their side, his official communication to the president was a disappointment. Although he recognized that Southern Californians nurtured justifiable grievances, their attempt to split the state was "for the present, at least, impolitic."[38] Latham may have been a southern sympathizer, but he was first and foremost a politician, and he saw the way the wind was blowing in Congress by early 1860. An outright endorsement of the bill would have smacked of proslavery intrigue, a risky play at a time when sectional feelings ran at fever pitch after Brown's raid on Harpers Ferry. Ultimately the bill died in the Senate Judiciary Committee, although California's legislature would continue agitating for state division well into 1860.[39]

Through the stillborn territory of Colorado, southern partisans enacted a familiar political drama. Once again, an influential political minority tapped local grievances and sectional sympathies in an attempt to carve out a corner of the Far West for slavery. And again, Congress was forced to deliberate on a local initiative that carried national significance. The Pico bill was merely the latest ploy in a proslavery campaign that had convulsed California politics since its admission to the Union in 1850. James Gadsden died several months before lawmakers in Sacramento passed the state division bill, but his spirit hovered over this act that resembled his earlier attempt to plant a slave colony on the Pacific coast. That reports of California state division reached the South via the Butterfield Overland

Mail Road, across Gadsden Purchase lands, seems additionally fitting. The decade-long campaign for state division ultimately died in the Senate, but the dream of a slaveholding corridor to the Pacific would live on.

"The High-Road to a Slave Empire"

The unresolved status of slavery in the western territories was the engine of the sectional conflict. Somehow, every major debate in Washington toward the end of the decade came back to this fundamental question: where in the West would slavery be allowed to expand? Most southern Democrats claimed that the Supreme Court had settled the matter in 1857 with *Dred Scott v. Sandford*. Slavery was national, as they saw it, and neither Congress nor any territorial legislature could say otherwise. Yet a rising class of Republican leaders would not concede this point to a group of nine justices. This was the issue at the heart of their national campaign in 1860 and the issue upon which the fate of America's "house divided" depended, or so they believed. After his victory that fall, President-elect Abraham Lincoln held firm on the matter, even as the Union disintegrated in front of his eyes. To fold on the territorial question would, he argued, pave "the high-road to a slave empire."[40]

From a certain perspective, the antebellum debate over the territories appears rather abstract. As numerous contemporaries noted, slaveholders were slow to push into the territorial West. Even New Mexico, with its comprehensive slave code, housed no more than a few dozen black bondpeople by the end of the decade. Furthermore, Lincoln was known to cast the machinations of the so-called Slave Power in bold strokes. Some might have believed that this emerging empire of slavery existed primarily in his imagination. According to the closest student of the subject, the sectional debate over the territories had become an "almost entirely academic" matter by 1860.[41] This debate exposed what historian Elliott West calls the "slavery paradox"—that is, political antagonists fought most fiercely over the territories at the moment when slavery's practical value in the West appeared, he argues, increasingly immaterial.[42]

That paradox can be resolved by following the long-range vision of slaveholders. Even if chattel slavery had not yet taken root in the soils of the Southwest, there was reason to suspect that such a flexible institution could eventually prosper in the region and open the door to greater advances for the South. The separatist movements of southern New Mexico and Southern California fed off this logic. So too did experiments with cotton cultivation in New Mexico. As they demonstrated in their ongoing campaign to strip New Mexico of its chattel slave code and peonage laws,

Republicans were willing to expend political capital to block the southwestern spread of coerced labor. They knew that not merely the labor order but also the political allegiance of the Far West hung in the balance. If slavery continued spreading west, so too would the influence of the South's planter class. That, in turn, would enable southerners to more effectively lobby for transportation links between the two regions—perhaps one day even build their great slavery road. Such future-thinking, as Elliott West argues, was often at the crux of the territorial question.[43] Lincoln's warning, therefore, cannot be dismissed as the product of an overactive imagination, nor can these debates be seen as abstract. For more than a decade, southern leaders pursued a transcontinental dominion for slavery and slaveholding influence. Their willingness to dismantle the Union over the territorial issue was merely the latest and most dramatic gambit of the Continental South.

As the election of 1860 approached, Democratic leaders pressed their advantage on the territorial question. In December 1859, President James Buchanan applauded the Taney court and reaffirmed the inviolability of slaveholding rights in the territories.[44] A few months later, Jefferson Davis issued a series of resolutions in the Senate, reasserting the orthodox southern interpretation of *Dred Scott*. Neither Congress nor any territorial legislature could prevent citizens from taking their human chattel into the territories, Davis maintained. If this fundamental right was ever denied, he added, Congress had the obligation to actively defend slave property in the territories. Davis's resolutions were not an outright demand for a territorial slave code. But they did mandate "the assurance of remedial legislation" should the status of slavery in the West ever be threatened.[45]

By forcing the issue, Davis set the terms of debate for the upcoming Democratic National Convention in Charleston and cornered Stephen Douglas on the most contentious question of the day. Douglas, until recently the presumptive presidential nominee, had made powerful enemies within the party by opposing the proslavery Lecompton Constitution for Kansas and by expounding on the principle of popular sovereignty in a lengthy article for *Harper's Magazine* in 1859. According to Douglas, each territory, rather than the Taney court, could establish its own laws with regard to slavery.[46] For this, Douglas was stripped of his chair on the Senate Committee on Territories and viciously rebuked by William Gwin, among other southern-born congressmen.[47] Due to Douglas's position on the territorial issue and Davis's resolutions in response, a showdown between the two wings of the party was virtually inevitable.[48]

At Charleston that May, the battle lines were drawn starkly. The pro-Douglas popular sovereignty camp consisted of delegates from the free states of the Northeast and Northwest, while all delegations from the slave states, along with California and Oregon, opposed his candidacy. The position of California's delegation was essentially indistinguishable from those of the South. Previously, at their own state convention, California Democrats had endorsed the *Dred Scott* decision, the Buchanan administration, and the rights of slaveholders in the territories. The state's representatives at Charleston reaffirmed these positions; none of them cast a single vote for Douglas. After nearly five dozen ballots and the theatrical walkout of fifty southern delegates, neither Douglas nor any of his competitors received the required two-thirds majority to secure the nomination.[49]

The party agreed to reconvene at Baltimore in June of that year, with the exception of hardliners from South Carolina and Florida, who boycotted. The second convention proved even less successful than the first. Again, neither faction would give ground on the territorial issue. And again, a legion of proslavery delegates stormed out of the convention in protest, including those from California and Oregon. The remaining delegates finally nominated Douglas, their champion, while the southern and far western states reassembled at Richmond. California's representatives in Virginia—including Congressman Charles L. Scott and Calhoun Benham, the second to David S. Terry in the duel that killed Senator Broderick—were even more solidly Chivalry than the two previous delegations. They joined with southern representatives to nominate John C. Breckinridge of Kentucky for president and Joseph Lane of Oregon as his vice presidential running mate. Both nominees embraced the southern (and far western) orthodoxy on the unrestricted rights of slaveholders in the territories.[50]

Because of their divergence on the territorial issue, Democrats split their ticket and effectively forfeited the presidency to Lincoln in that fall's election. Even with this lift from a divided Democratic Party, however, Lincoln's showing in large parts of the country was less than heartening for Republicans. Famously, he did not appear on the ballot in ten slave states. In the Far West, he eked out particularly narrow victories, with, for instance, just 36 percent of the vote in Oregon. Lincoln managed to carry California, breaking the electoral drought for Republican candidates there. But he did so with just 32 percent of the ballots, the lowest proportion of votes he received in any free state. He edged Douglas by a mere 643 votes out of 119,876 ballots cast in California—what Lincoln called "the closest political bookkeeping I know of." California's entire congressional delegation—two congressmen and two senators—supported Breckinridge, as did every single state officer, except Governor John G. Downey, who backed Douglas. Lincoln fared especially poorly in Southern California, where every major political figure campaigned for Breckinridge, handing the Kentuckian a sizable majority in Los Angeles County.[51] By the following month, South

Carolina made good on its long-standing secession threat and formally withdrew from the Union.

That winter, as Congress attempted to head off a further breakup of the Union, the West remained at the center of debate. Committees in the Senate and the House floated a number of compromise initiatives, none of which was more hotly debated than a set of proposals authored by Senator John J. Crittenden of Kentucky. The same month that South Carolina seceded, Crittenden put forward a set of six constitutional amendments and four supplementary resolutions. Of these, his most consequential and controversial was a proposal to extend the Missouri Compromise line to the Pacific coast. Slavery would then be legal across all lands south of 36°30′, while territories north of that line would be free soil.[52]

For nearly three months, as several additional states abandoned the Union, a shrinking Congress debated Crittenden's measures. A majority of congressmen who spoke formally on the issue believed that the so-called Crittenden Compromise would result in the further spread of slavery.[53] For them, the territorial issue was no mere abstraction. Three words in Crittenden's lengthy proposal attracted more criticism than any others: "territories hereafter acquired." That is, any future lands acquired by the United States—including those in Mexico and the Caribbean—would also adhere to the proposed division between slave and free soil. It did not require a particularly far-ranging imagination to foresee the potential upshot of this clause.[54]

Lincoln, waiting anxiously in Springfield before he could take office in March, fired off letters to prominent politicians, pleading with them to hold firm against any concessions on the territorial question. After all, he had been elected on a platform opposing the western extension of slavery. Both the Douglas position on popular sovereignty and the Crittenden plan "would lose us every thing we gained by the election," he wrote to Republican powerbroker Thurlow Weed. "Filibustering for all South of us, and making slave states of it, would follow in spite of us, under either plan."[55] The "tug has to come," he wrote to another friend, "and better now than later."[56]

Prominent Republicans in Congress were equally adamant. According to Senator Henry Wilson of Massachusetts, the central issue in the "battle of 1860" were the lands open to slavery by Crittenden's measure: "the Indian country, New Mexico, Arizona, and territory which might hereafter be acquired in Mexico and Central America." Any concession on these would invalidate the election, he argued.[57] Others were more emphatic still. Crittenden's line "would amount to a perpetual covenant of war against every people, tribe, and State owning a foot of land between here and T[i]erra del Fuego," according to Representative Roscoe Conkling of New York. The government would then become "the armed missionary of slavery," launching the United States upon a "shoreless and starless sea of war and filibustering."[58]

Although most critics of the Crittenden Compromise imagined the grim results for Latin America, congressmen were not blind to the potential consequences for lands *already* acquired. New Mexico was once again thrust into the national debate over slavery. For years, the territory had generated heated controversy over its peonage statutes and its more recent slave code, including the vigorous Republican campaign for repeal. Now Crittenden's plan, and a subsequent proposal to admit New Mexico as a state, threatened to forever surrender this substantial portion of the American map to slavery. As a Vermont Republican argued in the House, "Any people willing to vote *peon servitude* upon themselves, as they do in New Mexico, are hardly to be trusted with the destinies of a State."[59]

While some statesmen, including Lincoln himself, were willing to cede New Mexico "if further extension were hedged against," others balked at the idea.[60] Several Republicans looked beyond the present condition of New Mexico to imagine a future in which the region might occupy a central place in a slaveholding dominion. As soon as New Mexico won statehood, its slave population would likely "rapidly increase," according to Representative Daniel Gooch of Massachusetts. More alarming still, New Mexico might then join the growing southern rebellion. After all, he warned, "by geographical position, similarity of laws and institutions, she is identified with the States that have assumed to secede from this Union."[61] The southern dream of a transcontinental empire—seemingly closer at hand than ever before—had become a Republican nightmare.

New Mexico, some Republicans feared, was a potential slaveholding empire in and of itself. "Plant slavery in New Mexico and Arizona," Alfred Wells of New York warned, "let it be forever in contact with the fertile cotton-fields of Texas . . . and who can say what will be the future destiny of that vast Territory, large enough to make twenty-four states the size of Massachusetts." As the history of unfreedom around the globe illustrated, he continued, slavery was a highly adaptable institution. Wells was unconvinced by arguments about New Mexican aridity. "Who knows what new arts, what new appliances, what unimagined discoveries may convert the desert into a garden," he claimed. Congress, therefore had the obligation to purge New Mexico "not only [of] African slavery in its most objectionable form, but peon slavery" as well. Fail in this regard, he warned, and "we nationalize slavery."[62]

By March 1861 there was no possible compromise on the issue of slavery in the territories. Republicans refused to invalidate their national victory of 1860 by permitting the further spread of bondage, whereas southern

Democrats had already proved willing to break up their party and then the nation itself to affirm their unrestricted property rights in the territorial West. The Crittenden Compromise thus went down to defeat in both the Senate and the House.

These debates appear academic only when assessing the short-term prospects for the slave South. True, the Crittenden Compromise line would have changed little in early 1861, as New Mexico's legislature had already legalized debt peonage and chattel slavery. But should Arizona and Southern California spin off as separate territories, as their residents had pledged, southern expansionists would eventually gain title to three slave states within the Far Southwest. From there, who could say what further conquests might result. Southern expansionists had long coveted a coast-to-coast empire of precisely this sort.

Yet most of those expansionists were no longer interested in negotiation. By spring 1861, seven slave states had formed a government, drafted a constitution, and elected Jefferson Davis as president, the most persistent champion of slaveholding rights in the Far West.

Southern Secession, Western Separatism

Ten days after the formation of the self-proclaimed Confederate States of America, the new vice president of the rebel government, Alexander Stephens, delivered one of the defining speeches of the era. Before a large crowd in Savannah, he rhapsodized about the new Confederate constitution and the principle of human inequality upon which it rested. This government's foundations were laid, he argued, "upon the great truth that the negro is not equal to the white man; that slavery subordination to the superior race is his natural and normal condition." For good reason, this passage has become the most frequently quoted line in Stephens's long oratorical career. But lurking in the same speech is another powerful, albeit largely overlooked, formulation. If slavery, as Stephens argued, was the "cornerstone" upon which the Confederacy was built, the new government also possessed a stepping stone to future dominion. The "disintegration" of the United States "may be expected to go on with almost absolute certainty if we pursue the right course," Stephens proclaimed. "We are now the nucleus of a growing power which, if we are true to ourselves, our destiny, and high mission, will become the controlling power on this continent."[63] The process of national dissolution, according to Stephens, had only just begun.

Stephens was not the only one to foresee future ruptures. "So soon as the war with the South is concluded," J. D. B. De Bow predicted in the fall of 1861, "it is probable she [the United States] will be dismembered and split up into three or four independent states or nations."[64] Well into the war, leaders on both sides of the conflict continued to forecast a similar outcome for the dis-united states. "If secession is successful," General George B. McClellan wrote to Abraham Lincoln in July 1862, "other dissolutions are clearly to be seen in the future."[65] William Gwin relished the thought. He imagined a leading role for himself in an independent republic on the West Coast, once the Confederacy triumphed. "If we [Confederates] conquer," Gwin wrote to Joseph Lancaster Brent, "we can put down the Yankees there [California] & what a country it is & what a climate."[66]

The first division had occurred along a north-south axis; the next major rupture, as Gwin and others believed, would take place in the Far West. More than a decade of proslavery intrigue within California encouraged secessionists that the Pacific coast might peel off from the United States if it came to civil war.[67] Leading figures within the state had been frank on this point. Austin E. Smith, one of California's delegates at the Democratic convention at Charleston, floated the possibility in a long, fiery speech in support of his southern colleagues. If the slave states should continue to be mistreated, he argued, they would be justified in breaking from the Union. That would trigger further dissolutions, he suggested, which would only benefit the separatists of California. As Smith gleefully proclaimed, "The Pacific States, have, thank God, the domain upon which to build up a splendid empire of their own."[68]

Shortly after he delivered California's state division petition to Congress, Milton S. Latham, now a US senator, considered a grander sort of western separatism in a spring 1860 speech. He projected that, in the event of civil war, California would declare its independence and form part of a vast western republic, extending as far as the Rocky Mountains. California would therefore shield itself, Latham argued, from "fratricidal strife and mutual ruin." With the state's natural advantages, "why should we trust to the management of others what we are abundantly able to do ourselves?"[69] The senate speech kicked up a political firestorm in the West, and Latham, ever the opportunist, soon retracted his remarks.[70]

Others picked up where the senator left off and often made explicit connections between western separatism and southern secession.[71] In a December 1860 letter, Charles L. Scott, one of California's two US representatives, gave a full-throated endorsement to independence movements in both the South and the West. "In my heart of hearts I warmly sympathize with the South," he wrote, "and cordially endorse and fully justify them in not remaining in the Union under [Lincoln]." Although California boasted a large southern-born population, Scott noted, it would pursue its own path to independence. "If this Union is divided and two separate

confederacies are formed," he vowed, "I will strenuously advocate the secession of California and the establishment of a separate republic on the
Pacific slope." He believed California's mineral resources, agricultural
wealth, and access to the Pacific trade would ensure its independence and
success. But an independent California would retain close ties with the
South, he predicted, through the construction of a long-awaited railroad
between the two regions.[72] California's governor John Weller and US representative John C. Burch made similar projections, while Senator William
Gwin, although more circumspect at this point, privately hoped that California would break from federal control.[73] Thus, at one point or another,
the state's entire congressional delegation supported a western separation.

It is tempting to dismiss talk of a Pacific republic as a fleeting conspiracy
forged in the white heat of the secession crisis. After all, such a republic
existed only in the minds of eager secessionists and anxious Unionists,
caught in a moment of grave national peril. And it was dependent, as most
everyone at the time recognized, on the success of the Confederate experiment. Yet such a republic—even if only theoretical at this juncture—had
deeper roots than 1860–61.[74] Pacific separatism tapped a long-running
western bitterness toward the federal government and a very American
tendency to imagine bold geopolitical reconfigurations.

As several recent studies have argued, national loyalties and the American map itself had been in a state of flux since well before the secession
crisis. When thousands of Anglo-American migrants poured into Texas
in the 1820s and early 1830s, and then into California and Oregon in the
early 1840s, they left the United States behind. Many of them welcomed
the possibility that western lands would give rise to multiple republics, or
even that they would remain citizens of Mexico, rather than extend the
dominion of the United States. Meanwhile, American statesmen, from
Thomas Jefferson, to Thomas Hart Benton, to Daniel Webster, and finally
to William Gwin and Alexander Stephens, had envisioned an independent
empire at the western end of the continent. Western separatism and the
transcontinental railroad were often linked. Boosters like Thomas Jefferson Green argued—sometimes with threatening undertones—that a failure to construct a Pacific railway would result in California's secession.[75]
By the time South Carolina broke from the Union and triggered a crisis in
national authority, California had been part of the United States for barely
a decade. Only from the vantage point of the post–Civil War era—with
Union victory secured, a Pacific railroad constructed, and the electoral
crisis of 1876 averted—does a continental United States appear manifest.[76]

While California's leaders pondered independence, Anglo-Americans in
southern New Mexico took more active steps to break from US control. By

the spring of 1861, the Arizona territorial campaign had mutated into a full-blown secessionist movement. These southwestern separatists were spurred on by Philemon T. Herbert, a former US congressman from California and more recently a lawyer in El Paso, who had narrowly averted manslaughter charges for the killing of a hotel waiter. He had been dispatched by Texas as a secessionist commissioner—not unlike the agents sent to other slave states from South Carolina at the same time—to help organize the movement in Arizona.[77]

A single convention was apparently insufficient for Arizona's secessionists; they held three meetings in order to renounce the United States. They gathered first at Piños Altos on March 4, 1861, and then with more ceremony at Mesilla twelve days later. James A. Lucas of Texas, the long-standing leader of the region's territorial movement, presided over the Mesilla convention. Herbert and General W. Claude Jones gave impassioned speeches in defense of southern independence, making a special note of Arizona's multiple failed territorial bids while under US control. There were no dissenting voices. The convention unanimously resolved "that we will not recognize the present Black Republican Administration and that we will resist any officers appointed to this Territory by said Administration with whatever means in our power."[78] A week later, Anglo-American residents met at Tucson and also adopted secession resolutions.[79]

Transcontinental communication had been one of the major precipitating factors in the rift between North and the South, and the issue remained central to the separatists of the Far Southwest. One of the main attractions of secession, according to Jones at Mesilla, was the prospect of Confederate-controlled transportation links through Arizona. Jefferson Davis's government would doubtlessly "open extended and new facilities for the transportation of the mails," he argued. Wed Arizona's fortunes to the Confederate South, Jones boasted, and "across our Territory will be the Southern pathway to the Pacific."[80]

Jones ignored the fact that some Republican congressmen were actually willing to give ground on the Pacific railroad issue to avert a breakup of the Union. The Curtis Bill, passed the day that South Carolina seceded, called for the construction of a southern transcontinental railway with a plank road along a central route. William Seward endorsed the proposed roads as a "great measure of conciliation, of pacification, of compromise, and of union."[81] Yet southern Democrats in the House, many of whom had labored for just such an outcome in previous years, failed to muster the necessary support for the bill. According to the leading scholar on the subject, southern Democrats feared that any two-road system would favor the free states of the North and burden the South with a disproportionate share of the

resulting taxes.[82] They preferred to build a Pacific railroad as an independent republic rather than as junior partners to the free-labor North.

One of the first casualties of secession was the "lesser slavery road."
Shortly after the withdrawal of the seven states of the Deep South and the
territory of Arizona in March 1861, Congress undid this signal achievement
of proslavery expansion. The Senate, now overwhelmingly Republican,
voted to discontinue service along the old Butterfield Overland Mail Road
and move the entire letter mail to a central route. Republican senators also
voted for a subsidy for the Pony Express, which had initially been designed
as a rival to the far southern mail route.[83] For Jones in Arizona, these measures constituted a central justification for secession. A "Southern Post
Master General" had established the road through Arizona to the Pacific,
he reminded the Mesilla delegation. But "as soon as the North came into
power, it was taken away from you and placed ten degrees farther toward
the north pole."[84] Arizona's secession was, in large part, a referendum on
America's transcontinental networks.

With its three conventions, Arizona broke from the Union well before
the slave states of Virginia, Arkansas, Tennessee, and North Carolina,
which did not secede until after the firing on Fort Sumter in April 1861.
In the coming months, Arizona's secessionists shored up their control of
the region. They formed a commission, created three new counties, and
elected a delegate to the Confederate Congress. They also raised a militia of
several hundred volunteer troops to guard against Native Americans and
US forces, stationed at Fort Fillmore a mere six miles from Mesilla, the new
capital of Confederate Arizona.[85] Rather than writing new laws, Arizona's
leaders simply adopted those of New Mexico, including its slave code. Rebel
Arizona had finally achieved what it never could under the United States:
separate territorial status.

US agents entered Confederate Arizona at their own peril. When a federal Indian agent arrived in Mesilla in early summer 1861, he was met by
a belligerent committee of local secessionists who threated to drive him
from the territory. "They have at hand a fine barrel of tar," he reported,
"into which they will put the first officer appointed by President Lincoln,
feather him, and start him out to fly."[86] New Mexico's Unionist congressional delegate, W. W. Mills, found the situation in Mesilla equally distressing.
"A disunion flag is now flying from the house in which I write, and this
country is now as much in the possession of the enemy as Charleston is,"
Mills reported. "The *Mesilla Times* is bitterly disunion," he continued, "and
threatens with death any one who refuses to acknowledge this usurpation."
Compounding these local problems, Mills warned, was an invasion force
from rebel Texas expected to cross into New Mexico in a mere two weeks.[87]

The Limits of Rebellion in the Desert South

Yet across most of the Far Southwest, separatist threats did not result in outright secession. Although southern New Mexico—now, finally, the independent territory of Arizona—openly sided with the Confederacy, other schemes in the region had been thwarted, or at least stalled. The proponents of an independent Pacific republic, for instance, knew that their movement depended on the military success of the Confederacy. Therefore, even California's would-be disunionists, like William Gwin, remained on the sidelines in the early years of the war. The territory of New Mexico, although now cleaved in two, remained officially loyal to the United States, as its newly appointed governor began recruitment efforts to suppress rebellion in the region. And while there was some secessionist agitation in Utah, where slavery had been legalized, Brigham Young charted a neutral path for his territory. These displays of Unionism—or at least grudging neutrality—thus raise a perplexing question for the history of the Desert South: if the region appeared such a promising field of opportunity for slaveholders, why had more of it not joined their rebellion?

The answer has less to do with the appeal of Unionism than with the obvious perils of secession. Even outspoken disunionists in the West were reluctant, or simply unable, to swing their constituents toward outright rebellion. It was one thing to despise the Lincoln administration and to support the political agenda of slavery, as many across the Far Southwest certainly did. It was another thing altogether to take up arms against what remained, even after southern secession, one of the wealthiest and most powerful nations in the world. For a similar set of reasons, four of the fifteen slave states of the South—Delaware, Kentucky, Maryland, and Missouri—never joined the Confederacy. Within the Deep South as well, influential Unionists—including, for a time, Alexander Stephens—preached caution and reconciliation.[88]

The fate of New Mexico was more closely aligned with Missouri than any other part of the country. Jefferson Davis's western confidant Alexander Jackson made that clear. In February 1861, Jackson wrote to Davis to encourage "the assignment of New Mexico to the Southern Confederacy," an action that he believed "will certainly be in consonance with the wishes of a majority of her people." Yet he added a caveat: no matter how pro-Confederate New Mexico's residents may have been, the territory's political allegiance would be dictated by Missouri, the economic lifeline of Santa Fe. "These people are fully prepared to go South, provided Missouri so goes," Jackson assured Davis. "But in advance of Missouri, no expression could be obtained from any respectable body of them."[89] Missouri never seceded.

Nor did the northern half of New Mexico. Rather than foment rebellion within the territory, leading secessionists, like Jackson himself, left for the Confederate states. He would later return to New Mexico as a staff officer in an invading rebel army.

What many US officials in the West most feared—a military coup led by southern-born officers—never materialized. The leadership of western military forces lent itself to such a conspiracy. The commander of the Pacific Department, Albert Sidney Johnston, and the ranking officer in New Mexico, William Wing Loring, hailed from the slave states. Rumors circulated that Johnston had been installed in California by William Gwin precisely because of his southern sympathies. But when a group of secessionists approached Johnston in the spring of 1861, urging him to lead the rebellion from the West, he declined. "If you want to fight," he told them, "go South."[90] Johnston followed his own advice. He returned to the slave states and received a commission as the second-highest ranking officer in the Confederate army before being mortally wounded at the Battle of Shiloh in April 1862. Joseph Lancaster Brent joined Johnston in the exodus from California after declining the command of a 200-man force of secessionists in Los Angeles.[91] Loring, too, fled to the Confederate states rather than foment rebellion within the Far West. Also departing from New Mexico were former US officers and future Confederate generals Henry Hopkins Sibley, James Longstreet, and Richard S. Ewell, among other southern-born soldiers.[92]

As southern officers moved east, Republican appointees headed west. The Continental South was held together, in part, by Democratic patronage. With Lincoln's election, this vast political network disintegrated overnight. In a sweeping purge of the opposition party, Lincoln replaced virtually every single Democratic appointee under executive control, a total of more than 1,500 officeholders. These positions ranged from cabinet secretaries, to territorial governors, to federal marshals, to customs inspectors. Together, they had a far-reaching impact on the political life of the country and the day-to-day lives of ordinary Americans. (Lincoln understood the workings and importance of patronage, having served as postmaster for Salem, Illinois, early in his career.) No president in American history up to that point—not even Andrew Jackson, the famed master of the spoils system—had wielded federal patronage so aggressively.[93] This was nothing short of an administrative revolution, and one that checked disunionist tendencies in the Far West.

Lincoln's appointments devastated the old Democratic order in California. The federal patronage was the lever by which William Gwin and his Chivalry faction had controlled the political fate of California for the better part of a decade. No state or territory in the Far West had more federal appointees than California, many of whom had been hand-picked by Gwin himself—with the approval of the president—as a reward for their political loyalty. Gwin's feud with David Broderick was so fierce precisely because of the immense value of the numerous posts within the state. To the victor of that contest went the spoils. Roughly 150 federal employees occupied the state's Treasury Department alone. Other posts included more than 30 appointees within the Indian Office; the various attachés to the two US district courts within the state, including marshals, deputies, attorneys, and clerks; and a legion of postmasters and postal employees. Democratic loyalists had held a vast majority of these positions throughout the antebellum period, but with Lincoln's election they were swept from office and replaced by Republicans.[94] The party that had been virtually nonexistent within California now monopolized its plum posts, while the once-dominant Chivalry machine lay in ruins.

While Lincoln rewarded long-suffering Republicans within California, he took a different, yet equally effective, approach to New Mexico. Given the precarious position of the territory—which had recently lost roughly half of its landmass to Confederate Arizona—Lincoln had to proceed cautiously with his appointments. He largely refrained from tapping Republican loyalists for the territory's federal positions, as the party had little presence within New Mexico and easterners were viewed suspiciously. On the patronage issue, the president followed the advice of one of his old friends and political allies, John S. Watts, then practicing law in New Mexico. "Permit me to urge upon you the importance of making appointments in New Mexico from among the people of that Territory," Watts wrote to Lincoln in April 1861. "It is not just nor prudent to send strangers from the states to fill the offices in New Mexico (no matter how able and distinguished)."[95] Lincoln thus selected primarily Unionist Democrats with strong local ties for the territory's posts: governor, territorial secretary, territorial marshal, land office commissioner, and three federal district judges (which made up New Mexico's supreme court).

In adopting such a strategy, Lincoln bucked the prevailing opinion among party elites in Washington. His appointment of Henry Connelly as territorial governor, for instance, was not bound to curry favor with most of his Republicans allies. Connelly was a former slaveholder from Virginia and a member of the territorial legislature of 1859 that legalized chattel bondage within New Mexico. Heeding the advice of Watts, Lincoln also nominated Miguel Otero, the driving force behind that slave code, as territorial secretary. Otero's South Carolinian wife was a secession-ist, while he himself had feuded openly with Horace Greeley, disparaged Republicanism and "the accursed negro," and supported the creation of a Pacific republic to unite New Mexico and California in an independent nation.[96] Yet Watts argued that in a stark decision between "Texas and slavery or the United States and freedom," Otero would rally New Mexico behind the latter. Given his immense popularity and his strong ties within the Hispano community, Otero's appointment would determine, Watts wrote, "the success or defeat of the administration in New Mexico."[97] In the end, Otero was too suspect for Republicans in the Senate, who rejected his appointment. But most of Lincoln's other nominees, including the con-troversial Connelly, passed the Senate's scrutiny.

The cumulative effect of these appointments was to create in New Mex-ico a patronage system that more closely resembled the border slave states than any other part of the country.[98] In the border South and the territo-rial Southwest, Lincoln pursued a common strategy: appoint Unionists, regardless of party affiliation, and avoid stirring the hornet's nest of slav-ery. The parallels between the two regions were as apparent to Lincoln as they were to secessionists like Alexander Jackson. Both men understood the conflicted loyalties of the Far Southwest and the potential for outside factors—the political direction of Missouri, patronage decisions made in Washington—to tip the sectional balance within New Mexico. As Watts had predicted, Lincoln's shrewd appointments struck a delicate political balance and preserved the territory for the Union.

Henry Connelly, in particular, proved a wise choice for a secession-churned New Mexico. Although almost half of the territory had already spun off to join the Confederate rebellion, Connelly managed to hold to-gether the remainder of his jurisdiction. A threatened invasion from Con-federate Texas spurred the governor and the Hispano population to action. Here was a potential reprise of what had occurred on several occasions in the 1830s and 1840s, when Texas, as an independent republic, attempted to add New Mexican lands to its dominion. Appealing to New Mexicans' deep-rooted and well-founded mistrust of Anglo Texas, Connelly eventu-ally raised more than 5,000 volunteers.[99]

The loyalty of his citizens prompted warm congratulations from Con-nelly in his first annual message in December 1861. "When the secession began and for some time after it had been in progress," Connelly recalled, "it was presumed by the prime movers of the scheme, that our Territory would join them in their attempts to pull down the pillars of free govern-ment." Instead, New Mexico responded with a "patriotic outpouring of men" for the war machine. [100] Connelly no doubt inflated the territory's

Unionism. New Mexico was no patriotic stronghold. It clung to an uneasy Unionism, motivated more by hatred of Texas than love of the United States. But Connelly could justifiably celebrate at least one crucial fact: his territory's secession movement stopped short at Arizona.

Saints and Warriors

Latter-day Saints and the Southwest's diverse Indian peoples rarely found common ground. But by the spring of 1861 most of them could agree on at least one point: the impending war between North and South presented a rare opportunity. For years, an expanding United States had whittled away the sovereignty of Mormon settlers and Indigenous inhabitants alike. A war to sever the Union might create a power vacuum and a chance for various western peoples to reclaim some of their diminished autonomy. Neither the LDS church nor the major Native powers in the region—the Comanches, Apaches, and Navajos—officially sided with the Confederacy. But they inspired constant anxiety and some even clashed with US forces.

In a choice between two perceived threats—the United States and the Confederate rebellion—Utah chose neither. On the one side were Republicans, who had branded Mormon polygamy one of the "twin relics of barbarism" alongside slavery. On the other was a rebel government, with whom an alliance would likely prompt another US invasion of Utah. Brigham Young therefore charted a neutral course for his territory.

Still, LDS leaders had reason to cheer any conflict that threatened the United States. Their grudge against the federal government dated back to the formation of Utah. The Latter-day Saints had petitioned for a state named Deseret; instead Congress gave them a territory named for one of the major Indian powers in the region, the Utes. Tensions between federal officials and Mormon elders reached a breaking point in 1857–58 when a US Army detachment entered the territory during the Utah War. Utah's appeals for statehood, repeatedly rebuffed by Congress, further fueled Mormon resentment against the United States. Instead of statehood, the Saints had roughly a third of their territory amputated. Two days before leaving office, President Buchanan signed an act to create the territory of Nevada from lands in what had previously been western Utah.[101]

Although Utah remained neutral, numerous LDS leaders openly favored the Confederacy. Denunciations of the Union war effort rang from Mormon pulpits, from local meetings, and from the pages of Utah's press. At the outset of the conflict, the *Deseret News* had hard words for "Abraham the I."[102] Meanwhile, Mormon elders blamed the North for the carnage of the war. "The abolitionists of the North stole the niggers and caused it all," claimed Heber Kimball, first counselor to Brigham Young. Before the war, "the nigger was well off and happy," according to Kimball, echoing a common refrain of slaveholding paternalists. "The party in power laid aside the Constitution entirely, and were the main ones who rebelled," according to another apostle, George A. Smith, "and the South was right." Brigham Young concluded that "nine-tenths of the people of the Territory were southern sympathizers."[103]

Coupled with animosity to the Union, an ideological affinity for southern slaveholders shaped Utah's outlook on the war. Support for the Confederacy was most pronounced in the cotton mission lands of Washington County, where many migrants from the slave states had congregated. "There were but two Union men in Washington," a settler recalled, "myself and an old friend from Na[u]voo [Illinois]."[104] One of Brigham Young's closest wartime advisors came by way of South Carolina. He circulated in the upper echelons of the Mormon hierarchy and regularly reported to Young on secessionist activity in the Far West. Although northern and foreign-born whites made up the majority of Utah's population, they, too, often applauded the South's appeals to local sovereignty. Reprinted in the *Deseret News,* Jefferson Davis's inaugural address—and, specifically, his assertion that "government rests on the consent of the governed"—struck a chord with Mormon polygamists attempting to preserve their own peculiar institution from federal interference.[105] Crucially, slavery remained legal in the territory, and church leaders continued to speak in defense of human bondage.

Utah embraced what one might call wait-and-see separatism. The territory's neutrality rested on a widely shared assumption among Mormons about the course of the war: As northerners and southerners bled one another dry, Saints would step into the void and rebuild the broken nation, guided by divine favor. Joseph Smith, the founder of the LDS church, foretold of a similar outcome some three decades earlier. Mormon leaders repeated his prophecy countless times during the war in gleeful anticipation of a new national order.[106] "What will King Abraham do?" Young shrugged in the midst of the secession crisis. "I do not know, neither do I care. . . . God will accomplish his own purposes."[107] This position mirrored the strategy of California disunionists like William Gwin. Mormon theocrats and Pacific republic separatists alike took satisfaction in civil war, as something that might expand their spheres of control. What was bad for the Union was ultimately good for them.

No US state or territory gave fewer resources to the Union war effort than Utah. Young contributed a mere 95 volunteer troops to patrol mail and telegraph lines for a month and a half in 1862. Meanwhile, Utah stock-piled munitions and gunpowder and readied its territorial militia in case of any hostile action by the United States. An estimated 8,000 to 10,000 Mormons mustered into militia units, a larger force than the territory commanded during the Utah War of 1857–58.[108] Federal officials tracked Mormon movements with deep unease. It was an article of faith among many Unionists in the West that Mormons were working for the breakup of the United States.[109] The Saints had launched their western colony in a spirit of separatism in the 1840s, and as the Union fractured in 1861, they remained a people apart.

While Mormon apostles and Pacific separatists watched and waited, some of the most powerful Native American polities in the region took matters into their own hands. As early as January 1860, relations between the US military and the Apaches began to disintegrate. Previously, Apache bands and Anglo-American newcomers in New Mexico had maintained a cordial, if uneasy, peace. In exchange for rations and trade goods, Apache leaders had allowed John Butterfield to build stage stations and granted safe passage for white settlers along the Overland Mail Road. But when a Butterfield station keeper killed a Mexican captive belonging to the Chokonen leader Cochise, he set in motion a bloody cycle of retaliation. Chokonen Apaches began raiding wagon trains coming through Apache Pass as well as a number of stage stations in the region. When Apache warriors struck an American ranch in January 1861, US officials responded in kind. Subsequent skirmishes left a trail of American and Native corpses in their wake and signaled further violence to come.[110]

What Anglo separatists claimed as the Confederate territory of Arizona went by another name as well: Apachería. By the spring of 1861, these southwest rebels were drawn into what one soldier called "a three-cornered war" between Union, Confederate, and Native forces.[111] Fighting was especially fierce along the Butterfield road in Arizona, an important thoroughfare for Confederates and Chiricahua Apaches alike. The road cut across the stronghold of Mangas Coloradas. Standing six feet four and unbowed at age seventy, Mangas Coloradas had led the Chihenne and Bedonkohe bands of Chiricahua Apaches for the past forty years. He would not let a faction of Anglo-American separatists lay claim to his people's lands. Alongside his son-in-law Cochise, Mangas Coloradas led a series of devastating attacks on Arizona settlements and wagon trains passing through their people's homelands. Their assaults sparked an exodus of roughly forty settlers from Tubac, a mining town south of Tucson, in August 1861.[112]

When US forces withdrew from several southwestern garrisons that summer, they opened a military void in the region. Apache warriors watched from nearby hills as federal soldiers abandoned Forts Buchanan, Breckinridge, and McLane in Arizona. These troops had received orders to head east to meet the Confederate threat, but the US departmental commander deferred their departure, instead concentrating most of them in two larger forts along the Rio Grande. To US authorities, this was a tactical redeployment of forces, but to many Native peoples, it was a surrender of territory. The abandonment of forts created an opportunity for leaders like Mangas Coloradas to expand his people's access to resources and assert sovereignty in the region. With fewer than 2,500 federal troops across all of New Mexico, including Confederate Arizona, the United States was badly overmatched at the outset of the Civil War.[113]

Confederate secession had triggered a series of insurgencies and separatist movements, pitted against a dwindling federal presence in the Far Southwest. If Arizona's secession was not alarming enough, Mormon Saints and Native warriors could now be added to the list of far western threats. The two groups had become especially menacing by the summer of 1861, according to the *Alta California*. The withdrawal of federal troops from several forts in the region left "the great overland routes to California and Oregon without protection against Indians or hostile Mormons."[114] US officials had long regarded both groups as untrustworthy, but now they appeared downright dangerous.[115] As federal authority deteriorated across the continent, the Southwest had become a vast borderland of conflicting loyalties.

Conclusion

By the time Abraham Lincoln took the oath of office on March 4, 1861, the Union was coming apart in multiple directions. Most urgently, there was the open rupture with seven—and soon, another four—states of the South, as well as the defection of some of the nation's preeminent political and military leaders. But there were also several major separatist threats brewing in the Far West. Within weeks, southern New Mexico would throw its allegiance behind the Confederacy, while California's leaders anticipated the further dissolution of the Union and the foundation of an independent republic along the Pacific. In Utah, territorial leaders looked forward to a war that might create a power vacuum in the West and thereby broaden the Mormon sphere of influence. Meanwhile, the withdrawal of federal forces from frontier posts in the Southwest would soon prompt a fresh wave of raiding from Apache and Navajo warriors, who threatened to overrun the sparsely populated white settlements in the region. Alarming though they were, these western rebellions and separatist threats merely reinforced what Americans had long known: the North American map was a work in progress, and national loyalties, especially along the peripheries of the United States, were both conditional and flexible.

This much had been clear since well before the US-Mexico War. Contrary to the brassy rhetoric of certain American expansionists, there was nothing manifest or predestined about the extension of US authority to the Pacific. Thomas Jefferson himself, as much as he craved a Pacific outlet for the United States, saw little reason to believe that his nation's dominion would span the entire continent. More likely, he conceded, Anglo-American settlers would establish coexisting confederacies, "governed in similar forms and by similar laws," across the breadth of North America.[116] That the United States ultimately seized most of the Pacific coast did not sweep aside all concerns about the fragility of the American experiment. In some ways, it only amplified these anxieties. The Pacific railroad debates of the 1850s, for instance, hinged on a common belief that the United States would fracture unless it could be held together by a continuous bond of iron.[117] That the attempt to bridge a divide between East and West helped bring about a war between North and South is one of the era's great ironies.

Lincoln managed to avoid a full-scale rebellion in the Far West in 1861, thanks partly to his purge of Democratic officials in the region. But the Southwest's loyalty was a fickle thing, as William Need, a soldier stationed in New Mexico, understood all too well. In a September 1861 letter to Secretary of War Simon Cameron, Need specified the various threats to US control in the Far Southwest. Disloyal military officers, incompetent local officials, and conspiring politicians in Washington—all of these were to be blamed for the dire state of affairs in New Mexico at the outset of the war. Yet the greatest threat to the region, according to Need, was the man now occupying the Confederate White House, Jefferson Davis. Davis had coveted the region, especially Arizona, "his beau ideal of a railroad route to the Pacific," for more than a decade. "With an eye that never winked and a wing that never tired," Davis had pursued his plan for "indefinite expansion" in the western borderlands.[118]

And now there was a Confederate invasion force to confirm Need's greatest fears. Several months earlier, some 250 troops from Texas had marched into Arizona to buttress the secessionist movement there. "The Texas rebels and Arizona cut-throats, like the ancient Goths and Vandals, are at the very gates," Need warned, threatening the entire western half of the continent. To beat back the invaders required a mettle and constancy that the region's leaders conspicuously lacked, Need suspected. After all, it was these same leaders, "the tools of Jeff. Davis and company," who had passed New Mexico's infamous slave code just two years earlier. Thanks to them, and to the Mormons of Utah, the Southwest was now a land of "polygamy and slavery and peonage, twin relics of barbarism and the offspring of an oligarchy," Need despaired.[119] Whether or not these institutions could endure would be decided in a continental civil war.

→ PART III ←

War and Reunion

———————— ◆◆◆ ————————

✣ CHAPTER SEVEN ✣

West of the Confederacy

———◆●◆———

O N JULY 21, 1861, the Confederacy launched its first invasion
of the war. With a deployment of just over 250 men, Colonel
John R. Baylor's offensive into New Mexico made manifest what
many had long known: slaveholders laid claim to the Southwest, and they
were prepared to assert that claim through force of arms. Slipping across
the border of West Texas into the Mesilla Valley, Baylor's invaders exploited
the territory's patchwork defenses, capturing the region's military stronghold, Fort Fillmore and its 500 men, by late July. Less than two weeks after
setting out from Texas, Baylor pronounced the formation of the Confederate territory of Arizona, installing himself as military governor.[1] Although
Union forces soon mobilized against this far western wing of the rebellion,
the Confederate presence in the region strengthened in the months ahead.
The rebel president, Jefferson Davis, fortified the invasion with a force of
roughly 2,500 under Brigadier General Henry Hopkins Sibley, arriving in
the fall of 1861.[2] The Continental South now had an army behind it.

The rebel offensive in the Southwest constituted the military sequel to
a political process begun years before. As with slaveholders' antebellum
campaign for the Far West, California was the ultimate objective of this
Confederate invasion. Baylor appreciated the "vast mineral resources" of
Arizona, but the real strategic payoff of his invasion depended on opening a
thoroughfare to the Pacific—what southern expansionists had attempted
through the Gadsden Purchase, the "great slavery road," and the Overland
Mail during the preceding decade.[3] The architects of these antebellum
projects—Jefferson Davis and William Gwin, most notably—grew bolder
during the war years with greater resources at their disposal. Whereas a
number of studies examine military operations in the Civil War West, no
historian has yet explained in detail how armed engagements evolved from
earlier political movements.[4] Doing so helps make sense of what might

otherwise appear as quixotic forays into far-flung regions. Confederate grand strategy in the Far West grew naturally from a long-standing imperial dream, beginning around 1845 and continuing until the collapse of slavery two decades later.

As in the antebellum period, a transcontinental network of allies aided and abetted southern schemes in the West. In California, the proslavery coalition of the prewar period gave way to a menacing pro-Confederate movement during the war years, concentrated in the southern part of the state. California was divided against itself along a north-south axis, mirroring the political fault lines that had fractured the nation as a whole. To prevent Confederate sympathizers from stirring rebellion in the West, US authorities arrested suspected secessionists, banned seditious newspapers from the mails, and garrisoned Southern California with a major military installation just outside Los Angeles. Although California remained loyal to the Union, the persistent fear of rebellion delayed the eastern transfer of much-needed forces. We might view California, and indeed the entire Desert South, as a vast border region, where rebellion simmered and US control could be maintained only through armed force.[5]

From the outset of the war, Davis disavowed the imperial ambitions of the rebellion. "We seek no conquest, no aggrandizement, no concession of any kind from the States with which we were lately confederated," he wrote in April 1861. "All we ask is to be let alone."[6] Davis maintained this position well into the postwar period, arguing that, while self-preservation had been the aim of the Confederacy, the United States was driven by the "manifest purpose" of "empire."[7] Similarly, in an 1866 letter, Robert E. Lee framed the struggle as one between a confederacy for limited government and an American state bent on conquest.[8] This interpretation became a central plank of Lost Cause revisionism, which transformed the Civil War into America's great national tragedy, with the rebel states cast in the role of the victim. To maintain this victim status, apologists could point to the fact that the Confederacy made no overseas conquests during the war.

The myth of Confederate imperial innocence holds up only when facing southeast to the Caribbean, not west to the Pacific. True, the Davis administration dropped the long-standing southern fantasy of seizing more territory in the Atlantic world. But Davis did so from a sense of strategic necessity rather than restraint. As he recognized, any overseas acquisitions would have antagonized European powers and scuttled the Confederacy's chances of securing foreign recognition.[9] Territorial conquest in the American West, on the other hand, carried no such liability. In fact, westward expansion was imperative for slavery's long-term survival, according to many rebel leaders. Otherwise, why secede from a government that had made numerous promises, including a proposed constitutional amendment, to preserve slavery in the fifteen states where it already existed?[10]

Expand or perish—this Manichaean dilemma drove antebellum debates over slavery and, subsequently, the logic of rebellion. "We are constrained by an inexorable necessity to accept expansion or extermination," US senator Robert Toombs insisted before the Georgia legislature in a plea for southern independence.[11] This "necessity" also guided the framers of the Confederate Constitution. As article 4, section 3.3 of that document read, "The Confederate States may acquire new territory; and Congress shall have power to legislate and provide governments for the inhabitants of all territory belonging to the Confederate States, lying without the limits of the several States." Furthermore, the constitution stipulated that in all new territories, "the institution of negro slavery ... shall be recognized and protected by Congress."[12] The likeliest candidates for territorial integration lay in the region that slaveholders had been cultivating for decades. No amount of dissimulating from Davis or his subordinates could disguise what was unfolding in the Southwest beginning in the summer of 1861: the Confederacy was making a bid for a transcontinental empire.

California's Civil War

From the war's outset in April 1861, reports of disunionism in California consumed General Edwin Vose Sumner, the commander of the US Department of the Pacific. While "there is a strong Union feeling with the majority of the people of this State," Sumner reported, "the secessionists are much the most active and zealous party."[13] News of a brewing rebellion in California reached John Baylor in Confederate Arizona that fall. According to Baylor, the state contained "many Southern men ... who would cheerfully join us if they could get to us." Hundreds were poised to join his ranks, he predicted, if only rebel forces could open a pathway to the Pacific.[14] "California," he gloated, "is on the eve of a revolution."[15]

Although the revolution of Baylor's fantasies and Sumner's fears never materialized, a number of prominent California residents slipped across state lines to offer their services to the Confederacy. The list of Confederate officers from California amounts to something of a who's who of western politics: David Terry, the former chief justice of the state supreme court and the killer of Senator David Broderick; former US congressmen Charles L. Scott and Philemon T. Herbert; Los Angeles political kingmaker Joseph Lancaster Brent; General John B. Magruder; former US district attorney Calhoun Benham; at least three state senators; a handful of assemblymen; and agents in numerous federal posts, including the state controller, the

state navy agent, and a former surveyor general.[16] Furthermore, the top
brass from the prewar Department of the Pacific, including future Confederate generals Albert Sidney Johnston, George Pickett, Lewis Armistead,
and Richard B. Garnett, resigned their commissions and fled east.[17]

Southern California was the favored point of departure for many western
rebels. Johnston, the former departmental commander, was escorted out of
the state by the Los Angeles Mounted Rifles, a unit of about eighty California secessionists who had been outfitted with a full complement of rifles,
revolvers, and sabers by the order of Governor John G. Downey. En route to
Texas, this company traveled over the old Butterfield Overland Road, thus
transforming the antebellum mail route into a Confederate thoroughfare.
The Los Angeles Mounted Rifles would become the only militia from a free
state to fight under a Confederate banner.[18] Shortly thereafter, Joseph Lancaster Brent slipped from the port of San Diego. After a brief imprisonment
under Union guard, he rose to the rank of brigadier general of a Louisiana
cavalry unit. Two years later, Cameron Thom, future mayor of Los Angeles,
left his Southern California law practice as well as his infant son—named
in honor of Albert Sidney Johnston—to join the Confederate cause in his
home state of Virginia.[19] Johnston, Brent, and Thom represented just a
fraction of the Confederates who fled from Southern California. According to a rare Unionist from the region, Los Angeles County furnished the
rebellion with "colonels, majors and captains without end, besides about
two hundred and fifty of the rank and file who were . . . sent over the desert
to the Confederate forces in Texas."[20]

California's rebels waged a two-front war on the Union. While hundreds
mustered into Confederate armies, a vocal and numerous contingent remained in the West, putting US officials on high alert to the ever-present
threat of a regional uprising. As Governor Frederick Low would later recall,
the Civil War years in California marked "perhaps one of the most difficult
positions ever held by an executive in the state" given the "large secession
element here."[21] General Sumner estimated that as many as 32,000 Californians stood ready to rebel if the opportunity presented itself.[22] Although
Sumner undoubtedly exaggerated the strength of secessionism, there were
sufficient Confederate sympathizers to trigger recurring panics in the Pacific Department. According to local intelligence, rebel supporters ranged
from arms-bearing militants to clandestine conspirators to more matronly
figures, including one Mrs. Bettis, an enthusiastic secessionist who had
begun rallying Californians in support of southern independence.[23]

Much of this secessionist activity took place behind closed doors or
under the cover of darkness. Two related secret societies operated in war-

time California: the Knights of the Golden Circle and the Knights of the Columbian Star. Founded in the mid-1850s to promote slaveholding expansion
in Latin America, the two societies had established chapters in states, free
and slave, across the country.[24] Once the Civil War broke out, the Knights
turned their attention from the Caribbean to more local matters, with vigorous representation in California. Members of California chapters vowed
to aid the Confederacy, despite their distance from the conflict's major
military theaters. Riffing on the Declaration of Independence, the San
Bernardino Knights of the Golden Circle pledged "our lives, our property,
and our sacred honor to sustain our brethren of the Southern States in the
just defense of all their constitutional rights."[25] Other California chapters
stockpiled arms and ammunition, conducted military drills, and raised
money for the Confederate war effort.[26] Membership was a well-guarded
secret, although US agents successfully infiltrated several local chapters
and uncovered leading Californians within the organizations. Beriah
Brown, editor of the copperhead *Democratic Press* of San Francisco, purportedly headed the Knights of the Columbian Star, while ex-governor John
Bigler was a "prominent member."[27]

Anxieties ran high during the September 1861 gubernatorial election,
a three-man race that pitted the Republican Leland Stanford against
Democrats John Conness and John R. McConnell, a Kentucky native and
the former state attorney general. McConnell's platform—which justified
the right of secession, opposed US military intervention, and embraced
the Crittenden Compromise—was written by two southerners who would
later leave California to join the Confederacy. According to the *Sacramento
Daily Union,* the McConnell ticket galvanized "the enemies of the Government," who were more numerous in California "than any other free State in
the Union."[28] If California went for McConnell, fretted future Democratic
senator Eugene Casserly, the election would "do more to encourage the foe
and protract the war . . . than another Manassas [the Union's first major
loss of the war]."[29] Fortunately for California's Unionists, McConnell and
Conness split the Democratic vote, allowing Stanford to carry the state
with just 46 percent of the final tally.[30]

Yet the Republican victory hardly dispelled fears of a western rebellion.
Southern California, in particular, remained a proslavery stronghold. Los
Angeles County registered a two-to-one majority in favor of McConnell
over Stanford.[31] A year later, Los Angeles sent two Confederate sympathizers, E. J. C. Kewen and J. A. Watson, to the state assembly. "Well, the
Secessionists have carried this county, body and boots, for Jeff Davis, and
for the *dis*-United States," lamented the *San Francisco Bulletin*'s Southern

California correspondent after the election. "Let it never be forgotten that the county of Los Angeles, in this day of peril to the Republic, is two to one for Dixie and Disunion; or, for permitting disunion without a struggle."[32]

Support for the Confederacy took numerous public forms across Southern California. In El Monte, San Bernardino, Merced, and Visalia, rebel sympathizers paraded the Bear Flag, a symbol of California separatism. Before departing for the Confederate states, David Terry purportedly led nightly meetings of secessionists in El Monte, home to the Monte Boys, a gang of pro-Confederate vigilantes. In Los Angeles, rebel sympathizers staged rallies to celebrate Confederate victories and sang ditties—"We'll Hang Abe Lincoln to a Tree" and "We'll Drive the Bloody Tyrant from Our Dear Native Soil"—to taunt US forces. They also took part in the occasional defenestration. When a Unionist attempted to read a patriotic poem from the Bella Union Hotel, a rallying point for the city's secessionists, a gang of southern rowdies pitched him from an upstairs window. Rebel activity so alarmed future Union general Winfield Scott Hancock, then a quartermaster in Los Angeles, that he assembled a small arsenal of derringers for his own use, while also arming his wife.[33]

As Hancock equipped his household against a potential Confederate uprising, General Sumner began fortifying the entire county. In response to the rebel threat in the region, the Union high command created the military District of Southern California and Arizona. Sumner and his successor, General George Wright, stationed federal soldiers in San Bernardino, Santa Barbara, Visalia, El Monte, and Los Angeles. The town of Wilmington, just outside LA, soon housed one of the largest concentrations of troops California had ever seen.[34]

There, the Union command constructed Camp Drum (later Drum Barracks), a complex of nineteen buildings and ample drilling space, at the cost of roughly $1 million. Drum Barracks would become the headquarters of the new military district and the staging ground for some 8,000 California troops over the course of the war, most of them bound for service in the territorial Southwest. Before heading east into Confederate Arizona, soldiers from James Henry Carleton's celebrated California Column drilled at the camp.[35] Drum Barracks also hosted more peculiar guests. In June 1861, thirty-one camels arrived in Los Angeles and remained a common sight in the city's streets and at the base until they were auctioned off two years later. For at least a brief period, Jefferson Davis's pet project for southwestern development had been transformed into an agent of Yankee control. Between these camels and, most notably, thousands of US soldiers, Southern California had been garrisoned against its own disloyal residents.[36]

Even under increased scrutiny, rebel Californians continued to defy

The US military installation at Drum Barracks, Wilmington, California, circa 1865. Note the camel in the foreground, a Unionist repurposing of Jefferson Davis's antebellum pet project. USC Digital Library, California Historical Society Collection, Los Angeles.

federal authority. US troops had to proceed with caution whenever venturing beyond their garrisons. As one Unionist recalled, the soldiers stationed at Drum Barracks "scarcely dared appear in town on account of the wrath of the populace."[37] In San Bernardino and El Monte, southern sympathizers thwarted attempts to establish Union Clubs.[38] Meanwhile, Angelenos toasted Confederate leaders and their victories. A large crowd of rebel supporters gathered in central Los Angeles in the spring of 1862 as Andrew Jackson King, the county's undersheriff and "a notorious secessionist," unveiled a life-size portrait of Confederate general P. G. T. Beauregard, "elegantly engraved and framed," according to a US marshal. They hung it in the saloon of the Bella Union Hotel.[39] "Is Southern California a part of the rebel Confederacy that loyalty to the Union is neither respectable nor safe?" bemoaned the same US marshal in April 1862. "Our local State, county, and city officers, with very few exceptions, are avowed sympathizers with [the Confederacy], and the Union cause is very generally despised."[40]

The rebel spirit was equally strong 190 miles north of Los Angeles, in the Central Valley town of Visalia. "There are more secessionists in this and the adjoining counties than there are in proportion to the population in

any part of the United States this side of Dixie," concluded a Union officer stationed nearby. Daily, he reported, rebel sympathizers would "ride
through the streets of Visalia and hurrah for Jeff. Davis and Stonewall
Jackson."[41] That a federal garrison had been established one mile north of
Visalia in October 1862 seemed only to galvanize Confederate sympathizers. They mocked Union soldiers as "Lincoln hirelings" and instigated violent confrontations. One fight led to an exchange of gunfire and the death
of a US soldier as well as the wounding of two Visalia agitators—some of
the westernmost casualties of the war.[42]

Confederate sympathizers also waged a war of words in dozens of California newspapers, where the politics of the old Chivalry faction lived on.
According to some estimates, more than 100 newspapers were printed in
the state during the war years. Of these, roughly 30 openly opposed the
Lincoln administration.[43] The *Equal Rights Expositor* of Visalia was one of
the most anti-Union papers of this kind. Operated by S. J. Garrison and
Lovick P. Hall, a Mississippi native and advocate for slavery's westward expansion, the paper cheered the Confederate cause, even as federal authorities began concentrating troops in Tulare County. Rather than colonize
free blacks, the *Expositor* argued in a typical editorial, why not colonize
abolitionists?[44] According to a US officer in the region, the *Expositor* went
"as far if not further than the vilest sheet published in Richmond."[45]

The *Los Angeles Star* gave voice to the city's Confederate sympathies.
Founded in 1851 as LA's first newspaper, by 1856 the *Star* had come under
the editorial direction of Henry Hamilton, who lent it a reputation for cos-
mopolitanism, literary polish, and acerbic political commentary.[46] Hamilton, a native of Ireland, migrated to California during the gold rush and
quickly aligned himself with the state's southern-born power brokers.[47]
He supported the Chivalry faction along with the movement for a Pacific
republic and articulated, perhaps better than any writer in the region,
Southern California's natural affinity for the slave states. "We are on the
highway to and from the South, our population are from the South, and
we sympathize with her," he announced in a January 1861 issue. "Why then
should we turn our backs on our friends and join their enemies to invade,
impoverish, and despoil them?"[48]

Through the pages of his weekly paper, Hamilton heaped scorn on the
Union war effort. He kept close tabs on US authorities in the area, who
were busy committing "outrages" against the local citizenry and arrest-
ing innocents on purportedly unfounded charges of treason.[49] No federal
action, according to Hamilton, was more outrageous than the Republican campaign for emancipation. Lincoln's Emancipation Proclamation of
January 1, 1863, had transformed the US war effort into a campaign "for

a dissolution of the Union," Hamilton wrote, unleashing "the maddest revolution recorded in the annals of time."[50] Not only was emancipation a bald theft of private property, he argued, but it also would bring misery to the slaves themselves.[51] As for Lincoln, he was a "tyrant" and an "obscure, fourth-rate lawyer" who had somehow swindled his way into the highest office in the land.[52] When US armies—which he dubbed the "Abolition force"—went down in defeat, Hamilton gloated. The Union's "greatest leaders . . . attempted to measure swords with the Rebel leaders," Hamilton wrote of the Confederate triumph at Fredericksburg in December 1862, "and their inferiority is written in gore."[53]

Although California's rebels never came close to overthrowing the US government, the secession anxieties they provoked were not baseless, as some historians have argued.[54] To understand these anxieties requires a long view of California history. Since the early 1850s, the state's political apparatus had been under the thumb of southern migrants, including prominent slaveholders like William Gwin. Recall, for instance, that every member of the state's congressional delegation in 1860 supported the creation of a Pacific republic. US authorities, therefore, had good reason to fear a well-organized separatist movement from within the state. That these antebellum leaders did not prove more damaging to US control in California is partly explained by the fact that many of them, including Gwin and Joseph Lancaster Brent, fled to the Confederate South during the early years of the war.

Those who did remain fostered a siege mentality within the Department of the Pacific. To combat a fifth column of secessionists in their midst, US military authorities funneled thousands of troops into the southern part of the state. These men were needed in other military theaters, but California's Unionists pleaded with military authorities to delay their shipment east. Without a sufficient force within the state, a group of San Francisco businessmen wrote to the secretary of war, "the frightful scenes now transpiring in Missouri would be rivaled by the atrocities enacted upon the Pacific Coast."[55] While Colorado and New Mexico furnished thousands of volunteers to fight Sibley's invasion, California contributed virtually nothing to the campaign. By the time Carleton's California Column left Camp Drum in spring 1862—delayed by flooding, drilling, and policing disunionism in Los Angeles—soldiers from other parts of the West had already handled the brunt of the fighting.[56]

Yet in the final analysis, California's Confederate sympathizers were their own worst enemies. Would-be rebels hoped to secure a far western base of operations for the Confederacy, but instead they galvanized the loyal population and invigorated Republican interest in transcontinental development. Northern statesmen turned the West's vulnerability to their own advantage. Since the early 1850s, those advocating for a transcontinental railroad, including Jefferson Davis, often pointed to the exposed position of the Pacific coast. With the war, that exposure became an even greater liability. Build the road, or lose California in due course, one congressman argued in 1862. Perhaps the state would not immediately splinter into an independent Pacific republic, he reasoned, but who could tell what might happen over time if it remained separated from the seat of government in the East?[57] However murky the details, the threat of a European attack on the Pacific coast also loomed large in the American imagination, especially as tensions escalated between Britain and the United States in the wake of the Trent Affair of late 1861, in which the US Navy seized two rebel diplomats aboard a British ship.[58]

The United States now had a rare window of opportunity. The secession of eleven slaveholding states created an overwhelming Republican majority in Congress and a clear mandate for a northern railroad route. But as soon as the rebel states laid down their arms and rejoined the Union, Representative Thaddeus Stevens warned, they would again throw up roadblocks for any route aside from their own. "We shall find them with the same arrogant, insolent dictation which we have cringed to for twenty years," Stevens claimed, "forbidding the construction of any road that does not run along our southern border."[59] After more than a decade of fruitless debate, Congress swiftly capitalized on the southern rebellion and passed the Pacific Railroad Act, which Lincoln signed into law in July 1862. Hence an irony of the rebel experiment: the threat of a continental Confederacy helped ensure the creation of a continental Union. The great slavery road was dead; the great Union road was about to break ground.

The Continental South at High Tide

As rebel sympathizers rallied in California, Confederate invaders marched west from Texas. By August 1861, Colonel John R. Baylor had secured the southern half of New Mexico, now the Confederate territory of Arizona. Aided by the southern-born Anglo population, Baylor began shoring up control of the region and confiscating the property of Unionists, including mines owned by northerners around Tucson and Tubac.[60] Brigadier General Henry Hopkins Sibley, meanwhile, had mustered a force of roughly 2,500 Texans to extend the rebel conquest of the Southwest. His three regiments, along with a handful of slaves and 4,000 animals, arrived at Fort Bliss on the Texas-Arizona border in mid-December. Sibley then incorporated Baylor's forces into his own to form the Confederate Army of New

Mexico. While Baylor remained in Mesilla to preside over rebel Arizona, Sibley turned north into US-held New Mexico.[61]

One major objective propelled Sibley's invasion: to open a Confederate pathway to the Pacific. Although Jefferson Davis did not give him detailed instructions for the operation—instead trusting to Sibley's knowledge of New Mexico from his antebellum deployments—the two commanders were closely aligned in their long-range visions for the Far West.[62] For more than a decade, Davis had pursued links, both commercial and political, between the slave states and the Pacific coast. With Sibley's invasion, those links became military as well. *"The objective aim and design of the campaign was the conquest of California,"* one of Sibley's subordinates wrote. "As soon as the Confederate army should occupy the Territory of New Mexico, an army of advance would be organized, and 'On to San Francisco' would be the watchword."[63]

Deepwater ports, gold, diplomatic recognition, and rebel sympathizers all awaited Sibley in California, according to Confederate strategists. With the Union blockade of the Atlantic coastline, other maritime outlets had become essential to slaveholders' commercial interests. Mexican harbors provided one option, but a Confederate-controlled San Diego or Los Angeles was even more enticing. Rebel officials also looked longingly toward the gold mines of California and the treasure ships sailing from the coast. With a successful western thrust, Sibley might also become an important agent of Confederate foreign policy. If the rebellion could hold the Pacific coast, Davis's government could more effectively lobby for international recognition. A western conquest, in other words, would legitimize the Confederacy in the eyes of European leaders. Finally, as Baylor and others recognized, California harbored a sizable body of rebel sympathizers. Sibley and Baylor had already bolstered their ranks with local secessionists in Arizona and New Mexico. A rebel pathway to California would provide further reinforcements to beat back Yankee armies in the region.[64]

Sibley's campaign began auspiciously. Upon arriving at Fort Bliss, he issued a proclamation to the people of New Mexico, a document that echoed the logic of the South's antebellum expansionists. "By geographical position, by similarity of institutions, by commercial interests, and by future destinies New Mexico pertains to the Confederacy," he announced on December 20, 1861.[65] As if to confirm these claims, a group of secessionists from New Mexico rode to meet the invading Confederate army, mustering into a unit known as the Brigands.[66]

Much like Baylor's invasion less than a year earlier, Sibley's thrust into New Mexico caught Union forces flat-footed. At the Battle of Valverde—the largest military confrontation in the region's history to that point—

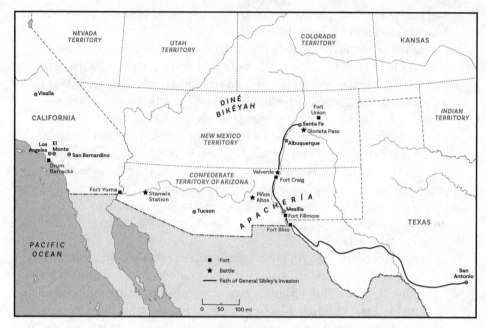

The Confederate invasion of Arizona and New Mexico

the Texans defeated a US army of 3,800. The victory opened the road to Albuquerque and Santa Fe. A panicked Governor Henry Connelly and his territorial officials fled east to Fort Union, the makeshift seat of New Mexico's government. When Sibley's men rode into Santa Fe in March 1862, they became the first and only Confederates to seize a capital city in Union territory. Their conquest capped a 1,000-mile march from San Antonio over an arid and unforgiving landscape. With Union forces demoralized and thousands of Texans concentrated in New Mexico, this was the high-water mark of the Continental South. The rebellion now controlled all of Arizona and much of New Mexico, from the Rio Grande nearly to the Colorado River.[67]

More so than General Robert E. Lee's much larger invasion of Pennsylvania in July 1863, Sibley's western operations had to balance a complicated set of foreign policy objectives. While Lee faced a single adversary in the Army of the Potomac, Sibley confronted a dense tangle of foreign powers across the Southwest: a multipronged Union counteroffensive, several major Native American polities, and agents of the Mexican government. How rebel leaders managed (and mismanaged) their foreign relations, especially with regard to the region's Native peoples, would ultimately determine the fate of the invasion.

Sibley's overtures to Mexico were moderately successful. In early 1862, he dispatched Colonel James Reily to negotiate with the governors of Chihuahua and Sonora in order to establish a depot for Confederate supplies at Guaymas and an exclusive trade relationship with the two Mexican states. The governor of Chihuahua, Luis Terrazas, proved broadly receptive to the Confederate mission, leading Reily to proclaim that he had secured "the first official recognition of the Government of the Confederate States by any foreign power."[68] (He had not. Neither he nor Terrazas wielded the authority to formalize diplomatic recognition.) Yet Reily had made important international inroads and received permission to purchase Mexican supplies, which might prove essential if Sibley's army continued pressing west.[69]

Reily hoped to win much more than trade rights. Privately, he argued for the seizure of Sonora and Chihuahua in order to secure a shorter railroad route to the Pacific. Such a bold move, however, clashed with the restrained foreign policy of Davis's administration. Davis had previously declined an opportunity to claim a large slice of Mexican territory. In the summer of 1861, the governor of Nuevo Leon proposed the annexation of Mexico's northern states to the Confederacy, but Davis passed for geostrategic reasons. He rightly feared that any seizure of Mexican territory would invite war with Benito Juárez's government and thus expose his rebellion to a multinational and multifront conflict. A Confederate seizure of foreign territory might also prompt the US government to blockade the Mexican coast, which had served as a valuable pipeline for military supplies into the rebel states.[70] For the time being, the Confederate invasion could cross US-held lands only. Sibley's dealings with Mexico, therefore, were restricted to matters of commerce rather than conquest.

When it came to the American Indians of the Southwest, Confederate diplomacy met its limits. Whereas Confederate officials successfully negotiated treaties with the Native nations of Indian Territory—the Cherokee, Chickasaw, Creek, Choctaw, and Seminole—they established no formal relations with the less centrally organized peoples of the Southwest.[71] Instead, they pursued a policy of open warfare across lands claimed by competing polities.

While Baylor quickly drove Yankee soldiers from Arizona, the Chiricahua Apaches proved far harder to dislodge. Indigenous Americans continued to hold the balance of power in the territory and regarded the Confederate presence an affront to their sovereignty. Baylor had attempted to use the Overland Mail Road as a rebel thoroughfare, along which he sent troops westward toward the California border. To the Apaches, however, this was an old hunting trail, along which Anglos could move only with Native consent. By the end of the summer, Apache warriors had killed more of Baylor's men than had federal armies.[72] In September 1861, Mangas Coloradas and Cochise struck the Arizona mining town of Piños Altos, killing several soldiers and residents and setting fire to the town's houses and stores. Only when a group of women dragged a twelve-pound howitzer into the fray were townspeople able to beat back the Apache assault. And who could say when the Apaches would return? As the *Mesilla Times* lamented, "Nineteen-twentieths of the Territory of Arizona is under [the Apaches'] undisputed control."[73]

To assert control over lands they claimed but did not possess, Confederate leaders turned to a familiar strategy: enslavement. When Sibley's invasion threatened the Navajo homeland of Diné Bikéyah in northern New Mexico, his men and animals became the target of Native raiding as well. "Such were the complaints of the people," Sibley reported, "that I had determined, as good policy, to encourage private enterprises against that tribe and the Apaches, and to legalize the enslaving of them."[74] Baylor took this policy a step further, advocating the "extermination" of Apache adults and the enslavement of their children. As "a firm believer in the civilizing effects of the system of slavery as regards the African race," Baylor saw no reason why a similar policy would not also benefit the Indigenous people of the Southwest.[75] If the logic was perverse, it was also consistent with the views of southern slaveholders who had, for more than a decade, defended unfree labor regimes across the continent—whether they relied on African, Indian, or indebted Hispano workers.

Baylor, however, had gone too far. His command in Arizona, which started propitiously with the capture of Fort Fillmore in the summer of 1861, soon devolved into a diplomatic quagmire. His troubles began in December that year, when he killed the editor of the *Mesilla Times*, Robert Kelley, in broad daylight. Founded in 1860, the paper had been a warm supporter of the Confederacy but a critic of Baylor's leadership in Arizona. In an encounter outside his headquarters, Baylor assaulted Kelley, pinned him to the ground, pulled his pistol, and shot the editor in the jaw. Baylor was tried for murder but acquitted by a jury of his own troops. Several months later, Baylor recruited a force of more than 100 men and rode 200 miles south to the Mexican mining town of Corralitos to satisfy what he called "a natural desire to see [Apaches] driven utterly from the face of the earth."[76] He found no Native warriors in Corralitos, only three unarmed and Christianized slaves hiding in a miner's home. Baylor executed all three—two women and one man. The governor of Chihuahua wrote to Sibley in a fury, protesting the violation of Mexican sovereignty.[77]

Baylor followed this fiasco by again advocating genocide. "You will use all means to persuade the Apaches or any tribe to come in for the purpose of making peace," he instructed one of his officers in March 1862. "And when you get them together kill all the grown Indians and take the Children prisoners and sell them to defray the expense of killing the Indians."[78] At a time when Jefferson Davis was attempting to secure the support of the Mexican government as well as the Native nations of Indian Territory, Baylor's savage vendettas undermined Confederate policy. He did not have time to put his exterminationist policies into action, however. Baylor left Arizona under a cloud of shame that spring, relieved of his governorship and stripped of his rank. Less than a year later, he was elected to the Confederate Congress.[79]

Sibley's command in northern New Mexico disintegrated simultaneously. While not openly genocidal like Baylor, Sibley possessed his own litany of faults. His alcoholism was a poorly kept secret as well as a major liability on a long campaign in enemy territory. At several key moments during the campaign, including his army's victory at Valverde, Sibley was drunkenly incapacitated in his wagon, purportedly in an effort to combat the pain of his kidney stones. Sibley's men were also poorly equipped for a campaign that carried them into a forbidding landscape a thousand miles from their base of operations in Texas. For much of the invasion, two of his companies carried only lances. He had expected to sustain his army off the fat of the land, but he found the countryside alarmingly lean. Even the conquest of Santa Fe did not provide his troops with the supplies they needed to continue waging such a lengthy operation.[80]

A lack of provisions ultimately proved fatal to his invasion. A few miles southeast of Santa Fe, at the Battle of Glorieta Pass in late March 1862, a tactical victory turned into a strategic disaster. Although the rebels initially held the field, a detachment of Colorado volunteers under the command of John M. Chivington—who would later lead US troops in a massacre of Cheyenne and Arapaho Indians at Sand Creek—destroyed Sibley's supply train. Without provisions to sustain thousands of troops in hostile territory, Sibley was forced to abandon the invasion and his dream of opening a Confederate thoroughfare to the Pacific.

His men began a long retreat, first to Mesilla, then to Confederate Texas in scorching desert heat.[81] To stay ahead of pursuing US troops, Sibley abandoned sick and dehydrated soldiers along the way. By the time he reached Texas, the Confederate Army of New Mexico had lost an estimated 800 to 1,000 men to sickness, exhaustion, Union forces, and Indian warriors. That amounted to a nearly 30 percent casualty rate, higher than that suffered by almost any other Confederate army.[82]

The dramatic collapse of Sibley's invasion obscures its initial successes. For the better part of a year, invading Texans maintained control of southern New Mexico in the face of provisional shortages, environmental challenges, formidable Indian polities, and US armies—not to mention the faults of their own commanders. Compared to the far larger rebel invasions in the eastern theaters—namely Robert E. Lee's push into Maryland (1862) and Pennsylvania (1863), which were quickly turned back at Antietam and Gettysburg, respectively—Baylor and Sibley conducted lengthy occupations. They also commanded sizable forces by the standards of that early point in the conflict. The 3,000 troops in the Confederate Army of New Mexico were equal to roughly 10 percent of the rebel force at Bull Run, the first major battle of the war. Every man whom Davis sent into the deserts of the Far Southwest was one fewer whom he could deploy in the all-important theaters east of the Mississippi. These far western invasions would not turn the tide of war in the way that eastern campaigns did. And in hindsight, Sibley's dream of California conquest appears rather farfetched. But, for a time, his invasion threw a major US military department into disarray and brought more than decade of proslavery scheming in the West to a bloody climax.[83]

The Continental South at Low Ebb

Jefferson Davis refused to turn his back on the region that defeated Sibley and Baylor. Although preoccupied with pivotal campaigns in Virginia and along the Mississippi, the Confederate high command continued to authorize (or at least condone) smaller operations in the Far West: additional New Mexican invasion schemes, a guerrilla unit in California's gold country, and a privateering expedition in the Pacific Ocean. Albeit unsuccessful, these offensives harried US officials in the West until the last days of the war. Only by beating back multiple rebel threats was the United States finally able to secure control over the far end of the continent.

From the earliest days of the war, rebels threatened—at least rhetorically—Union control of the Pacific Ocean. As federals tightened their grip on the Atlantic coast, Confederates sought outlets elsewhere, hence Sibley's interest in Mexico and the ports of California. He was merely the latest in a long line of southern expansionists who lusted after the Pacific trade. Secessionists also considered piracy. In an open letter to President Lincoln in May 1861, the proslavery polemicist Edward Pollard envisioned a sea of Confederate privateers opening a Pacific theater to the war. The ships "will destroy the commercial and navigating interests of the North," he boasted. "They will scour the South Pacific as well as other oceans of the world; they will penetrate into every sea, and will find as tempting prizes in the silk ships of China as in the gold-freighted steamers of California."[84]

US authorities recognized the value and the vulnerability of their gold shipments from California. One of Lincoln's first acts after the firing on Fort Sumter was to ensure the protection of the nation's maritime commerce, especially the Pacific treasure ships.[85] "I do not know what we would do in this great national emergency," Ulysses S. Grant is rumored to have said, "were it not for the gold sent from California."[86] To be sure, there was more bombast than actual threat in declarations like Pollard's. The Confederacy lacked the naval capacity to launch a full-scale maritime contest in the Pacific. But the rebellion did possess important contacts in California, eager to assist in a smaller privateering campaign. With only six sloops of war and fewer than 1,000 sailors to protect a vast coastline and lucrative commerce, US naval control in the Pacific was patchy at best.[87]

Enter the adventurer and western secessionist Ashbury Harpending. The scion of a wealthy Kentucky family, Harpending attached himself to proslavery schemes at an early age. At fifteen he sailed for Nicaragua in one of William Walker's filibustering expeditions, though American officials intercepted his ship and prevented the young Harpending from taking part in ground operations. He later helped organize a secessionist movement within California, appealing to Albert Sidney Johnston to hand over the entire Department of the Pacific to the nascent western rebellion. When Johnston refused, Harpending shifted his attentions toward the Pacific Ocean, where he reasoned that a weak US naval presence could be turned to the Confederacy's advantage.[88]

In 1862 Harpending traveled overland to the Mexican port city of Veracruz, then via blockade runner to Charleston, and finally to Richmond. Once there, he laid his plans before Jefferson Davis. He proposed to sail a sloop to Mexico, transform his vessel into a fighting craft, and seize the first Pacific Mail steamer that crossed his path, confiscating the ship's gold and silver payloads. Then Harpending and his associates planned "to equip the captured liner as a privateer and . . . intercept two more eastbound Pacific Mail steamers before the world knew what was happening in those days of slow traveling news."[89] Although Davis was wary of any operation that could be construed as piracy—due to the international scandal that might result—he was intrigued by the plan. According to Harpending, Davis "fully realized the importance of shutting off the great gold shipments to the East from California," which, in his estimation, "would be more important than many victories in the field."[90] Harpending received a commission as a captain in the Confederate navy, even though "I had never been on a man-of-war in my life."[91]

Harpending returned to California in July 1862 and enlisted the help of two coconspirators, Ridgley Greathouse and a young English gentleman, Alfred Rubery—fittingly flamboyant names to match the nature of their operation. They purchased the *J. M. Chapman*, a ninety-ton schooner moored in San Francisco Bay, and outfitted the ship with two twelvepound cannon. They also bought a small arsenal of rifles, revolvers, and cutlasses. "Without much difficulty" Harpending found "twenty picked men—all from the South, of proved and desperate courage." The *Chapman* never made it out of port, however. As Harpending and his would-be privateers were preparing to set sail in March 1863, the plot was betrayed by the ship's navigator. Harpending was soon staring down the trained guns of a US warship and several boatloads of police and marines.[92]

He and his associates were taken to Alcatraz Island and then to San Francisco's Old Broadway jail. As they sat in prison, the San Francisco press called for the execution of the *Chapman* conspirators. They had "committed a treason as grave as any that ever was, or ever could be," the *Alta California* thundered. "That of Arnold was not baser or more malicious." Harpending was finally convicted of treason, though his crew was acquitted. Fortunately for Harpending, Lincoln's Amnesty Proclamation of December 1863 granted full pardon to all political prisoners on the condition they take a loyalty oath. He won his freedom by February 1864, after nearly a year of confinement, bankrupted and foiled in his plans to bring the Confederacy into the Pacific.[93]

As Harpending languished in prison, Jefferson Davis authorized yet another audacious plot under yet another inexperienced commander. This time it was Lansford Hastings, an eccentric western booster and aspiring conqueror, who won the approval of the Confederate high command. Hastings had achieved notoriety before the war when his faulty guidebook to the American West sent the Donner Party to a disastrous winter in the High Sierra in 1846–47. In December 1863, he wrote to Davis with a plan that by comparison made Sibley look like a paragon of restraint. Hastings proposed to raise a force of 3,000 to 5,000 partisans from California's southern-sympathizing population and then march east to reclaim Arizona for the rebellion. The campaign would open "an unbroken intercourse between California and the Confederacy," according to Hastings. It would also lay the groundwork, he claimed, for a far southern transcontinental railroad.[94]

The plan was nothing short of preposterous, coming from a man with a shortage of military experience and a high-profile navigational blunder in his recent past. But Hastings knew how to appeal to Davis. By highlighting railroad development, as well as the agricultural and mineral riches of the Southwest, Hastings spoke in the language that southern expansionists had long employed when discussing their prospects in the region. Davis approved the plan and commissioned Hastings a major in the Confederate army. Although the campaign never materialized—probably a result of Hastings's own shortcomings as a military commander and ongoing difficulties in the major eastern theaters—that Davis even entertained such an operation speaks to the enduring pull of the Far West on the southern imagination.[95]

Western rebels had more success in 1864 with a smaller, better-organized operation around Sacramento. Under the command of Captain Rufus Ingram, a group of southern-sympathizing desperadoes brought a taste of Missouri's guerrilla warfare to California's gold country. Ingram himself had fought under the notorious partisan leader William Quantrill in Missouri. He took part in the rebel raid on Lawrence, Kansas, in August 1863, in which Quantrill's ruffians murdered more than 180 civilians and burned nearly every building in town. Known as the "Red Fox," Ingram saw opportunity in California, which boasted a sufficient population of Confederate sympathizers without an experienced leader. He began recruiting in March 1864, mainly from the Knights of the Golden Circle around San Jose, eventually attracting an outfit of some fifty men. Ingram had hoped to lead his unit to the military theaters of the East, but with scanty funding, he opted instead for a guerrilla campaign in California. As Ingram's lieutenant and Monterey undersheriff Tom Poole later recalled, "If we could not raise means enough to go South, we were to raise [an] insurrection in California."[96]

The band that the California press would soon dub "Ingram's Partisan Rangers" achieved its greatest coup in June 1864, when the rebels robbed a Wells Fargo stagecoach of its substantial cargo of gold and silver. When demanding the bullion, Ingram identified himself as a Confederate captain, raising money for the southern war effort.[97] The six-man outfit buried the bullion at a nearby spring and then fled to their hideout, where local authorities, hot in pursuit, tracked them down. Ingram and his raiders opened fire, killing one officer and grievously wounding another before making their escape. Poole, who had lost half his cheek to a shotgun blast in the exchange, was later captured and confessed to the buried treasure's location.[98]

Rebel activity and small-scale carnage continued through most of the summer. After a failed heist in mid-July, the gang fled to another hideout, where they were again tracked down by a posse of sheriffs, constables, and citizens. Ingram and his partisans came out firing, wounding two sheriffs.

Two of their own died in the exchange. In late July, California authorities, backed by four companies of infantry (a testament to just how seriously Union officials viewed this threat), arrested ten of Ingram's raiders. Several members of the gang robbed two more stagecoaches in early August, but by then their partisan campaign was all but played out. By early September, authorities had killed or arrested nearly every active member of the band except for Ingram and one other. Local citizens packed the courtroom that month, as the majority of the Ingram raiders stood trial for murder and highway robbery, though not for treason.[99] Poole, the operation's former second-in-command, was hanged for his crimes the next year. Ingram, however, eluded justice, melting into the countryside and thereafter disappearing from history.[100]

The roundup of Ingram's guerrillas coincided with a broader US campaign against insurrection within the state. A major target of these crackdowns was California's copperhead press. As early as February 1862, the US postmaster banned the *Los Angeles Star* from the mails. Several months later the *Visalia Equal Rights Expositor*, the *Stockton Argus*, and the *San Jose Tribune*, followed by the *Placerville Mountain Democrat* and the *Stockton Democrat*, joined the *Star* on the list of banned materials. Southern sympathizers rallied in defense of their beleaguered press. In Visalia, donations from local disunionists floated the *Equal Rights Expositor* while its subscriptions sagged under the ban. Similarly, the *Los Angeles Star* survived with the support of Democrats in the area. When the mails were reopened to the *Star* in January 1863, the editor, Henry Hamilton, redoubled his defiance of Lincoln's administration. "The prohibition was impotent," Hamilton boasted, "so do we despise this proffered sop."[101] Where prohibition failed to silence the southern sympathizing press, mobs often proved more persuasive. After editor Lovick P. Hall published an abusive article on California's federalist volunteers, titled "California Cossacks," a Unionist mob, led by soldiers, demolished the press and offices of the *Visalia Equal Rights Expositor*. One of Merced's copperhead papers met a similar end.[102]

Along with prohibitions and mob action came a flurry of arrests. Ingram's rangers, Harpending and his coconspirators, and other less violent offenders were all jailed for treasonous activity. Alcatraz, the famous prison island in San Francisco Bay, got its start as a penal complex during the Civil War when General George Wright constructed the first prison building at the fort to contain this motley assortment of rebels.[103] In 1862, the outspoken disunionist E. J. C. Kewen, who had been the state's first attorney general, was arrested, taken to Drum Barracks, and then transported to Alcatraz. So too was Henry Hamilton. Upon their release, the citizens of El Monte treated them to a celebratory barbecue. The undersheriff of Los

Angeles County, Andrew Jackson King, who had so brazenly displayed a life-size portrait of rebel General P. G. T. Beauregard, was also arrested on charges of conspiracy. Like Hamilton and Kewen, he secured his release upon taking a loyalty oath. Of all Confederate sympathizers in California, none was more extraordinary than Peter Biggs, a former slave turned Los Angeles barber and Democratic partisan, who was escorted to Drum Barracks in 1864 for suspected treason.[104] The *Expositor's* editor, Lovick P. Hall, was arrested twice during the course of the war, remaining under guard until September 1865, several months after the conflict had ended.[105]

Individually, these rebel plots in the Far West appear little more than errands into the wilderness. But together, they sustained a sense of panic among western Unionists and turned the region into another theater of the war. Like earlier secessionist episodes in California and Arizona, they also diverted resources and troops from the pivotal campaigns in the East. The most enduring legacy of these insurgencies, however, was unintended. Rather than extending the South's sphere of influence, as they had hoped, these western disunionists triggered a series of countermeasures that hastened the rebellion's undoing. By exposing the vulnerability of the Far West, Confederate sympathizers enabled the Lincoln administration to expand its wartime powers and shape the region in its own image. The "Yankee leviathan"—the vastly expanded central state of the war years—drew strength from the administration's response to these western threats.[106]

The Republican administration increasingly tightened its grip over New Mexico. That process, which began with Lincoln's prewar patronage appointments, accelerated with the threat of a Texas invasion. Governor Henry Connelly tapped deep-rooted fears of Texas to raise a force of more than 5,000 volunteers from the territory's population. Even the proslavery *Santa Fe Gazette* tempered its positions and largely ceased its attacks on abolitionists and Lincoln.[107] In December 1861, the territorial legislature unanimously voted to overturn New Mexico's slave code, which had withstood a national campaign for repeal since its passage two years earlier. Lawmakers finally caved to necessity in the face of a Confederate invasion, knowing that they risked losing federal support if they retained the slave code.[108] The Republican-controlled Congress followed this local victory by abolishing slavery and involuntary servitude in all US territories the next year.[109] In 1863, Lincoln divided New Mexico along a north-south axis, creating the new US territory of Arizona from the western half of these lands, with the borders we know today. The division helped neutralize the rebel threat from Arizona by splitting the former Confederate territory.

US troops, meanwhile, continued to pour into the Southwest. First they beat back the Confederate Army of New Mexico. After 1862, they battled against a rebellion of a different sort: the numerous Indian peoples of the region who had converted a civil war into a conflict for Native self-determination. US forces waged a scorched-earth campaign against the Navajos and Apaches in New Mexico, eventually confining more than 9,000 of them to Bosque Redondo—one of the largest and deadliest prison camps anywhere on the continent. Other Indians were simply murdered. After capturing the famed Apache leader Mangas Coloradas under a flag of truce, federal troops tortured him and then riddled his body with bullets, claiming (falsely) that he had attempted to escape. To wage this war, the Union enrolled some 24,000 volunteers from California, New Mexico, and Colorado. It was a combined force 50 percent larger than the entire antebellum US Army.[110]

In California, the Democratic Party's flirtation with rebellion led to a surge in Republicanism, unthinkable just a few years before. Many of the same figures who had supported Chivalry politicians in the antebellum period, including Californio elites like Andrés Pico, shifted their allegiances once the faction's leaders began agitating for secession.[111] Disunion was a bridge too far for most Californians. Republicans played to voters' fears of a secessionist coup to win their first gubernatorial election in 1861, having secured just 10 percent of the vote in the 1859 contest. By mid-war, Republicans and loyal Democrats fused to form the Union Party, wielding power over the state in a way that only the Chivalry faction had done before.

Unionist lawmakers finally began dismantling systems of Native American servitude and antiblack discrimination that had prevailed under Democratic rule. By April 1863, Governor Leland Stanford signed an act outlawing the custodianship of Native minors and the indenture of California Indians.[112] After a sustained campaign from African American leaders, California's lawmakers finally lifted the ban on black testimony against whites in civil and criminal cases (although the ban on Native American and Chinese witnesses remained in place). State officials also recognized, for the first time, African Americans' right to preempt public lands.[113]

Republican power in California came, in part, from the barrel of a gun. To deter any potential Ashbury Harpending imitators, the legislature declared it a capital offense to arm a ship against the United States.[114] Union soldiers garrisoned the Chivalry strongholds of Los Angeles and Tulare, policing the movements of leading political figures in the two counties. The clampdown on anti-Lincoln newspapers and the arrests of subversives, including Andrew Jackson King, Henry Hamilton, and E. J. C. Kewen, crippled the Democratic machine in Southern California. In 1864, Kewen and Hamilton opted not to run for reelection to the state legislature. That year, financial difficulties forced Hamilton to sell the *Los Angeles Star* to a

pro-Union Democrat. Later, the wealthy Unionist Phineas Banning purchased the press and its materials, moved it to Wilmington, and filled its
columns with praise for Lincoln.[115] The proslavery spirit that had burned
so brightly during the antebellum period and the early war years had
waned to mere embers.

A California Rebel in Napoleon's Court

But that spirit was not dead. It simply migrated. While military crackdowns had suppressed the most vocal signs of secessionism in the Far
West, California's rebels had gone international by mid-war. Most threatening, in the eyes of federal authorities, was former US senator William
Gwin, who, in 1864, reached the court of Napoleon III. There, he launched a
campaign to convince the French emperor to back a scheme for a colonial
settlement in Sonora, Mexico. He proposed to populate the region, then
under the jurisdiction of France's puppet emperor, with American miners
and adventurers in order to trigger a mineral rush. Although Gwin was not
an official representative of the Confederate government, US authorities
feared his Sonora colony would become a far western base of operations
for the rebellion. General Ulysses S. Grant even considered invading the
Mexican colony in January 1865.[116] Gwin threatened to transform a civil
war into an international conflagration.

US officials watched Gwin's movements carefully, well before he moved
to Paris. Few could forget that he had been the leading figure in California's proslavery political faction, the absentee owner of a Mississippi plantation, and a close confidant of Confederates across the country. Two of
those rebels accompanied Gwin as he slipped out of California in October
1861: future Confederate general Joseph Lancaster Brent and the prominent Chivalry lawyer Calhoun Benham. The three traveled aboard the USS
Orizaba en route to New York via Panama. But they never intended to sail
for a US harbor. Instead, according to Brent, they planned to "leave the
steamer at Panama, make our way to the West Indies, and from there run
the blockade into one of the Southern ports."[117] Unfortunately for them,
General Edward Vose Sumner, with 400 US soldiers, had also boarded the
Orizaba. Sumner, the former commander of the Pacific Department, had
been particularly vigilant in his surveillance of California rebels during
the opening phase of the war, and he maintained that vigilance aboard the
Orizaba. While at sea, he ordered the arrest of Gwin, Benham, and Brent,
"all leading, active, and influential men of the party in rebellion against
the government."[118]

In protesting their arrest, the three men nearly sparked a diplomatic crisis. When the *Orizaba* pulled into port at Panama City, several American southerners there—including the former minister to Panama, who owed his appointment to Gwin—caught wind of the ex-senator's arrest. They appealed to the governor, who in turn dispatched a company of soldiers to the landing wharf to protest the "violation of the sovereignty of Panama." Sumner threatened to bombard the city if his orders were resisted and sent the three prisoners ashore, guarded by a flotilla of small boats and 400 soldiers, while a man-of-war pulled into the port and turned its broadside on the city. According to Brent, their arrest was carried out with "a 'pomp and circumstance of war' such as Pizarro himself never possessed on the Isthmus when at the height of his power."[119] Thus secured, the prisoners were sent off to New York under parole and later imprisoned at Fort Lafayette. Lincoln, after vigorous lobbying from a personal friend (who also happened to be Benham's brother-in-law), reluctantly agreed to free the prisoners in late 1861. "I never want to hear their names mentioned again," Lincoln sighed as he ordered the release.[120]

Gwin returned to Mississippi to look after his plantation for the next few years, while his son served a brief stint in the Confederate cavalry. Musing on his next steps, he wrote to Brent in March 1863. America was no place for him, he concluded, with US troops closing in on every side. "I want to get away from war," he wrote. Although "my negroes are as yet safe," there was no telling how far the Yankees ("the vilest thieves on Earth") would go with regard to southern property. Ultimately, Gwin hoped to return to a California free from US control. With a Confederate victory, he expected to "put down the Yankees" in his former state and live out his days as a citizen of a new republic.[121] Although sketchy in their details, here were plans for a separate empire on the Pacific: first, southern independence, and then the termination of US rule in California.

But California had to wait; in the meantime, France beckoned. After Union forces sacked his Mississippi plantation in July 1863, Gwin boarded the side-wheeler *R. E. Lee*, ran the federal blockade, and sailed for Paris. He joined a large community of southern expatriates, many endeavoring to enlist French aid in the Confederate cause. Although never pledging official support for the slaveholders' rebellion, the French emperor Napoleon III proved receptive to these overtures—more so than other European heads of state—turning a blind eye to the money and munitions that French sources were sending to the Confederate South.[122]

Thus, Gwin had reason for optimism when he won an audience with Napoleon to outline his ambitious plan for a new mining colony in Sonora and Chihuahua, Mexico. France had invaded Mexico in the spring of 1862, on the pretext of securing repayment of past debts, and installed the Austrian archduke Maximilian I on the throne of the newly created Mexican Empire. Gwin proposed to unearth the hidden wealth of this empire by attracting American immigrants to the mineral regions of northern Mexico and to provide a buffer against the United States, which was hostile to Napoleon's puppet government. All he asked in return was a military detachment of some 1,000 troops to protect his colonists from Comanche and Apache raiders.[123] Enchanted by Gwin's assurances of mineral riches, Napoleon and his cabinet endorsed the plan by the spring of 1864 and dispatched Gwin to Mexico City to prepare the way for the new colony.[124]

Although the former senator pitched his colony as an opportunity for France's imperial prospects, Gwin had a different empire in mind when he set out for Mexico in the summer of 1864. As he recorded in his memoirs, the Sonora colony was to be a key component in a vast Pacific republic. Had the Confederacy won its independence, "it was believed by many that the country would have still been divided by the separation of California from the Union and the establishment of an independent government on the Pacific coast," he wrote. "In that event, northern districts of Mexico would have formed an important addition to the Western Republic."[125] With an army of emigrants, most of them southern-born, Gwin could exert his political will over a powerful and mineral-rich Pacific empire, entirely free from US control.

Only in hindsight does such a geopolitical reordering appear fanciful or far-fetched. As historian Rachel St. John has argued, Gwin's visions for Pacific independence were "entirely possible" and consistent with decades of American imperialism. The Pacific coast, as American expansionists from Thomas Jefferson to Thomas Jefferson Green routinely predicted, could easily form its own republic. Gwin and other influential westerners—men with "grand ambitions and flexible loyalties"—saw "their nation's boundaries not as a fait accompli but as a work in progress."[126] Gwin's plans were also consistent with the longer history of proslavery expansionism in the American West. Proponents of a southern transcontinental railroad, for instance, had hoped to exert control over the West through immigration, infrastructural development, and commercial penetration. Territorial conquest and the extension of chattel slavery, while desirable, were not essential to this blueprint for expansion. Gwin attempted to harness the cumulative force of migration to remake this western region in a southern and disunionist image.

In fleeing one war in the United States, Gwin nearly created another in Mexico. When US officials caught wind of his movements in Sonora, they prepared for a border-crossing conflict. Ulysses S. Grant was particularly worried about Gwin, "a rebel of the most virulent order." As his army besieged Robert E. Lee's forces at Petersburg, Virginia, Grant considered launching another invasion, thousands of miles to the west. If Gwin organized "the dissatisfied spirits of California" and threatened an incursion of American territory, Grant was prepared to respond in force. "I would not rest satisfied with simply driving the invaders onto Mexican soil," he wrote to General Irvin McDowell in January 1865, "but would pursue him until overtaken, and would retain possession of the territory from which the invader started until indemnity for the past and security for the future . . . was insured."[127]

McDowell, commander of the Pacific Department, mobilized the military to frustrate Gwin's plans. Two of Gwin's agents were then operating in San Francisco to recruit would-be colonists and thereby "plant upon our frontiers a people hostile to our institutions, our influence, and our progress," McDowell wrote. In response, the general drove the two immigration agents from San Francisco, then instituted a policy requiring passports for all Mexican-bound travelers. Meanwhile, he dispatched a brigadier general to Arizona to monitor Gwin's movements and organized a force of several regiments to "provide for any contingency."[128]

Gwin was not officially commissioned by the Confederate government, but Confederates cheered his progress. Gwin recognized that he was "highly valued because I am with the South in this contest."[129] John Slidell—the Confederate minister to France, who had been privy to Gwin's dealings in Paris—held high hopes for the Sonora mission. "His object is to colonize Sonora with sons of southern birth . . . residing in California," Slidell wrote to Confederate secretary of state Judah P. Benjamin, another enthusiast of Pacific expansion. "If carried out its consequences will be most beneficial."[130] Geographic factors alone, as Slidell probably recognized, would have lent the Sonora colony a southern character. In close proximity to rebel Arizona and Confederate-sympathizing Southern California, Sonora would be a magnet for nearby disunionists. As the Confederacy's armies crumbled in the East, Gwin's colony could have opened a rebel escape valve in the West.

Yet for all the Unionist fears and Confederate expectations that he stirred, Gwin's Mexican career was short-lived. A medley of factors beyond his control—interpersonal struggles within the court of Maximilian, the tenacious resistance of President Benito Juárez's Liberal armies, administrative missteps—doomed his best-laid plans.[131] Gwin began recruiting in California, but without French military aid to protect his colonists from Apache and Comanche warriors, mining operations could not safely commence. Gwin—ridiculed by the Unionist press as "El Duque de Guino"—continued to argue his case until early summer 1865, several months after the Confederacy's collapse. By July, however, he finally abandoned his plans and rode from Mexico City under an armed escort.[132] Maximilian eventually faced a firing squad of Juárez's victorious soldiers; Gwin was fortunate to escape with his life—a fact he attributed to the poor marksmanship of the Mexican Liberals.[133] But he had merely leaped from the frying pan and into the fire. Back in the United States, and with Confederate rebellion quashed, the former senator was arrested and transported under guard to Fort Jackson, Louisiana, in October 1865.[134]

He languished there for nearly eight months, until April 1866.[135] Aside from Jefferson Davis, no Confederate high official served such a long prison term after the war.[136] And for good reason. In many ways, Gwin's border-crossing adventure was the apotheosis of more than a decade of southern scheming in the Far West. James Gadsden and Thomas Jefferson Green had conspired to plant a slave colony on the ostensibly free soil of antebellum California; Postmaster General A. V. Brown had outmaneuvered northern congressmen to finance an overland mail road along a far southern route; David Terry had killed the antislavery senator David Broderick; and Chivalry Democrats had leveraged their political power to pass a state division bill in California. But only Gwin had dared to conspire with foreign dignitaries, to provoke the US high command, and to launch a colony intended as the southern extension of an independent Pacific republic. As the United States attempted to reassert sovereignty over the former Confederacy, Gwin's actions highlighted the globetrotting nature of the recent rebellion, when the slave South reached into the courts of emperors.[137]

Conclusion

Slaveholders' western projects almost outlived slavery itself. As his armies deteriorated across the eastern theaters and his government collapsed around him, Jefferson Davis prepared yet another invasion of New Mexico. He turned again to John Baylor, the genocidal ex-governor of Confederate Arizona. For his encore performance, Baylor planned to enlist thousands of troops from the only part of the country where able-bodied rebel recruits could still be found: the Far Southwest, namely Arizona and Southern California. Davis overrode his own War Department to authorize Baylor's operation in March 1865.[138] Yet there would be no invasion. Robert E. Lee surrendered his Army of Northern Virginia at Appomattox Courthouse in April, ending major military operations. A month later, Davis himself was captured.

With the Confederacy's defeat, the Continental South unraveled. In California, the once-dominant Chivalry faction simply ceased to exist. Former

Democratic elites, like William Gwin and E. J. C. Kewen, had been jailed, while seditious newspapers were silenced. The crackdown on disloyal Californians accelerated in the wake of Lincoln's assassination on April 15. US authorities arrested Confederate sympathizers in Southern California, including Peter Biggs, the so-called black Democrat. And mobs destroyed the presses of five Democratic papers, including the one belonging to Beriah Brown, the reputed head of the Knights of the Columbian Star.[139] Even Henry Hamilton's once-defiant *Los Angeles Star* was now in the hands of Unionists. Through war, Republicans achieved what they never could in peace: political influence in the Far West.

In New Mexico and Arizona, a similar process played out. When he and his California Column arrived in spring 1862, James Henry Carleton declared martial law over the former Confederate territory of Arizona and arrested rebel sympathizers. The repeal of New Mexico's slave code was followed by the division of the territory along a border running north to south, cleaving Confederate Arizona in two. Although rebels in the region attempted to muster an invasion force six weeks after Lee's surrender, the concentration of federal troops in the Southwest rendered a Confederate takeover impossible.[140] The Union war machine not only brought together North and South but also held together East and West.

Republicans would now seek to remake the Desert South in the image of the free-labor Northeast. They could do so with the vastly expanded reach and resources of the federal state. Republicans had stamped out rebellion, redrawn territorial borders, broken ground on the transcontinental railroad, overturned systems of Native American servitude, and outlawed African American chattel slavery. Yet the grandeur of their vision rested on a fragile coalition. To carry their wartime successes into the postbellum Southwest would require the continued cooperation of a dubious base of voters in California and landholders in New Mexico. While most westerners had renounced secessionist Democrats during the war, they sat uncomfortably within the Republican fold. They remained skeptical of federal power, resistant to the advancement of African Americans, and sympathetic to the old planter class of the South. The threads connecting South and West had worn thinner during the war, but still they held.

→ CHAPTER EIGHT ←

Reconstruction and the Afterlife
of the Continental South

———— •●• ————

Surveying california's postwar political order, the writer Bret Harte delivered a grim prognosis for the state's once-dominant Democratic Party. "Rip Van Winkle, awakened from his long nap, hurrahing for his Majesty King George, did not exhibit a more incongruous and ridiculous spectacle than these men who seem to have hibernated during the war," Harte wrote in 1866. Whereas Democrats—largely southern in origin and proslavery in outlook—had ruled the state through most of the 1850s, they were now, in Harte's estimation, little more than "fossils" of a bygone era.[1] According to Harte, California's future was firmly in the hands of the Union Party, a coalition of Republicans and moderate Democrats who had fused during the war years. Together, they had preserved California's loyalty, raised thousands of troops for the Union war effort, and even lifted the long-standing ban on black testimony against whites. The stain of the proslavery Chivalry faction would soon be wiped clean— or so it seemed.

But Harte's projections were entirely premature. Within a year, California's Democratic Party rode to a stunning electoral victory on a white supremacist, state-rights platform. And in the coming years, Democratic lawmakers would tap bitter antiblack and anti-Chinese sentiment to pursue a campaign against Reconstruction, rejecting the Fourteenth and Fifteenth Amendments. Thanks to their efforts, California was the only free state to ratify neither amendment in the nineteenth century.[2] Meanwhile, white vigilantes assaulted Chinese workers across the state, mimicking terrorist tactics employed by unreconstructed rebels in the South and sometimes identifying as members of the Ku Klux Klan. Taken together, these developments flashed warning signs to Republicans at the national level: the rebellion against Reconstruction stretched far beyond the former Confederacy.

New Mexico's master class joined California's Democrats in this western revolt against federal policy. As Republicans attempted to extend slave emancipation across the continent, they met with evasion and outright defiance in the territorial Southwest. The Thirteenth Amendment, reinforced by an anti-peonage statute in 1867, had outlawed the enslavement of Native captives and the coercion of indebted laborers. But, as Republican policy makers discovered, these measures required active enforcement in New Mexico, where bonded laborers could still be found in an estimated 10 percent of the territory's households.[3] Drawing on a set of arguments made familiar by antebellum planters, New Mexico's landed elite stressed the benevolent, paternalistic nature of their labor system, which "redeemed" nonwhite workers into Christian households and provided them with the protections of a humane master class. Republican officials managed to free several hundred peons and Native captives in the late 1860s, but the institution of bonded servitude endured in New Mexico for decades to come.

In defying Reconstruction-era policies, New Mexico and California revived the Continental South, albeit in a modified and more modest form. True, the unifying political objective of the Continental South—the extension of slaveholding interests on a national scale—had been nullified with the collapse of the Confederacy. Furthermore, southern policy makers had lost their voice in national affairs, no longer able to press their agenda through Congress and the executive branch, as they had done during the 1850s. But the postbellum South still exerted a powerful influence over the Far West. In California, a familiar set of southern-born notables—William Gwin; his son, Willie; and the old Chivalry stalwart Benjamin Franklin Washington—shook off their reputations for wartime treason and re-emerged onto the public stage. Many of the state's Democratic politicians and writers, including those born in the Northeast, stressed their affinity for the beleaguered South and articulated the emerging tenets of the so-called Lost Cause. Above all, political elites across the former Confederate states and the Far Southwest found common ground in their campaigns against the major civil rights measures of the era: the Thirteenth, Fourteenth, and Fifteenth Amendments.

A new generation of scholarship has expanded the traditional boundaries of the Reconstruction era.[4] These historians explore how contests over emancipation, enfranchisement, and federal authority played out beyond the former rebel states.[5] Much of their writing builds on the pioneering work of Elliott West, who dubbed the period between 1846 and 1877 "Greater Reconstruction." West's formulation describes a series of interlinked efforts by the US federal state to subdue rebellious polities, consolidate control over the continent, and extend a vision of liberal citizenship to a diverse, and often resistant, range of people.[6] Across large parts of the country, however, this project failed.

The enduring (yet generally overlooked) affinities between South and West help explain why. The local conditions that made the Far West unique—namely, its diverse population of Hispanos, African Americans, Native Americans, and Chinese immigrants—also created a sense of solidarity between the region's white voters and those in the former Confederate states. An anxious white electorate understood that efforts to emancipate and enfranchise the South's black population would remake racial politics in the Far West as well. Democratic lawmakers exploited these anxieties and cast South and West alike as the victims of an overweening federal government. Some white westerners wore their southern affiliations as a badge of honor. By invoking the Ku Klux Klan, western vigilantes linked their attacks on Chinese workers with the racial terror of the postbellum South—a calculated strategy to spread panic among immigrant communities and their allies.

This transcontinental perspective on Reconstruction challenges common assumptions about the era and uncovers familiar developments in unfamiliar locales. By moving beyond a black-white, North-South binary, it underscores the breadth and durability of white supremacy in the age of emancipation. Former Confederates had kindred spirits at the far edge of the continent. Democratic lawmakers and vigilantes in California echoed the rhetoric and violent strategies of the most unreconstructed rebels. In some ways, they even anticipated developments in the Deep South. California's Democrats, for instance, stormed back to power on an anti-Reconstruction platform at a time when the former Confederate states were still under military occupation. The retreat from Reconstruction was national in scope, with some of its leading figures located in the Far Southwest. The view from the West thus underlines the incompleteness of what historian Eric Foner calls America's postwar "revolution."[7] Given this transcontinental resistance, perhaps the wonder is not that Reconstruction ultimately failed but that it survived for as long as it did.

Go West, Old South!

By the spring of 1865, the Confederacy had been routed, slavery abolished, and the wealth of the rebellious states drained. Yet fears persisted of a lingering threat from the South. Less than a month after Appomattox, the *Sacramento Daily Union* predicted that a flood of rebel refugees would soon inundate the West. The border slave states, warned the *Union*, would send westward a "class of shiftless, lawless Union-haters," and "across the Plains will come the poor, ignorant, brute whites" of the South, along with their political apostasy. The West's relative scarcity of African Americans made it a natural escape for thousands of former Confederates fleeing the fallout of emancipation.[8] Unreconstructed rebel leaders regarded California as a field of political opportunity, according to the *Union*'s New York correspondent. Among those contemplating a fresh start in the West were former Confederate general P. G. T. Beauregard and William Gwin, recently freed from prison after the failure of his Sonora colony.[9]

Ultimately the threat of a mass southern migration to the Far West never materialized. According to census data, the number of Californians born in the former Confederate states increased by only 700 between 1860 and 1870, bringing the total to just over 21,000.[10] Yet this lingering distrust of the slave South was not misplaced. Prominent Californians continued to tout their connections to the former Confederacy and openly encouraged the westward migration of rebels. From San Francisco, Lucy Smith Crittenden Thornton—wife of an Alabama Supreme Court judge, mother of a Confederate officer, and sister of former US senator John J. Crittenden of Kentucky—helped launch a charity drive for the rebel states and wrote to family members in the South trumpeting the advantages of the West.[11] Few longtime residents of California could forget that proslavery leaders had steered the state's political course through the antebellum period. California may have entered the postwar years under antislavery Union Party leadership, yet many residents cherished fond memories of California's Chivalry past.

Of all places in California where a Confederate might settle, Los Angeles was the most hospitable. There, rebel sympathizers, such as the former undersheriff Andrew Jackson King, continued to crow about their southern attachments well after Appomattox. "We have been and are yet secessionist," King, who had been arrested during the war for his disunionism, proclaimed in November 1865.[12] "The Civil War continued to rage" in postwar Los Angeles, according to Horace Bell, a Union veteran who returned to Southern California shortly after the war. Bell found that old friends "turned their backs on me" and disparaged his wartime service. He encountered a common refrain on the city's streets: "The idea . . . of a Los Angeles man of your stamp fighting on the side of the blacks!" A "red rag to the Secessionist bulls of the vicinity," Bell wound up, according to his own estimates, in as many as forty brawls for his wartime loyalties.[13] The arrival of more Union veterans relieved some of the pressure on Bell, but Los Angeles remained a Democratic stronghold with a southern orientation. Democrats carried the county in every state and national election between 1866 and 1880. In 1882 the citizens of Los Angeles went so far as to elect as mayor Cameron E. Thom, a former captain in the Confederate army.[14]

The southern influence in California persisted in less violent form along the Merced River in the Central Valley, where emigrant planters began experimenting with cotton. John L. and J. M. Strong, brothers from Georgia, served as the pioneers and propagandists of these efforts, gathering around them a community of fellow southern transplants. They advertised California as an extension of the plantation South, lying almost entirely "within the cotton zone," according to John L. Strong.[15] By the early 1870s, efforts at cotton cultivation had created what the *Fresno Expositor* called a "mania" in California, as glowing reports poured in from across the country.[16] When the Strong brothers shipped their samples to experts in New Orleans, Liverpool, and Scotland, they received gratifying feedback, attesting to the superior quality of the California crop.[17] Aspiring planters also began growing cotton around Los Angeles, with promising yields.[18] From the perspective of California's planters, it appeared that the American West was poised to join India, Egypt, and other parts of the world in what historian Sven Beckert describes as a global reconstruction of cotton.[19] The South's wartime collapse might be turned to California's profit.

Aside from the temperate climate, California's advantage lay in its laboring population, according to western planters. The Strong brothers insisted that immigrant Chinese workers in the West presented an elegant solution to the so-called problem of free black labor in the South. John L. Strong made his case by drawing on common tropes of Chinese immigrants as industrious, feminized, and readily available. Compared to recently emancipated slaves, Chinese laborers were "less expensive," "controlled with less difficulty," and generally "more efficient," as he explained to a correspondent in Kentucky.[20] These cotton experiments thus constituted both an endorsement of western agriculture and a small-scale revolt against the post-emancipation order in the South.

The Strongs' interest in Chinese labor coincided with a similar movement unfolding in the former slave states. Shortly after the war, a group of sugar planters, statesmen, and intellectuals began clamoring for the importation of Asian laborers to staff their old slave plantations.[21] The motivating force behind this interest in Asian indentured labor was not difficult to discern. According to Frederick Douglass, "coolie" importation was merely the latest form of anti-abolitionism. "The loss of the negro is to gain them the Chinese," Douglass lamented, "and if the thing works well, abolition, in their opinion, will have proved itself to be another blessing in disguise."[22] African American leaders in California also tracked this southern development with alarm, seeing in these plans an "unrelenting spirit of oppression" designed to "keep up the distinction of caste, which the fruits of Emancipation and Enfranchisement would soon have obliterated."[23]

Neither project, however, matched the expectations of its boosters. The program for coolie importation into the South eventually petered out, while fantasies of a new cotton kingdom in the West ultimately came to naught, despite the Strong brothers' best efforts. The combination of a labor shortage and California's distance from major markets proved fatal for the crop, which planters had largely abandoned by the late 1870s.[24]

The Strong brothers created a brief sensation with their cotton experiments, but they were not the most famous planters to arrive in postwar California. That distinction belonged to William Gwin. In the spring of 1865, few would have predicted that Gwin could ever return to politics in the West. For the second time in the course of four years, he had been imprisoned on suspicion of treason. He remained under guard at Fort Jackson, Louisiana, until early 1866, for a total of nearly eight months. California's loyal press had cast him off as a "hoary-headed traitor" and the disgraced leader of the "fallen house of Southern chivalry."[25] Gwin himself conceded that he had no home in his former state. "I do not know where to settle," he wrote to his rebel coconspirator Joseph Lancaster Brent in June 1866. "Like you I cannot go to California which . . . I would prefer to anyplace on earth."[26]

Gwin's aimlessness was short-lived. By late 1866 he had returned to California and, within a year, resumed his familiar place at the center of the state's political ferment. When he appeared in Sacramento in the fall of 1867, he stirred "a sensation among the ranks of the Democracy."[27] Rumors circulated that he would soon reclaim his old Senate seat or that President Andrew Johnson would appoint him to a cabinet position. Gwin disavowed any desire to reassume public office, but he remained an active Democratic campaigner and railroad lobbyist for the next decade.[28] In 1869, he helped orchestrate the election of his son, Willie, to the state senate.[29] The younger Gwin, who had served in the Confederate cavalry during the war, would become one of the leading opponents of the Fifteenth Amendment in California. Until his death in 1885, the elder Gwin continued to attract glowing tributes as a political powerbroker and fixture in San Francisco's high society.[30] In his second career, Gwin not only redeemed himself; he had helped redeem California's Democratic Party.

The Limits of Emancipation

The collapse of the Confederacy and the passage of the Thirteenth Amendment brought freedom to enslaved laborers in the South but not to those in the Far West. Despite concerted efforts by congressional Republicans and local authorities, New Mexico's traditions of captive slavery and indebted servitude survived the so-called age of emancipation. The Republican campaign grew from antebellum struggles against slavery in the Southwest, led by Ohio representative John Bingham and *New York Tribune* editor Horace Greeley. Although western masters could no longer rely on a powerful bloc of southerners to thwart antislavery legislation in Congress, they resisted federal intervention by arguing, as they had for years, that their labor practices rested on a voluntary compact between employer and servant. In doing so, they revealed the limits of emancipation and federal authority, even at the height of Radical Reconstruction.

Whereas southern congressmen had blocked all antebellum attempts to uproot New Mexican peonage, their secession and failed rebellion exposed the institution to a fresh wave of assaults. The Republican-controlled Congress outlawed slavery and involuntary servitude in all federal territories in 1862. Abraham Lincoln, acting on advice from Senator Charles Sumner, also ordered his War Department to stamp out coercive labor practices in New Mexico.[31] As its authors framed it in 1865, the Thirteenth Amendment was broad enough to target chattel slavery in the South and unfree labor practices in the Far Southwest. After Lincoln's assassination, President Andrew Johnson, although no Radical, took up the antislavery campaign. He directed one of his first executive orders against the abduction of Indigenous people, what he called a "barbarous and inhuman practice."[32] Meanwhile, Julius Graves, a Radical Republican and Indian agent, advocated for the creation of a special "freedmen's bureau" for New Mexico to protect Indigenous people from labor exploitation.[33]

The US military played an inconsistent role in the campaign against unfreedom in New Mexico. On the one hand, army officers and federal agents stationed in the region routinely exploited indebted servants and Native captives. "Nearly every Federal officer held peons in service," according to Graves. "The superintendent of Indian affairs had half a dozen."[34] On the other hand, leading military authorities attempted to abolish the institution. When a congressional commission visited New Mexico in the summer of 1865 to inspect Bosque Redondo, departmental commander James Carleton defended the reservation as a hedge against slavery. Carleton had forcibly relocated thousands of Navajos, along with hundreds of Mescalero Apaches, to the reservation, where they endured an annual casualty rate between 10 and 20 percent. "Much of the hostility manifested by many people of New Mexico against the reservation system grows out of the fact that when this system goes into successful operation there will be no more tribes from which they can capture servants," Carleton reported.[35] When General William Tecumseh Sherman came to the territory three years later to close Bosque Redondo and shift the imprisoned Navajos to new reservations in their ancestral homelands in northern New Mexico, he too framed his operation as an antislavery measure. Sherman reminded Navajo leaders that the United States had fought a war to abolish slavery and that the military would endeavor to reclaim Navajo captives from Hispano households.[36]

Sherman's actions stemmed from an invigorated congressional campaign to enforce emancipation on a continental scale. In early 1867, Senator Henry Wilson of Massachusetts, a veteran from the antebellum struggle against unfreedom in the Southwest, proposed a federal law to abolish peonage. Leading Republicans, including Wilson and Sumner, had been frustrated by the impotence of earlier enforcement efforts. Authorities estimated that as many as 3,000 Navajos (out of a population of 87,000) remained enslaved. Santa Fe alone contained an estimated 400 captive Indians.[37] Clearly, neither the Thirteenth Amendment nor Johnson's executive order had ended coercive labor practices in the region. Behind a united Republican vote, the new federal law declared peonage "to be unlawful, and the same is hereby abolished and forever prohibited in the Territory of New Mexico, or in any other Territory or State." The law also imposed fines and prison terms on any federal official engaged in the traffic or exploitation of peon laborers.[38] "Upon the publication of such a statute in that Territory," one senator exulted, "the whole system will fall to the ground at once."[39]

Would-be emancipationists drew confidence from the popular mandate they wielded. In the election of 1866, Republicans had solidified their majority by claiming well over two-thirds of all congressional seats, giving them enough votes to override any veto by President Johnson.[40] Their decisive victory helped transform the Radicals from a "determined minority" to a position of "irresistible mastery," according to one historian.[41] Over the next year, Radical Republicans leveraged these gains to secure the military occupation of the South, to advance their program of black suffrage, and to strike against unfree labor in the Far Southwest. If only briefly, they presided over what historian Eric Foner calls an "unprecedented experiment in interracial democracy."[42]

New Mexico's master class would not, however, go gently. They parried this congressional campaign in the same fashion that they had defended against its antebellum antecedent: by insisting upon the voluntary nature of their labor arrangements and through simple noncompliance. Unfreedom in New Mexico was difficult to classify, which made it difficult to eradicate. To Republican congressmen, peons were slaves; but to Hispano landholders, they were often considered kin. Many of these Native captives were *genízaros*—enslaved Indians who had been baptized and incorporated into Hispano households. Although many *genízaros*, as well as their mestizo offspring, had been trapped in inescapable cycles of debt and forced into a lifetime of servitude, their masters nevertheless stressed the voluntary nature of their labor. Peonage, New Mexican elites argued, resulted from legally binding (albeit often unwritten) contracts between consenting parties. They also borrowed the paternalistic language of the South's old planter class to stress the benevolent nature of southwestern bondage. As the Indian agent Graves complained, "The arguments to sustain the system are the same as those formerly used in behalf of [southern] slavery." New Mexicans also claimed that federal interference violated local sovereignty—namely the territory's Master and Servant Act of 1851.[43]

New Mexico's recalcitrant masters found allies in a familiar place: the South. During the congressional debate over peonage, Senator Garrett Davis of Kentucky emerged as the fiercest critic of the abolition act. "I have been for a good many years of my life in about the same state of slavery" as indebted peons, Davis mocked. "I have owed considerable debts and I have worked mighty hard to pay them. All the proceeds of my labor went to the payment of my debts, and I had not the advantage which the peon has; the creditor was not supporting me during the time I was laboring to discharge my debts; I had to support myself."[44] Yet Davis's was a rare voice of dissent in the Thirty-Ninth Congress of 1866–67, in which southern Democrats occupied a fringe position. The fire-eating faction that had blocked earlier attempts to outlaw peonage was barred from Washington in the immediate postwar years. Aside from a few border state supporters like Davis, proprietors in the postbellum Southwest had to fend for themselves.

Republicans enjoyed some early successes in the crusade against New Mexican slavery. Beginning in 1868, a Radical Republican commissioner used the Civil Rights Act of 1866 and the new anti-peonage law to free 289 captive and indebted laborers. Yet the institution as a whole survived this campaign. New Mexican juries often sided with landholders, exonerating defendants accused of violating the anti-peonage statute. As the Radicals' hold over Reconstruction policy waned, so too did the enforcement of the 1867 abolition law. Native captives and peon laborers could be found in New Mexican households into the twentieth century.[45]

Wartime mobilization and slave emancipation created what political scientist Richard Bensel calls a "Yankee leviathan"—an increasingly centralized and expanding US state—on the eastern half of the continent.[46] But in the arid borderlands of the Far Southwest, that leviathan was a fish out of water. In New Mexico, US officials lacked the coercive authority that they wielded over former Confederates in the South. While defeated southern planters were forced to accept slave emancipation as one of the preconditions for their readmission to the Union, landholders in mostly loyal

New Mexico faced no such dilemma. So long as they avoided detection by federal authorities, they could continue buying Native captives and exploiting indebted servants for years to come. The emancipationist project hit a wall of noncompliance in the Far West.[47]

A Referendum on Reconstruction

California Democrats began their comeback by tapping into a widely held fear among the state's voting public: that whites sat uneasily atop a racial pyramid crumbling under the weight of federal Reconstruction. White voters recognized that measures designed to reconstruct the South would reshape the West as well. In fact, Congress extended the suffrage to black men in the territories two months before those in the former Confederacy.[48] In a diverse state such as theirs, white Californians felt particularly threatened by the prospect of a widening franchise that would inexorably dilute their voting power. These threats to white supremacy came in many shades of brown: Hispanos, African Americans, Native Americans, and Chinese immigrants. The Chinese alone constituted about 10 percent of California's population and 25 percent of the state's workforce.[49] Hispano citizens (legally defined as white) had earned at least the grudging respect of many Anglo Democrats due to their long-standing ties to the party, especially in Southern California. But blacks, Indians, and Chinese residents remained political outcasts and the targets of rhetorical and physical assaults.[50]

In the statewide races of the immediate postwar period, local issues generated far less interest (and friction) than national policies. For instance, on crucial labor issues—namely, the eight-hour workday—California's Democrats and Unionist/Republicans agreed. And unlike northeastern Republicans, westerners expended little political capital on policies related to prohibition, prostitution, or trade unionism. Instead, California's electoral battles centered on Reconstruction and the racial and economic policies that it entailed. By conjuring the bogeyman of an overweening federal government, Democratic leaders differentiated themselves from their Republican opposition and rallied white working-class voters. They harped on the cost of Reconstruction in the South, especially expenditures on the Freedmen's Bureau, and what this might mean for taxation in the West. Above all else, they played to deep racial anxieties by presenting scenarios in which the state's nonwhite residents had equal political power.[51] These were the anxieties that united many white voters across the nation and made the Republican political experiment such a fragile undertaking.

As the self-anointed defenders of white rule, Democrats clawed back some of their power in the fall 1865 elections. While Union candidates ran on their wartime records, Democrats made opposition to black voting rights the central plank in their platform. (Because Union Party leaders also vocally opposed Chinese suffrage, Sinophobia was not the political wedge that it would later become for Democratic candidates.) "The negro is about the only staple in Democratic argument," the *Stockton Independent* reported. "Without him the party would be *non est*."[52] Although the Union Party retained control of the statehouse, Democrats picked up seats in Sacramento, San Francisco, and Sonoma. But more valuable than any legislative gains were the lessons learned: race-baiting, and attacks on Reconstruction policy more generally, could provide a way forward for the party. Once in office, Democratic representatives issued a wave of resolutions on federal issues while also introducing more localized bills to prevent the immigration of African Americans into California and to permanently bar them from the franchise.[53]

When congressional Republicans passed three Reconstruction Acts in the spring and summer of 1867, they invigorated the Democratic cause in California. Here was confirmation of white supremacists' worst fears: not only did the acts place the South under military rule, but they had also enfranchised black voters in the former Confederacy while simultaneously barring many whites from the polls. Benjamin Franklin Washington, editor of the Democratic *San Francisco Examiner*, raged against what he called the "great Mongrel military despotism" and the "Five Monarchy Acts," a reference to the five military districts into which the former Confederacy had been divided.[54] Military Reconstruction was an act of naked northern aggression, Washington seethed, born in a spirit of vengeance. "Ranting, raving New England Puritans," he wrote, "hate a Southern gentleman and all his belongings, on the same principle that the devil does holy water."[55] The acts, according to another California Democrat, "crush[ed] beneath the iron heel of naked power every principle of right and freedom [for which] the revolution [had been] fought."[56]

Democratic politicians carried this outrage into campaign season that fall. Roughly half of their platform planks targeted Reconstruction, namely the issues of black suffrage and military rule in the South. Radical Republicans, the Democratic state committee argued, had "imperil[ed] the union by their mad and seditious course." Reflecting growing sympathy for the defeated South, the committee insisted that "the states lately in rebellion should be dealt with in a spirit of kindness and forbearance" rather than by Congress's current "harsh, illiberal, and oppressive" policy. Democrats across the country made similar arguments that fall, but California's ethnic diversity lent a particular urgency to the suffrage issue, which party leaders readily exploited. Voting rights for "negroes, Chinese, and Indians," the California committee warned, "would end in the degradation of the white race and speedy destruction of the government."[57] By linking the Union Party with congressional legislation, California's Democrats turned the September elections into a referendum on Reconstruction.

Opposition to Military Reconstruction, rejection of black suffrage, and sympathy for the white South proved a winning formula in the election.[58] Indeed, this grand strategy catapulted California's Democrats to one of the most stunning electoral reversals of the postwar years. The Union Party held a decisive 65 percent of the seats in the previous state legislature, but when the polls closed in September 1867, the Democrats had gained a twenty-two-seat majority in the assembly. They also won two of the three US House elections. Out of the state's forty-seven counties, thirty-two went Democrat, while Union-Republicans polled a dismal 35 percent in San Francisco, once a party stronghold. Democratic legislators were now poised to elect a US senator in December and to fill most state offices with party loyalists.[59] Although some Unionists insisted that their defeat resulted from internal party divisions and low voter turnout, Democrats knew that their attacks on federal policy had been the deciding factor in the election.[60] By returning the Democratic Party to power, California's white voters repudiated Reconstruction and its race-leveling policies.

The returns of 1867 came as a sobering rebuke for a Republican Party recently on the rise. Twenty states across the country held elections between March and November that year, and Republicans took losses in nearly all of them.[61] In Connecticut's congressional elections, Democrats won three of four available seats, while their candidate eked out a narrow victory in the gubernatorial contest. Ohio's voters struck down a state constitutional amendment that would have enfranchised black men and barred "disloyal" whites from the polls. And in New York and New Jersey, Republicans lost dozens of legislative seats. Yet what were setbacks for Republicans in most states was an utter rout in California. Only in California did Unionist-Republicans lose the governorship, the statehouse, *and* their congressional majority. In no other free state did the Democratic gubernatorial candidate win by a larger margin than California's Henry Huntly Haight, who beat his opponent, George Gorham, by more than ten percentage points.[62]

The political forecast was gloomy for Republicans across much of the West. Following California, Oregon's Democrats took back the legislature in 1868 and rescinded the state's earlier ratification of the Fourteenth Amendment. Other western states and territories expressed a similar distaste for Reconstruction policy. Voters in Kansas, for instance, struck down a referendum on black suffrage in 1867, while Indiana ousted its Republican leadership three years later. Minnesota was the only western state to grant African American voting rights before the Fifteenth Amendment made it national law, and only after rejecting the measure in two previous referenda. Black leaders in California, Nevada, Kansas, and Colorado petitioned their state legislatures for greater civil and political rights. But western politicians, unwilling to imperil their chances at reelection, tabled all of their appeals.[63]

The 1867 defeat proved fatal to California's Union Party, which soon dissolved. The party's downfall stemmed from several strategic miscalculations. When gubernatorial candidate George Gorham attempted to set the moral direction for his fellow Unionists by appealing to the "universal brotherhood of man," he played into the hands of his race-baiting opposition.[64] Union candidates, never able to parry the damning Democratic critique that they had abandoned the white voter, largely ignored national issues in 1867. Members of the now-defunct Union Party who did not defect to the Democrats soon adopted the Republican banner. The reconstituted Republicans would eventually enjoy some electoral success, but only after shedding the racially progressive ideals of the wartime era and crafting a new image based on the hard experiences of 1867. There would be no "brotherhood of man" in California politics for decades to come.[65]

Taking the long view of California history, the Union Party can be seen as the product of wartime exigencies, an aberration in the state's long-running association with the white South. California's electoral politics were tightly bound up with white supremacy and hostile to the progressive policies of the Republican postwar order. Within this climate, the Union Party lacked the blueprint for a political future. That future belonged to the Democrats and their politics of white retrenchment. From this perspective, the Democratic victories of the late 1860s look less like a "political revolution," as one historian has suggested, and more like a return to the political dispensation that had long prevailed in California.[66] This was redemption, not revolution.[67]

California's Southern Revival

By 1867 white Californians were eager to bury the past. Although Republicans continued to blame Democrats for secession and the ravages of the war, their strategy yielded diminishing returns.[68] Treason had lost much of its odiousness for California's electorate. Reconciliation, rather than revenge, had become a byword for many state leaders. Through a sort of political alchemy, Democrats transformed the white South from traitorous

An example of the race-baiting, anti-Reconstruction tactics that carried the California Democratic Party to victory in 1867. This Democratic campaign cartoon mocks the supposed racial egalitarianism of the state's Unionist coalition. The Union Party gubernatorial candidate, George Gorham, stacks ethnic minorities—an African American, a Chinese immigrant, and a Native American—on his shoulders. Even a monkey prepares to clamber up. Gorham lost to his Democratic opponent by more than ten percentage points, the widest margin of any gubernatorial contest in a former free state that year. "The Reconstruction Policy of Congress, as Illustrated in California," Library of Congress, Prints and Photographs Division, LC-USZC4–5758.

aggressor into helpless victim. This was a national process, but in California, support for the former Confederate states proved especially robust. Spurring this southern revival were members of the so-called fallen house of Chivalry, including William Gwin and Benjamin Franklin Washington, who embarked on second careers in the postwar era. California statesmen linked sympathy for former rebels with a warning that the reforms imposed on the South might soon migrate west.[69]

At the center of this shift in public opinion was the newly elected governor, Henry Huntly Haight. Haight took a roundabout path to the top of the Democratic Party. A supporter of the Republican presidential candidate John C. Frémont in 1856, Haight went on to serve as the party's state chairman four years later during Lincoln's campaign. But less than a month into the war, he shed his previous affiliations, denounced Lincoln's war machine, and began a dramatic pivot to the Democratic fold, citing northern military coercion as the reason for his political transformation.[70] When his adopted party mounted its comeback in the postwar years, Haight emerged as one of the most forceful Democratic speakers in the state, especially on the issues of Military Reconstruction and black suffrage. During the 1867 campaign, Haight harped on Radical Reconstruction in a series of rallies held around San Francisco and Sacramento, fashioning himself as the "anti-black, states' rights spokesman for the West."[71]

Haight may have been born in Rochester, New York, but his sympathies now lay with the Deep South. Before enthusiastic crowds he conjured the image of a vindictive and bullying national government, exacting undue vengeance on the former Confederate states long after the war had ended. "The South seceded, was conquered, and now lies helpless and bleeding at every pore," he pleaded.[72] Instead of vengeance, he called for "a spirit of broad, catholic patriotism that knows no North, no South, no East, no West."[73] Haight's position on state rights sharpened his support for the South. He claimed that amendments could be made only to limit, and not to extend, the powers originally granted by the Constitution. Even John C. Calhoun, some Republicans argued, did not go so far in defense of state sovereignty.[74] Because of Reconstruction, Haight declared, the nation was falling victim to "the worst form of despotism," or what he would later call "a congressional absolutism."[75]

State rights were sacrosanct, according to Haight—especially when it came to the right to deny suffrage to nonwhites. Haight devoted much of his inaugural address to this issue. White southerners had been stripped of their constitutional rights and subjected to military despotism, he claimed, which devolved "political control to a mass of negroes just emancipated and almost as ignorant of political duties as the beasts of the field."

The federal policy of Reconstruction, he elaborated, was the "subversion of all civil government under military rule, the abolition of those personal rights guaranteed by the Constitution," and "the subjection of the white population of the Southern States, men, women, and children, to the domination of a mass of ignorant negroes just freed from slavery." The former Confederacy, Haight fulminated, amounted to nothing more than "negro States," dangerously close to becoming "another St. Domingo on our Southern border."[76]

Haight's message struck a chord with anxious whites in the West and South alike. After reading the text of one of Haight's political addresses, a woman in Nashville, Tennessee, wrote directly to the California governor to express her appreciation. She congratulated Haight on his effective leadership and thanked him for his enduring support of the South. "Like everything from your pen," she wrote in June 1868, the speech conveyed "*true* patriotism, justice, and integrity, and gives us *down trodden* people *some hope* of a bright future."[77] That same month, a correspondent from New Orleans confided in Haight: "Between the 'cotton wound' and the Radicals, poor Louisiana has suffered a perfect martyrdom." That martyrdom included, most egregiously, the political elevation of black men over their former masters, a system enforced by strict federal oversight. "So you see how we are persecuted," the writer added, "having strangers, and negroes in office, to rule us, and make laws for us."[78] Embittered rebels knew they had a sympathetic audience in the California governor.

While Haight could occasionally out-Calhoun even Calhoun himself in his attacks on federal authority, no Californian surpassed Benjamin Franklin Washington in his devotion to the former slave states. Washington's Old Southern pedigree ran deep. The scion of a slaveholding Virginia family and a lineal descendent of the first president's brother, Washington carried his planter allegiances to California when he moved west during the gold rush. He rose to prominence within the Chivalry faction, editing one of the party's newspapers and securing top patronage appointments through William Gwin. Like several Chivalry leaders, he once dueled a political adversary, though neither combatant was seriously hurt in the affair. Washington retired from the public eye during the war, likely to avoid running afoul of the government because of his Confederate sympathies. He reemerged by June 1865 to take on the editorship of the *San Francisco Examiner*. (The *Examiner* had previously gone under the name of the *Democratic Press*, a fiercely anti-Lincoln paper, until it was destroyed by a mob of Unionists in the wake of the president's assassination.)[79] Under Washington's watch, the *Examiner* would rise from the ashes, quite literally, to become the leading Democratic newspaper in the state. Washington also transformed it into a mouthpiece for the revisionist interpretation of the Civil War, known as the "Lost Cause."[80]

Like the *Examiner* itself, the myth of the Lost Cause was born shortly after the war. The Confederate apologist Edward Pollard articulated some of the major themes of the Lost Cause in his book of the same name, published in 1866.[81] Over the coming decades, a diverse cast of writers, artists, orators, and politicians added to the mythology of the Confederacy, as they sought to craft a sympathetic public memory of the war and imbue the rebellion with romance and dignity. Their contributions embraced a core set of tenets. They denied the central role of slavery in triggering secession; they blamed the war on abolitionists in the North rather than on fire-eaters in the South; they exalted the gallantry of the common Confederate soldier and the virtues of their commanders; they dismissed the Union victory as a nearly inevitable consequence of sheer numbers and resources; and they looked back nostalgically on the era of plantation slavery.[82]

Through the pages of Washington's *Examiner*, one can trace the emergence of the Lost Cause in the American West. Like other Confederate apologists, Washington blamed northern abolitionists rather than southern rebels for the outbreak of the war. "We believe now, and always shall believe," he wrote, "that the recent war was unnecessary, uncalled for, and wicked in its inception."[83] Washington filled his columns with praise for Confederate soldiers in their struggle against the Yankee juggernaut. "No men ever embarked in a cause with a more thorough conviction of right and justice than did they," he argued. "No men conscious of wrong could ever have made the heroic and prolonged resistance against such overwhelming odds."[84] The real rebels, Washington insisted, were Radical Republicans. To call the current Congress "the hell-spawn of civilization," he spat, is "a slander on the infernal regions."[85] He also penned tributes to deceased slaveholding luminaries such as John C. Calhoun and defended Jefferson Davis, calling his trial for treason a "shameful, disgraceful and contemptible farce."[86] In his more sober moods, Washington invoked familiar tropes of reconciliation. "'Let the dead past bury the dead,'" he insisted, as we "shak[e] hands over the graves of common brothers and countrymen."[87]

As slavery's staunchest postmortem apologist within California, Washington infused the *Examiner* with nostalgia for the Old South. The San Francisco *Elevator*, California's leading African American newspaper, noted that Washington "would doubtless like to see the old era re-established, and slavery triumphant over the land."[88] Just a few days earlier, Washington had written in praise of human bondage, what he called the "negro birthright." The institution, he argued, granted each black person "the protecting care and guardianship of his master who provided for all his wants, and made him a useful member of the community." Now, "with an insane love for the negro," Yankees had uprooted this benevolent and prosperous order and attempted to "force" freedom on blacks, which would bring them "nothing but wretchedness and misery."[89] In Washington's view, African-descended people were "not only totally incapable of self-government, but wholly unfit to be free."[90] While many southerners in the immediate post-war years sought to distance themselves from their slaveholding pasts, Washington embraced the institution. He was perhaps less reconstructed than Jefferson Davis himself, who all but erased the issue of slavery from his memoir of the war.[91]

Yet Washington was no maverick. He edited the leading Democratic paper in California and represented many of the views of the state's most powerful party. Although the overtly proslavery Chivalry faction had crumbled during the war, the leaders and the ideology of that fallen house proved surprisingly resilient. The most detailed study of Democratic politics in post–Civil War California reveals that native southerners continued to wield disproportionate influence within the state. Of the seventeen Democrats identified as the party's most influential leaders, more than half hailed from former slave states. Only seven, including Haight, were born in free states.[92] Through luminaries like Washington, elements of the Old South survived in the postwar West.

Retreat from Reconstruction

California's Democrats, armed with a popular mandate, led the West in the struggle against Reconstruction. They accelerated that campaign in December 1867 with a wave of resolutions opposing the military occupation of the South.[93] Several months later, they issued one of their fiercest declarations yet: "Resolved, That it is not only the patriotic duty, but the deliberate purpose of the democratic party *never to submit* to be governed by negroes, nor by those claiming to be elected by negro suffrage."[94] California's lawmakers were flirting with rebellion. Democrats suited their actions to their words over the next two years, refusing to ratify the Fourteenth Amendment and then overwhelmingly rejecting the Fifteenth.

The Fourteenth Amendment, Democrats warned, would topple California's racial hierarchy. John Bingham, the Ohio congressman who led the antebellum campaign against New Mexico's slave code, drafted much of the amendment. The measure granted citizenship rights and equal protection under the law to "all persons born or naturalized in the United States."[95] Although the amendment's architects primarily intended to benefit the freedpeople of the South, California Democrats argued that it would empower Chinese and Native American residents as well. Even some lawmakers in Washington considered California's unique racial landscape when debating the law. "What is its length and breadth?" Senator Edgar Cowan of Pennsylvania asked. "Is the child of the Chinese immigrant in California a citizen?" Senator James Rood Doolittle of Wisconsin feared that the amendment "would bring in all the Digger Indians of California."[96] California Democrats also complained about the clause barring former Confederate officers and government officials from holding state or federal positions. These measures, Senator Eugene Casserly argued, constituted a Radical "negro supremacy" conspiracy.[97]

California Democrats' battle against the Fourteenth Amendment was hardly a battle at all. After winning the necessary two-thirds majority in Congress, the amendment was sent to the states for ratification, arriving in the summer of 1866, while California's legislature was in recess. The Union Party governor could have called a special session to consider the amendment, but—perhaps realizing that his ailing party could not survive such a contest—he left the issue for the next legislature.[98] With Democrats in control of that session, the amendment never came up for a full vote. California was the only former free state that did not ratify the Fourteenth Amendment before the end of the decade.[99] Not until 1959 would legislators extend a token ratification.

When the Fifteenth Amendment came before the states for ratification in late 1869, California Democrats again complained about federal overreach and the subordinate status of the South and West. The law, which would extend voting rights to all black men, was unpopular across large swaths of the country, but California's ethnic diversity made it especially unpalatable to many white voters there. Democrats warned that the amendment would also enfranchise California's Chinese workers, despite assurances from Republicans that Chinese immigrants could never vote, because they were legally barred from citizenship. Reconstruction had made a colony of former Confederate states, Senator Casserly warned, and now its sinister effects were moving west. "California, is governed at Washington," he argued, "very much in the spirit in which old Rome, in her decline, might govern a distant province by a pro-consul."[100]

State senator Willie Gwin was the first within the legislature to speak out against the amendment. The former Confederate cavalryman and son of the old Chivalry leader warned that if the measure passed, California would "degenerate into a government of mixed races." The Reconstruction of the South would be replicated in California, he continued. "The only difference will be the substitution of the Chinaman for the negro."[101] John S. Hager followed on Gwin's comments, blending appeals for sectional reconciliation with racist metaphors. "I do not think the donkey is the equal of the thoroughbred," he argued, "nor do I think our radical Congress can legislate him into a horse, or into social equality with the horse."[102]

Gwin's and Hager's jeremiads sealed the inevitable. The California legislature rejected the amendment by an overwhelming eighty-one to sixteen vote.[103] Just one assemblyman, a Republican, defended black voting rights during the deliberations. And he did so only while emphasizing his belief in the natural inferiority of African Americans.[104] California would not ratify the Fifteenth Amendment until 1962, the only free state to withhold support for so long.

California's campaign against black suffrage took place not just within the statehouse but also in polling places across the state. Clerks in Sacramento, San Joaquin, Santa Clara, and San Francisco Counties refused to register black voters. They did so in defiance of the Fifteenth Amendment, which had become national law in February 1870.[105] State attorney general Jo Hamilton, a native of Kentucky, endorsed these violations of African American voting rights. In a letter to the clerk of Nevada County, Hamilton advised "against the registration of negroes." According to Hamilton, "the so-called Fifteenth Amendment" was not "self-operative"; it required confirmation in the California Constitution itself in order to become enforceable within the state. Until then, he insisted, it was the "duty" of county clerks to prevent the registration of aspiring black voters.[106] During his tenure as state attorney general, Hamilton also attacked the Civil Rights Act of 1866 and claimed that the *Dred Scott* decision remained the law of the land. "The term 'citizen' does not include 'negroes' or mulattoes," he concluded.[107]

Judge Ygnacio Sepulveda of the County Court of Los Angeles reinforced Hamilton's interpretation of the Fifteenth Amendment in a dubious ruling one month later. Lewis Green, an African American, had filed for a court order to secure his place on the voting registry. In the spring of 1870, he took his case before Sepulveda, citing his new constitutional right. Sepulveda struck down the request. Like Hamilton, Sepulveda ruled that further "legislative enactments" would be necessary to secure black voting rights. The amendment, he continued, "cannot punish its violation, and hence it is not self-executing; for really it has no *modus operandi*, and cannot be enforced."[108] With the blessings of county judges as well as the attorney general, state officials brought proto–Jim Crow strategies of disenfranchisement to the Pacific coast.

Black Politics and Anti-Chinese Violence
in the Age of Emancipation

The black struggle for political rights, like the white backlash it inspired, unfolded on a continental scale. African Americans waged their fiercest campaigns in the post-emancipation South, but greater attention on the cognate battles in the Far West reveals a broader, more nuanced movement than the standard narrative allows.[109] As California grappled with Reconstruction policy, the state's black leaders renewed a political campaign that had lagged under Chivalry control in the prewar years. Centered in San Francisco—the largest black community west of St. Louis—race leaders demanded a place in the political life of the state and nation.[110] Western blacks joined in the national movement for voting rights while also responding to unique challenges engendered by California's demographics. Their path to civil rights would wind between the rock of white supremacist politics and the hard place of a perceived Chinese labor threat.

The postwar bid for citizenship and voting rights was part of a longer history of black political mobilization in the West, dating back to the early 1850s, at a time when many African Americans in California remained enslaved. Black political activists cut their teeth in a prolonged campaign against a pair of discriminatory testimony statutes, which barred African Americans from taking the stand in civil and criminal cases involving whites. The community launched three separate campaigns to end the testimony ban, although the Democratic state legislature ignored all of its petitions. To better identify and pursue black needs within California, the First Colored Convention assembled in November 1855. A year later, the state's first black newspaper, the *Mirror of the Times*, appeared.[111] The black community also rallied financially and politically around several high-profile fugitive slave trials within the state, notably the Archy Lee case. Not until Confederate secession and the wartime ascent of the Republican Party, however, would African Americans have allies within the state legislature. By 1863 Union-Republican legislators, responding to pressure from the black community, finally overturned the statutes banning African American testimony in civil and criminal cases.[112]

Black leaders transferred the lessons learned in their campaign against the testimony laws to a postwar political order that was at once more promising and more challenging. This was the age of emancipation but also an era of Democratic resurgence and white backlash. To address the trials and opportunities of the times, Phillip A. Bell founded *The Elevator* in San Francisco on April 7, 1865, two days before Robert E. Lee's surrender at

Appomattox and amid a national movement for African American rights. A former correspondent for William Lloyd Garrison's *Liberator*, Bell turned *The Elevator* into the most widely read African American periodical within the state, surpassing the other black-owned publication, the *Pacific Appeal*. Within months, Bell emerged as the most vocal champion of black voting rights in the West. Again and again, he called on both the California legislature and the US Congress to finally enfranchise its "law loving and law abiding, honest, industrious" black citizens.[113]

The Elevator published searing critiques of the state's Democratic leadership, painting them with the broad brush of wartime treason. Bell blasted the 1870 Democratic statehouse as "the legislature of a thousand swindles," a play on the so-called legislature of a thousand drinks of 1849–50, led by the slaveholding Thomas Jefferson Green. "Of what material is this infamous body composed, and who are its leaders?" Bell wrote. "They are traitors and the sons of traitors. Wm. M. Gwin, son of an ex-Senator, *soi-disant* Count of the Mexican empire, and . . . traitor, leads the Senate."[114] Here was a fierce and capable editor who could spearhead the black campaign for political rights and simultaneously challenge the Democratic majority.

Yet Bell also turned his acid pen on less powerful opponents. California's Chinese immigrants—"alien to our customs, habits and language, heathen in their worship, and naturally licentious"—served as Bell's foil for the black population, "with their American ideas, Christian religion, and family connections."[115] For Bell and other black leaders within the state, Sinophobia and black political advancement went hand in glove. These rhetorical assaults stemmed largely from the perceived labor threat caused by rising Chinese immigration. Whereas San Francisco's African American population remained fairly stagnant during the 1860s, the Chinese population had more than tripled. By 1870, the city's Chinese outnumbered blacks by more than nine to one, while at the statewide level, there was a 50,000-to-5,000 imbalance in favor of the Chinese.[116] Anti-Chinese feeling in the black community only deepened with the debate over the Fifteenth Amendment. Democrats attempted to link African Americans and Chinese immigrants by arguing that the measure would enfranchise both groups simultaneously. Bell, in response, insisted that the Fifteenth Amendment would leave Chinese disenfranchisement in place, dismissing rumors to the contrary as "the sheerest nonsense" and a "brazen-faced falsehood."[117]

The driving force behind California's anti-Chinese movement was white workers, not black journalists. Whites had targeted Chinese immigrants since their arrival during the gold rush, but it was not until the postbellum period that racial anxieties gave rise to official anti-Chinese clubs.

The first major organization of this kind, the Central Pacific Anti-Coolie Association, emerged in the wake of a violent race riot in San Francisco in the winter of 1867. Some 400 white laborers drove Chinese contract workers from their jobs on the Portrero Street railway, injuring twelve Chinese people, one of whom later died of his wounds. When ten of the rioters were convicted and sentenced to prison, the newly formed Central Pacific Anti-Coolie Association rallied to their defense and won the release of all ten perpetrators on technicalities.[118]

White southerners played an outsized role in California's anti-Chinese movement. Many of them were veterans of antebellum political campaigns, where they honed race-baiting tactics to achieve a disproportionate influence in the state. Take, for instance, General Albert M. Winn, a former Mississippi militia officer who served under Jefferson Davis during the US-Mexico War. Winn transported several black slaves into gold rush California, and though he sided with the Know-Nothing Party by mid-decade rather than with the Chivalry, he retained well-placed friends within California's proslavery faction. After the war, Winn emerged as one of the leading voices in anti-Chinese politics. He served first as the co-secretary of the Central Pacific Anti-Coolie Association and later as president of the Anti-Chinese Convention.[119] In his presidential role, Winn addressed menacing warnings to the Six Chinese Companies of California, predicting violent assaults that would result from increased immigration.[120]

In Southern California, a pair of former secessionists stirred anti-Chinese outrage through their sensationalist reporting in the *Los Angeles News,* the city's first daily. Andrew Jackson King, who paraded a portrait of Confederate general P. G. T. Beauregard through Los Angeles during the war, served as publisher, while Charles E. Beane, a former rebel officer, edited the paper, beginning in 1870. They portrayed the Chinese as "an alien, an inferior and idolatrous race," pouring into California to squeeze white men out of work and leave "a foul blot upon our civilization." There was no evidence to suggest that Chinese immigrants seriously threatened white people's jobs in Los Angeles, which enjoyed a strong labor market and high employment. Nonetheless, these editorials were followed by an uptick in attacks on the city's Chinese residents.[121]

California vigilantes assaulted Chinese immigrants in ways that mirrored the rash of racial violence spreading across the South. In the late 1860s, California's Republican press regularly reported on outrages committed by western iterations of the Ku Klux Klan and other unaffiliated vigilantes. Rather than target African Americans, these California mobs generally attacked Chinese immigrants and their white employers while also threatening Republican politicians and journalists. Not isolated to a single western state, the Klan and similar vigilante groups also operated in Oregon and Utah, according to several reports.[122]

Whether there were any direct connections between southern and western Klansmen is difficult to discern. Like many paramilitary groups in the postbellum South, self-identified members of the Ku Klux Klan in California operated independently and without a clear governing structure. The Reconstruction-era Klan, as historian Steven Hahn has written, "was less a formal organization than a rubric embracing a variety of secret vigilante and paramilitary outfits showing the marks of their local settings."[123] The nature of contemporary newspaper coverage compounds the difficulty of measuring California's early Klan membership. The Republican press likely exaggerated the presence of the Klan in California in order to tar its Democratic opposition with the brush of southern rebellion. Through the label of the KKK, disparate acts of violence against Chinese workers and churches could be connected to a much broader network of vigilantism. Nevertheless, some California vigilantes did indeed invoke the Klan. And regardless of the labels they adopted, western vigilantes mimicked the terrorist strategies of their southern counterparts in ways that historians have yet to appreciate.[124]

Like southern Klansmen, western vigilantes operated in a cryptic and clandestine fashion, often achieving their political ends through anonymous threats. In April 1869, "another open Ku Klux proclamation, without address or envelop[e], was thrown into the Post Office receiving box last night after ten o'clock," reported the *Patriot* of San Jose, where vigilantes were particularly active. "It threatens a destruction of all the crops of persons employing even a single Chinaman."[125] A message sent to one Rice Eli and signed "Ku Klux Klan" demanded the cessation of "your obscene and slanderous conversations at once, or the excrements will be ripped out of you."[126] Another anonymous writer sent a similarly threatening note to a former Union soldier and correspondent to the *Alta California*, warning that "parties are watching your course" and that "serious consequences" could result from further Republican writings. The *Alta* took this as proof of "the affinity of character between the Ku Klux of the South and the Democracy of California."[127]

Western vigilantes also resorted to outright violence. In an article titled "Kuklux Klan—California Branch," the *Sacramento Daily Union* reported on several raids on Northern California ranches in the spring of 1868. A white mob captured, beat, and "nearly murdered" the Chinese workers on these ranches, carrying away a small amount of money in the process.[128] The spring and summer of 1869 seems to have been an especially busy period for anti-Chinese vigilantes. In one instance, vandals raided a ranch near Santa Cruz, "drove some Chinamen off after horribly maltreating them, abused and terrified the children, declared their intention to Democratize the whole county, broke open the wine cellar and stole, broke and raised Cain generally with things."[129] Vigilantes also targeted churches. When, in 1869, arsonists burned down a Methodist Episcopal church that catered to San Jose's Chinese population, the local press branded it an act of the western Klan.[130] In Nevada City, California, a newly opened school for Chinese children was scheduled to operate strictly in the daytime and on Sundays "so as to avoid the Ku Klux Klan, who are burning churches, and will next attempt to destroy all school books," reported the *Marysville Daily Appeal* in March 1869.[131]

The steady stream of vigilante atrocities in the West and South handed Republicans a stick with which to cudgel their political opposition.[132] Despite the hailstorm of bad press, however, California's Democrats refused to concede that former rebels were responsible for this bloodbath. Instead, they turned the blame back on Republicans. By elaborate contortions of logic, US senator Eugene Casserly argued that the "secret clans and leagues" in the South were proof that Republican Reconstruction policies had failed.[133] According to Edward Stanly, the former North Carolina slaveholder and Republican candidate for governor, the Klan was "merely an organization for mutual protection against negroes."[134] Benjamin Franklin Washington, meanwhile, repeatedly dismissed reports of vigilante violence in the South while thundering against "the infamous atrocities perpetrated upon defenceless [white] people by the infamous tools of Radicalism."[135]

This rhetoric betrayed a deep sense of vulnerability, however. As white supremacists in the South and West recognized, their racial hierarchies sat in the crosshairs of an activist federal government. The same set of laws could unsettle the racial order in both parts of the nation, as the federal campaign against the KKK illustrated. A series of Enforcement Acts, passed between 1870 and 1871, not only broke the back of the southern Klan but also outlawed special taxation of Chinese immigrants in California. Not for the first or last time, California's Democratic central committee found itself in league with the unreconstructed rebels of the South. While the committee paid lip service to the unfortunate "riotous and unlawful combinations" in the former Confederacy, it more forcefully "denounce[d] ... the 'Ku-Klux bill,' as enacted for no other purpose than to complete the work of centralization, and by establishing a military despotism to perpetuate the present administration without regard to the will of the people." In branding these acts "revolutionary and dangerous in their tendency," California Democrats implicitly dismissed Klan violence as a by-product of

unjust federal intervention rather than as the manifestation of a continuing rebellion in the South.[136]

As California's Democrats shrugged off reports of racial violence in the
South and railed against protections for freedpeople, one of the largest
mass lynchings in American history took place in Los Angeles. On the evening of October 24, 1871, a mixed crowd of some 500 frenzied Angelenos—
Hispanos and Anglos, common laborers and local elites alike—pressed in
around a small cluster of buildings where several dozen Chinese residents
had taken refuge. The mob had gathered in response to a brief and dis-
organized shootout between suspected Chinese gang leaders and local
law enforcement, which left two men—one Chinese and one white—dead.
The crowd charged the main building, stabbing and shooting some of the
Chinese while dragging others to a makeshift gallows to be hanged and
mutilated. In total, the mob left eighteen mangled bodies in its wake, including those of a respected doctor and a twelve-year-old boy, a death toll
amounting to roughly 10 percent of the city's Chinese population. Only one
of the victims had participated in the earlier shootout. Of the 500 rioters,
only 8 were convicted of manslaughter and none would serve a full sen-
tence. Represented by former California attorney general and Mississippi
native E. J. C. Kewen, they were released from San Quentin on technicalities
one year later.[137] As in San Francisco in 1867 and in countless cases across
the South, the perpetrators of racial violence once again walked free.

Rituals of racial violence at the local and national level provided a template for the Los Angeles mob. Longtime residents of Los Angeles would
likely remember previous episodes of collective violence—the sacking of an
Indian rancheria in 1847 or any one of the thirty-seven lynchings, mostly of
Mexican men—that took place between 1854 and 1870.[138] Between lynchings and other forms of homicide, midcentury Los Angeles was one of the
most violent places anywhere in America, with a murder rate comparable
to that of the Mexican border towns at the height of the cartel wars in the
early twenty-first century.[139] In short, Angelenos were accustomed to violence and extralegal redress, and when the local courts appeared unable
to extinguish small-scale criminal activity within the city's Chinese community, they saw an opening for mob action.[140]

That Los Angeles erupted in violence at around the same time that numerous southern locales—New Orleans, Memphis, Colfax (Louisiana)—
witnessed their own race riots is not a coincidence. To be sure, the landscapes of racial violence at opposite ends of the country differed in crucial
respects. Whereas fears of labor competition drove anti-Chinese attacks
in the West, political concerns were usually behind the violence against
African American voters and their white Republican allies in the South.

Corpses of Chinese men and boys in the Los Angeles jail yard in October 1871.
They had been murdered by a mob of 500 fellow Angelenos in a massacre that
claimed the lives of roughly 10 percent of the city's Chinese population. It remains
one of the largest mass lynchings in American history. Security Pacific
National Bank Collection, Los Angeles Public Library, CA.

Furthermore, racial violence in the West involved more than a binary
struggle between white and black, as the joint assault by Hispano and
Anglo rioters in Los Angeles attests. Nevertheless, a common denomina-
tor of deep racial anxiety, stirred by the progressive measures of Republican Reconstruction, undergirded both the anti-Chinese violence of the
West and the antiblack violence of the South. And whether in California
or Tennessee, race riots shared a particular set of rituals—inducements
to violence by a racist press, indiscriminate targeting of ethnic minorities, performative public hangings and torture in order to reassert hege-
monic rule, and little or no legal action taken against perpetrators. Racial
violence in both regions also depended on a widespread belief that local
law enforcement was incapable of meeting the need for "public order."
White supremacists, from one end of the nation to the other, refused to be
reconstructed.[141]

Paranoid Sinophobia was not limited to mobs, self-identified Klansmen,
or even Democratic lawmakers. Republicans soon joined the fray. If imitation is the sincerest form of flattery, Democrats should have been deeply
honored by the political strategy adopted by their opponents in the 1870s.

Once associated with the "universal brotherhood of man," California Republicans reinvented themselves by taking a page from the Democratic playbook, reclaiming the state assembly and governorship with a vigorous anti-Chinese campaign.

That campaign rested on a curious contortion of old antislavery principles. Republican leaders argued that Chinese immigrants—universally defined as "coolies" working under near-starvation wages—violated the Thirteenth Amendment's prohibition on involuntary servitude. If postwar America was to preserve its commitment to emancipation, Republicans insisted, these immigrants would have to be barred from the country. In truth, most of the Chinese workers who came to the United States did so under a flexible credit-ticket system and were therefore a good deal more free than California's politicians claimed. Nevertheless, the argument that they were virtual slaves and a threat to free labor in America eventually carried the day.[142]

With feigned antislavery fervor, western Republicans helped drive the nation toward its first immigration ban on an entire ethnic group. The Page Law of 1875, sponsored by a California Republican, barred the immigration of forced laborers and female sex workers from any "Oriental country." Then in 1882, Congress passed the Chinese Exclusion Act, which outlawed the immigration of skilled and unskilled Chinese laborers for a period of ten years. The act also rendered Chinese immigrants ineligible for US citizenship, making them permanent aliens. Three years later, an orgy of collective violence drove thousands of Chinese from their communities across the American West. A bipartisan effort from Congress strengthened the 1882 act, barring virtually all arrivals from China by 1888. Although immigrants would exploit loopholes in the code and patchy US border control, American legislators renewed and reinforced these restrictions for decades to come. Chinese exclusion remained national policy until World War II. The age of emancipation had slipped seamlessly into an era of exclusion.[143]

Conclusion

Reconstruction was a political reordering that unfolded on a continental scale. The former Confederacy may have been the epicenter of the era's struggles, but the South's road to redemption accompanied corollary conflicts that stretched to every corner of the Union. In New Mexico, landholders blunted the reach of the Republican emancipation program. Armed with a constitutional amendment, an executive order, and an anti-peonage law, federal officials finally had the legal authority to challenge southwestern systems of servitude that had bedeviled antislavery activists since the antebellum period. But those of New Mexico's master class refused to recognize federal jurisdiction over their labor relations. They defended debt peonage as a paternalistic system rooted in voluntary contracts, eluding Republican attempts to liberate their workers. A half century after the collapse of chattel slavery in the South, captive laborers could still be found in the households of the Southwest.

As New Mexicans contested emancipation, Californians challenged African American enfranchisement and the military occupation of the former Confederacy. To the state's anxious white voters, Reconstruction came largely as a specter, a series of politically exploitable fears: the fear that the federal juggernaut that purportedly invaded the South would find its way west; the fear that manhood suffrage would give the state's unassimilated underclasses a decisive say in local affairs; and the fear that federal spending on programs for freedpeople would shatter an already weakened economy and deprive the West of needed resources. What made California unique—its racial diversity, marked especially by its large Chinese population—also made it particularly resistant to the race-leveling policies of the Republican Party. California's elected representatives thus repudiated the landmark measures of the Reconstruction era, the Fourteenth and Fifteenth Amendments.

Elements of the Continental South lived on in postwar California. The imprint of the former slave states could still be found in cotton experiments along the Central Valley, anti-Unionist hooliganism in Los Angeles, vigilante terror around San Jose, and legislative debates in Sacramento. The Continental South's antebellum luminaries had largely faded from the scene: Jefferson Davis in prison; James Gadsden dead; Joseph Lancaster Brent retired from public life; even William Gwin in a supporting role to the state's political leadership. But many western leaders still looked to the South for political direction. That cast included William Gwin Jr., the first state legislator to argue against the Fifteenth Amendment; Cameron Thom, the Confederate-officer-cum-Los-Angeles-mayor; and Benjamin Franklin Washington, the proslavery apologist and Lost Cause enthusiast who became one of the most influential editors in the West. Even northern-born politicians in the Democratic fold, like Governor Henry Haight, railed against Reconstruction and received fan mail from the South.

Rumors of the Democratic Party's death, which circulated during and immediately after the war, had been greatly exaggerated. California Democrats staged their comeback by linking their state with the former Confederacy, in common cause against congressional policy. And they pursued a platform familiar to any unreconstructed rebel. Ex-Confederates and California Democrats alike spoke a shared language of local sovereignty, white supremacy, and sectional reconciliation. The retreat from Reconstruction in the West took on a distinct character, given the racial diversity of the region. But Californians employed a combination of tactics, including noncompliance with federal law and racial violence, to subordinate ethnic minorities and preserve a system of white rule that southern rebels would have envied. In the age of emancipation, California voters resurrected the party that had ruled in an age of slavery.

In the Shadow of the Confederacy

·◆·

REVEREND Martin Luther King Jr., standing on the steps of the first Confederate capitol in March 1965, could see a new era unfolding before him. "The end we seek is a society at peace with itself, a society that can live with its conscience," King proclaimed in one of his most lyrical and hopeful speeches. "I know you are asking today: How long will it take? I come to say to you this afternoon however difficult the moment, however frustrating the hour, it will not be long. . . . Not long, because the arc of the moral universe is long, but it bends toward justice."[1]

Roughly 25,000 people had gathered in Montgomery, Alabama, to hear King, among others, speak on that spring day and to celebrate a milestone in the civil rights movement. Many of them had marched from neighboring Selma in a major demonstration for African American voting rights. Their first attempt at a march was blocked by a posse of state troopers at Edmund Pettus Bridge (named for a former Confederate general). The troopers, equipped with billy clubs and gas masks, lobbed tear gas and charged into the crowd, bludgeoning peaceful protesters in one of the most infamous state-sponsored attacks of the decade, known thereafter as Bloody Sunday. When those activists rallied around King on the steps of the Alabama statehouse later that month, standing in the shadow of the Confederacy, they marked a hard-won victory over the Jim Crow regime.[2] To commemorate that triumph, the road between Selma and Montgomery was designated the "Voting Rights Trail" in 1996.

Yet that historic road, hallowed by the footsteps of thousands of civil rights activists, goes by another name as well: the Jefferson Davis Highway.

THE LARGEST Confederate monument in the country is neither carved in stone nor cast in bronze; it's paved in asphalt. The fifty-four-mile stretch of highway between Selma and Montgomery is just a small portion of a road system named in honor of the rebel commander in chief. Stretches of Jefferson Davis Highway run for hundreds of miles through the South, while dozens of markers to the original road dot states across the country—from Virginia through the old cotton belt, then westward across Texas and into California. A Confederate monument that spans much of the continent, the Jefferson Davis Highway is the apotheosis of Lost Cause revisionism.

The origins of this road system date to 1913, when members of the United Daughters of the Confederacy (UDC) unveiled their plans for a coast-to-coast highway in honor of Davis. The road was intended as a rival to the recently announced Lincoln Highway from New York to San Francisco, which was backed by northern capital. Not to be outdone by Yankee entrepreneurs, the UDC sketched out a southern analogue that would stretch from Arlington, Virginia, to San Diego, California. In doing so, the group carried the contest over Civil War memory far beyond the parks and public squares of the South; the Confederacy would be embedded in the very infrastructure of the nation.[3]

The campaign for a Jefferson Davis Highway drew strength from a broader movement to rehabilitate—or rather, to fabricate—a new image for the Old South. In 1915, D. W. Griffith's epic *The Birth of a Nation* hit theaters, presenting a sweeping apologia for the Confederate rebellion and a triumphant depiction of the Ku Klux Klan of the Reconstruction era. The NAACP protested the film and its crude caricatures of African Americans, many of them played by white actors in blackface. Yet this did little to blunt the film's overall appeal to white Americans, who poured into theaters and made *The Birth of a Nation* a blockbuster success. Later that year, the Klan reorganized at Stone Mountain, Georgia, and soon chapters began popping up across the country. Meanwhile, members of the UDC unveiled numerous new monuments to Confederate commanders and common soldiers. The South was rising again—in theaters, in vigilante organizations, in public spaces, and, as the Daughters of the Confederacy hoped, through transcontinental infrastructure.[4]

The Jefferson Davis Highway, while not the continuous coast-to-coast thoroughfare envisioned by its architects, was a monumental achievement nonetheless. Rather than building new roads, UDC leaders lobbied state governments to name portions of their highways after the old rebel president. The fruits of those efforts, carried out over several decades, can be seen in dozens of Davis Highway markers across the country and in long stretches of road that still bear the Confederate president's name. The Jefferson Davis Highway runs through part of Virginia and then along the length of North Carolina and South Carolina. A number of markers line the roads of Georgia, while a long portion of the highway cuts through the heart of Alabama. Texas alone contains over twenty markers to Davis's road. Although signs have now been removed, parts of the I-10 through New Mexico once carried the name, as did a stretch of highway in Arizona. Until summer 2020, Davis Highway markers could still be found in four municipalities in California. In tribute to his antebellum railroad campaigning, several of these California monuments celebrated Davis as the "Father of National Highways." Davis may have failed to construct a great slavery road, but his ghost now graces a great rebel highway.[5]

JEFFERSON DAVIS IS NOT the only rebel with a posthumous presence beyond the South. Dozens of markers to Confederate soldiers and commanders were erected across the Far West in the twentieth century. In New Mexico and Arizona, several towns unveiled tributes to the Texan invasion of 1861–62: a monument to Henry Hopkins Sibley's volunteers at Fort Craig, New Mexico; a memorial to Confederate troops in Phoenix; and another monument to rebel soldiers at Picacho Pass, near Tucson. Although largely untouched by the Civil War, Utah commemorates its southern heritage in the form of Dixie State University in Washington County, where migrants from the slave states cultivated cotton in the mid-nineteenth century. Dixie State once flew a Confederate flag as a school symbol and adopted a rebel soldier as its mascot.

No other free state housed more Confederate monuments than California. Along with five markers to the Jefferson Davis Highway, there were schools in San Diego and Long Beach named for Robert E. Lee; the township of Confederate Corners in Monterey County; a mountaintop in the Sierra Nevada range commemorating Jefferson Davis; the Robert E. Lee redwood in Kings Canyon National Park, plus three other large trees that bear the rebel general's name; a scenic network of rock formations near Lone Pine named for the CSS *Alabama,* one of the Confederacy's most feared warships; a plaque to Robert S. Garnett, the designer of California's state seal who became the first Confederate general killed in the war; and large stone memorials to Confederate soldiers in Orange County, San Diego, and Hollywood.[6] As late as 1999, California still contained eighteen active UDC chapters. For comparison, the next closest free states in terms of UDC activity, Ohio and New York, had only three chapters each. California was also home to more UDC chapters than several former slave states, including Missouri, Kentucky, and Arkansas.[7]

Los Angeles, a hotbed of secessionist activity during the war, erected the first Confederate monument in the Far West. Local memorial associations unveiled the landmark, a six-foot-tall granite pillar in Hollywood

Cemetery, in 1925. It saluted rebel veterans who had moved west after the war and took their final rest under Southern California soil. The graves of those soldiers—about thirty of them in total, representing virtually every Confederate state—surrounded the granite memorial. Four years later, the California Division of the UDC established a rest home for Confederate veterans in nearby San Gabriel, the only such facility beyond the former slave states and territories.[8] They called it Dixie Manor. Some 500 guests gathered for the dedication of the home in April 1929. Over the next seven years, twenty-one rebel veterans would pass through Dixie Manor. Most of them are buried in the Confederate section of what is now Hollywood Forever Cemetery.[9]

For nearly a century, California's Confederate monuments attracted little interest beyond the communities who tended to them. That changed in 2017, when a white supremacist rally around a statue to Robert E. Lee in Charlottesville, Virginia, spilled into the city's streets, culminating in the murder of a counterprotester named Heather Heyer. The event sparked a national backlash to Confederate iconography and the violent history it represents.

The rebel memorial in Hollywood was among the first targeted in California. While the granite pillar had remained hidden in plain sight since 1925, an article I wrote for the *Los Angeles Times* in August 2017 brought attention to its presence and triggered a petition campaign for its removal.[10] My piece did not call for such action, but when Charlottesville erupted in violence several days later, the monument's fate was sealed. It was hauled out of Hollywood Forever Cemetery the next week. Also that week, the mayor of San Diego ordered the removal of a Jefferson Davis Highway marker, located in one of the city's central squares. The newest and largest Confederate monument in California, a nine-foot pillar in an Orange County cemetery, met a similar end. Erected in 2004, the monument bore the names of numerous rebels, including some, like Stonewall Jackson, who had never set foot in the state. A 100-foot crane lifted it from the cemetery grounds in August 2019, purging California of its most audacious Confederate tribute.[11]

Now, very little remains of a cause that once claimed a prominent place in California's landscape. The murder of George Floyd in May 2020 was the catalyst for the latest wave of removals. Galvanized by the Black Lives Matter movement, activists swept away numerous Confederate monuments across the country, including most of California's remaining markers and place-names. From one end of the state to the other—San Diego, Bakersfield, Monterey, Hornbrook—rebel tributes fell. The Confederacy's long and curious afterlife in the West has perhaps finally hit its terminal point.

A granite pillar in Hollywood Forever Cemetery, honoring some
thirty Confederate veterans buried in the surrounding plot. Erected
in 1925, this was the first major Confederate memorial in the Far West.
It was removed in August 2017, following the white supremacist riot
in Charlottesville, Virginia. Photograph by the author.

THE STRUGGLE OVER western monuments and place-names is the postscript to a contest—the presence of the Old South in the Far West—begun
more than a century and a half earlier. Shortly after the US-Mexico War,
slaveholders looked to the far end of the continent, envisioning a southern
sphere of influence that would stretch from the Carolina coastline to the
ports of the Pacific. They pursued this vision first through transcontinental
infrastructure projects. Along a continuous band of iron, the "great slavery road" would unite the southern corridor of the country, they argued,
while also providing the plantation economy with a direct outlet to the

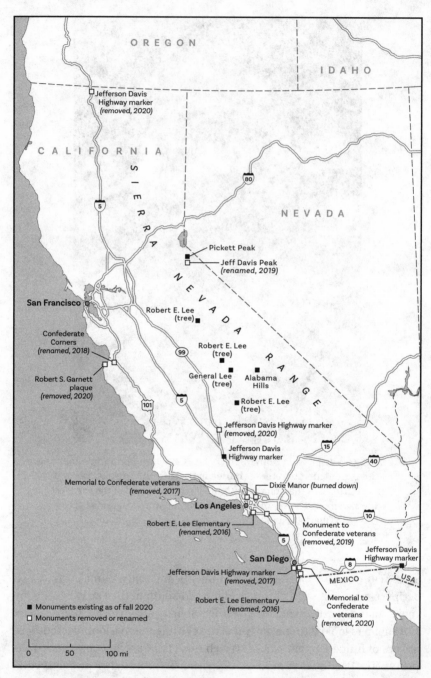

Confederate monuments of California

Pacific trade. Congressional stalemate in the mid-1850s scuttled all plans for a transcontinental railroad. But by leveraging their influence within the executive branch, slaveholders and their allies forged alternate paths to the West. Secretary of War Jefferson Davis and Postmaster General A. V. Brown sent camels, stagecoaches, and settlers across the continent along the line originally proposed for a far southern railroad.

As migrants from the slave states moved west, they extended the long reach of the South. In antebellum California, slaveholders and their allies proved especially powerful. Headed by the Mississippi planter William Gwin, the proslavery Chivalry faction occupied a disproportionate share of the state's legislative seats, judicial positions, and federal offices. California may have outlawed human bondage by 1850, but the state's leaders opened legal loopholes for slaveholders and followed the South on most of the major debates of the era. In Utah as well, slaveholding migrants enjoyed legal protections for their human property thanks to the territory's slave code, passed in 1852. Seven years later, New Mexico's Anglo newcomers and their Hispano allies pushed through a robust chattel slave law, while also licensing other coercive labor regimes in the region. Meanwhile, Anglo-American residents in the southern half of New Mexico, known as Arizona, agitated for separate territorial status with support from congressmen in the Deep South. When the war came, Arizona's migrants rushed into the arms of the Confederacy.

Confederate grand strategy evolved from slaveholders' antebellum ambitions. Jefferson Davis's government launched several invasions of the Far Southwest in an attempt to secure a continental Confederacy while also authorizing smaller guerrilla operations in California. The rebellion's collapse enabled the Republican Party to establish, for the first time, a position in the region. But the party's progressive agenda soon hit a wall of noncompliance in the Far West. New Mexico's master class defied federal emancipation efforts, while California's Democrats stormed back to power by 1867 on a white supremacist, anti-Reconstruction platform. The plantation South had been shattered, but elements of the Continental South lived on. Into the twenty-first century, California's Confederate monuments and place-names spoke to the enduring (if often overlooked) hold of the Old South in the Far West. This is the long, intricate history that *West of Slavery* has sought to uncover.

THAT HISTORY carries lessons as relevant today as they were when Confederate veterans populated the suburbs of Los Angeles. To lay the sin of slavery entirely at the South's door is to ignore the western half of the country and its commitment to coercive labor regimes. Slavery was national in the mid-nineteenth century. Bondpeople of various sorts could be found in the goldfields of California, the households of Utah, the mines of Arizona, and the ranches of New Mexico. Black chattel slavery never flourished as an economic system in those places. Yet it was legally protected nonetheless—a testament to the political dexterity of southern slaveholders and the broad appeal of race-based systems of bondage.[12] Peonage in the Far West buttressed slavery in the Deep South, and together they constituted the transcontinental terrain of unfreedom. To frame the history of American slavery as regional rather than national encourages a misguided brand of American exceptionalism and imposes a retrospective quarantine on an institution that recognized no natural limits.

Conventional wisdom about southern culpability sustains myths of western innocence. Those myths have been deposited like layers of sediment—romantic fictions piled atop romantic fictions, dating back at least two centuries. Since the earliest days of the republic, the West has occupied a central place in the American imagination as a landscape of opportunity and social mobility. As Thomas Jefferson famously claimed, the West belonged to white yeomen, whose economic independence and agrarian virtues would usher forth an "empire of liberty." Roughly a century later, Frederick Jackson Turner's frontier thesis provided scholarly validation for the stories that Americans tell about the West. Purportedly free from the squabbles over slavery that convulsed the eastern half of the country, Turner's frontier was the nursery of republicanism and virtuous self-sufficiency.[13] Meanwhile, a pervasive pop-culture industry—beginning with dime novels and then migrating to the silver screen—embellished these myths of a free and vigorous white frontier. Various bonanzas and technological breakthroughs have only added luster to the shimmering image of the West. The land of gold became the land of the automobile, became the land of film, became the land of silicon. The busts are quickly forgotten, the next boom just around the corner. Through it all, personal freedom, rugged individualism, and forward progress have been the keywords of the American West. Slavery has little place in this story.[14]

Aside from a few surviving Confederate markers, the imprint of slavery is easy to miss in the West's natural and built landscape as well. California bears only a faint resemblance to what it once was. Los Angeles, in particular, has seemingly thrown off its proslavery past and its southern leanings, touting instead a reputation for cosmopolitan liberalism.[15] As early as the 1930s, when a group of aging Confederate veterans moved into San Gabriel's Dixie Manor, fellow immigrants from the South no longer represented a majority of the region's Anglo-American population. At the same time, the black community of Los Angeles was growing quickly and thriving in several business ventures, despite persistent legal and residential discrimination. In the place of the old pueblo, a modern metropolis was rising fast, propelled by booming industries in petroleum, the automobile, and film. The city was beginning to glitter and to drive back the long shadow that slavery once cast over the land.

Amid these transformations, Southern California's Confederate veterans cut a discordant figure. They were, in many ways, anachronisms in a place that pointed relentlessly to the future and busily paved over its own past. Yet here they were, still calling out for recognition of their receding history. Within the walls of Dixie Manor, the Civil War had never really ended. Confederates to the very last, these veterans continued their rebellion in the only way they could—through memory. They honored fallen comrades, recited paeans to their lost cause, and accepted new medals for old service. That they now lived thousands of miles from the Confederate South and decades after the last guns fell silent did not diminish their symbolic significance. On the contrary, their presence in suburban Los Angeles spoke powerfully to the geographic reach and persistence of this rebellion. These aged veterans were, in essence, the last representatives of the Continental South. And so they lingered on, toasting their faded glory, clinging to another century, and, like those who went before them, slouching toward their final resting place beneath the glow of a metropolis forever on the move.

NOTES

Abbreviations

Banc	Bancroft Library, University of California, Berkeley
DBR	*De Bow's Review*
HEHL	Henry E. Huntington Library, San Marino, CA
JDC	Dunbar Rowland, ed., *Jefferson Davis, Constitutionalist: His Letters, Papers and Speeches*, 10 vols. (Jackson: Mississippi Department of Archives and History, 1923)
LOC	Library of Congress, Washington, DC
MHS	Massachusetts Historical Society, Boston
OR	*The War of the Rebellion: A Compilation of the Official Records of the Union and Confederate Armies*, 128 vols. (Washington, DC: Government Printing Office, 1880–1901). Unless otherwise cited, all references are to series 1. *OR* citations take the following form: volume number (part number, where applicable): page number.
PJD	Lynda Lasswell Crist et al., eds. *The Papers of Jefferson Davis*, 14 vols. (Baton Rouge: Louisiana State University Press, 1971–2015).
SHC-UNC	Southern Historical Collection, Wilson Library, University of North Carolina at Chapel Hill
VHS	Virginia Historical Society, Richmond

Introduction

1. Robinson, *Los Angeles in Civil War Days*, 50–51; *OR*, 50 (1): 472, 556–58, 563–66, 589–91, 643, 993, 996–97; *OR*, 50 (2): 236, 938; Faragher, *Eternity Street*, 385–86.

2. Bell, *On the Old West Coast*, 72.

3. William Need to Simon Cameron, September 27, 1861, *OR*, 50 (1): 635–41.

4. This formulation is adapted from Richter, *Facing East from Indian Country*.

5. Slaveholders' involvement in the Atlantic world took many forms and is the subject of a number of important studies. For bloody slaveholding incursions in the Caribbean, see May, *Southern Dream of a Caribbean Empire*; May, *John A. Quitman*; Chaffin, *Fatal Glory*; and W. Johnson, *River of Dark Dreams*. For slavery's long commercial reach, see Schoen, *Fragile Fabric of Union*; Jarnagin, *Confluence of Transatlantic Networks*; and Horne, *Deepest South*. For political and diplomatic accounts of the South's Atlantic influence, see Fehrenbacher, *Slaveholding Republic*; and Karp, *This Vast Southern Empire*. For the flourishing of southern cultural and intellectual life in the Atlantic orbit, see O'Brien, *Conjectures of Order*; and Guterl, *American Mediterranean*. On the simultaneous growth of southern slavery

and American empire, see Hammond, "Slavery, Sovereignty, and Empires"; and Bonner, *Mastering America*, 3–40. On slavery in the Atlantic and the coming of the Civil War, see Rugemer, *Problem of Emancipation*.

6. Benjamin is quoted in the *New Orleans Picayune* (n.d.), reprinted in the *Arkansas Whig*, January 22, 1852.

7. For important works on proslavery California, see S. Smith, *Freedom's Frontier*; L. Richards, *California Gold Rush*; and Lapp, *Blacks in Gold Rush California*. For the antebellum political history of New Mexico and Arizona, see Ganaway, *New Mexico and the Sectional Controversy*; Sunseri, *Seeds of Discord*; Kiser, *Borderlands of Slavery*; and Kiser, *Turmoil on the Rio Grande*. For Utah and the politics of slavery, see Bringhurst, "Mormons and Slavery"; and Reeve, *Religion of a Different Color*, 140–70.

8. Some might argue for the inclusion of Oregon in a study of slaveholders' far western influence. Antebellum Oregon, after all, was dominated by Democrats, some of whom sided openly with the South on the crucial debates of the era. The state's delegation at the Democratic Convention of 1860, for instance, voted with the slave states on all major issues and supported slaveholders' unrestricted rights in the territories. However, Oregon falls beyond the remit of this study for several reasons. First, Oregon never legalized slavery, as did New Mexico, Arizona, and Utah, nor did the state harbor a large population of enslaved African Americans, as did California during the gold rush years. Second, Oregonians supported a transcontinental railroad route across the free states of the North. Third, Oregon rarely factored into the expansionist plans of white southerners, as did the western regions addressed in this book.

9. Although it treats the slavery controversy only briefly, the most complete overview of the region during this period remains Lamar, *Far Southwest*. On the geostrategic importance of the Far Southwest, namely New Mexico, see Kiser, *Coast to Coast Empire*.

10. Carr, *Pioneer Days in California*, 347.

11. My analysis draws on several key works concerning state formation and the growth of federal authority during the nineteenth century, including Ericson, *Slavery in the American Republic*; J. Larson, *Internal Improvement*; Balogh, *Government Out of Sight*; Edling, *Hercules in the Cradle*; Novak, "Myth of the 'Weak' American State"; and Bensel, *Yankee Leviathan*. For a critique of some of this literature, see Gerstle, "State Both Strong and Weak." On the power of courts and political parties in pre–Civil War American governance, see Skowronek, *Building a New American State*, 1–36. On how personal relationships lubricated major legislative and legal decisions during this period, see Shelden, *Washington Brotherhood*.

12. I employ the term "state rights" rather than "states' rights." The former was the more common usage with the white southerners who so often spoke (even if they did not always act) in defense of strict construction. My thanks to Rachel Shelden for clarifying this point on terminology.

13. On slaveholding modernity, see Majewski, *Modernizing a Slave Economy*; and Karp, *This Vast Southern Empire*. On state rights and slavery, see Sinha, *Counterrevolution of Slavery*; and Huston, *Calculating the Value of the Union*.

14. L. Richards, *Slave Power*; Karp, *This Vast Southern Empire*; Fehrenbacher,

Slaveholding Republic; Rothman, "'Slave Power' in the United States"; C. Brooks, *Liberty Power*; A. Smith, *Stormy Present*, 42, 79–85.

15. The federal government was often most visible in the West, or in the words of Richard White, "The West itself served as the kindergarten of the American state." White, *"It's Your Misfortune,"* 57–58.

16. Lincoln to William Henry Seward, February 1, 1861, in Basler, *Collected Works of Abraham Lincoln*, 4:183.

17. For the ways in which the "long arm of the South" touched regions generally considered "western"—namely, Indian Territory—see Miles, "Long Arm of the South?"; and Waite, "Jefferson Davis and Proslavery Visions of Empire in the Far West."

18. On the theory of "many Souths," see Freehling, *Road to Disunion: Secessionists at Bay* and *Road to Disunion: Secessionists Triumphant*.

19. On contingency in the Civil War era, see J. McPherson, *Battle Cry of Freedom*; for a revision and the concept of "deep contingency," see Ayers, *In the Presence of Mine Enemies*.

20. On the unifying force of the proslavery agenda, see Cooper, *South and the Politics of Slavery*.

21. On the federal government's commitment to slavery, see again Ericson, *Slavery in the American Republic*. On the blurred lines between "southern" and "northern" identity, see C. Phillips, *Rivers Ran Backward*.

22. The correspondence of the California-based abolitionist John Bachelder Peirce is instructive on this point; see John Bachelder Peirce Papers, MHS. See also Thomas, *Confederate Nation*, 9.

23. Major works on Native slavery include Reséndez, *Other Slavery*; James Brooks, *Captives and Cousins*; Blackhawk, *Violence over the Land*; Madley, *American Genocide*; Magliari, "Free Soil, Unfree Labor"; Magliari, "Free State Slavery"; and Kiser, *Borderlands of Slavery*.

24. For a major effort to integrate these histories, see Martin and Brooks, *Linking the Histories of Slavery*. An excellent literature on Native masters also challenges common assumptions about the nature and geography of American slavery. See Miles, *Ties That Bind*; Snyder, *Slavery in Indian Country*; and Krauthamer, *Black Slaves, Indian Masters*. S. Smith, *Freedom's Frontier*, and Kiser, *Borderlands of Slavery*, both situate African American chattel slavery and other forms of labor coercion within the same analytical frame. But how the most powerful slaveholders—the planters of the South—drew these various regimes into a continental defense of unfreedom is beyond the remit of their studies.

25. See the seminal works on the era that remain, for good reason, standards in the field: J. McPherson, *Battle Cry of Freedom*; Freehling, *Road to Disunion: Secessionists at Bay* and *Secessionists Triumphant*; M. Morrison, *Slavery and the American West*; Holt, *Political Crisis of the 1850s*; Varon, *Disunion!*; Levine, *Half Slave and Half Free*; and Potter, *Impending Crisis*. It should be noted that Potter covers the Pacific railroad debates as a prologue to the Kansas-Nebraska Act.

26. In contrast to the abovementioned works, Elliott West foregrounds the West in the major political developments of the nineteenth century; West, *Creating the West*.

27. For important overviews of the Civil War in the West, see Arenson and Gray-bill, *Civil War Wests*; Scharff, *Empire and Liberty*; Cutrer, *Theater of a Separate War*; Josephy, *Civil War in the American West*; and Adams, "War in the West." For recent works that foreground Native peoples in the contest for the West, see Kelman, *Misplaced Massacre*; Masich, *Civil War in the Southwest Borderlands*; Waite, "War in Indian Country"; and M. Nelson, *Three-Cornered War*. For works from the perspective of St. Louis, Colorado, and California, respectively, see Arenson, *Great Heart of the Republic*; Schulten, "Civil War and the Origins of the Colorado Territory"; and Matthews, *Golden State in the Civil War*. These studies join several older monographs, primarily concerned with military operations in the Far Southwest. See Hall, *Sibley's New Mexico Campaign*; Colton, *Civil War in the Western Territories*; Frazier, *Blood and Treasure*; Finch, *Confederate Pathway to the Pacific*; and Masich, *Civil War in Arizona*.

28. William Deverell has argued that this focus on the military engagements in the region has distracted from the deeper meaning of the Civil War in the West. "Western historians look for the Civil War in the West in the wrong places," he wrote. "A skirmish here or there, a real battle in northern New Mexico, and that is supposedly the whole story." Deverell, "Redemptive California?," 64.

29. There have been a few exceptions. Megan Kate Nelson provides brief but useful background on proslavery expansion in the antebellum Southwest in "Death in the Distance." So too does Frazier in *Blood and Treasure*, chap. 1. Frazier, however, focuses on an earlier period while glossing over proslavery activities during the formative final decade before the Civil War.

30. My understanding of empire and imperialism is drawn from several important works. In the American context from Meinig, *Continental America*, 170–97; Hopkins, *American Empire*; Herring, *From Colony to Superpower*; Kagan, *Dangerous Nation*; Nugent, *Habits of Empire*; Hietala, *Manifest Design*; and Hahn, *A Nation Without Borders*. And in a global perspective, from Burbank and Cooper, *Empires in World History*; and Proudman, "Words for Scholars."

31. On Americans' understanding of the concept of empire during the early republic and antebellum eras, see Onuf, *Jefferson's Empire*, 2–7; and May, *Southern Dream of a Caribbean Empire*, 9.

32. Elliott West has encouraged scholars to expand the geographic optic on Reconstruction, while Rachel Shelden has urged historians to trace continuities across the "long Civil War era." I attempt to heed both of those calls. See West, *Last Indian War*, introduction; West, "Reconstructing Race"; and Shelden, "Politics of Continuity and Change."

33. The interconnectedness of the American South and West is more commonly studied from a twentieth-century perspective, namely by historians of the Sunbelt and its politics. See, for example, Lassiter and Crespino, *Myth of Southern Exceptionalism*; Dochuk, *From Bible Belt to Sunbelt*; Nickerson and Dochuk, *Sunbelt Rising*; and Cunningham, *American Politics in the Postwar Sunbelt*. For a study that skillfully interweaves South and West in the Reconstruction era, see Teitelman, "Properties of Capitalism." And for a work that links the oligarchic politics of the two regions during the nineteenth and twentieth centuries, see H. Richardson, *How the South Won the Civil War*.

34. For introductions to the New Western History, see Limerick, Milner, and Rankin, *Trails*; and White, *"It's Your Misfortune."*

35. But for several thousand African Americans, their road to freedom did run south, into Mexico. See Nichols, "The Line of Liberty"; and especially Baumgartner, *South to Freedom.*

Chapter One

1. Thomas Jefferson to André Michaux, January 23, 1793, Manuscript/Mixed Material, LOC, https://www.loc.gov/item/mtjbib006813. Several years earlier, Jefferson endorsed the expedition of John Ledyard, who proposed to travel overland through Russia, across the Bering Strait, then across North America to Virginia. Ledyard was arrested in Russia in 1788, ending his North American mission before he even reached the continent.

2. See Kupperman, *Jamestown Project*, 150–58; and Mancall, *Fatal Journey.*

3. Such efforts distinguish Jefferson as the first American statesman to direct national attention toward the other end of the continent—or in the words of Henry Nash Smith, "the intellectual father of the American advance to the Pacific." H. Smith, *Virgin Land*, 15.

4. Thomas Jefferson to Meriwether Lewis, June 20, 1803, in Thwaites, *Original Journals of the Lewis and Clark Expedition*, 7:247–52. See also Thomas Jefferson to Meriwether Lewis, July 4, 1803, Manuscript/Mixed Material, LOC, https://www .loc.gov/item/mtjbib012551; Jefferson to Congress, January 18, 1803, LOC, http:// hdl.loc.gov/loc.mss/mtj.mtjbib012083; and Onuf, *Jefferson's Empire*, 118.

5. Melville, *Moby Dick*, 452.

6. David Igler's important account of the early Pacific world, for instance, casts South Carolina senator George McDuffie as a stand-in for slaveholding apathy toward Asian trade; Igler, *Great Ocean*, 126. For one of the most complete studies of American trade in the Pacific during this period, see Pletcher, *Diplomacy of Involvement*. Pletcher, however, deals only briefly with American slaveholders.

7. See introduction, note 5.

8. As historian Bruce Cumings argues, "Most of the American literature on international affairs remains deeply imbued with Atlanticism," while "the concerns of western historians come to a creaking halt when they hit the shoreline—they barely get their toes wet in the Pacific. The American West and America in the Pacific are two entirely different literatures." Cumings, *Dominion from Sea to Sea*, ix, xix, 476. For another critique of the literature's Atlantic orientation, see Hahn, "Slave Emancipation, Indian Peoples and the Projects of the New American Nation State," n11; and Hahn, *Nation Without Borders*. For a powerful corrective, see Igler, *Great Ocean*.

9. Quoted in Graebner, *Empire on the Pacific*, 70. See also Andrew Jackson, "Notes for Instructions to Joel Roberts Poinsett," August 13, 1829, in Feller, *Papers of Andrew Jackson Digital Edition*, https://rotunda.upress.virginia.edu/founders /JKSN-01-07-02-0267.

10. Torget, *Seeds of Empire*, 137–78.

11. Memucan Hunt to Richard A. Irion, April 13, 1838, in Garrison, *Diplomatic*

Correspondence, 2:323–25. See also "Memucan Hunt, of Texas," *DBR* 13 (October 1852): 416–19; and Bonner, *Mastering America*, 23–27.

12. "Inaugural Address of President Mirabeau Lamar, November 10, 1838," in Gulick, *Papers of Lamar*, 2:320.

13. David G. Burnet to James Treat, August 19, 1839, in Garrison, *Diplomatic Correspondence*, 2:476–77.

14. See Lamar's "Notes for the Inaugural Address on the Annexation of Texas" in Gulick, *Papers of Lamar*, 2:324–28; also Torget, *Seeds of Empire*, 204–6.

15. Webster's comment is quoted in a letter from James Reily to Anson Jones, March 11, 1842, in Garrison, *Diplomatic Correspondence*, 2:540–42.

16. Quoted in Binkley, *Expansionist Movement in Texas*, 121.

17. For more on Texas's mounting problems, see Torget, *Seeds of Empire*, 219–54.

18. M. H. D. Kerr, "Thomas Jefferson Green," in W. Powell, *Dictionary of North Carolina Biography*.

19. Ferrier, *Origin and Development of the University of California*, 11–22.

20. Green, *Journal of the Texian Expedition against Mier*, 412–16.

21. Binkley, *Expansionist Movement in Texas*, 23–24; Green, *Journal of the Texian Expedition against Mier*, 412.

22. William M. Gwin, "Memoirs on the History of the United States, Mexico, and California," 1–4, Banc.

23. *Cong. Globe*, 27th Cong., 3rd Sess., appendix, 139. Calhoun's Pacific preoccupations are rarely noted by his biographers. See, for instance, one of the standard accounts, Niven, *John C. Calhoun*.

24. Karp, *This Vast Southern Empire*, 38–39.

25. On informal empire and Anglo-American rivalry in the Pacific, see Brauer, "The United States and British Imperial Expansion." For the navy's role in building an American commercial empire, see Schroeder, *Shaping a Maritime Empire*. For more on the nature of American empire, see introduction, notes 30 and 31, above. For contemporary commentary by a proslavery southerner on imperial rivalry and Anglo-Saxon power in the Pacific, see Trescot, *A Few Thoughts on the Foreign Policy of the United States*, 8–14; and Trescott, "Our Foreign Policy."

26. Meinig, *Continental America*, 170–71.

27. On slaveholders and the American state, see Karp, *This Vast Southern Empire*.

28. Crapol, *John Tyler*, 118–20; Graebner, *Empire on the Pacific*, 70–72; Sellers, *Market Revolution*, 413. Don Fehrenbacher called Tyler "arguably the most resolute defender of slavery ever to occupy the presidency." Fehrenbacher, *Slaveholding Republic*, 126.

29. John Tyler to the Senate and House of Representatives of the United States, December 30, 1842, in J. Richardson, *Compilation of the Messages and Papers of the Presidents*, 211–12.

30. Keliher, "Anglo-American Rivalry," 233, 253. For more on the long career of the Monroe Doctrine, see Sexton, *Monroe Doctrine*.

31. *Cong. Globe*, 32nd Cong., 2nd Sess., 146. See also Gwin, "Memoirs on the History of the United States, Mexico, and California," 68, Banc.

32. For an early example, see *Missouri Register* (Boonville), January 18, 1845,

Ralph Bieber Collection, HEHL. *De Bow's Review* regularly featured commentary on the Sandwich Islands; see "New Fields for American Commerce," 4 (December 1847): 481; "The Islands of the Pacific," 13 (November 1852): 464; A. W. Ely, "The Islands of the Pacific," 18 (February 1855): 213; Dr. Wood, "Our Island Neighbors," 22 (March 1857): 288–93; "The Sandwich Islands," 24 (February 1858): 156–59; and Francis Poe, "The Hawaiian Islands: What They Are, and Ought We to Receive Them?," 24 (May 1858): 347–48. For a treatment of pro-annexation sentiment during this period, see Greenberg, *Manifest Manhood*, 243–54.

33. Parker, *Sandwich Islands as They Are*, 17. Others, however, were equally convinced of slavery's inadmissibility in the Sandwich Islands. See John Bachelder Peirce to Hitty Peirce, October 12, 1851, John Bachelder Peirce Papers, MHS.

34. Dr. Wood, "Our Island Neighbors." See also Poe, "Hawaiian Islands." On health and labor in Hawaii, see Archer, *Sharks upon the Land*.

35. Quoted in Crapol, *John Tyler*, 133–34.

36. Due to logistical difficulties, the final force that eventually arrived in China was considerably smaller. Donahue, "Caleb Cushing Mission," 198; Belohlavek, "Race Progress and Destiny."

37. Tyler to the Senate and House of Representatives, December 30, 1842, in J. Richardson, *Compilation of the Messages and Papers of the Presidents*, 213–14.

38. Keliher, "Anglo-American Rivalry," 238; Pletcher, *Diplomacy of Involvement*, 129.

39. For more on these antebellum antecedents, see Keliher, "Anglo-American Rivalry." Prominent diplomatic historians, however, have largely ignored Tyler's policies and instead date the beginnings of America's China policy to the turn of the nineteenth century. See Fairbank, *United States and China*; Fairbank, "'American China Policy' to 1898"; and McCormick, *China Market*. For the commercial imperialists of the late nineteenth century, see LaFeber, *New Empire*; and W. Williams, *Roots of the Modern American Empire*.

40. Speech of Caleb Cushing before the Mercantile Library Association of Boston, in *New York Herald*, October 25, 1845. See also Pena, "Implications of Slavery and Cotton."

41. Treaty of Wangxia, May 18, 1844; see also Pletcher, *Diplomacy of Involvement*, 15–17; Donahue, "Caleb Cushing Mission"; and Belohlavek, "Race Progress and Destiny."

42. *New Orleans Bee*, May 13, 1836, excerpted in the *Richmond Enquirer*, May 27, 1836. See also Francaviglia and Bryan, "'Are We Chimerical in This Opinion?'"

43. *Cong. Globe*, 28th Cong., 2nd Sess., 218–19; Russel, *Improvement of Communication*, 10–19; J. Larson, *Internal Improvement*, 240–42. For a deeply researched account of the sectional struggle over the Pacific railroad, see Lutzweiler, "Fierce Sectional Competition." My thanks to Jim for sharing his work and ideas.

44. *Charleston Courier*, January 12, 1847; see also "Intercommunication between the Atlantic and Pacific Oceans," *DBR* 7 (July 1849): 22–23.

45. Cotterill, "Early Agitation for a Pacific Railroad," 396–98.

46. James Gadsden to John C. Calhoun, October 9, 1845, in Jameson, *Correspondence of John C. Calhoun*, 2:1062.

47. *Journal of the Proceedings of the South-Western Convention*, 29–41; "Convention

of Southern and Western States," *DBR* 1 (January 1846): 1–22; "Southern Atlantic and Mississippi Railroad," *DBR* 1 (January 1846): 22–33; *Southern Patriot (Charleston)*, May 11, 1846.

48. "Southern Atlantic and Mississippi Railroad," 24.

49. *Journal of the Proceedings of the South-Western Convention*, 14; Cotterill, "Improvement of Transportation in the Mississippi Valley," 24; Schoen, *Fragile Fabric of Union*, 210–12.

50. For the commercial rivalry between New Orleans and other major southern cities like Memphis, see Cotterill, "Southern Railroads and Western Trade," 428–32.

51. Cotterill, 427–28.

52. De Bow's magazine would undergo several name changes over the antebellum period, from the *Commercial Review of the South and West* (January 1846–January 1847), to *De Bow's Commercial Review of the South and West* (February 1847–June 1850), to *De Bow's Southern and Western Review* (July 1850–December 1852), to *De Bow's Review* (January 1853–August 1864). For the sake of uniformity and simplicity, however, the publication is cited here as *De Bow's Review* (*DBR*).

53. Kvach, *De Bow's Review*, 3.

54. Also that year, De Bow, along with Judah Benjamin and several others, formed the Louisiana Historical Society. The society reflected the interests of its founders in the American West and Mexican North. See Judah P. Benjamin, L. Janin, J. D. B. De Bow, J. L. Riddell, and Alfred Hennen to Poinsett, September 5, 1846, Joel Poinsett Papers in Gilpin Family Papers, Historical Society of Pennsylvania, Philadelphia. According to Norman Graebner, "No American publication called the attention of its readers to the importance of Asiatic commerce in more ebullient terms than did *De Bow's Commercial Review*"; Graebner, *Empire on the Pacific*, 130.

55. White, *Railroaded*, 2–3. For more on the sectional character of railroads, see W. Thomas, *Iron Way*, 32.

56. Russel, *Improvement of Communication*, 20–21.

57. Grant, *Personal Memoirs*, 1:37.

58. George Bancroft to John D. Sloat, June 24, 1845; Bancroft to Sloat, May 15, 1846. On the importance of California more generally to the Polk war effort, see William L. Marcy to Colonel Stephen W. Kearny, June 3, 1846. All letters in Captain of Volunteers, *Alta California*, 14–16. See also Graebner, *Empire on the Pacific*, ix, 115–20; Howe, *What Hath God Wrought*, 736; and Sellers, *James K. Polk, Continentalist*, 230–35.

59. Waddy Thompson, *Recollections of Mexico*, 233.

60. Greenberg, *Wicked War*, xvii.

61. "Atlantic and Pacific Railroad," *DBR* 3 (June 1847): 478.

62. Davis recalled this objective in an 1851 speech. *Mississippi Free Trader*, October 8, 1851, in *JDC*, 2:89.

63. James Buchanan to Nicholas Trist, July 13, 1847, printed in *Richmond Enquirer*, March 28, 1848.

64. Russel, *Improvement of Communication*, 13–14; St. John, *Line in the Sand*, 19–23.

65. For a tribute to Maury's international impact, see Wrottesley, *Lord Wrottesley's Speech*. Maury established his position as a leader in his field, first with *A New Theoretical and Practical Treatise on Navigation* and then, definitively, with *The Physical Geography of the Sea*.

66. See Majewski and Wahlstrom, "Geography as Power"; W. Johnson, *River of Dark Dreams*, 298–302.

67. Matthew Fontaine Maury to John C. Calhoun, March 29, 1848, printed in *Western Journal of Agriculture, Manufactures, Mechanic Arts, Internal Improvement, Commerce, and General Literature* 1 (July 1848): 352–58. See also Maury to Joseph Segar, October 4, 1848, printed in *Richmond Enquirer*, February 13, 1849; *Richmond Enquirer*, March 30, 1849; and the annual report from the secretary of the Treasury Robert J. Walker printed in the *Richmond Enquirer*, December 29, 1848.

68. Already by the 1830s, Alexis de Tocqueville found southerners fretting over their declining influence with "the melancholy uneasiness of men who suspect oppression." Tocqueville, *Democracy in America*, 1:381. See also L. Richards, *Slave Power*, 102–3; Quigley, *Shifting Grounds*, 91; Carpenter, *South as a Conscious Minority*; and "Who Profits by Our Commerce?," *DBR* 24 (May 1858): 449–50.

69. "Intercommunication between the Atlantic and Pacific Oceans," *DBR* 7 (July 1849): 32, 36. Some southerners imagined that, after the railroad had been constructed, they would control shipping across the Pacific as well. For more on direct trade and the South, see Maury, *Commercial Conventions*; George Elliot, "A Port for Southern Direct Trade," *DBR* 27 (August 1859): 164–68; "Ship-Building at the South—Pensacola Navy-Yard," *DBR* 27 (December 1859): 710–11; "Movement in Virginia Looking to Direct Trade," *DBR* 27 (December 1859): 713–15; and James Gadsden's remarks in *Charleston Courier*, February 5, 1851.

70. Matthew Fontaine Maury to Thomas Butler King, January 10, 1848, in "Steam Navigation to China," 22.

71. King, "Steam Navigation with China and the Sandwich Islands," 9.

72. Keliher, "Anglo-American Rivalry," 238; Dennet, *Americans in Eastern Asia*, 74.

73. Figures come from *Historical Statistics of the United States*, 251; Pletcher, *Diplomacy of Involvement*, 99–100; Teng, "American China-Trade," 94–96; and Pena, "Implications of Slavery and Cotton," 14–15. For more on the Pacific trade, see Igler, *Great Ocean*, chap. 1; Norwood, "Trading in Liberty"; and Yokota, "Transatlantic and Transpacific Connections," 204–19.

74. G. Wright, *Slavery and American Economic Development*, 84–90.

75. Statistics from Beckert, *Empire of Cotton*, xiv, 104, 109, 114, 119.

76. *Historical Statistics of the United States*, 251.

77. See Platt, *Autumn in the Heavenly Kingdom*; Spence, *God's Chinese Son*; Teng, "American China-Trade," 94.

78. Barnes, Schoen, and Towers, *Old South's Modern Worlds*.

79. On the Wilmot Proviso debates and the sectionalizing of Congress, see Freeman, *Field of Blood*, 142–76; M. Morrison, *Slavery and the American West*, 66–125; and Potter, *Impending Crisis*, 63–89.

80. *Cong. Globe*, 31st Cong., 1st Sess., appendix, 119.

81. *Cong. Globe*, 31st Cong., 1st Sess., 480.

82. James K. Polk, January 5, 1847, in Polk, *Polk*, 183. For similar sentiments, see

Waddy Thompson to Calhoun, December 18, 1847, in Wilson, Hemphill, and Cook, *Papers of John C. Calhoun*, 25:20–22; and R. H. Weightman to Henry Foote, December 16, 1851, in *Cong. Globe*, 32nd Cong., 1st Sess., 754–55. For a detailed study of these debates, see C. Hart, "Congressmen and the Expansion of Slavery into the Territories."

83. *New York Daily Times*, March 6, 1856.

84. *Cong. Globe*, 29th Cong., 2nd Sess., 354.

85. Horace Mann to James Richardson et al., May 3, 1850, in Mann, *Horace Mann's Letters*, 5–7; see also Mann to the *Boston Atlas*, June 6, 1850, also in *Horace Mann's Letters*, 22.

86. Reséndez, *Other Slavery*, 100–105.

87. *Cong. Globe*, 31st Cong., 1st Sess., 1005–6.

88. John R. Bartlett to Davis, December 29, 1850, *PJD*, 4:146–47.

89. Estimates are based on imprecise census data and from contemporary accounts of slaves in the diggings. The figure of 500 to 600 slaves comes from Lapp, *Blacks in Gold Rush California*, 50, 65; the higher estimate comes from S. Smith, *Freedom's Frontier*, 40. See also S. Johnson, *Roaring Camp*, 68–70.

90. Hackel, *Children of Coyote*.

91. Madley, *American Genocide*, 37–38, 51–52; Hurtado, *Indian Survival*, 211.

92. John S. Griffin, December 3 and 4, 1846, in Griffin, *Doctor Comes to California*, 44. Griffin, who came to California with the US military during the Mexican War, traveled with an African American slave, Caswell Wade. For biographical details on Griffin, see Lynch, "Southern California Chivalry," 31.

93. Hastings, *Emigrants Guide to Oregon and California*, 132.

94. Madley, *American Genocide*, 67–102. See also Lindsay, *Murder State*.

95. For reports of enslaved African Americans on the overland trails, see Delano, *Life on the Plains*, 178; Hayes, *Pioneer Notes*, 34–35; *St. Louis Republican*, April 17, 22, 25, 1849; *Brownlow's Knoxville Whig and Independent Journal*, June 23, 1849; and *Fredericksburg News*, November 30, 1849 (all newspaper articles in Ralph Bieber Collection, HEHL). For a brief account of slaves traveling to California by steam, see *Clarksville Jeffersonian*, August 7, 1850, Ralph Bieber Collection, HEHL.

96. If Wise's math was fuzzy, his knowledge of American geography was even more dubious. The California gold mines were north of the 36°30′ line of the Missouri Compromise. Simpson, *Good Southerner*, 87, 104–5; L. Richards, *California Gold Rush*, 35–37.

97. S. Smith, *Freedom's Frontier*, 40–44; Inscoe, *Mountain Masters*. John C. Calhoun purchased a gold mine within the southern border of the Cherokee Nation, using slaves for the work there. Saunt, *Unworthy Republic*, 271.

98. Isaac Thomas Avery to his son, October 14, 1852, George Phifer Erwin Papers, subseries 1.1, box 1, folder 11, SHC-UNC.

99. Avery to his son, November 26, 1852, Erwin Papers, SHC-UNC.

100. *Charleston Courier*, February 23, 1850, Ralph Bieber Collection, HEHL.

101. *Jackson Mississippian*, October 26, 1849, Ralph Bieber Collection, HEHL.

102. Robert M. Dickson to Father and Mother, January 24, 1853; Robert M. Dickson to Margaret Dickson, December 10, 1852, both in William G. Dickson Papers, series 1.1, folder 7, SHC-UNC.

103. *Jackson Mississippian*, October 26, 1849, Ralph Bieber Collection, HEHL.

104. Bell, *On the Old West Coast*, 21.

105. A similar saga plays out in the papers of Robert M. Dickson, who settled in Tuolumne County with his slave John. Like Murrell and Reuben, Dickson barely scraped by in gold country, relying on John's forced labor to make ends meet. See the correspondence of Robert M. Dickson in Dickson Papers, series 1.1, folder 7, SHC-UNC.

106. George McKinley Murrell to Samuel Murrell, September 17, 1849, George McKinley Murrell Correspondence, HEHL.

107. Murrell to Elisebeth Murrell, October 15–17, 1849, Murrell Correspondence, HEHL.

108. Murrell to John Grider, August 24, 1850, Murrell Correspondence, HEHL.

109. Murrell to Samuel Murrell, January 29–February 1, 1851, Murrell Correspondence, HEHL.

110. Murrell to Elisebeth R. Murrell, November 8, 1850, Murrell Correspondence, HEHL.

111. Jesse Holcomb Chaney to Robert Chambliss Chaney, July 10, 1850, in Chaney, "Louisiana Planter in the Gold Rush."

112. Helper, *Land of Gold*, 276–78.

113. Prince to Nicholas Woodfin, April 25, 1853, Nicholas Washington Woodfin Papers, box 1, folder 4, SHC-UNC.

114. Murrell to Sam Murrell, October 4, 1849, Murrell Correspondence, HEHL.

115. The first report of Reuben's death is in Murrell to Jesse Grider, May 25, 1851, Murrell Correspondence, HEHL.

116. See Redpath, *Roving Editor*, 321. For more on the shifting dynamics of slavery in California, see S. Smith, "Remaking Slavery in a Free State," 28–63.

117. Albert to Charles McDowell, May, 15, 1855, Woodfin Papers, SHC-UNC.

118. Undated receipt of slaves' personal earnings, Parks and McElrath Family Papers, Thomas Parks Collection, sub-collection 2, sub-series 2.3, folder 83, SHC-UNC.

119. S. Smith, *Freedom's Frontier*, 51–54.

120. Lapp, *Blacks in Gold Rush California*, 70–74.

121. Haskins, *Argonauts of California*, 70.

122. See the unsigned letter reprinted in *Daily Republican Banner and Nashville Whig*, March 28, 1850, Ralph Bieber Collection, HEHL.

123. S. Smith, *Freedom's Frontier*, 42–44.

124. Peter Green bought his freedom from Thorn for $1,000, though not until 1856, a full seven years after California had outlawed slavery; see E. Taylor et al., "California Freedom Papers." For more on Thorn, see L. Richards, *California Gold Rush*, 57–58. For another case of insecure mastery, see W. P. Robinson to G. P. Dodson, May 18, 1852, Parks and McElrath Family Papers, sub-collection 2, series 1, folder 63, SHC-UNC.

125. Memo of patent, January 15, 1849, Thomas Jefferson Green Papers, box 3, folder 30, SHC-UNC.

126. Sherman, "Sherman Was There," 351–52. For more on the regulations against staking claims in the name of slaves, see Ayres, *Gold and Sunshine*, 46–47.

127. Sherman, "Sherman Was There," 351–52. For more on the encounter, see L. Richards, *California Gold Rush*, 57–59; and S. Smith, *Freedom's Frontier*, 47–48.

128. S. Smith, *Freedom's Frontier*, 48. Sherman himself claimed the episode led to the passage of California's antislavery constitution.

129. Sherman, "Sherman Was There," 351.

130. Quoted in Pletcher, *Diplomacy of Involvement*, 97.

Chapter Two

1. Green's speech near Marshall, Texas, was excerpted in the *Texas State Gazette* (Austin), July 29, 1854.

2. Quoted in Russel, *Improvement of Communication*, 26. On the "bonds of interest" created by railroads, see Majewski, *Modernizing a Slave Economy*, 97.

3. Scholars have been grappling with the relationship between slavery and capitalism since at least E. Williams, *Capitalism and Slavery*. For more recent studies, see Oakes, *Ruling Race*; Bender, *Antislavery Debate*; W. Johnson, "Pedestal and the Veil"; Beckert, *Empire of Cotton*; Baptist, *Half Has Never Been Told*; Schermerhorn, *Business of Slavery*; Beckert and Rockman, *Slavery's Capitalism*; Guterl, "Slavery and Capitalism"; and Rosenthal, *Accounting for Slavery*.

4. William Seward was perhaps the most ambitious imperial visionary of the North during the late antebellum period. And his empire, as Eric Foner has argued, was fundamentally incompatible with slavery; Foner, *Free Soil*, 51. See also Sexton, "William H. Seward in the World"; and Paolino, *Foundations of the American Empire*.

5. Jefferson Davis, "Report on the Secretary of War, December 3, 1855," *JDC*, 2:567–70. See also Green, *Letter from General Thomas J. Green*, 5–11.

6. Memphis Convention Corresponding Committee, *Circular to the Citizens of the United States*, 3–5, 7, 10. See also Trezevant et al., "Letter to 'Sir.'"

7. Russel, *Improvement of Communication*, 47–50; Cotterill, "Early Agitation for a Pacific Railroad," 409–11; Roberson, "South and the Pacific Railroad," 166–67. For the resolutions of a similar meeting in Texas, which also advanced a far southern route, see *Democratic Telegraph and Texas Register* (Houston), March 15, 1849, Ralph Bieber Collection, HEHL.

8. Russel, *Improvement of Communication*, 15–16.

9. Creuzbaur, *Route from the Gulf of Mexico*.

10. Whitney, *Project for a Railroad to the Pacific*, 25–28.

11. Browne, *Report of the Debates in the Convention of California*, 43–44.

12. Crosby, *Memoirs*, 48–49. According to Crosby, only J. M. Jones, "an extreme Southerner," was "persistent about the incorporation of a slave clause in the Constitution," 45.

13. For commentary on the slavery issue before the convention, see *Nashville Daily Gazette*, September 2, 1849, Ralph Bieber Collection, HEHL. For Thomas Jefferson Green's opposition to the antislavery clause, see Green to Thomas Butler King, April 13, 1855, in Thomas Jefferson Green Papers, box 3, folder 33, SHC-UNC.

14. *Constitution of the State of California*, article 1, section 18, 4.

15. Browne, *Report of the Debates in the Convention of California*, 48, 137–39.

Slaveholding emigrants to Tejas used similar strategies after Mexico outlawed slavery there; see Torget, *Seeds of Empire*, chaps. 3 and 4.

16. Browne, *Report of the Debates in the Convention of California*, 143–45 and 147–48.

17. *Sacramento Transcript*, April 25, 1850. Thanks to John Suval for pointing me to this particular article.

18. John Augustus Sutter, Personal Reminiscences, Banc, 198–99. Another delegate observed Gwin's personal strategy: "He seemed to show a consummate skill for ingratiating himself, making friends which aided a good deal to his success afterwards"; Crosby, *Memoirs*, 40–41.

19. For the convention's composition, see L. Richards, *California Gold Rush*, 71; and E. Powell, "Southern Influences in California Politics," 31–32.

20. Gwin's biographer, Lately Thomas, gives a very generous reading of his motivations at the convention, claiming that "Gwin had exerted all his influence to dispose of the issue of slavery decisively and permanently, so that there could be no future agitation of the question." Throughout the work, the only full-length biography on Gwin, Thomas consistently overlooks Gwin's strong loyalties to the South and its peculiar institution; L. Thomas, *Between Two Empires*, 48. In contrast, Arthur Quinn offers a more cynical and sharper interpretation in his account of the Gwin-Broderick rivalry; Quinn, *Rivals*, 67–70.

21. L. Richards, *California Gold Rush*, 91.

22. The plan is discussed at length in Joseph Allen to Theodore Parker, March 14, 1850, P-175, microfilm reel 4, volume 12, Theodore Parker Papers, MHS. See also *Jackson Mississippian*, April 1, 1850; and Beasley, "Slavery in California," 40.

23. Jefferson Davis to Malcolm D. Haynes, August 18, 1849, *PJD*, 4:28–30.

24. "Statement on the Admission of California," August 2, 1850, *PJD*, 4:124. See also Davis's congressional speech in *Cong. Globe*, 31st Cong., 1st Sess., 248–50.

25. *Cong. Globe*, 31st Cong., 1st Sess., appendix, 1485–1504; see also 31st Cong., 1st Sess., 602–4; Freehling, *Road to Disunion: Secessionists at Bay*, 505–7; and L. Richards, *California Gold Rush*, 106–8.

26. See the commentary of Crosby, *Memoirs*, 49.

27. J. H. Hammond to John C. Calhoun, March 5, 1850, in Jameson, *Correspondence of John C. Calhoun*, 2:1210.

28. Wise, *Seven Decades of the Union*, 242.

29. Davis, Speech at Holly Springs, October 25, 1849, and Speech at Fayette, July 11, 1851, both in *PJD*, 4:49, 194. Indeed, the slave states provided nearly two-thirds of the invading US force; Bonner, *Mastering America*, 4–40.

30. Cooper, *Jefferson Davis*, 217. For more on the debate over California, see M. Morrison, *Slavery and the American West*, chap. 4.

31. *Cong. Globe*, 31st Cong., 1st Sess., 451–55. See also Trescot, *Position and Course of the South*, 14.

32. See, for instance, M. Morrison, *Slavery and the American West*, 97–125.

33. For a comprehensive history of the Compromise of 1850 and its broader significance, see Maizlish, *Strife of Tongues*. For a helpful historiographic review, see Woods, "Compromise of 1850."

34. Crosby, *Memoirs*, 41–43, 61. Gwin's election was a narrow one, however,

and even some southerners opposed him; see Edmund Randolph to Tarmesia G. (Meux) Randolph, December 22, 1849, Edmund Randolph Papers, VHS.

35. John Davis, *Union Pacific Railway*, 44; Garber, *Gadsden Treaty*, 23; *American Railroad Journal*, August 27, 1853, 545.

36. Russel, *Improvement of Communication*, 25.

37. *Cong. Globe*, 32nd Cong., 2nd Sess., 280–84. For a brief summary of Gwin's railroad measures, see Quinn, *Rivals*, 142–44.

38. *Cong. Globe*, 32nd Cong., 2nd Sess., 319, 339–43, 469–70, 676–704, 708–15, 767–75; J. Larson, *Internal Improvement*, 247–52.

39. Karp, *This Vast Southern Empire*, 189.

40. As William J. Cooper writes, "Jefferson Davis made his chief concern the great American West"; Cooper, *Jefferson Davis*, 274–77.

41. Duff Green to John M. Clayton, March 12, 1850, read in Congress on January 23, 1852, *Cong. Globe*, 32nd Cong., 1st Sess., 339.

42. James Gadsden to Thomas Jefferson Green, Charleston, January 29, 1849, Green Papers, box 3, folder 30, SHC-UNC.

43. "Internal Improvements," *DBR* 3 (May 1847): 447. See also *Charleston Courier*, February 8, 1851, for more praise for Gadsden's "untiring" contributions to southern railroad development.

44. James Gadsden to M. Estes, December 10, 1851, in *Charleston Courier*, February 7, 1852. See also James Gadsden to Thomas Jefferson Green, December 7, 1851, William Alexander Leidesdorff Collection, HEHL. For his earlier opposition to free-labor measures in California, see *Southern Patriot*, November 2, 1848. For biographical detail, see Garber, *Gadsden Treaty*, 74–80.

45. James Gadsden to Jefferson Davis, May 23, 1853, Jefferson Davis Papers, Transy Library Special Collections and Archives, Transylvania University, Lexington, KY. My thanks to Susan Brown for making Gadsden's correspondence available to me.

46. Marcy to Gadsden, July 15, 1853, in Miller, *Treaties and Other International Acts*, 6:342–47. The official organ of the Mexican government immediately recognized that Gadsden's negotiations were part of a scheme "for the construction of a Railroad from the Mississippi to the Pacific," as quoted in the *Texas State Gazette*, September 17, 1853. See also *Freeman's Journal*, August 11, 1853, quoted in the *Philadelphia Public Ledger*, August 16, 1853.

47. *Philadelphia Public Ledger*, April 11, 1854.

48. *National Era*, March 2, 1854, 34; May 4, 1854, 70.

49. *Cong. Globe*, 33rd Cong., 1st Sess., appendix, 1031–36. Even some proslavery expansionists opposed the purchase, however. William Gwin, for instance, refused to endorse the treaty because it failed to secure a sufficient amount of land from Mexico; William McKendree Gwin, "Memoirs on the History of the United States, Mexico, and California," 68–69, LOC. On land speculation in San Diego, see John McLemore to Thomas Jefferson Green, June 25, 1849, Green Papers, folder 30, SHC-UNC.

50. Garber, *Gadsden Treaty*; Russel, *Improvement of Communication*, 130–49; Schmidt, "Manifest Opportunity"; St. John, *Line in the Sand*, 40–41.

51. W. Brown, *Life of Albert Pike.*

52. "The Great Southern Convention at Charleston, No. 2," *DBR* 17 (July 1854): 97.

53. "The Great Southern Convention at Charleston, No. 3," *DBR* 17 (August 1854): 210–13.

54. "The Great Southern Convention at Charleston, No. 6," *DBR* 17 (November 1854): 491–96, 505. See also *Charleston Courier,* April 18, 1854.

55. "Great Southern Convention at Charleston, No. 6," 502.

56. The convention's resolutions can be found in *DBR* 16 (June 1854): 636–40.

57. Roberson, "To Build a Pacific Railroad"; Russel, *Improvement of Communication,* 190.

58. Gwin, "Memoirs," 72, Banc.

59. Goetzmann, *Army Exploration in the American West,* 262–303.

60. Goetzmann, 266, 278. See "Report on the Secretary of War, December 3, 1855," *JDC,* 2:567–70.

61. Jefferson Davis, *Report of the Secretary of War,* 8–34, 37–39.

62. Goetzmann, *Army Exploration in the American West,* 300–303.

63. "Superiority of Slave Labor in Constructing Railroads," *DBR* 18 (March 1855): 404.

64. Thomas Jefferson Green to the Executive Committee of the Southern Pacific Rail Road, 1856, Green Papers, box 3, folder 34, SHC-UNC.

65. R. G. Morris, "Slave Labor upon Public Works at the South," *DBR* 17 (July 1854): 76.

66. W. Thomas, *Iron Way,* 24.

67. Green to Executive Committee, 1856, Green Papers, SHC-UNC.

68. The payrolls and annual slave contracts of the Richmond, Fredericksburg and Potomac Railroad are scattered throughout the large collection of the company's records at the Virginia Historical Society. I have drawn my estimates from the documents found in Richmond, Fredericksburg and Potomac Railroad Records, MSS 3 R4152 a, folder 45, August 1839; folder 366, March 1858; and folder 422a, January–February 1861, VHS.

69. Kornweibel, "Railroads and Slavery," 45, 55; Marrs, *Railroads in the Old South,* 55–67, 81–82. To be sure, slave labor was not without its risks. Bondpeople could and did run away, could be called back to their plantations during harvest season, and could incur fines for violating local laws; see, for example, "To the Corporations of Bowling Green," April 25, 1860, Richmond, Fredericksburg and Potomac Railroad Records, MSS 3 R4152 a, folder 422a, January–February 1861, VHS.

70. For estimates, see Kornweibel, "Railroads and Slavery," 34–36; Marrs, *Railroads in the Old South,* 55; Yanochik, Thornton, and Ewing, "Railroad Construction," 727. Several antebellum planters owned more than 1,000 slaves, but they were generally spread over multiple plantations. For figures, see Levine, *Fall of the House of Dixie,* 6.

71. Frederick Nims to Horace Nims, December 3, 1837, series 1, folder 1, Nims, Rankin, and Spratt Family Papers, SHC-UNC.

72. See, for instance, Frederick Nims to Horace Nims, April 24 and May 11, 1851, series 1, folder 1, Nims, Rankin, and Spratt Family Papers, SHC-UNC.

73. Gray, *Southern Pacific Railroad*, 85.

74. F. H. King to Horace Nims, June 23, 1850, series 1, folder 1, Nims, Rankin, and Spratt Family Papers, SHC-UNC.

75. "Recollections of Slavery by a Runaway Slave," *Emancipator*, October 11, 1838. The entire recollection was serialized in six parts, appearing on August 23, September 13, September 20, October 11, October 18, and October 21.

76. Richmond Fire Association, Life Insurance Agreement, February 17, 1858, in Richmond, Fredericksburg and Potomac Railroad Records, MSS 3 R4152 a, folder 366, March 1858, VHS. Under this policy, a Virginia master paid $16 to ensure his slave, Emmanuel, for up to $800. For more on slave insurance, see Slavery Era Insurance Documents, box 2439, Registry, California State Library, Sacramento.

77. Marrs, *Railroads in the Old South*, 66. Railroad corporations were in the business of tracking down runaways. See, for instance, a runaway slave ad, unknown publication details, in Richmond, Fredericksburg and Potomac Railroad Records, MSS 3 R4152 a, folder 296, April 1855, VHS.

78. "Recollections of Slavery by a Runaway Slave," October 11, 1838. The narrator himself eventually ran away from the line because "I knew I could not be worse treated than I was on the rail road" (October 21, 1838).

79. Redpath, *Roving Editor*, 136–38.

80. Kornweibel, "Railroads and Slavery," 46.

81. Redpath, *Roving Editor*, 138.

82. A few slaves, however, rode the rails en route to their freedom—most famously, Frederick Douglass. Henry Williams, with the help of Henry David Thoreau, also escaped to freedom via train; W. Thomas, *The Iron Way*, 36.

83. Marrs, *Railroads in the Old South*, 111–12, 154; Kornweibel, "Railroads and Slavery," 53–54.

84. Stroyer, *My Life in the South*, 42–44. During his travels in America, Charles Dickens encountered a similar scene involving an enslaved family hauled to a new plantation via Virginia's rails. "The children cried the whole way," Dickens wrote, "and the mother was misery's picture." Dickens, *American Notes*, 2:17. Solomon Northup was also carried into slavery partly by train. Northup, *Twelve Years a Slave*, 32–35, 58, 92–94. See also Deyle, *Carry Me Back*, 111–12.

85. Yanochik, Thornton, and Ewing, "Railroad Construction," 723–30; W. Thomas, *Iron Way*, 21. On the soaring slave prices of the 1850s, see Deyle, *Carry Me Back*, 56–59. The arrival of a railroad could also accelerate the pace of slave labor on plantations, as one slave man related to James Redpath. Because of the railroad, "it is so much easier to carry off the produce and sell it now; 'cause they take it away so easy; and so the slaves are druv more and more to raise it"; Redpath, *Roving Editor*, 127.

86. Railroads were a boon not only to planters in agricultural areas but also to businessmen in urban ones. In fact, railroads had the power to create towns where none existed before and to transform isolated backwaters into thriving emporiums. On the growth of Atlanta and its relationship to the railroad, see G. H. Stueckrath, "The Cities of Georgia—Atlanta," *DBR* 27 (October 1859): 462–68.

87. [King], *First Annual Report to the Board of Directors*, 17.

88. Marrs, *Railroads in the Old South*, 11–12.

89. Ford, *Origins of Southern Radicalism*, 220; see also Schoen, *Fragile Fabric of Union*, 203–4.

90. For the obstacles to railroad development in the slave states, highlighted by the South Carolina planter James Henry Hammond, see Nelson, *Iron Confederacies*, chap. 1.

91. W. Thomas, *Iron Way*, 20–28; Marrs, *Railroads in the Old South*, 5. For more on slaveholding support for railroad development, see Downey, *Planting a Capitalist South*, 92–117; and Ford, *Origins of Southern Radicalism*, 219–43.

92. Majewski, *Modernizing a Slave Economy*, 81–82; J. Larson, *Internal Improvement*, 226, 238.

93. Karp, *This Vast Southern Empire*, 151.

94. Emerson, "Address on the Anniversary of the Emancipation," 11:125–26.

95. Licht, *Industrializing America*, 36, 117. For more on southern industrialization and slave labor, see Dew, *Bond of Iron*; and Towers, *Urban South*.

96. Karp, "World the Slaveholders Craved"; Karp, *This Vast Southern Empire*, 150–70.

97. See note 3.

98. Beckert and Rockman, *Slavery's Capitalism*, 27.

99. On the fundamental tensions between the scholarship on slavery/capitalism and the literature on the American Civil War, see Oakes, "Capitalism and Slavery and the Civil War."

100. For a particularly thoroughgoing and angry articulation of the differences between the free industrial North and enslaved agricultural South, see Fitzhugh, *Cannibals All!* Also see James Henry Hammond's famous "Cotton is King" speech, *Cong. Globe*, 35th Cong., 1st Sess., 962.

101. *Texas State Gazette*, August 6, 1853.

102. For the rising tide of southern optimism, see Russel, *Improvement of Communication*, 161.

103. *San Antonio Ledger*, July 28, 1853. Magruder was a native Virginian and future Confederate general.

104. Even Hinton Rowan Helper, no friend to the slaveholding class, acknowledged that "it is now generally admitted that the Southern route is the most practicable." Helper, *Land of Gold*, 283–93. His most famous publication, *The Impending Crisis of the South*, in which he harshly criticized slavery as an impediment to the economic growth of the region, was still two years off.

Chapter Three

1. Thoreau, *Walden*, 1:146.

2. Gwin, "Memoirs on the History of the United States, Mexico, and California," 110, Banc.

3. For a typical piece of southern railroad boosterism late in the decade, see William Gwin's speech in the Senate, *Cong. Globe*, 35th Cong., 2nd Sess., 55.

4. *Cong. Globe*, 31st Cong., 2nd Sess., 826–27.

5. Quoted in L. Hafen, *Overland Mail*, 92.

6. Jefferson Davis, Report of the Secretary of War, December 1, 1853, *JDC*, 2:292–320.

7. Masich, *Civil War in the Southwest Borderlands*, 38–39.

8. For intra-regional divisions, see Freehling, *Road to Disunion: Secessionists at Bay* and *Road to Disunion: Secessionists Triumphant*; Sellers, "Who Were the Southern Whigs?"; and Dunning, "Southern Perception of the Trans-Mississippi West."

9. For his most detailed effort, see Whitney, *Project for a Railroad to the Pacific*; and for his continued agitation, see Russell, *Improvement of Communication*, 152.

10. Judah, *Practical Plan for Building the Pacific Railroad*. See also J. Williams, *Great and Shining Road*, 29–36; and Thomas Greaves Cary, "The Pacific Railroad to Its Completion in 1869," No. 19, MSS, Thomas Greaves Cary Papers, MHS.

11. Gilpin, *Central Gold Region*, 14, 32–34.

12. Benton was also critical of the mission to China under the Tyler administration. Benton, *Discourse of Mr. Benton*; see also Arenson, *Great Heart of the Republic*, 28–47.

13. Phelps, *Letter from Hon. John S. Phelps*, 9–14. See also Swallow, *Geological Report*.

14. For De Bow on this route, see "Tehuantepec Railroad, Movement in New Orleans," *DBR* 10 (January 1851): 94–96; "Thoughts on a Rail-Road System for New Orleans," *DBR* 10 (February 1851): 175; and also Kvach, *De Bow's Review*, 60. Initially Jefferson Davis and Henry Foote supported the Tehuantepec option as well.

15. Russel, *Improvement of Communication*, 236–41.

16. *New York Times*, November 22, 1894. See also May, *Southern Dream of a Caribbean Empire*, 139, 156, 160.

17. Aspinwall and his associates purchased a grant from the Republic of New Granada for the exclusive rights to construct a railroad across the Isthmus of Panama; Aspinwall et al., "Panama Rail-Road Company with a Chart Prepared by Lt. M. F. Maury." For more on Aspinwall and Vanderbilt, see L. Richards, *California Gold Rush*, 132–38. On Davis's opposition, see *Cong. Globe*, 30th Cong., 2nd Sess., 313.

18. Stiles, *First Tycoon*, 277–333; Russell, *Improvement of Communication*, 203–18, 247–60; Gobat, *Empire by Invitation*. On steam technology, trade, and American power, see Maggard, "One Nation under Steam"; and Fraga, "Ocean Fever."

19. Russell, *Improvement of Communication*, 261.

20. For cost estimates, see Jefferson Davis, *Report of the Secretary of War on the Several Pacific Railroad Expeditions*. For more on the financing of railroads and the often blurred line between public and private works, see Roy, *Socializing Capital*; and Dobbin, *Forging Industrial Policy*.

21. Gwin, "Memoirs on the History of the United States, Mexico, and California," 61, 123, Banc.

22. *Cong. Globe*, 32nd Cong., 2nd Sess., 285.

23. Kidwell, *Report on the Impracticability of Building a Railroad*, 22–23. See also *Southern Quarterly Review* 10 (October 1846): 377–417, 442.

24. G. Smith, *Keep Government within Its Limits*, 9, 12.

25. Peebles, *Exposé of the Atlantic and Pacific Railroad Company*, 6–9, 12.

26. See Walker, King, and Dimond, *Circular to the Stockholders*; and [King], *First Annual Report to the Board of Directors*.

27. Kiser, *Turmoil on the Rio Grande*, 52, 59–64, 72, 81. When the Civil War broke out, Gray joined the Confederate army. He died in 1862 in a steamboat explosion.

28. Gray, *Southern Pacific Railroad*, 6, 75–79, 81, 85, 93, 96.

29. See, for instance, the report from the foundational Memphis Convention of 1849; Memphis Convention Corresponding Committee, *Circular to the Citizens of the United States*, 6.

30. S. Nelson, *Nation of Deadbeats*, 133–36.

31. For Calhoun's evolving views on federal power and infrastructure development, see J. Larson, *Internal Improvement*, 64–66, 174–76, 240–41.

32. On the federal government's role in expanding slave territory, see Rothman, *Slave Country*. On southerners' flexible position on state rights, see Majewski, *Modernizing a Slave Economy*; and Karp, *This Vast Southern Empire*.

33. Hodder, "Railroad Background of the Kansas-Nebraska Act." See also John R. Wunder and Joann M. Ross, "'An Eclipse of the Sun': The Nebraska-Kansas Act in Historical Perspective," in Wunder and Ross, *Nebraska-Kansas Act of 1854*, 1–12.

34. *Cong. Globe*, 32nd Cong., 2nd Sess., 558, 560. Similar arguments about Nebraska's territorial organization were made in [Starr], *Letters for the People on the Present Crisis*, July 27, 1853.

35. S. Nelson, *Nation of Deadbeats*, 137–46; Gwin, "Memoirs on the History of the United States, Mexico, and California," 86, 110, Banc.

36. J. Larson, *Internal Improvement*, 226. For Bleeding Kansas, see Hodder, "Railroad Background of the Kansas-Nebraska Act," 18; Russel, *Improvement of Communication*, 150–67; and Woods, *Bleeding Kansas*.

37. *Cong. Globe*, 31st Cong., 2nd Sess., 826–27, which notes the laughter of Davis's colleagues.

38. Jefferson Davis to Franklin Pierce, December 1, 1856, in *PJD*, 6:86–87; Faulk, *U.S. Camel Corps*, 28–45; Fowler, *Camels to California*, 9–13; Woods, "Antebellum Camel Capers."

39. Jefferson Davis to William R. Cannon, December 7, 1855, *PJD*, 5:142 (my italics).

40. Henry C. Wayne to Jefferson Davis, November 21, 1853, *JDC*, 2:288–91. Davis was a close student of military history. During the Crimean War, he sent a delegation of officers to study European strategy. Cooper, *Jefferson Davis*, 274.

41. Davis to Wayne, May 10, 1855, *JDC*, 2:461–62; Woods, "Antebellum Camel Capers."

42. Karp, *This Vast Southern Empire*, 208–16, 222.

43. For reports on the carrying capacity of camels in Texas, see *Daily Democratic State Journal (Sacramento)*, January 6, 1857; and the *Georgia Telegraph* (Macon), May 26, 1857.

44. *San Antonio Ledger*, September 12, 1857; *Georgia Telegraph*, September 15, 1857; *Columbus (GA) Daily Enquirer*, October 8, 1857; *San Joaquin Republican* (Stockton, CA), December 19, 1857; *Trinity Advocate* (Palestine, TX), March 31, 1858.

45. Beale to John B. Floyd, May 23, 1859, printed in the *Daily True Delta* (New Orleans), October 14, 1859; see also *Georgia Telegraph*, January 26, 1858.

46. "Camels for the Dry Plains," *Southern Cultivator* 16, no. 4 (April 1858): 128.

47. Report of the Secretary of War, December 1, 1859, reprinted in *The Constitution*, January 4, 1860.

48. On the various camel expeditions of the 1850s, see Greenly, "Camels in America."

49. See "Remarks of Jefferson Davis on the Pacific Railroad Bill," January 11, 1859, *JDC*, 3:453–56.

50. See Davis to Pierce, December 1, 1856, in *PJD*, 6:86–87.

51. T. Connelly, "American Camel Experiment," 458–60.

52. Henry C. Wayne, "The Camel—His Nature, Habits, and Uses," *National Intelligencer*, November 29, 1858, reprinted in *Southern Planter* 19 (April 1859): 238–39.

53. Both letters in *Southern Cultivator* 17, no. 3 (March 1859): 81–82. The *Southern Intelligencer* of Austin, TX, March 10, 1858, reported on earlier calls to import camels into the United States.

54. *Southern Cultivator* 17, no. 7 (July 1859): 212.

55. Woolsey's report reprinted in *Daily True Delta*, June 9, 1859.

56. *Texas State Gazette*, January 15, 1859; *Columbus (GA) Daily Enquirer*, April 23, 1859; Derry, "Camels in Cahawba," 30–33.

57. *Southern Cultivator* 17, no. 8 (August 1859): 234.

58. Michael E. Woods has been the closest student of this subject—a regular don of modern American camel studies; see Woods, "Antebellum Camel Capers." My thanks to him for sharing a draft of his article prior to publication. See also Woods, "Dark Underbelly of Jefferson Davis's Camels."

59. Woods, "Antebellum Camel Capers"; Derry, "Camels in Cahawba," 34–35.

60. Perrine, "Uncle Sam's Camel Corps."

61. "The Late Postmaster-General, Hon. A. V. Brown," *Harper's Weekly*, March 19, 1859, 188.

62. Winfrey, "Butterfield Overland Mail Trail," 22–28; Lavender, *American Heritage History of the Great West*, 288; Moody, *Stagecoach West*, 72–75.

63. *Sacramento Daily Union*, December 28, 1857.

64. John, *Spreading the News*, 3–6, 90–100; W. Gallagher, *How the Post Office Created America*, 45, 104, 107–8; Balogh, *Government Out of Sight*, 220–23.

65. Report of the Postmaster General, *Cong. Globe*, 35th Cong., 1st Sess., appendix, 27.

66. Report of the Postmaster General, 28.

67. Report of the Postmaster General, 28.

68. Report of the Postmaster General, 27.

69. *Alexandria Gazette*, December 10, 1857; *Memphis Daily Appeal* (n.d.), reprinted in *Charleston Mercury*, March 8, 1858.

70. *Memphis Daily Appeal* (no date) reprinted in *Charleston Mercury*, March 8, 1858.

71. *National Era*, October 21, 1858, 166.

72. *Ohio State Journal (Columbus)*, March 1, 1859.

73. *National Era*, October 21, 1858, 166; see also *National Era*, July 16, 1857, 144, and November 4, 1858, 174. For a critique of the journey itself, see Waterman Ormsby, "Overland to San Francisco," in *New York Herald*, September 26, 1858.

74. *San Francisco Bulletin*, March 2, 1859; see also *Sacramento Daily Union*, October 16, 1858. See also Stanly, *Speech of the Hon. Edward Stanly*, 8.

75. Quoted in Moody, *Stagecoach West*, 81.

76. *Cong. Globe*, 35th Cong., 1st Sess., appendix, 422.

77. *Cong. Globe*, 35th Cong., 2nd Sess., 262–63.

78. *Cong. Globe*, 35th Cong., 2nd Sess., 304–5.

79. L. Hafen, *Overland Mail*, 121–24, 134–35.

80. For figures, see A. Brown, postmaster general's report of 1859, 1408. Brown died in office in March 1859, at which point his successor, Joseph Holt, began drastically curtailing this system; see L. Hafen, *Overland Mail*, 103–22, 134–38.

81. *Cong. Globe*, 35th Cong., 2nd Sess., 1504.

82. L. Hafen, *Overland Mail*, 92–99; Winfrey, "Butterfield Overland Mail Trail," 31–33.

83. DeLay, *War of a Thousand Deserts*; Hämäläinen, *Comanche Empire*; Truett, "Ghosts of Frontiers Past," 322–23. See also Barr, "Geographies of Power."

84. Truett, "Ghosts of Frontiers Past," 323–24. See also Truett, *Fugitive Landscapes*, chap. 1; and Park, "Apaches in Mexican-Indian Relations."

85. Ely, *Texas Frontier*, 6, 15–16.

86. L. Hafen, *Overland Mail*, 92–99.

87. On the expense of managing stage lines more generally, see Blevins, *Gossamer Network*, chap. 4; and W. Gallagher, *How the Post Office Created America*, 127.

88. Winfrey, "Butterfield Overland Mail Trail," 32–44; see also Russel, *Improvement of Communication*, 224–25; W. T. G. Weaver to *Sherman Patriot*, November 19, 1858, reprinted in *Dallas Herald*, December 15, 1858; and "Department of Internal Improvements," *DBR* 25 (December 1858): 719–23.

89. M. Nelson, *Three-Cornered War*, 20.

90. J. T. Sprague to W. W. H. Davis, May 13, 1860, quoted in Lamar, *Far Southwest*, 92.

91. Jefferson Martenet to mother, March 6, 1860; August 1 and September 3, 1859; all in Jefferson Martenet Correspondence, HEHL.

92. *San Francisco Bulletin*, June 13, 1859, quoted in L. Hafen, *Overland Mail*, 99.

93. Cody, *Life of Hon. William F. Cody*, 117–34. See also Warren, *Buffalo Bill's America*, 3–29; and DeFelice, *West Like Lightning*.

94. When it came to transportation schemes, Gwin was more likely to buck his sectional allegiances than were some of his congressional colleagues, such as Jefferson Davis. For Gwin's flexibility, see Russell, *Improvement of Communication*, 227–28.

95. Blevins, *Gossamer Network*, chap. 4.

96. Twain, *Roughing It*, 71.

97. L. Hafen, *Overland Mail*, 170–90.

98. For more on the Slave Power and the camel corps, see Woods, "Antebellum Camel Capers."

Chapter Four

1. James Gadsden to Thomas Jefferson Green, December 7, 1851, William Alexander Leidesdorff Collection, HEHL; James Gadsden to M. Estes, December 10, 1851, in *Charleston Courier*, February 7, 1852.

2. *Cong. Globe*, 31st Cong., 1st Sess., 451–55.

3. Hahn, *Political Worlds of Slavery and Freedom*, chap. 1.

4. Lewis Sanders to Jefferson Davis, March 19, 1858, Jefferson Davis Papers, Transy Library Special Collections and Archives. Sanders stressed to Davis another key feature of proslavery influence in the West. Any mass movement of white southerners, and their attempts to turn the Far West to slavery's advantage, must be accomplished "by *silent* means." He fretted that, if antislavery forces in England and the American Northeast caught wind of such a project, they would descend on California in droves and thus recreate the bloody standoff of Kansas.

5. Sanders to Davis, March 19, 1858, and March 5, 1853, Transy Library Special Collections and Archives.

6. The phrase is adapted from Joan Didion, who remarked that twentieth-century Lancaster, California, had become the "west coast of Iowa" due to its large Midwestern population; Didion, "John Wayne," 31.

7. State of California, *Journal of the Senate*, 1849–50, 372–74; Beasley, "Slavery in California," 38–39.

8. John Bachelder Peirce to Hitty Peirce, January 13, 1851, John Bachelder Peirce Papers, MHS.

9. On the demography of early California, see D. Wright, "Making of Cosmopolitan California," 339.

10. Report of the Finance Committee, January 28, 1850, Thomas Jefferson Green Papers, box 3, folder 31, SHC-UNC.

11. Crosby, *Memoirs*, 58. For more on Green, see John Augustus Sutter, Personal Reminiscences, 201, Banc. For more on the first state legislature, see Edmund Randolph to Tarmesia G. (Meux) Randolph, December 22 and December 28, 1849, both in Edmund Randolph Papers, VHS.

12. See *Democratic Telegraph and Texas Register*, February 21, 1850, Ralph Bieber Collection, HEHL. In a legislative body that numbered sixteen senators and thirty-six assemblymen, the Lone Star State was thus well-represented. For biographical details on this first legislature, see "Biography of the First Cal. Legislature," California State Library, Sacramento.

13. See, for instance, James Caleb Smith to Green, January 23, 1850; and Thomas B. Eastland to Green, February 3, 1850, both in Thomas Jefferson Green Papers, box 3, folder 31, SHC-UNC.

14. Quoted in Quinn, *Rivals*, 98.

15. Helper, *Land of Gold*, 275; Nokes, *Troubled Life of Peter Burnett*; D. Johnson, *Founding the Far West*.

16. Berwanger, *Frontier against Slavery*; West, *Creating the West*, chap. 4.

17. For commentary on the political makeup within early California, see Ayres, *Gold and Sunshine*, 115–16; and S. Smith, *Freedom's Frontier*, 56–61.

18. For population figures, see S. Moore, "'We Feel the Want of Protection,'"

103–8; and Lapp, *Blacks in Gold Rush California*, 49. For Californios, see Pitt, *Decline of the Californios*.

19. As recalled by Thomas Jefferson Green to the editor of the *Daily News*, October 24, 1856, in Thomas Jefferson Green Papers, box 3, folder 34, SHC-UNC.

20. John Bachelder Peirce to Hitty Peirce, December 29, 1850, John Bachelder Peirce Papers, MHS.

21. Quinn, *Rivals*, 99–103.

22. Weller would also join Gwin in endorsing the Kansas-Nebraska Act, the *Dred Scott* decision, the Lecompton Constitution, and Breckinridge's 1860 presidential campaign. See L. Richards, *California Gold Rush*, 114–17.

23. Carr, *Pioneer Days in California*, 346.

24. Gadsden to Green, December 7, 1851, William Alexander Leidesdorff Collection, HEHL. Green and Gadsden probably met during their time in Florida in the 1830s. For background, see Parish, "Project for a California Slave Colony."

25. James Gadsden to M. Estes, December 10, 1851, in *Charleston Courier*, February 7, 1852. The letter was reprinted in a number of outlets, including the *National Era*, February 19, 1852. For more on Gadsden's railroad plans, see Gadsden to Thomas Jefferson Green, January 29, 1849, Thomas Jefferson Green Papers, box 3, folder 30, SHC-UNC.

26. For Green's later attempt to get Holmes appointed to President Franklin Pierce's cabinet, see Green to Pierce, February 15, 1853, Thomas Jefferson Green Papers, box 3, folder 33, SHC-UNC.

27. *California State Assembly Journal*, 1852, 159–60.

28. For more on Gadsden's memorial to the California legislature, see S. Smith, *Freedom's Frontier*, 48; L. Richards, *California Gold Rush*, 125–27; and E. Powell, "Southern Influences in California Politics," 105–6.

29. There is evidence that abolitionist forces in Massachusetts were attempting to send men to California in an effort to combat slavery in the West. A reference to this activity can be found in Charles F. Hovey to Samuel May, June 14, 1852, Samuel May Papers, Boston Public Library. For reports on slaveholders moving into California as late as 1852, see *Frederick Douglass' Paper*, December 3, 1852, reprinting an article that initially appeared in the *New York Tribune*.

30. "Slavery and California," *National Era*, February 19, 1852, 30.

31. Peirce to Hitty Peirce, July 8, 1851, John Bachelder Peirce Papers, MHS.

32. Robert R. Givens to his father, September 10, 1852, Robert R. Givens Letters to Family, Banc. See also Carr, *Pioneer Days in California*, 346; and Marston, *Records of a California Family*, 171.

33. See Peirce to Hitty Peirce, April 8, 1851, in John Bachelder Peirce Papers, MHS.

34. Henry Crabb would later orchestrate a failed filibustering operation in Sonora, Mexico. He and nearly his entire invading force of eighty-five were killed; *Execution of Colonel Crabb and Associates*. For commentary on Henry Crabb's political and military career, see Foote, *Casket of Reminiscences*, 386.

35. *California State Assembly Journal*, 1852, 146–47. For Estell, see S. Smith, *Freedom's Frontier*, 70, 264, n. 59.

36. "An Act Respecting Fugitives from Labor, and Slaves Brought to This State prior to Her Admission into the Union," *Statutes of California*, 1852, 67–69.

37. S. Smith, *Freedom's Frontier*, 46, 64–73.

38. McCurdy, "Prelude to Civil War," 4.

39. In re Perkins, 2 Cal. 424 (October 1, 1852), 441.

40. S. Smith, *Freedom's Frontier*, 46, 64–73; L. Richards, *California Gold Rush*, 127–31; Lapp, *Blacks in Gold Rush California*, 139–46; E. Powell, "Southern Influences in California Politics," 110–12; Bakken, "Courts, the Legal Profession, and the Development of Law," 74–80.

41. I. Gilman to Thomas Gilman, bill of sale, June 27, 1853, Thomas Gilman Papers, box 353, folder 1, California State Library, Sacramento.

42. For a transcript of the ruling, see *National Anti-Slavery Standard*, April 5, 1856; and Demaratus, *Force of a Feather*. The Mason story is the subject of the collaborative project *The Long Road to Freedom: Biddy Mason and the Making of Black Los Angeles*, codirected by myself and Sarah Barringer Gordon. Our project is funded by a National Endowment for the Humanities Collaborative Research Grant and available at biddymasoncollaborative.com.

43. On the ideological power of the contract, see Stanley, *From Bondage to Contract*.

44. "Thomas Thorn, State of California, County of Mariposa," in Taylor et al., "California Freedom Papers," 48–49. Other documents in this collection record the efforts of several others to win their freedom and who, like Green, endured a deferred emancipation. For more on these arrangements, see S. Smith, *Freedom's Frontier*, 57–60; and Beasly, *Negro Trail Blazers*, 84.

45. "Guardianship of Rose, a negro minor child," Los Angeles Probate Court Records, 1850–1910, No. 45, HEHL. For more on John Rowland, see Donald Rowland, *John Rowland*.

46. See, for example, George McKinley Murrell to Elisabeth R. Murrell, November 8, 1850, George McKinley Murrell Correspondence, HEHL; Jesse Holcomb Chaney to Robert Chambliss Chaney, July 10, 1850, in Chaney, "Louisiana Planter in the Gold Rush"; W. P. Robinson to G. P. Dodson, May 18, 1852, Parks and McElrath Family Papers, sub-collection 2, series 1, folder 63, SHC-UNC; and Robert R. Givens to his father, September 10, 1852, Robert R. Givens Letters to Family, Banc. See also Finkelman, "Law of Slavery and Freedom," 453.

47. Reports of California freedom suits appeared in northern and abolitionist papers up until 1855. See, for instance, *National Anti-Slavery Standard*, July 6, 1855.

48. *British Banner* (London), March 22, 1854.

49. The speech was given in Pittsburg in August 1855 and reprinted in the *Provincial Freeman (Canada West)*, August 24, 1855.

50. Faulk, *Destiny Road*; L. Richards, *California Gold Rush*, 49–57; Bieber, *Southern Trails*; Woolsey, *Migrants West*.

51. Benjamin Hayes to B. M. Hughes, January 24, 1853, in Hayes, *Pioneer Notes*, 90–93.

52. Lynch, "Southern California Chivalry," 12–15.

53. Both quotes in Brent, *Memoirs of the War between the States*, 22–23. See also Faragher, *Eternity Street*, 376.

54. Joseph Lancaster Brent to Edward Brent, April 16, 1851, Joseph Lancaster Brent Papers, HEHL.

55. Lynch, "Southern California Chivalry," introduction; Monroy, *Thrown among Strangers*, 50, 75, 115, 136.

56. For white southern honor, see Wyatt-Brown, *Southern Honor*.

57. Knight, "Debt Bondage in Latin America," 103, 116.

58. "An Act for the Government and Protection of Indians," *Statutes of California*, 1850, 408–10. See also S. Smith, *Freedom's Frontier*, 110–25; Reséndez, *Other Slavery*, 264–73; Gordon and Shipps, "Fatal Convergence," 335–38; and Madley, *American Genocide*, 157–60.

59. Madley, *American Genocide*, 240.

60. *Cong. Globe*, 36th Cong., 1st Sess., 2366–69.

61. Magliari, "Free State Slavery"; Heizer, "Indian Servitude in California," 414–16; Madley, *American Genocide*, 304, 332.

62. Magliari, "Free Soil, Unfree Labor."

63. Hubert Howe Bancroft, "Personal Observations during a Tour through the Line of Missions of Upper California," 22–23, Banc. See also Hayes, *Pioneer Notes*, 224–25.

64. Bell, *Reminiscences of a Ranger*, 48–49. See also Faragher, *Eternity Street*, 246–47; Lynch, "Southern California Chivalry," 127; and Hernandez, *City of Inmates*, 38–39.

65. G. Phillips, "Indians in Los Angeles," 448.

66. Lyman, *San Bernardino*; Lyman, "Rise and Decline of Mormon San Bernardino," 321–39.

67. See Hayes, *Pioneer Notes*, 104–5; and K. Carter, *Negro Pioneer*, 8, 16, 20, 31, 44. The extant literature on San Bernardino makes little note of the colony's enslaved population. For a brief account, see Sarah Barringer Gordon and Kevin Waite, "California's Forgotten Slave History," *Los Angeles Times*, January 19, 2020.

68. Bishop, "Politics, Land, Apostasy"; Lyman, "Rise and Decline of Mormon San Bernardino," 330–39. One of the dissidents within San Bernardino was Robert M. Smith, whose conflict with LDS authorities deprived him of necessary allies during the trial over his fourteen enslaved black women and children in 1856. He lost and left for Texas without his former human property; *National Anti-Slavery Standard*, April 5, 1856; Demaratus, *Force of a Feather*.

69. For commentary on the frequency of state division petitions, see *Sacramento Daily Union*, March 3, 1859. For early state division efforts, see Griffin, *Los Angeles in 1849*, 14; *Alta California*, October 1, 1851; and *Alta California*, September 25 and October 27, 1851. Californians were not the only ones considering a division of their territory in 1851. A movement for the division of Oregon was underway that same month; see *Alta California*, October 14, 1851.

70. Robert R. Givens to his father, September 10, 1852, Robert R. Givens Letters to Family, Banc. For more observations about the machinations of slaveholders in the state division movement, see Helper, *Land of Gold*, 278–79; John Bachelder Peirce to Hitty Peirce, September 17, 1851, John Bachelder Peirce Papers, MHS; and Carr, *Pioneer Days in California*, 346.

71. Unsigned extract of a letter to James Gadsden, August 22, 1852, in Thomas Jefferson Green Papers, box 3, folder 33, SHC-UNC. For Green's efforts on behalf of California state division, see *Texas State Gazette*, July 29, 1854.

72. For Foote's amendment and the extensive debate that followed, see *Cong. Globe*, 31st Cong., 1st Sess., appendix, 1485–1504; and *Cong. Globe*, 31st Cong., 1st Sess., 602–4. See also Freehling, *Road to Disunion: Secessionists at Bay*, 505–7. Elisha Crosby believed that Gwin, during the state constitutional convention, was already conspiring to introduce slavery into Southern California. "It was pretty well understood by those who knew that Gwin had at the time we were seeking to have the state admitted, promised the southerners that if they would admit the state he would further the plan of colonizing the southern portion of California with Southern people," Crosby wrote, "and quietly without attracting attention get a majority in the Legislature of California to pass a bill dividing the state, making the southern part of it slave." Crosby, *Memoirs*, 62.

73. "A bill for an act to be entitled an act to divide the state of California," April 6, 1852. Tellingly, the bill is preserved in the papers of Thomas Jefferson Green, box 3, folder 33, SHC-UNC. See also E. Powell, "Southern Influences in California Politics," 117–18.

74. Abraham Lincoln, Draft of Resolutions for presentation in the US House of Representatives, January 1855, in Basler, *Collected Works of Abraham Lincoln*, 2:301; see also McAfee, "California's House Divided," 118–19.

75. For Gwin's scheming over this election, see Gwin to Thomas Jefferson Green, November 19, 1849, Thomas Jefferson Green Papers, box 3, folder 31, SHC-UNC.

76. Lynch, "Southern California Chivalry," 66.

77. J. Carter, "Abraham Lincoln and the California Patronage," 495; L. Richards, *California Gold Rush*, 116, 183–86; E. Powell, "Southern Influences in California Politics," 74, 77, 99. For a list of the hundreds of federal positions within California and corresponding salaries, see *Register of Officers and Agents*.

78. Crosby, *Memoirs*, 62.

79. Carr, *Pioneer Days in California*, 347.

80. John Bigler to William Bigler, April 14, 1854, William Bigler Papers, box 6, Historical Society of Pennsylvania, Philadelphia. See also [Winston?] S. Pierce to William Bigler, box 5, William Bigler Papers.

81. On Bigler, see Quinn, *Rivals*, 132–33, 145–46.

82. Ayres, *Gold and Sunshine*, 121. See also Milton Latham to James Mandeville, November 18, 1856, box 8, James Mandeville Papers, HEHL.

83. Andrew Jay Hatch to James W. Mandeville, March 3, 1854, box 4, James Mandeville papers, HEHL. See also Quinn, *Rivals*, 41–55.

84. John Currey, "Incidents in California," 11–12, Banc; see also Annis Merrill, "Statement of Recollection on Early Days of San Francisco," 10, Banc; and Jefferson Martenet to his mother, April 2, 1857, Jefferson Martenet Correspondence, HEHL.

85. E. Powell, "Southern Influences in California Politics," 78–89, 128; G. Stanley, "Republican Party in California," 61.

86. *Statutes of California, 1854*, 223–24; State of California, *Journal of the Assembly*, 1854, 446. For John B. Weller's support of the bill, see Weller, *Speech of Mr. Weller, of California, in the Senate, February 13, 1854*, Benjamin Hayes Scrapbooks, vol. 17, p. 70, Banc.

87. Atchison's letter initially appeared in the *Charleston Mercury* and was reprinted in the *National Anti-Slavery Standard*, November 10, 1855.

88. For more on the Chivalry support for Kansas-Nebraska, see S. Smith, *Freedom's Frontier*, 74–75.

89. On California's dueling culture, see Shuck, *History of the Bench and Bar of California*, 227–64; and McGrath, "A Violent Birth." On Gwin's violent feuds, see Sylvester Mowry to Edward Bicknell, May 30, 1853, Letters of Sylvester Mowry to Edward Bicknell, Banc; and *Frederick Douglass' Paper*, June 18, 1858. Gwin's brother was killed in a political dispute in Mississippi roughly two decades earlier.

90. *Sacramento Daily Union*, April 13, 1854. See also Lapp, *Blacks in Gold Rush California*, 146; and S. Smith, *Freedom's Frontier*, 74–75.

91. Quinn, *Rivals*, 154–59.

92. Denver was elected to the state senate in 1852, the same year he killed a newspaper editor in a duel. The capital of Colorado would later be named for him. Herbert had an even more violent career. After shooting and killing a waiter in a Washington, DC, hotel, Herbert's congressional career was effectively finished, although he was acquitted of manslaughter. He later moved to Texas, where he practiced law. Then in the spring of 1861 he traveled to Arizona and played a leading role in the secessionist movement there. He returned to the South during the war, joined the Confederate army, was wounded at the Battle of Mansfield in April 1864, and died of his wounds several months later. For Herbert's killing of the hotel waiter, see *New York Daily Times*, May 12, 1856. See also Weller, *Speech of John B. Weller, in Sacramento . . . July 25th, 1857*.

93. On the 1854 state elections and Broderick's failed bid for the Senate, see Luther B. Curtiss to James W. Mandeville, September 28, 1854, box 4; Edward Rutledge Galvin to Mandeville, February 1, 1854, box 3; Fleming Amyx to Mandeville, February 4, 1854, box 3; and Andrew Jay Hatch to Mandeville, March 3, 1854, box 4, all in James Mandeville Papers, HEHL.

94. Thomas Butler King to Thomas Jefferson Green, March 19, 1855; see also Green to King, April 13, 1855, both in Thomas Jefferson Green Papers, box 3, folder 33, SHC-UNC.

95. Know-Nothing candidates won fifty-six of ninety assembly races and seventeen of thirty-three senate seats. See L. Richards, *California Gold Rush*, 176–80; and E. Powell, "Southern Influences in California Politics," 91–96.

96. "The Southern Convention at Vicksburg, Part 2," *DBR* 27 (August 1859): 216.

97. Caleb Gilman to Mandeville, February 13, 1856, box 7, James Mandeville Papers, HEHL. Much like his fellow Mississippian William Gwin, Henry Foote saw in the West a chance for political advancement. See also Foote, *Casket of Reminiscences*, 340.

98. Curiously, Gwin claimed, in his own memoirs, to have served continuously from 1849 to 1861. Perhaps he did not consider the 1855–57 period as a break in his service, as the legislature failed to elect a replacement and thus his old seat remained vacant for those two years. Gwin, "Memoirs on the History of United States, Mexico, and California," 1–4, Banc.

99. Cole, *Memoirs*, 112–13. For more commentary on the founding of the party,

see also Carr, *Pioneer Days in California*, 326; and Merrill, "Statement of Recollection on Early Days of San Francisco," 10, Banc.

100. The best account of the state's early Republican Party remains the dissertation of Gerald Stanley, "Republican Party in California."

101. L. Richards, *California Gold Rush*, 169–72; G. Stanley, "Republican Party in California," 52–53. On Frémont, see Inskeep, *Imperfect Union*.

102. Carr, *Pioneer Days in California*, 342.

103. Carr, 328. For comments on California's border ruffians, see p. 332.

104. Cole, *Memoirs*, 113–14. As Cole happily noted, however, no hangings followed from this threat. For more on anti-Republican violence, see G. Stanley, "Republican Party in California," 37–39.

105. Currey, "Incidents in California," 7, Banc.

106. For reports on these Colored Conventions, see Stokes, *Proceedings of the First State Convention*; Booth, *Proceedings of the Second Annual Convention*; and *Frederick Douglass' Paper*, July 17, 1857. See also Lapp, *Blacks in Gold Rush California*, 187–230; S. Moore, "We Feel the Want of Protection," 116–17; and Q. Taylor, *In Search of the Racial Frontier*, 91–94.

107. G. Stanley, "Republican Party in California," 37–42. See also Field, *Personal Reminiscences*, 114; and Tilford, *Speech of Hon. Frank Tilford*.

108. E. J. C. Kewen before the Democratic Committee of Los Angeles, September 15, 1856, in *Los Angeles Star*, September 20, 1856. See also Robinson, "Colonel Edward J. C. Kewen"; Lynch, "Southern California Chivalry," 106–9; and Faragher, *Eternity Street*, 376–84.

109. G. Stanley, "Republican Party in California," 30–32, 53–58, 81, 85–86, 89. This was not the racially progressive Republican Party portrayed in some of the most important works on the subject, including Foner, *Free Soil*; and Oakes, *Freedom National*.

110. All quotes are from Stanly, *Speech of the Hon. Edward Stanly*. For Stanly's proslavery position in Congress, see *Cong. Globe*, 25th Cong., 2nd Sess., appendix, 87; and *Sacramento Daily Union*, August 27, 1857.

111. The Democratic nominee, John B. Weller, won in a landslide. For more on the election, see G. Stanley, "Republican Party in California," 59–60; G. Stanley, "Politics of the Antebellum Far West," 19–20; and Carr, *Pioneer Days in California*, 342.

112. Reports on the buildup to the election and the politicking of the 1857 contest can be found in "To Gwin [signed only "your friend"]," November 10, 1856, box 8; David Blanchard to Mandeville, November 16, 1856, box 8; William B. Norman to Gwin, December 20, 1856, box 8; and Gwin to Mandeville, December 25, 1856, box 8, all in James Mandeville Papers, HEHL.

113. See John G. Hyatt to Charles M. Hitchcock, January 20, 1857, Hitchcock Family Papers, Banc. For years afterward, Gwin would deny that he entered into any such contract with Broderick. In August 1859 he asserted that he had willingly given up the patronage with no expectation that Broderick would, in return, support his candidacy for the US Senate; Gwin, *Address of Hon. W. M. Gwin*.

114. According to Charles Scott, Gwin "was utterly powerless, by reason of the contract that he had entered into to relinquish the patronage of the state." But Scott, McKibbin, and others in Washington presented "a solid & undivided force"

against Broderick. Charles L. Scott to Mandeville, March 18, 1857, box 8; see also Gwin to Mandeville, March 19, 1857, box 8, both in James Mandeville Papers, HEHL.

115. Scott to Mandeville, April 2, 1857, box 8, James Mandeville Papers, HEHL.

116. Gwin to Mandeville, April 3, 1857, box 8, James Mandeville Papers, HEHL. By this point, Gwin had effectively reneged on his pledge to refrain from the patronage struggles and would continue to nurture a close personal friendship with Buchanan. See Gwin to Mandeville, April 5, 1857, box 8, James Mandeville Papers, HEHL, for comments on "visiting the Cabinet and the President with whom I had talks they will not forget."

117. L. Richards, *California Gold Rush*, 196–200; Quinn, *Rivals*, 227–51; L. Thomas, *Between Two Empires*, 142–65.

118. The quote about "New York tacticians" comes from Lewis Sanders to Jefferson Davis, March 5, 1853; the rest from Sanders to Davis, April 9, 1853, both in Jefferson Davis Papers, Transy Library Special Collections and Archives. My thanks to Susan Brown at Transylvania for making these and other letters available to me.

119. Jefferson Davis to William R. Cannon, December 7, 1855, *PJD*, 5:142.

120. W. R. Isaacs MacKay to Jefferson Davis, January 13, 1857, in *PJD*, 6:99–101; see also Sanders to Davis, March 19, 1858, Transy Library Special Collections and Archives.

121. *National Anti-Slavery Standard*, April 10, 1858.

122. For California's endorsement of the Lecompton Constitution, see *Statutes of California*, 1858, 353–54. For more Democratic race-baiting, see the *Sonora Democrat*'s response to anti-Lecomptonites, reprinted in the *Daily Globe (Toronto)*, February 5, 1858.

123. The quote from Gwin comes from his 1859 Grass Valley speech, excerpted in Douglas, *Letter of Judge Douglas in Reply to the Speech of Dr. Gwin*.

124. Dred Scott v. Sandford, 60 US 393 (argued 1856; decided 1857); Fehrenbacher, *Dred Scott Case*.

125. The case and its aftermath was covered extensively in California's press. For detailed reports, see *Sacramento Daily Union*, March 8, 18, 19, 20, 22, 25, 1858; and *Alta California*, February 6, March 6, 9, April 20, May 31, 1858. See also *Stovall v. Archy, a Slave*; Lapp, *Archy Lee*; Lapp, *Blacks in Gold Rush California*, 148–52, 236; S. Smith, *Freedom's Frontier*, 76–78; and McGinty, *Archy Lee's Struggle for Freedom*.

126. For the voting record on Assembly Bill No. 411, "An Act to restrict and prevent the immigration to and residence in this State by Negroes and Mulattoes," see State of California, *Journal of the Assembly*, 1857, 811–12, 822–24.

127. Billington Crum Whiting to Susan Helen Whiting, May 19, 1858, Billington Crum Whiting Papers, HEHL.

128. That California's blacks would seek another mining community is understandable, as many had originally migrated to the Pacific coast in search of gold. On African American migrants and the California gold rush, see *Frederick Douglass' Paper*, April 1, 1852.

129. *Frederick Douglass' Paper*, June 4, 1858; Lapp, *Blacks in Gold Rush California*, 239–55. During the Civil War, Victoria's black community raised money to aid contrabands. See also S. Smith, "*Dred Scott* on the Pacific."

130. Philip A. Roach to Jefferson Davis, June 27, 1859, *JDC*, 4:59–61.

131. Roach to Davis, May 17, 1859, *JDC*, 4:52–53.

132. Roach to Davis, May 27, 1859; see also Roach to Davis, July 22, 1859, both in Jefferson Davis Papers, Transy Library Special Collections and Archives. See also Roach to Davis, July 19 and July 25, 1859, both in *JDC*, 4:91–92.

133. In the legislature of 1859, nineteen of the thirty state senators were southern-born, while northerners had a slight edge in the assembly, forty to thirty-four. With the support of northern doughfaces, Chivalry leaders reigned; E. Powell, "Southern Influences in California Politics," 143.

134. L. Richards, *California Gold Rush*, 183; G. Stanley, "Politics of the Antebellum Far West," 22–24; and G. Stanley, "Republican Party in California," 72–78.

135. Shuck, *History of the Bench and Bar of California*, 232–33; Billington Crum Whiting to Susan Helen Whiting, March 18, 1852, Billington Crum Whiting Papers, HEHL.

136. Quinn, *Rivals*, 128, 218, 255–60.

137. Field, *Personal Reminiscences*, 124. It was Field's bodyguard who shot and killed Terry in 1889, after the Texan assaulted Field at a railway station in Lathrop, California; "Judge Terry Killed," *Los Angeles Herald*, August 15, 1889.

138. Newspapers across the country reported on the duel, as well as the political feud from which it originated. When Broderick read the transcript of Terry's speech, he lashed out against "the damned *miserable wretch*." Broderick had defended Terry against the Vigilance Committee in 1854 and had "hitherto spoken of him as an honest man—as the only honest man on the bench of a miserable corrupt Supreme Court," Broderick reportedly said. "But now I find I was mistaken. I take it all back. He is just as bad as the others." *Columbus Daily Enquirer*, October 14, 1859.

139. Merrill, "Statement of Recollections on Early Days of San Francisco," 7–8, Banc.

140. L. Richards, *California Gold Rush*, 3–7, 219–21.

141. Merrill, "Statement of Recollections on Early Days of San Francisco," 7–8, Banc.

142. Billington Crum Whiting to Susan Helen Whiting, September 18, 1859, Billington Crum Whiting Papers, HEHL.

143. Shuck, *History of the Bench and Bar of California*, 240–45; Carr, *Pioneer Days in California*, 345.

144. Haun served until March 1860, at which point he was replaced by Milton S. Latham.

145. Carr, *Pioneer Days in California*, 363. Broderick's death elicited a national outpouring of grief. New York held a second funeral for its native son, while the Republican National Convention at Chicago hung a portrait of Broderick, ringed in black crepe. In California, trophy hunters began seeking Broderick's autograph, and his supporters erected a monument at his gravesite in Lone Mountain Cemetery, San Francisco. For the text of the New York funeral address, see Dwinelle, *Funeral Oration*. On Broderick autograph collectors, see John G. Downey to Lewis Jacob Cist, October 18, 1861, John G. Downey Correspondence, Banc. Baker would himself become an antislavery martyr just a few years later, when he was killed at the Battle of Ball's Bluff in October 1861.

146. Baker, *Oration of Colonel Edward D. Baker*, 7–9, 13.

147. If there is a critique to be made of Stacey Smith's interpretation of ante-bellum California politics, it is that she dismisses the Chivalry faction from her narrative too quickly. See S. Smith, *Freedom's Frontier*, 77.

148. Jefferson Martenet to his mother, October 3, 1859, Jefferson Martenet Correspondence, HEHL.

149. *National Anti-Slavery Standard*, October 22, 1859.

Chapter Five

1. *New York Daily Tribune*, December 31, 1860.

2. On Rhett's views, see Quigley, *Shifting Grounds*, 85; and May, "Irony of Confederate Diplomacy," 76.

3. For the important studies that explore the controversy over slavery in specific western states and territories, see S. Smith, *Freedom's Frontier*; L. Richards, *California Gold Rush*; Lapp, *Blacks in Gold Rush California*; Ganaway, *New Mexico and the Sectional Controversy*; Sunseri, *Seeds of Discord*; Kiser, *Borderlands of Slavery*; Kiser, *Turmoil on the Rio Grande*; Bringhurst, "Mormons and Slavery"; and Reeve, *Religion of a Different Color*, 140–70.

4. Alexander Jackson to Jefferson Davis, February 17, 1861, in J. P. Wilson, *When the Texans Came*, 18.

5. Antislavery politicians wielded these accusations as a potent political tool. See A. Smith, *Stormy Present*, 42, 79–85; C. Brooks, *Liberty Power*; Holt, *Fate of Their Country*; Foner, *Free Soil*, 73–102; and D. Davis, *Slave Power Conspiracy*.

6. Charges of a Slave Power conspiracy resonated because they were at least partially true; L. Richards, *Slave Power*; Fehrenbacher, *Slaveholding Republic*, 118. On the long reach of the Slave Power, see Woods, "Antebellum Camel Capers."

7. *Book of Mormon*, 2 Nephi 26:33.

8. Abdy, *Journal*, 3:58. For the progressivism of the early LDS church, see Mueller, *Race and the Making of the Mormon People*, 31–118. For Mormonism as a "new religious tradition," see Shipps, *Mormonism*.

9. The manifesto is included in a letter "To His Excellency, Daniel Dunklin, Governor of the State of Missouri," reprinted in *Evening and the Morning Star* (Independence, MO) 2, no. 15 (December 1833): 226–31. It was written largely in response to "Free People of Color," *Evening and the Morning Star* 2, no. 14 (July 1833): 218–19. See also Bush, "Mormonism's Negro Doctrine," 11–13.

10. "Extra," *Evening and the Morning Star*, July 16, 1833. See also "The Outrage in Jackson County, Missouri," *Evening and the Morning Star* (Kirtland, Ohio), January 1834.

11. For a useful overview of this ideology and a selection of important writings from contemporary southerners, see Faust, *Ideology of Slavery*. For more on pro-slavery religious doctrine in the Old South, see Daly, *When Slavery Was Called Freedom*; Harlow, *Religion, Race, and the Making of Confederate Kentucky*; McCurry, *Masters of Small Worlds*; and Heyrman, *Southern Cross*.

12. See Genesis, 9:20–27. Contemporary scholarship often refers to this as the "curse of Ham," although nineteenth-century writers generally referenced

Canaan. For a slaveholding southern preacher on this subject, see Stringfellow, *Brief Examination of Scripture Testimony*, 2. See also Haynes, *Noah's Curse*.

13. Joseph Smith to Brother Oliver Cowdery, n.d., in *Latter Day Saints' Messenger and Advocate* 2, no. 7 (April 1836): 289–91. The purpose of this letter was primarily to distance the LDS church from a well-known abolitionist, who was then in Kirtland, Ohio. See also Bringhurst, *Saints, Slaves, and Blacks*, 14–15. For Smith's position on slavery at this moment, see Bushman, *Rough Stone Rolling*, 327–28.

14. "The Abolitionists," in *Latter Day Saints' Messenger and Advocate* 2, no. 7 (April 1836): 299–301; see also W. Parrish, letter *to Latter Day Saints' Messenger and Advocate* 2, no. 7 (April 1836): 295–96; and *Messenger and Advocate* 2, no. 11 (August 1836): 356–57. For another Mormon attempt to disavow abolitionism, see Pratt, *History of the Late Persecution Inflicted by the State of Missouri*, 7.

15. For instance, compare this argument with similar statements made by Thornton Stringfellow, a Baptist minister and Virginia planter, in *Brief Examination of Scripture Testimony*.

16. Park, *Kingdom of Nauvoo*, 141.

17. Newell, *Your Sister in the Gospel*.

18. J. Smith, *General Smith's Views*, 1–6. See also Bushman, *Rough Stone Rolling*, 514–17.

19. Beller, "Negro Slaves in Utah," 122–24. The Brigham Young monument lists these enslaved men as "Colored Servants." Two of those men changed their names upon winning their freedom. The plaque would thus more accurately list them as Green Flake, Hark Wales, and Oscar Smith. My thanks to Amy Tanner Thiriot for sharing her insights on the subject. See also "One of the First African Americans to Arrive in the Salt Lake Valley Honored on Memorial Day," *Deseret News*, May 31, 2019.

20. Utah's twenty-six slaves listed in the census of 1850 are designated "*En route* for California." Their destination was likely San Bernardino, which would be settled in 1851 by a group of Mormons, including several prominent slaveholders. De Bow, *Statistical View of the United States*, 332. See also R. Coleman, "Blacks in Utah History," 116–17.

21. The most detailed accounting of the enslaved population in antebellum Utah can be found in the tables of Thiriot, *Slaves in Zion*. See also Bringhust, *Saints, Slaves, and Blacks*, 66–67, 219, 224.

22. Brown, *Autobiography*, 36–55.

23. Parrish, "Mississippi Saints," 490–506; Kohler, Southern Grace; Brown, *Autobiography*, 88–101.

24. McCurry, *Masters of Small Worlds*.

25. Quoted in Hardy, "Lords of Creation," 128. This helps explain why a disproportionate number of early converts to the LDS church were men; see Hill, "Rise of Mormonism in the Burned-over District," 427–28.

26. Jacob, *An Extract: From a Manuscript Entitle the PEACE Maker*, 16; and Stringfellow, *Brief Examination of Scripture Testimony*, 4. Stringfellow called this passage in Exodus "a patriarchal catalogue of property."

27. See *New York Evening Post* (n.d.), quoted in *Zion's Herald and Wesleyan Journal*, February 5, 1851, 22; and *The Liberator*, February 14, 1851, 27.

28. Orson Hyde, "Slavery among the Saints," in *Latter-day Saints' Millennial Star* 13, no. 4 (February 15, 1851): 63.

29. *Broad Ax* (Salt Lake City), March 25, 1899. Note: this interview was transcribed and paraphrased by the paper's publisher, Julius Taylor, and thus does not reflect exact quotes from Bankhead. For more on Bankhead and the *Broad Ax*, see R. Coleman, "Blacks in Utah History," 121–23. For testimony from another African American slave in Utah, see R. Freeman, "James Madison Flake," 41; S. Moore, *Sweet Freedom's Plains*, 276; and Thiriot, *Slaves in Zion*. For an illuminating study of slaves' experiences in early Utah, see Reiter, "Redd Slave Histories."

30. Brigham Young reversed the more egalitarian racial policies of Joseph Smith. In 1852, he announced a ban on the ordination of black men into the priesthood. He was also a vicious opponent of interracial mixing. "If the white man who belongs to the chosen seed mixes his blood with the seed of Cain [i.e., those of African descent], the penalty, under the law of God, is death on the spot," Young told an audience in 1863. Quoted in Reeve, *Religion of a Different Color*, 158. Not until 1978 would the LDS church finally lift the ban on black men from holding lay priesthood; see Mueller, *Race and the Making of the Mormon People*, 9–10, 143, 189–94, 212–32. For a catalog of African Americans in the LDS church, see Paul Reeve's excellent digital project, "Century of Black Mormons," https://exhibits.lib.utah .edu/s/century-of-black-mormons/page/welcome. For the first scholarly biography of an African American Mormon, see Newell, *Your Sister in the Gospel*. For more on Young's views and the African American experience in Utah, see Bringhurst, *Saints, Slaves and Blacks*; and Christensen, "Negro Slavery in the Utah Territory," 299.

31. Brigham Young, "Governor's Message to the Council and House of Representatives of the Legislature of Utah, Jan. 5, 1852," in *Deseret News* (Salt Lake City), January 10, 1852.

32. Greeley, *Overland Journey*, 211–12.

33. "An Act in Relation to Service," sections 6, 8, and 9, in *Acts, Resolutions and Memorials, Passed at the Several Annual Sessions of the Legislative Assembly of the Territory of Utah*, 160–62. Not unlike the American Constitution, Utah's slave code cloaked slavery in euphemisms, referring to "service" and "servants." For further commentary, see Rich, "True Policy for Utah"; Reeve, Rich, and Caruth, *"Enough to Cause the Angels in Heaven to Blush"*; and Reeve, *Religion of a Different Color*, 144–52.

34. "Act in Relation to Service," section 4, 161. For the roots of anti-miscegenation statutes in the South, see K. Brown, *Good Wives*; and on anti-miscegenation law more broadly, see Pascoe, *What Comes Naturally*, 19–22.

35. *The Liberator*, May 2, 1856, 70; see also Lythgoe, "Negro Slavery in Utah," 53.

36. Berlin, *Many Thousands Gone*.

37. Bringhurst, "Mormons and Slavery," 332.

38. S. Gordon and Shipps, "Fatal Convergence," 340; Hardy, "Lords of Creation," 143; S. Gordon, *Mormon Question*.

39. "A Word with Our Opponents," *Latter-Day Saints' Millennial Star* 15, no. 17 (April 23, 1853); "Celestial Marriage," *The Seer* 1, no. 5 (May 1853): 76.

40. For decades to come, anti-Mormon critics routinely linked polygamy and slavery; see Reeve, *Religion of a Different Color*, 161–69.

41. *Deseret News*, February 4, 1857.

42. *Deseret News*, May 20, 1857. For the paper's earlier support of the Kansas-Nebraska Act, see *Deseret News*, April 13, 1854.

43. *National Era*, November 20, 1856, 188.

44. For the origins of the region's name, dating to 1860, see A. Larson, *I Was Called to "Dixie."*

45. "Report of Council Committee on Cotton Culture in Utah," *Deseret News*, December 28, 1859.

46. See Brigham Young to Amasa Lyman and Charles Rich, June 13, 1861, in *Latter-Day Saints' Millennial Star*, 23, no. 32 (1861): 509; "Labours before the People in Zion—Influence of Tithing," December 7, 1861, *Latter-Day Saints' Millennial Star*, 23, no. 49 (1861): 787.

47. Arrington, "Mormon Cotton Mission"; Juanita Brooks, "Cotton Mission"; and Hicks, "George Armstrong Hicks," 65, 172–78.

48. Waves of immigration in the 1860s significantly diminished Dixie's southern orientation; see Thiriot, "A Response to the *Salt Lake Tribune* on Utah's Dixie and Slave Culture," *Keepapitchinin*, February 7, 2013, http://www.keepapitchinin .org/2013/02/07/guest-post-a-response-to-the-salt-lake-tribune-on-utahs-dixie-and -slave-culture.

49. Hicks, "George Armstrong Hicks," 170–74.

50. Maxwell, *Civil War Years in Utah*, 57.

51. Reprinted in the *National Era*, December 24, 1857, 206.

52. Poll and MacKinnon, "Causes of the Utah War Reconsidered," 16–44; West, *Creating the West*, chap. 5.

53. Buchanan, "Proclamation—Rebellion in the Territory of Utah."

54. On the war, see Poll and MacKinnon, "Causes of the Utah War Reconsidered"; MacKinnon, "Loose in the Stacks," 43–81; and Bigler and Bagley, *Mormon Rebellion*. On Mountain Meadows, see Brooks, *Mountain Meadows Massacre*; Gordon and Shipps, "Fatal Convergence"; and Bagley, *Blood of the Prophets*.

55. *Deseret News*, June 1, 1859.

56. See, for instance, Brigham Young's gubernatorial message in *Deseret News*, December 25, 1852, in which he distances himself from both abolitionism and overt proslavery sympathy. See also Rich, "True Policy for Utah."

57. See, again, Alex Bankhead's testimony in *Broad Ax*, March 25, 1899.

58. According to the 1850 census, New Mexico had a population of over 60,000 (inclusive of Native Americans), although fewer than 800 were Anglo-American; see De Bow, *Statistical View of the United States*, 332; and Bancroft, *History of Arizona and New Mexico*, 642.

59. [King], *First Annual Report to the Board of Directors*, 18.

60. Sunseri, *Seeds of Discord*, 67–81.

61. Hugh Smith, *Address of Hugh N. Smith*, 2. Smith, although elected by political leaders in New Mexico, was not officially recognized by Congress, as the territory had yet to be organized.

62. On the activities of the Free Territory League, see *National Era*, September 25, 1851, 154. See also Murphy, "Antislavery in the Southwest."

63. Kiser, *Borderlands of Slavery*, 39.

64. On the *Gazette*'s political about-face, see Ganaway, *New Mexico and the Sectional Controversy*, 58.

65. *Santa Fe Gazette*, September 12, 1857. For predictions that New Mexico would soon become a slave state, see *Richmond Enquirer*, quoted in the *Sacramento Daily Union*, December 28, 1857.

66. *Santa Fe Gazette*, January 16, August 21, and November 27, 1858.

67. *Santa Fe Gazette*, November 13, 1858. The paper would later argue that the US campaign against the international slave trade was simply too costly to justify the results; see *Santa Fe Gazette*, July 3, 1860.

68. Stegmaier, "Law That Would Make Caligula Blush?," 209–10.

69. Miguel Antonio Otero to Charles P. Clever, December 24, 1858, William G. Ritch Collection, HEHL. For biographical information on Otero, see Sunseri, *Seeds of Discord*, 117–21, 133–35.

70. See Otero to Alexander Jackson, December 16, 1858, in Bingham, "Bill and Report of John A. Bingham," 1.

71. Again, for the Hispano-southern alliance in Los Angeles County, see Lynch, "Southern California Chivalry." For Hispano politics in New Mexico, see Gonzales, *Política*.

72. Stegmaier, "Law That Would Make Caligula Blush?," 210–12; Ganaway, *New Mexico and the Sectional Controversy*, 60–68. Buchanan's administration also staffed Indian Territory with a disproportionate number of proslavery partisans; see Warde, *When the Wolf Came*, 43.

73. "An Act to Provide for the Protection of Property in Slaves in This Territory," in *Laws of the Territory of New Mexico*, 64–80. In an effort to curry greater southern support for his territory, Otero urged Jackson to distribute copies of the code to newspapers in the slave states; Kiser, *Borderlands of Slavery*, 125–29.

74. *Cong. Globe*, 36th Cong., 2nd Sess., 1313.

75. For fugitive slaves and the US-Mexico border, see Baumgartner, *South to Freedom*; and Nichols, "Line of Liberty."

76. *Cong. Globe*, 31st Cong., 1st Sess., 1005–6.

77. Sunseri, *Seeds of Discord*, 24–28, 120–21.

78. Walker himself had invested in the Sonora Exploring and Mining Company, a group formed by a Kentuckian in 1856 and bound for the silver mines of Arizona. For more on that venture, see Truett, *Fugitive Landscapes*, 38–40.

79. Gray, *Southern Pacific Railroad*, 60. For more on the cotton-growing potential of the region, see Cozzens, *Marvellous Country*, 99. For Jefferson Davis's interest in cotton cultivation in neighboring Utah, see Lamar, *Far Southwest*, 98.

80. Gadsden's letter to Maury and the subsequent report from the *Washington States* was reprinted as "The Cotton Fields of Arizona Territory," *DBR* 24 (April 1858): 320–21.

81. Governor Abraham Rencher also recommended experiments with sugar planting in New Mexico, subsidized by the federal government; Sunseri, *Seeds of Discord*, 22.

82. *Memphis Daily Appeal*, March 6, 1859. The correspondent insisted that New

Mexico would provide a lucrative market for human chattel, evidenced by the recent sale of a "third rate negro girl" for the large sum of $1,000 in gold.

83. *Washington States* (n.d.) quoted in *Sacramento Daily Union*, May 11, 1859.

84. *New York Daily Tribune*, February 25, 1861. For Greeley on similar themes, see *New York Daily Tribune*, March 10, 1859, and July 31 and December 31, 1860; and Kiser, *Borderlands of Slavery*, 127, 132. For Otero's rebuttal to Greeley, see Otero, *Abolition Attack*.

85. Stegmaier, "Law That Would Make Caligula Blush?," 216–18.

86. US Government Docs., 36th Cong., 1st Sess., House Resolution 64; see also Bingham, "Bill and Report of John A. Bingham."

87. "Slavery in the Territory of New Mexico," 35–38.

88. *Cong. Globe*, 36th Cong., 1st Sess., 2045–46, 2059.

89. *Cong. Globe*, 36th Cong., 2nd Sess., appendix, 82–83.

90. For more on these repeal efforts, see Stegmaier, "Law That Would Make Caligula Blush?," 216–22.

91. Reséndez, *Other Slavery*.

92. Kiser, *Borderlands of Slavery*, 13, 16; James Brooks, *Captives and Cousins*, 154.

93. Lamar, "From Bondage to Contract."

94. Calhoun to Orlando Brown, March 31, 1850, in Abel, *Official Correspondence of James S. Calhoun*, 183.

95. On the destructive force of these raids, see DeLay, *War of a Thousand Deserts*. For how slavery functioned in the American Indian political economy, see James Brooks, *Captives and Cousins*; and Hämäläinen, *Comanche Empire*, 248–55.

96. D. Jones, *Forty Years among the Indians*, 49–53; Kiser, *Borderlands of Slavery*, 59–79; Reséndez, *Other Slavery*, 245–46.

97. Van Hoak, "And Who Shall Have the Children?," 6–7.

98. "An Act for the Further Relief of Indian Slaves and Prisoners [1852]," *Acts, Resolutions, and Memorials of the Legislative Assembly of the Territory of Utah*, 87–88. See also Jones, *Trial of Don Pedro Leon Lujan*.

99. Book of Mormon, 2 Nephi 30:6. In 1981, the LDS church released an updated version of the Book of Mormon, which slightly altered this passage, along with nineteen other revisions to the text. The revised version reads, "They shall be a *pure* and delightsome people." Some note that Smith made the same scriptural adjustment in the 1840 edition of the Book of Mormon. Yet subsequent editions reverted to the wording of the 1830 original. For more, see Mueller, *Race and the Making of the Mormon People*, 231. On Native identity and the broad community of Mormonism, see Hafen, "Being and Place of a Native American Mormon."

100. Young, "Governor's Message to the Council and House of Representatives of the Legislature of Utah, Jan. 5, 1852."

101. Gordon and Shipps, "Fatal Convergence," 335–38, 345.

102. Kitchen, "Mormon-Indian Relations in Deseret," appendixes C and D; see also Reséndez, *Other Slavery*, 273.

103. S. Jones, "'Redeeming' the Indian," 234–35; Van Hoak, "And Who Shall Have the Children?," 16–17; Reséndez, *Other Slavery*, 266–73; Mueller, *Race and the Making of the Mormon People*, 196, 207.

104. James Brooks, *Captives and Cousins*, 347–48.

105. Gregg, *Commerce of the Prairies*, 1:235–36. See also Cooke, *Conquest of New Mexico and California*, 61.

106. W. W. H. Davis, *El Gringo*, 232. See also Bancroft, *History of Arizona and New Mexico*, 681.

107. Kiser, *Borderlands of Slavery*, 100–101.

108. "An Act Amendatory of the Law Relative to Contracts between Masters and Servants," section 4, *Laws of the Territory of New Mexico*, 1858–59, 24–26. In his campaign against New Mexico's slave code, Bingham also took aim at this peonage statute; see Bingham, "Bill and Report of John A. Bingham."

109. Calhoun to Orlando Brown, March 15, 1850, in Abel, *Official Correspondence of James S. Calhoun*, 160–62.

110. "Incidents of Travel on the Tehuantepec Route," *Harper's Weekly*, January 15, 1859, 41–42.

111. W. W. H. Davis, *El Gringo*, 232. See also Pumpelly, *Across America and Asia*, 32; and Ruxton, *Adventures in Mexico and the Rocky Mountains*, 106.

112. W. W. H. Davis, *El Gringo*, 233.

113. Kiser, *Borderlands of Slavery*, 123.

114. *Cong. Globe*, 31st Cong., 1st Sess., appendix, 1180. See also W. W. H. Davis, *El Gringo*, 108. On Mexico's preference for peonage over slavery, see "Texas—A Province, Republic, and State," *DBR* 23 (September 1857): 246.

115. Inman, *Old Santa Fe Trail*, 374–78. See also Kiser, *Borderlands of Slavery*, 89–91.

116. *Cong. Globe*, 30th Cong., 1st Sess., 871.

117. *Cong. Globe*, 30th Cong., 1st Sess., appendix, 913.

118. Green, *Journal of the Texian Expedition against Mier*, 427–29.

119. *Cong. Globe*, 30th Cong., 1st Sess., appendix, 1159, 1197, 919.

120. *Cong. Globe*, 31st Cong., 1st Sess., part 2, 1141–44.

121. Karp, "World the Slaveholders Craved"; Karp, *This Vast Southern Empire*, chaps. 6 and 7; E. Young, *Alien Nation*, chaps. 1, 2. For contemporary southern views on indentured Asian labor in the tropics, see W. W. Wright, "The Coolie Trade," *DBR* 27 (September 1859): 296–321. For the southern embrace of "coolie" labor in the post–Civil War period, see Jung, *Coolies and Cane*.

122. Karp, *This Vast Southern Empire*.

123. *Cong. Globe*, 36th Cong., 1st Sess., 2932.

Chapter Six

1. Speech of General W. Claude Jones at the secessionist convention at Mesilla, March 16, 1861, in *Mesilla (AZ) Times*, March 30, 1861. My thanks to Sarah Allison, special collections librarian at New Mexico State University, for making available to me this scarce issue.

2. See, for instance, J. McPherson, *Battle Cry of Freedom*; Freehling, *Road to Disunion: Secessionists at Bay* and *Secessionists Triumphant*; M. Morrison, *Slavery and the American West*; Holt, *Political Crisis of the 1850s*; and Potter, *Impending Crisis*. For an overview of the scholarship, see Towers, "Partisans, New History, and Modernization."

3. On US attempts to shore up western rebellions involving the nation's Indian peoples, see Hahn, "Slave Emancipation"; Hahn, *Nation without Borders*, chap. 10; Masich, *Civil War in the Southwest Borderlands*; Waite, "War in Indian Country"; and M. Nelson, *Three-Cornered War*.

4. See L. Richards, *California Gold Rush*; Ganaway, *New Mexico and the Sectional Controversy*; Kiser, *Turmoil on the Rio Grande*; Long, *Saints and the Union*; Maxwell, *Civil War Years in Utah*; and Jewell, "Thwarting Southern Schemes."

5. For a panoramic view of the secession crisis in the Far West, see Josephy, *Civil War in the American West*. Yet given the sheer scope of his subject, Josephy necessarily moves quickly through secession in order to reach the war itself.

6. See Horace Mann to James Richardson et al., May 3, 1850, in Mann, *Horace Mann's Letters*, 5–7; see also Mann to the *Boston Atlas*, June 6, 1850, also in *Horace Mann's Letters*; *Cong. Globe*, 31st Cong., 1st Sess., 1005–6; and John R. Bartlett to Jefferson Davis, December 29, 1850, *PJD*, 4:146–47. For the diversity and complexity of this region, see Mora, *Border Dilemmas*.

7. For the southern composition of early Arizona, see the travel memoir of Pumpelly, *Across America and Asia*, 29. For background on early Arizona, see Hall, "Mesilla Times," 338–39, 343; and Bancroft, *History of Arizona and New Mexico*, 474–93.

8. See Lansford Hastings to Governor Rencher, July 11, 1858, RI 907, William G. Ritch Collection, HEHL.

9. Kiser, *Turmoil on the Rio Grande*, 133–42; Ganaway, *New Mexico and the Sectional Controversy*, 105.

10. *Richmond Whig*, August 18, 1857; *Charleston Mercury*, August 19, 1857; *Charleston Courier*, August 19, 1857.

11. President Buchanan's Message to Congress, December 8, 1857, *Cong. Globe*, 35th Cong., 1st Sess., appendix, 6; President Buchanan's Message to Congress, December 6, 1859, *Cong. Globe*, 35th Cong., 2nd Sess., appendix, 5.

12. *Cong. Globe*, 34th Cong., 3rd Sess., 817; 35th Cong., 1st Sess., 13, 62; US Govt. Doc., 35th Cong., 1st Sess., Senate Journal, 41–47; *Cong. Globe*, 35th Cong., 2nd Sess., appendix, 48; *Cong. Globe*, 36th Cong., 1st Sess., 2071; *Richmond Whig*, March 2, 1860.

13. *Cong. Globe*, 36th Cong., 2nd Sess., 195–96.

14. *Charleston Courier*, November 13, 1857.

15. Lawrence, Kansas, to the *Boston Journal*, January 24, 1858, reprinted in the *Charleston Mercury*, March 23, 1858.

16. *Texas State Gazette*, May 22, 1858. See also the *Daily Confederation* (Montgomery, AL), June 30, 1858; and Alfred A. Smith, "A Southern Confederacy: Its Prospect, Resources, and Destiny," *DBR* 26 (May 1859): 571–72.

17. "The New Territory of Arizona," *DBR* 23 (November 1857): 543.

18. *Columbus (GA) Times* (n.d.) reprinted in the *Charleston Mercury*, June 28, 1859.

19. *Alexandria Gazette*, January 31, 1859. See also *Sacramento Daily Union*, July 4, 1859.

20. *Baltimore Sun* (n.d.) quoted in *New Orleans Daily Picayune*, February, 17, 1858. See also *New Orleans Daily Picayune*, September 11, 1859.

21. Hall, "Mesilla Times," 337; Kiser, *Turmoil on the Rio Grande*, 137–39.

22. Mowry, *Memoir of the Proposed Territory of Arizona*, 8, 13–15.

23. Mowry, *Geography and Resources of Arizona and Sonora*, 14.

24. Mowry, 34.

25. *Constitution and Schedule of the Provisional Government of the Territory of Arizona*, 8, 9.

26. *Constitution and Schedule of the Provisional Government of the Territory of Arizona*, article 3, section 9.

27. For some of the most helpful accounts of California state division, see McAfee, "California's House Divided"; Guinn, "How California Escaped State Division"; W. Ellison, "Movement for State Division in California"; R. Hunt, "History of the California State Division Controversy"; L. Richards, *California Gold Rush*; and Lynch, "Southern California Chivalry," 109–17.

28. See Lynch, "Southern California Chivalry," 66–70; and the firsthand postbellum account of Hubert Howe Bancroft, "Personal Observations during a tour through the Line of Missions of Upper California," Banc.

29. "An Act Granting the Consent of the Legislature to the Formation of a Different Government for the Southern Counties of this State," *Statutes of California*, 1859, 310–11.

30. McAfee, "California's House Divided," 117.

31. *Sacramento Daily Union*, March 26, 1859; see also August 13, 1859, and March 3, 1859.

32. Foote's speech is found in "The Southern Convention at Vicksburg, Part 2," *DBR* 27 (August 1859): 216; see also *Sacramento Daily Union*, August 17, 1859. Foote was so convinced of the proslavery nature of the Pacific coast that, while serving in the Confederate Congress in October 1862, he proposed the formation of "a league offensive and defensive, between said States and Territories [of the Far West] and the confederate States of America"; in F. Moore, *Rebellion Record*, 5:90.

33. *Baltimore Sun*, April 1859, excerpted in *Los Angeles Star*, May 28, 1859; see also McAfee, "California's House Divided," 127.

34. *Columbus Daily Enquirer*, November 1, 1859. For more southern reports on California state division, see *Daily True Delta*, November 12 and December 11, 1859; *San Antonio Ledger and Texan*, February 11, 1860; *Georgia Telegraph* (Macon), May 17, 1859.

35. "An Act Granting the Consent of the Legislature to the Formation of a Different Government for the Southern Counties of this State," 310–11.

36. A total of 2,457 Southern Californians voted for the territory, and only 828 against; *Columbus Daily Enquirer*, November 1, 1859; Hunt, "History of the California State Division Controversy," 41–45.

37. Latham's views on slavery are most clearly articulated in an April 1860 Senate speech, a response to William Seward's "irrepressible conflict" address; *Cong. Globe*, 36th Cong., 1st Sess., 1727–29. See also William Thompson, "Political Career of Milton Slocum Latham"; and Rappel-Kroyzer, "California Democratic Party."

38. *Communication of Governor Latham to the President of the United States*, 4.

The communication was one of the few pieces of official business that Latham completed as governor. In fact, his five-day term makes him the shortest-serving executive in California history. Latham was not a consistent Chivalry ally, nor did he enjoy a particularly easy relationship with William Gwin. For more on their rivalry, see George Wallace to Milton S. Latham, February 23, March 29, and March 30, 1860, in Papers of Milton S. Latham, California Historical Society, San Francisco.

39. State of California, *Journal of the Assembly*, 1860, 228–33. See also *Sacramento Daily Union*, January 27, 1860; *Los Angeles Star*, March 10, 1860; and *Sacramento Daily Union*, March 15, 1860.

40. Lincoln to William Henry Seward, February 1, 1861, in Basler, *Collected Works of Abraham Lincoln*, 4:183; see also Hammond, "High-Road to a Slave Empire."

41. Fehrenbacher, *Dred Scott Case*, 526.

42. West, *Creating the West*, chap. 4. See also Holt, *Fate of Their Country*.

43. West, *Creating the West*, chap. 4.

44. James Buchanan, Third Annual Message, December 19, 1859, in J. Richardson, *Compilation of the Messages and Papers of the Presidents*, 7:3085.

45. *Cong. Globe*, 36th Cong., 1st Sess., 2344.

46. Stephen Douglas, "The Dividing Line between Federal and Local Authority: Popular Sovereignty in the Territories," *Harper's Magazine*, September 1859, 519–37.

47. See Douglas, *Letter of Judge Douglas in Reply to the Speech of Dr. Gwin*.

48. Fehrenbacher, *Dred Scott Case*, 515–16, 531–32. For a sweeping account of the feud between Davis and Douglas and the direction of the Democratic Party, see Woods, *Arguing until Doomsday*.

49. Halstead, *History of the National Political Conventions*, 54; Parkhurst, *Official Proceedings of the Democratic National Convention*, 47; D. Williams, "California Democrats of 1860," 239–46.

50. D. Williams, "California Democrats of 1860," 247–49; Potter, *Impending Crisis*, 405–47. For an explanation as to why Oregon, despite its southern orientation during these debates, falls beyond the remit of this book, see introduction, n8.

51. L. Richards, *California Gold Rush*, 224–29; G. Stanley, "Republican Party in California," 88–109; McCurdy, "Prelude to Civil War," 24–25; *Los Angeles Star*, September 8, September 29, and November 3, 1860.

52. *Cong. Globe*, 36th Cong., 2nd Sess., 114.

53. C. Hart, "Why Lincoln Said 'No,'" 736–40.

54. May, *Southern Dream of a Caribbean Empire*, 208–26.

55. Lincoln to Thurlow Weed, December 17, 1860, in Basler, *Collected Works of Abraham Lincoln*, 4:154.

56. Lincoln to William Kellog, December 11, 1860, in Basler, *Collected Works of Abraham Lincoln*, 4:150. See also Lincoln to Elihu B. Washburne, December 13, 1860, 151; Lincoln to Lyman Trumbull, December 17, 1860, 153; and Lincoln to John D. Defrees, December 18, 1860, 155.

57. *Cong. Globe*, 36th Cong., 2nd Sess., 1088–94.

58. *Cong. Globe*, 36th Cong., 2nd Sess., 651.

59. *Cong. Globe*, 36th Cong., 2nd Sess., 1007.

60. Lincoln to William H. Seward, February 1, 1861, in Basler, *Collected Works of Abraham Lincoln*, 4:183. See also Crittenden on the sterility of New Mexico; *Cong. Globe*, 36th Cong., 2nd Sess., 1375–76.

61. *Cong. Globe*, 36th Cong., 2nd Sess., appendix, 263–63. See also *Cong. Globe*, 36th Cong., 2nd Sess., 132–33.

62. *Cong. Globe*, 36th Cong., 2nd Sess., appendix, 191. For more on these debates, see C. Hart, "Why Lincoln Said 'No.'"

63. Cleveland, *Alexander H. Stephens in Public and Private*, 717–29.

64. "The Perils of Peace," *DBR* 31 (October–November 1861): 396–97.

65. George B. McClellan to Abraham Lincoln, July 7, 1862, *OR*, 11 (1): 73–74.

66. William Gwin to Joseph Lancaster Brent, March 27, 1863, Joseph Lancaster Brent Papers, HEHL. For more on the possibility of multiple American confederacies, see Quigley, *Shifting Grounds*, 120.

67. The movement also extended to Oregon and Washington. See Hull, "Movement in Oregon"; and J. Ellison, "Designs for a Pacific Republic," 319–42. My thanks to Knute Berger for introducing me to the Pacific Northwest component of this story.

68. Quoted in Halstead, *History of the National Political Conventions*, 79.

69. Before moving to his comments on Californian independence, Latham devoted much of the speech to an attack on abolitionism. He argued that "the South claims nothing but her constitutional rights" and defended slaveholders' prerogative to the "protection and enjoyment" of their human property within the federal territories. *Cong. Globe*, 36th Cong., 1st Sess., 1727–29. See also "Pacific Confederacy," *Alta California*, January 12, 1861.

70. With convenient historical amnesia, Latham insisted "there is not a word of truth" in the assertion that California "would form a Pacific Republic" in the event of southern secession; *Cong. Globe*, 36th Cong., 2nd Sess., 27. For the national critique of western separatism, see *Alta California*, December 11, 1860; *San Francisco Bulletin*, November 27 and December 24, 1860; and *New York Herald*, December 14, 1860 and January 5, 1861.

71. Ashbury Harpending, one of the major pro-Confederate conspirators in California, claimed that the "Republic of the Pacific" was to be "a preliminary" for a Confederate takeover of the state; Harpending, *Great Diamond Hoax*, 30–31. See also *Los Angeles Southern News*, March 1, 1861.

72. Charles L. Scott to Charles Lindley, Chairman of the Democratic State Central Committee of California, December 21, 1860, printed in the *San Francisco Bulletin*, January 16, 1861. Similarly, the *Los Angeles Star* predicted that an independent California would pave the way for a southern Pacific railroad; *Los Angeles Star*, December 8 and December 22, 1860; William Carey Jones to the *San Francisco Herald*, December 15, 1860, in Benjamin Hayes Scrapbooks, vol. 19, no. 10, Banc.

73. For Burch's position, see *Red Bluff (CA) Independent*, January 8, 1861; *Sacramento Daily Union*, February 13, 1861; and W. J. Davis, *History of Political Conventions in California*, 128–29. For Gwin's views, see William Gwin to Calhoun Benham, February 8, 1861, *OR*, series 2, 2:1015; and Gwin to Joseph Lancaster Brent, March 27, 1863, Joseph Lancaster Brent Papers, HEHL.

74. Shortly after the US-Mexico War, rumors circulated that California might

secede from the United States; see James K. Polk, December 12, 1848, in Polk, *Polk*, 356.

75. Green, *Letter from General Thomas J. Green*, 7.

76. T. Richards, *Breakaway Americas*; Isenberg and Richards, "Alternative Wests"; T. Richards, "'Farewell to America'"; St. John, "Unpredictable America of William Gwin"; Rodriguez, "'Children of the Great Mexican Family'"; Downs, "Mexicanization of American Politics"; Reséndez, *Changing National Identities*; Meinig, *Continental America*, 197; Kreitner, *Break It Up*.

77. For an excellent account of South Carolina's secessionist commissioners, see Dew, *Apostles of Disunion*. For more on Herbert, see Ayres, *Gold and Sunshine*, 120. Texas also sent secessionist commissioners to meet with the Five Nations in Indian Territory; see McCaslin, "Bitter Legacy," 19.

78. This resolution was included in the report of Lorenzo Labadie to James L. Collins, June 16, 1861, in J. P. Wilson, *When the Texans Came*, 27. See also *OR*, 4:39.

79. For a report on the Tucson meeting, see *Mesilla Times*, March 30, 1861. The Arizona secessionists did not bother consulting the Hispano population, probably realizing that they could not count on them for support.

80. *Mesilla Times*, March 30, 1861.

81. *Cong. Globe*, 36th Cong., 2nd Sess., 250–53.

82. Russel, *Improvement of Communication*, 287–91.

83. L. Hafen, *Overland Mail*, 189; and Russel, *Improvement of Communication*, 292–93.

84. *Mesilla Times*, March 30, 1861. See also *Sacramento Daily Union*, April 4 and 16, 1861; and Finch, "William Claude Jones."

85. Ganaway, *New Mexico and the Sectional Controversy*, 108–10; Kiser, *Turmoil on the Rio Grande*, 144–46.

86. Lorenzo Labadie to James L. Collins, June 16, 1861, in J. P. Wilson, *When the Texans Came*, 27; Ganaway, *New Mexico and the Sectional Controversy*, 108–13.

87. W. W. Mills to John S. Watts, June 23, 1861, *OR*, 4:56.

88. On divisions within the slave states during the war, see Freehling, *South vs. the South*; and McCurry, *Confederate Reckoning*. For the backlash against secessionists in the border slave states in 1861, see Levine, *Fall of the House of Dixie*, 67.

89. Alexander Jackson to Jefferson Davis, February 17, 1861, in J. P. Wilson, *When the Texans Came*, 19–20.

90. Harpending, *Great Diamond Hoax*, 25–43; Quinn, *Rivals*, 284–85.

91. Brent, *Memoirs of the War between the States*, 52–53. See also Hayes, *Pioneer Notes*, 251–56.

92. Josephy, *Civil War in the American West*, 34–36; Richard S. Ewell to Bettie Ewell, January 22, 1861, in Pfanz, *Letters of General Richard S. Ewell*, 161–62; Ball, *Army Regulars on the Western Frontier*, 189–203.

93. Paludan, "War Is the Health of the Party," 64; Guelzo, *Fateful Lightning*, 127–29; W. Gallagher, *How the Post Office Created America*, 108.

94. Abraham Lincoln, "Memoranda on Federal Appointments," ca. April 1, 1861, in Basler, *Collected Works of Abraham Lincoln*, 4:304–6; J. Carter, "Abraham Lincoln and the California Patronage."

95. John S. Watts to Abraham Lincoln, April 1, 1861, the Robert Todd Lincoln Collection of the Papers of Abraham Lincoln, LOC; see also Kellogg, "Lincoln's New Mexico Patronage," 511–17.

96. Miguel Otero to Colonel Collins, November 8, 1860, in *Santa Fe Gazette*, December 8, 1860; Otero, *Abolition Attack*; and Sunseri, *Seeds of Discord*, 133–35.

97. Watts to Lincoln, April 1, and Watts to Lincoln, April 2, 1861, in Robert Todd Lincoln Collection, LOC.

98. Kellogg, "Lincoln's New Mexico Patronage," 524–28.

99. Ganaway, *New Mexico and the Sectional Controversy*, 94–100. On Hispano grievances and contested sovereignty in the US-Mexico borderlands, see B. Johnson, "Reconstructing North America."

100. Connelly, *First Annual Message*, 12; see also Connelly, *Proclamation by the Governor*.

101. Long, *Saints and the Union*, 6–16.

102. See, for instance, *Deseret News*, February 27, 1861.

103. All three quotes were recorded by Samuel Bowles during his travels through Utah at the end of the war; Bowles, *Across the Continent*, 391–94. See also Maxwell, *Civil War Years in Utah*, 57, 171–72, 314.

104. Hicks, "George Armstrong Hicks," 174.

105. *Deseret News*, March 6, 1861; Maxwell, *Civil War Years in Utah*, 40–44.

106. Long, *Saints and the Union*, 18; Bushman, *Rough Stone Rolling*, 191–92.

107. Brigham Young, "Human Intelligence and Freedom—National Administrative Movements, &c." *Journal of Discourses* 8 (February 10, 1861): 323; Long, *Saints and the Union*, 19–20.

108. Maxwell, *Civil War Years in Utah*, 59, 73–74.

109. See, for instance, Clarence Bennett to General Edwin Sumner, August 6, 1861, *OR*, 50 (1): 556–58; see also *OR*, 50 (1): 550, 564; and J. Campbell, "Abode of Chivalry."

110. M. Nelson, "Civil War from Apache Pass," 512–22.

111. Quoted in M. Nelson, 520.

112. M. Nelson, *Three-Cornered War*, 15–25.

113. Utley, *Frontiersmen in Blue*, 211–18; Kiser, *Turmoil on the Rio Grande*, 127–28, 151; Masich, *Civil War in the Southwest Borderlands*, 38–39; Waite, "War in Indian Country."

114. *Alta California*, June 11, 1861.

115. (False) rumors of a joint Mormon-Indian conspiracy against white American settlement had circulated since the 1830s, when the LDS church began a series of sporadic missions to various Indigenous peoples. For more on this conspiracy theory, see Reeve, *Religion of a Different Color*, 59–90.

116. Jefferson to James Monroe, November 24, 1801, in Oberg, *Papers of Thomas Jefferson*, 719–20.

117. Jefferson Davis, Report of the Secretary of War, December 1, 1853, *JDC*, 2:292–320.

118. William Need to Simon Cameron, September 27, 1861, *OR*, 50 (1): 635–41.

119. Need to Cameron, September 27, 1861, *OR*, 50 (1): 637–38.

Chapter Seven

1. John R. Baylor, "Proclamation to the People of the Territory of Arizona," August 1, 1861, *OR*, 4:19–20.

2. Frazier, *Blood and Treasure*.

3. On the strategic significance of this conquest, see Baylor to General Earl Van Dorn, August 14, 1861, *OR*, 4:22–23. See also Teel, "Sibley's New Mexican Campaign," 700.

4. See introduction, notes 27, 28, and 29.

5. For the Civil War along the border states, see C. Phillips, *Rivers Ran Backward*; and Burke, "Scattered People." For secessionist scares in the Lower Middle West, see M. Stanley, *Loyal West*, 80–93. See also Cowsert, "Should Indian Territory Be Considered a Border State?"

6. Jefferson Davis, "Message to Congress, April 29, 1861," on the ratification of the Confederate Constitution, *JDC*, 5:84. See also J. McPherson, *Embattled Rebel*, 28, 103.

7. Jefferson Davis, *Rise and Fall of the Confederate Government*, 1:vii.

8. Robert E. Lee to Lord Acton, December 15, 1866, in Figgis and Laurence, *Selections from the Correspondence of the First Lord Acton*, 303. My thanks to John Barr for directing my attention to this letter.

9. May, "Irony of Confederate Diplomacy," 73–75.

10. Crofts, *Lincoln and the Politics of Slavery*. See also Abraham Lincoln, "First Inaugural Address," in Basler, *Collected Works of Abraham Lincoln*, 4:262–71.

11. Robert Toombs speech, November 13, 1860, in Freehling and Simpson, *Secession Debated*, 31–50. On Confederate expansionist ambitions, see Brettle, "Fortunes of War."

12. *Constitution of the Confederate States of America*, article 4, section 3.3, p. 19. The administration put this clause into effect when it organized the Confederate territory of Arizona by June 1862; "Executive Dept Ariz. Terr. Proclamation," June 11, 1862, *OR*, 9:692.

13. Sumner to Colonel E. D. Townsend, April 28, 1861, *OR*, 50 (1): 472.

14. Baylor to Colonel H. E. McCulloch, November 10, 1861, *OR*, 4:135.

15. Baylor to Major S. B. Davis, November 2, 1861, *OR*, 4:149.

16. Robinson, *Los Angeles in Civil War Days*, 62–64, 83–85, 118; Walters, "Confederates in Southern California," 51–52; Woolsey, "Politics of a Lost Cause," 376; Lewis, "Los Angeles in the Civil War Decades"; Clendenen, "Dan Showalter."

17. Josephy, *Civil War in the American West*, 235–36.

18. Faragher, *Eternity Street*, 385–86.

19. "You can appreciate in part the agony that is mine at the thought of turning my back (most probably forever) upon my motherless infant," Thom wrote to his brother before departing for the Confederacy. Cameron Erskine Thom to Pembroke Thom, January 5, 1863; Cameron Erskine Thom to Pembroke Thom, September 27, 1863; William Alexander Thom to brother, June 30, 1863, all in Thom Family Papers, section 3, folder 5, VHS. See also Krick, *Staff Officers in Gray*, 284.

20. Bell, *On the Old West Coast*, 74. See also *Los Angeles Star*, November 29, 1862; and Robinson, *Los Angeles in Civil War Days*, 85.

21. Low, *Some Reflections of an Early California Governor*, 12.

22. Sumner to Colonel George Wright, September 30, 1861, *OR*, 50 (1): 643.

23. See four letters to Sumner about the powerful presence of secessionists in southern California, *OR*, 50 (1): 563–66.

24. Keehn, *Knights of the Golden Circle*.

25. Clarence Bennett to General Edwin Sumner, August 6, 1861, *OR*, 50 (1): 556–58. This resolution was obtained by a Unionist agent who had infiltrated the San Bernardino chapter.

26. Robert Robinson to Brigadier General John S. Mason, August 10, 1864, *OR*, 50 (2): 938.

27. Robinson to Mason, *OR*, 50 (2): 940.

28. *Sacramento Daily Union*, August 28, 1861; see also *Alta California*, September 9, 1861.

29. Casserly, *Issue in California*, 11–14.

30. E. Powell, "Southern Influences in California Politics," 176–80.

31. Robinson, *Los Angeles in Civil War Days*, 70–71; Woolsey, "Politics of a Lost Cause," 378; W. J. Davis, *History of Political Conventions in California*, 179–80.

32. *San Francisco Bulletin*, September 13, 1862.

33. *OR*, 50 (1): 621–22; *Los Angeles Southern News*, March 1, 1861; Woolsey, "Politics of a Lost Cause," 376; Robinson, *Los Angeles in Civil War Days*, 16–17, 25, 50–51, 58–59; Gilbert, "Confederate Minority in California," 168; Bell, *On the Old West Coast*, 72.

34. On the necessity of reinforcing Southern California, see Sumner to Colonel E. D. Townsend, September 17, 1861, *OR*, 50 (1): 623.

35. Ironically, Carleton was a southwestern slaveholder himself. He carried an enslaved black man into New Mexico in the early 1850s and subsequently sold him to Governor William Carr Lane, a native of Missouri; Masich, *Civil War in the Southwest Borderlands*, 276.

36. Robinson, *Los Angeles in Civil War Days*, 58–61, 68–69, 93–94; Matthews, *Golden State in the Civil War*, 116–17. The figure of 8,000 troops comes from Drum Barracks Civil War Museum (drumbarracks.org).

37. Bell, *On the Old West Coast*, 75.

38. Gilbert, "The Confederate Minority in California," 157. For more on the disloyalty of San Bernardino's residents, see *Alta California*, November 23, 1864.

39. Henry Dwight Barrows to Colonel J. H. Carleton, April 9, 1862, *OR*, 50 (1): 993. Shortly thereafter, King was arrested on charges of treason, though released upon taking a loyalty oath; *OR*, 50 (1): 994.

40. Barrows to Brigadier General George Wright, April 10, 1862, *OR*, 50 (1): 996.

41. Lieutenant Colonel George S. Evans to Lieutenant Colonel R. C. Drum, December 1, 1862, *OR*, 50 (2): 236.

42. Evans to Drum, *OR*, 50 (2): 236. For more reports of pro-Confederate activity beyond Los Angeles and Visalia, see *OR*, 50 (2): 707, 924–25.

43. E. Powell, "Southern Influences in California Politics," 194–98.

44. Gilbert, "Confederate Minority in California," 160–62.

45. Evans to Drum, *OR*, 50 (2): 236.

46. Los Angeles had one other newspaper during the war years, the *Semi-Weekly Southern News*, published by C. R. Conway and Alonzo Waite.

47. For Hamilton's biography see Robinson, "California Copperhead."

48. *Los Angeles Star*, January 5, 1861; the same issue featured Hamilton's support for a Pacific republic. See also Faragher, *Eternity Street*, 384; and an official report presented in the state senate, which quotes this issue in an attempt to discredit Hamilton's 1864 bid for office; *Report of the Senate Committee on Elections, in the Contested Election Case*, 5.

49. *Los Angeles Star*, November 29, 1862; November 7, 1863; May 14, 1864.

50. *Los Angeles Star*, November 8, 1862; January 16, 1864, quoting the *London Herald*, no date. See also *Los Angeles Star*, December 13, 1862; January 3, 1863.

51. *Los Angeles Star*, April 23, 1864.

52. *Los Angeles Star*, November 7, 1863.

53. *Los Angeles Star*, December 27, 1862.

54. See, for example, Venit-Shelton, "'A More Loyal, Union Loving People Can Nowhere Be Found,'" 489.

55. [San Francisco businessmen] to Simon Cameron, August 28, 1861, *OR*, 50 (1): 589–91. The letter was written in response to rumors that Sumner was to be sent east to Texas with 5,000 California troops, thus depriving the state of much-needed defenders.

56. Carleton's men skirmished with a small detachment of Arizona Confederates at Stanwix Station, a stop on the Butterfield Overland Mail Road, eighty miles east of the California border. There were no fatalities in what is considered the western-most battle of the war; Hall, *Sibley's New Mexico Campaign*, introduction. On the torrential rains that contributed to Carleton's delay, see William J. Cowan "Remembering the Great California Flood of 1862," *San Diego Union-Tribune*, May 22, 2014.

57. *Cong. Globe*, 37th Cong., 2nd Sess., 1948.

58. For more on these debates, see Russel, *Improvement of Communication*, 294–307.

59. *Cong. Globe*, 37th Cong., 2nd Sess., 1950.

60. Ganaway, *New Mexico and the Sectional Controversy*, 119–21.

61. Frazier, *Blood and Treasure*, 117–34.

62. Samuel Cooper to Henry H. Sibley, July 8, 1861, *OR*, 4:93.

63. Teel, "Sibley's New Mexican Campaign," 700 (italics in original).

64. W. H. Watford writes, "In the western correspondence of the Confederacy nothing appeared quite so frequently as the phrase 'outlet to the Pacific'"; Watford, "Confederate Western Ambitions," 168. See also Captain Gurden Chapin to Henry Halleck, February 28, 1862, *OR*, 9:634–35.

65. Proclamation of Brigadier General H. H. Sibley to the People of New Mexico, December 20, 1861, *OR*, 4:89.

66. M. Nelson, *Three-Cornered War*, 99–100.

67. M. Nelson, 94–100.

68. James Reily to Henry H. Sibley, January 20, 1861, *OR*, 4:171–72.

69. Hall, "Colonel James Reily's Diplomatic Missions"; Frazier, *Blood and Treasure*, 145–46; M. Nelson, *Three-Cornered War*, 83–85. For US diplomatic countermeasures in Sonora, see Carleton to Don Ignacio Pesqueira, May 2, 1862 *OR*, 50 (1): 1044–45; and Wright to Pesqueira, May 3, 1862, *OR*, 50 (1): 1047–48.

70. May, "Irony of Confederate Diplomacy," 86–91.

71. For more on Confederate Indian policy, see Warde, *When the Wolf Came*, 51–59, 121–22, 127; Waite, "War in Indian Country"; and Agnew, "Our Doom as a Nation Is Sealed."

72. Frazier, *Blood and Treasure*, 64–66.

73. *Mesilla Times*, October 3, 1861, reprinted in J. P. Wilson, *When the Texans Came*, 150–51; see also M. Nelson, *Three-Cornered War*, 24–25.

74. Henry H. Sibley to General Samuel Cooper, May 4, 1862, *OR*, 9:512.

75. John R. Baylor to Major General J. B. Magruder, December 29, 1862, *OR*, 15:914–17.

76. Baylor to Magruder, *OR*, 15:914–17.

77. M. Nelson, *Three-Cornered War*, 79–89; Kiser, *Turmoil on the Rio Grande*, 181–86.

78. Quoted in Jacoby, *Shadows at Dawn*, 119.

79. Masich, *Civil War in the Southwest Borderlands*, 82.

80. On Sibley's inadequacies as a commander, see Teel, "Sibley's New Mexican Campaign," 700; and West, *Creating the West*, chap. 5.

81. For the environmental obstacles that Sibley faced, see M. Nelson, "Death in the Distance."

82. K. Adams, "War in the West"; Josephy, *Civil War in the American West*, 91; M. Nelson, *Three-Cornered War*, 101–21; Masich, *Civil War in the Southwest Borderlands*, 110.

83. For a counterpoint to this argument, see G. Gallagher, "How the West Wasn't Won." Gallagher is right to note that Confederate leaders were consumed by major operations closer to Richmond and therefore had little energy to devote to such a distant (and relatively small) campaign. Judging by the standards of the East, Sibley's operation was indeed a minor affair. But judging by the standards of the Far Southwest itself, the Confederate invasion takes on greater significance. It brought about some of the largest and bloodiest military encounters the region had ever seen, and it set in motion a series of events that would forever alter the balance of power across this broad swath of the American map.

84. [Pollard], Letter to the President, May 30, 1861, in [Pollard], *Southern Spy*, 68.

85. Lincoln recalled this decision in a later message to Congress, dated May 27, 1862, in F. Moore, *Rebellion Record*, 5:145.

86. Quoted in Walters, "Confederates in Southern California," 41. Grant knew firsthand of the wealth coming from western mines as he had spent time in gold rush California before the war; see Grant, *Personal Memoirs*, 1:159–66.

87. With Sibley's invasion of the Southwest, the Pacific squadron was placed on alert. For more on the federal naval presence in the Pacific theater, see A. Hunt, *Army of the Pacific*, 301–20.

88. Harpending, *Great Diamond Hoax*, 9–26.

89. Harpending, 73–74.

90. Harpending, 46–48.

91. Harpending, 48.

92. Harpending, 74–78.

93. *Alta California*, September 9, 1863; see also *Alta California*, March 16, March 17, and October 13, 1863; and Harpending, *Great Diamond Hoax*, 65–89. For more on the operation, see A. Hunt, *Army of the Pacific*, 305–10, 314.

94. Lansford Hastings to Jefferson Davis, December 16, 1863, *OR*, 50 (2): 700–701. For the guidebook, see Hastings, *Emigrants Guide to Oregon and California*.

95. Clendenen, "Confederate Spy in California," 225–29.

96. Quoted in *Alta California*, September 10, 1864. See also Boessenecker, *Badge and Buckshot*, 133–55; and Haskins, *Argonauts of California*, 224.

97. W. J. Davis, *History of Political Conventions in California*, 204–5.

98. Boessenecker, *Badge and Buckshot*, 141–47.

99. *Alta California*, September 10, 1864.

100. Boessenecker, *Badge and Buckshot*, 149–55.

101. *Los Angeles Star*, January 17, 1863.

102. Robinson, "California Copperhead," 219–28; Robinson, *Los Angeles in Civil War Days*, 114–15, 149–50; Gilbert, "Confederate Minority in California," 162–64. For the parallel campaign against the administration's political opponents in the Northeast, see J. Weber, *Copperheads*.

103. Chandler, "Uncertain Influence," 248–50.

104. For more on Biggs, see Field and Lynch, "'Master of Ceremonies.'"

105. Gilbert, "Confederate Minority in California," 164; Robinson, "California Copperhead," 220–21; Robinson, *Los Angeles in Civil War Days*, 101–11, 140; see also *OR*, 50 (1): 1015.

106. Bensel, *Yankee Leviathan*.

107. Ganaway, *New Mexico and the Sectional Controversy*, 94–100. See also Connelly, *First Annual Message*, 12; and Connelly, *Proclamation by the Governor*.

108. Kiser, *Borderlands of Slavery*, 138.

109. "An Act to secure Freedom to all Persons within the Territories of the United States," June 19, 1862, *Statutes at Large, Treaties, and Proclamations of the United States of America*, 12:432.

110. Masich, *Civil War in the Southwest Borderlands*, 48; Blyth, "Kit Carson and the War for the Southwest."

111. Lynch, "On the Edge of Empires."

112. Madley, *American Genocide*, 332–33.

113. S. Moore, "'We Feel the Want of Protection,'" 117–20.

114. West, *Creating the West*, chap. 5.

115. Woolsey, "Politics of a Lost Cause," 379–80; Robinson, "A California Copperhead," 227–28; John W. Shore to Brent, July 9, 1865, in Joseph Lancaster Brent Papers, HEHL.

116. Ulysses S. Grant to Irvine McDowell, January 8, 1865, *OR*, 50 (2): 1118.

117. Brent, *Memoirs of the War between the States*, 59.

118. Edwin Vose Sumner to Lawrence Kip, November 4, 1861, Joseph Lancaster Brent Papers, HEHL. For an account of the arrest of the Californians and the search of their property, see Henry B. Judd to Charles S. Merchant, November 5, 1861, Joseph Lancaster Brent Papers, HEHL.

119. Brent, *Memoirs of the War between the States*, 67–69.

120. George Dennison Prentice, Memorandum, December 7, 1861, Joseph Lan-

caster Brent Papers, HEHL; Brent, *Memoirs of the War between the States*, 77–82. Earlier, the three had signed a statement of parole; Calhoun Benham, Joseph Lancaster Brent, and William M. Gwin to William Henry Seward, December 5, 1861; see also William Henry Seward, Memorandum, December 10, 1861, both in Joseph Lancaster Brent Papers, HEHL.

121. William M. Gwin to Joseph Lancaster Brent, March 27, 1863, Joseph Lancaster Brent Papers, HEHL.

122. See Nathanial Beverley Tucker to "Dear Friend," March 8, 1863, Thom Family Papers, section 3, box 6, VHS. For more on Napoleon's attitude toward the Confederacy, see Sainlaude, *France and the American Civil War*, chap. 6.

123. William M. Gwin to Napoleon III, January 5, 1864, Paris, William M. Gwin Papers, Banc.

124. Gwin followed up on his January letter with more detailed plans. See "Rules and Regulations for carrying into effect the Treaty between their Majesties the Emperor of the French and the Emperor of Mexico," MSS; Gwin, "Eclaircissement sur le Projet de Colonisation des Etats de Sonora et de Chihuahua," March 1864; and Gwin, "Memorandum on the Colonization of Sonora, 1864," all in William M. Gwin Papers, Banc. For more on Gwin's operations in Paris, see L. Thomas, *Between Two Empires*, 284–304; and H. McPherson, "Plan of William McKendree Gwin for a Colony in North Mexico."

125. Gwin's memoirs, originally dictated to the California bookseller and historian Hubert Howe Bancroft in 1878, are notoriously self-serving and revisionist. Throughout, he underplays his proslavery allegiances and Confederate sympathies. In contrast, his candor here is remarkable; Gwin, "Memoirs on the History of the United States, Mexico, and California," Banc. (These musings are written on a tipped-in leaf, numbered as page 249½.)

126. St. John, "Unpredictable America of William Gwin," 58, 61.

127. Ulysses S. Grant to Irvin McDowell, January 8, 1865, *OR*, 50 (2): 1118. For more on Grant and Mexico, see Hardy, "South of the Border."

128. Irvin McDowell to Ulysses S. Grant, March 12, 1865, *OR*, 50 (2): 1158–60. See also Chandler, "Uncertain Influence," 252.

129. Gwin to his brother, June 1, 1864, in E. Coleman, "Senator's Gwin's Plan for the Colonization of Sonora." In his memoirs, Gwin claimed to be "a consistent and unwavering union man throughout," Gwin, "Memoirs on the History of the United States, Mexico, and California," 249½, Banc. Even before Gwin arrived in Sonora, disunionists like Cameron Thom believed French intervention in Mexico would lift rebel prospects in the West; Cameron Erskine Thom to Pembroke Thom, January 5, 1863, section 3, folder 5; also Charles Slaughter Moorehead to Captain Thom, October 7 and 17, 1863, section 3, folder 3, all in Thom Family Papers, VHS. See also Egerton, "Rethinking Atlantic Historiography in a Postcolonial World," 88.

130. John Slidell to Judah Benjamin, Paris, June 2, 1864, quoted in G. Stanley, "Senator William Gwin," 252. See also Calhoun Benham to Joseph Lancaster Brent, November 25, 1864, Joseph Lancaster Brent Papers, HEHL. For Benjamin on the Pacific, see *New Orleans Picayune* (n.d.), reprinted in *Arkansas Whig*, January 22, 1852.

131. Gwin, "Memoirs on the History of United States, Mexico, and California," 225–45, Banc. For his complaints that he had not received adequate support from

Maximilian's court, see William M. Gwin to Napoleon, July 3, 1865, William M. Gwin Papers, Banc.

132. Three months after Gwin fled Mexico, Maximilian commissioned another veteran proslavery expansionist, Matthew Fontaine Maury, to carry out a similar plan; see L. Thomas, *Between Two Empires*, 361.

133. William M. Gwin to the Marquis de Montholon, October 15, 1865, in E. Coleman, "Senator Gwin's Plan for the Colonization of Sonora," 210.

134. L. Thomas, *Between Two Empires*, 314–54; St. John, "Unpredictable America of William Gwin," 73–74; Bloss, "Senator Defiled," 385–418.

135. Gwin insisted on his innocence to the very end, complaining that "no intimation has been given to me as to the cause of my arrest." He also noted that the garrison at Fort Jackson was "composed of negro troops," likely a galling sight to someone who had until recently commanded a large plantation of black slaves; William M. Gwin to Charles Jean Tristan Montholon, October 15, 1865, William M. Gwin Papers, Banc. In a later letter to Brent, the liberated Gwin wrote, "Thank God I have never taken an oath [of allegiance]"; William M. Gwin to Joseph Lancaster Brent, June 13, 1866, Joseph Lancaster Brent Papers, HEHL.

136. For more on political prisoners during the Civil War, see Blair, *With Malice toward Some*.

137. For months after the war, the California press maintained a keen interest in the ill-fated Sonora colony and the man derided as "Duke Gwin." See *San Francisco Bulletin*, February 22, March 3, November 23, and December 28, 1866; *Alta California*, May 6, 1866; *Sacramento Daily Union*, May 18 and November 20, 1866; and *Marysville (CA) Daily Appeal*, January 16, 1867.

138. John R. Baylor to James Seddon, December 21, 1864, *OR*, series 4, 3:960; Baylor to Seddon, January 24, 1865, *OR*, series 4, 3:1035; Baylor's Commission, *OR*, series 4, 3:1168–69. See also Watford, "Far-Western Wing of the Rebellion," 141–42.

139. Bottoms, *Aristocracy of Color*, 62–63; Gilbert, "Confederate Minority in California," 165. One of the keenest students of Brown's career is Knute Berger, whose work on the subject appears in "The Untold Story of Seattle's Racist Mayor," *Crosscut*, August 12, 2015, http://crosscut.com/2015/08/the-untold-story-of-seattles-racist-mayor/. On Californians celebrating Lincoln's assassination, see the report of E. D. Waite, *OR*, 50 (2): 1202; also *OR*, 50 (2): 1198; *OR*, 50 (2): 1201; Bell, *On the Old West Coast*, 75; Newmark, *Sixty Years in Southern California*, 336; and Lewis, "Los Angeles in the Civil War Decades," 292–93.

140. Finch, "Arizona in Exile," 81; see also *OR*, 50 (2): 1204.

Chapter Eight

1. Bret Harte to the *Springfield Republican*, September 9, 1866, in Harte, *San Francisco in 1866*, 55–56. For similar sentiments, see John W. Shore to Joseph Lancaster Brent, July 9, 1865, Joseph Lancaster Brent Papers, HEHL.

2. Oregon initially ratified the Fourteenth Amendment and then rescinded its ratification two years later.

3. Montoya, "Not-So-Free Labor," 163.

4. Berwanger, *West and Reconstruction*, was among the first to investigate the

struggle over Reconstruction policy in the West. For helpful overviews of this scholarship, see S. Smith, "Beyond North and South"; West, "Future of Reconstruction Studies"; and Waite, "West and Reconstruction after the American Civil War."

5. For important works that foreground the West in the history of the Reconstruction era, see S. Gordon, *Mormon Question*; H. Richardson, *West from Appomattox*; H. Richardson, *How the South Won the Civil War*, chap. 4; Paddison, *American Heathens*; Bottoms, *Aristocracy of Color*; S. Smith, *Freedom's Frontier*; Hahn, "Slave Emancipation"; Hahn, *Nation without Borders*; Downs and Masur, *World the Civil War Made*; Kelman, *Misplaced Massacre*; Kelman, *For Liberty and Empire*; and Teitelman, "Governing the Peripheries."

6. West, *Last Indian War*; West, "Reconstructing Race"; West, *Creating the West*; White, *Republic for Which It Stands*, 103–35.

7. Foner, *Reconstruction*. For more on this retreat from Reconstruction, albeit an account that largely ignores the Far West, see Gillette, *Retreat from Reconstruction*.

8. *Sacramento Daily Union*, April 29, 1865.

9. *Sacramento Daily Union*, October 2, 1867.

10. The number of inhabitants born in the former Confederacy, by state or territory, is as follows: California, 21,045; Oregon, 4,457; Nevada, 1,531; Washington, 848; Montana, 851; Idaho, 484. Berwanger condenses this census data in *West and Reconstruction*, 19–20. For the original figures, see Walker, *Compendium of the Ninth Census*, 378–88. See also D. Wright, "Making of Cosmopolitan California," 339.

11. Lucy Smith Crittenden Thornton to Harry Inness Thornton Jr., November 21, 1866, and April 14, 1867, in Lucy Smith Crittenden Thornton Papers, HEHL. See also Lucy Thornton to Harry Innes Thornton Jr., May 12, 1866, and March 14, 1867; and Lucy Thornton to Bessie Thornton, June 21, 1866, Lucy Smith Crittenden Thornton Papers, HEHL. Californians sent some $45,000 to the South; see Summers, *Ordeal of the Reunion*, 41.

12. Quoted in Waldie, "'We Have Been and Are Yet Secessionist.'"

13. Bell, *On the Old West Coast*, 76–81. See also Faragher, *Eternity Street*, 440–44.

14. Wallace, "Cameron Erskine Thom." See also Graves, *My Seventy Years in California*, 122; and Lewis, "Los Angeles in the Civil War Decades," 281–82.

15. In John L. Strong's letter to the *Pacific Rural Press (San Francisco)*, January 7, 1871. J. M. Strong was known as "an ultra Democrat, with strong Southern sympathies"; *San Francisco Bulletin*, November 19, 1878.

16. *Fresno Expositor*, November 20, 1872. These reports came from a range of California papers, as well as some publications within the South; see articles from the *San Francisco Bulletin*, *San Francisco Rural Press*, *Visalia Delta*, *Woodland Democrat*, *Yuba City Banner*, *San Francisco Commercial Herald*, *Sacramento Record*, and *Stockton Republican*, all reprinted in "Transactions of the California State Agricultural Society during the Year 1872," *Journal of the Legislature of the State of California* (1874), Appendix: Reports, 3:310–22. See also reports from Georgia in the *Georgia Weekly Telegraph*, September 12, 1871; *Savannah Daily Advertiser*, June 27, 1871; and *Columbus Daily Enquirer*, January 4, 1871.

17. *Merced (CA) Argus*, November 25, 1871; *Sacramento Daily Union*, May 12, 1873; John L. Strong, "Cotton Experiments in California," *Overland Monthly* 6, no. 4 (April 1871): 329–30.

18. See the positive personal report of Matthew Keller to Joseph Lancaster Brent, August 17, 1865, Joseph Lancaster Brent Papers, HEHL; and Newmark, *Sixty Years in Southern California*, 317.

19. Beckert, *Empire of Cotton*.

20. John L. Strong to Robert Muldron, November 16, 1871, in "Transactions of the California State Agricultural Society during the Year 1872," 306. Strong would later claim that white labor would be far more effective than Chinese workers, although he did not discount the proven results of Chinese cotton pickers in California; John L. Strong, "Labor in Cotton Culture," *Overland Monthly* 13, no. 1 (July 1874): 18–19, 24.

21. Jung, *Coolies and Cane*; E. Young, *Alien Nation*, chaps. 1, 2; Aarim-Heriot, *Chinese Immigrants*, 126; "Coolies as a Substitute for Negroes," *DBR* 2 (August 1866): 215–17.

22. Frederick Douglass, "Our Composite Nationality," December 7, 1869, in Blassingame, *Frederick Douglass Papers*, 240–59.

23. Speech of W. H. Hall in *The Elevator* (San Francisco), November 19, 1869. See also *The Elevator*, December 3, 17, 1869.

24. California cotton would make a comeback in the 1920s and 1930s, and to this day the state ranks second only to Texas in its cotton output. See D. Weber, *Dark Sweat*.

25. *Sacramento Daily Union*, November 16, 1861; April 26, 1867.

26. William M. Gwin to Joseph Lancaster Brent, June 13, 1866, Joseph Lancaster Brent Papers, HEHL.

27. *Sacramento Daily Union*, November 10, 1867.

28. *Alta California*, September 15, 1867; *San Francisco Bulletin*, October 30, 1867; December 27, 1875; April 29, 1876; December 3, 1877; *Los Angeles Journal*, October 15, 1879.

29. *Sacramento Daily Union*, August 24, 1869. Just two years earlier, Willie was worrying about being hanged for his role in the rebellion. See Willie Gwin to his mother, May 18, 1865, in *San Francisco Bulletin*, December 28, 1866.

30. *San Francisco Bulletin*, March 7, 1883; for obituaries see *Bulletin*, September 1 and 4, 1885. On Gwin in high society, see Benjamin Davis Wilson to Joseph Lancaster Brent, April 10, 1868, Joseph Lancaster Brent Papers, HEHL. See also L. Thomas, *Between Two Empires*, 368–80.

31. *Cong. Globe*, 39th Cong., 2nd Sess., 239.

32. A. Johnson, "Executive Order, June 9, 1865"; Johnson's quote from Downs and Masur, *World the Civil War Made*, 1.

33. S. Smith, "Emancipating Peons," 50–54.

34. Graves's report included in *Cong. Globe*, 39th Cong., 2nd Sess., 239–40.

35. The report of Brigadier General James Carleton, July 3, 1865, in Doolittle, *Condition of the Indian Tribes*, 324.

36. M. Nelson, *Three-Cornered War*, 240–41.

37. Estimates from Doolittle, *Condition of the Indian Tribes*, 325; *Cong. Globe*, 39th Cong., 2nd Sess., 239–40.

38. "An Act to Abolish and Forever Prohibit the System of Peonage in the Territory of New Mexico and Other Parts of the United States," *US Statutes at Large*, 39th Cong., 2nd Sess., chap. 187 (March 2, 1867), 546.

39. *Cong. Globe*, 39th Cong., 2nd Sess., 1571–72.

40. Riddleberger, *1866*, 202.

41. Beale, *Critical Year*, viii, 399, 406.

42. Foner, *Reconstruction*, 278.

43. Graves quoted in *Cong. Globe*, 39th Cong., 2nd Sess., 239–40; see also S. Smith, "Emancipating Peons," 50–53; and Pope, "Contract, Race, and Freedom of Labor," 1485–87.

44. *Cong. Globe*, 39th Cong., 2nd Sess., 1571–72.

45. Montoya, "Not-So-Free Labor"; Rael-Gálvez, "Identifying Captivity and Capturing Identity," chap. 7; Castro, "Liberty Like Thunder," 101–3; S. Smith, "Emancipating Peons," 57–59; Kiser, *Borderlands of Slavery*, 142–69. For the afterlife of peonage, see Peck, *Reinventing Free Labor*.

46. Bensel, *Yankee Leviathan*.

47. For more on the limits of federal authority in the post–Civil War West and what Greg Downs and Kate Masur call the "stockade state," see Downs and Masur, *World the Civil War Made*, introduction; and Waite, "West and Reconstruction after the American Civil War."

48. Berwanger, *West and Reconstruction*, 10.

49. According to the 1870 census, more than 4,000 African Americans and nearly 50,000 Chinese, Japanese, and "Civilized Indians" lived in the state. The census did not include a separate category for the significant Hispano population; see Walker, *Compendium of the Ninth Census*, 9–18; and also Lew-Williams, *Chinese Must Go*, 34–35.

50. Hispanos—unlike African Americans, Chinese immigrants, or Native peoples—were legally allowed to vote in California, as one of the conditions of the Treaty of Guadalupe Hidalgo and the California Constitution. Indians could win the right to vote by a two-thirds concurrent decision from the legislature—although there was little chance of that in California's postwar political climate; see *Constitution of the State of California*, article 2, section 1.

51. On the similarities between the western Democratic and Republican Parties—that is, on issues not pertaining to Reconstruction—see Berwanger, *West and Reconstruction*, 5–6, 31–34, 207–8; and W. J. Davis, *History of Political Conventions in California*, 264–86.

52. *Stockton Independent*, August 18, 1865, quoted in Malone, "Democratic Party in California," 22. See also Eugene Casserly's speech in *San Francisco Bulletin*, September 20, 1865.

53. Malone, "Democratic Party in California," 15, 29–30, 42–46.

54. *San Francisco Examiner*, July 1 and July 23, 1867.

55. *San Francisco Examiner*, July 24, 1867.

56. Quoted in Berwanger, *West and Reconstruction*, 106.

57. Quoted in W. J. Davis, *History of Political Conventions in California*, 264–66.

58. Tamara Venit-Shelton convincingly argues that antimonopolism, in addition to race-baiting, helped the Democrats secure support from industrial workers and farmers; Venit-Shelton, *Squatter's Republic*, 87.

59. G. Stanley, "Republican Party in California"; Berwanger, *West and Reconstruction*, 202–3; Malone, "Democratic Party in California," 62–63.

60. For a representative Unionist response to the election, see *Alta California*, September 6, 1867. The *Pacific Appeal* (San Francisco), one of California's two African American papers, was far franker in its assessment of the defeat. "All are aware that the real issue in the nation at present is hinged upon the reconstruction measures of Congress"; *Pacific Appeal*, September, 14, 1867.

61. Benedict, "Rout of Radicalism," 341; Benedict, *Compromise of Principle*, chap. 13.

62. My assessment here is drawn from the detailed state-by-state statistics on the 1867 elections in *Tribune Almanac and Political Register for 1868*, 43–65.

63. Berwanger, *West and Reconstruction*, 130–43, 158–72, 185–86, 202–9; Stanley, *Loyal West*, 115–16.

64. Gorham, *Speech Delivered by George C. Gorham*, 13. Even the former Republican candidate for governor Edward Stanly berated Gorham for his inclusive racial politics. In a pro-Haight speech, Stanly derided Gorham as "uniformly black . . . black in speech, black in principle, black all over," in *Sacramento Daily Union*, August 10, 1867.

65. On California Republicans' abandonment of radicalism, see G. Stanley, "'Whim and Caprice of a Majority in a Petty State,'" 450, 455; and G. Stanley, "Republican Party in California," x, 215.

66. Bottoms, *Aristocracy of Color*, 55.

67. Stacey Smith argues that the Democratic resurgence in California marked a western Redemption, as it overturned the previous period of Republican rule within the state and returned to power the political party that had reigned throughout the antebellum period; S. Smith, *Freedom's Frontier*, 210. Of course, this western Redemption did not have to contend with a federal military presence, as did the Democratic Redeemers of the former Confederate states.

68. See, for example, *Marysville Daily Appeal*, June 22, 1867; and Gorham, *Speech Delivered by George C. Gorham*, 14–16.

69. Even the fiercest wartime Unionists eventually relinquished their outrage over secession. Henry Dwight Barrows, who waged a tireless campaign against pro-Confederate Californians during the war, wrote glowing obituaries for the men he once pursued. See his tributes to both Joseph Lancaster Brent and John S. Griffin, a prominent Los Angeles doctor and Lincoln-hater. Barrows, "Joseph Lancaster Brent"; Barrows, "Memorial Sketch of Dr. John S. Griffin." Former California secessionists, in turn, memorialized their erstwhile opponents. See the motion of Andrew Jackson King to commemorate the memory of Billington Crum Whiting, an antislavery Democrat of the Broderick faction; Resolutions by the Los Angeles County Bar, entered by Andrew Wilson Potts, clerk, June 9, 1881, Billington Crum Whiting papers, HEHL.

70. For Haight's renunciation of the Republican Party, see Haight to George [R. Bissell?], May 3, 1861, Henry H. Haight Papers, HEHL.

71. Berwanger, *West and Reconstruction*, 108. For a detailed treatment of Haight's racial politics, see Bottoms, *Aristocracy of Color*, 72–84.

72. Haight, *Speech of H. H. Haight*, 2.

73. Haight, 1.

74. *San Francisco Bulletin*, January 22, 1870.

75. Haight, *Inaugural Address*, 6; Haight to William Tell Coleman, October 20, 1868, Henry H. Haight Papers, HEHL; see also Haight to Andrew Johnson, January 18, 1868, Henry H. Haight Papers, Banc.

76. Haight, *Inaugural Address*, 9–10. For similar sentiments, see Haight to John Bigler, May 7, 1868, Henry H. Haight Papers, HEHL.

77. Narcissa P. Saunders to Haight, June 10, 1868, Henry H. Haight Papers, HEHL.

78. Andrew A. Roland to Haight, June 29, 1868, Henry H. Haight Papers, HEHL.

79. *San Francisco Bulletin*, June 3, 1865.

80. For biographical detail, see his obituary in the *New York Times*, February 18, 1872; and Shuck, *History of the Bench and Bar of California*, 412. For some of Washington's proslavery views, see *Daily Democratic State Journal*, January 28, 1858; and *San Francisco Bulletin*, April 30, 1861.

81. Pollard, *Lost Cause*.

82. For useful introductions to the history and evolution of the Lost Cause, see Gary W. Gallagher, "Introduction," and Alan T. Nolan, "The Anatomy of the Myth," both in Gallagher and Nolan, *Myth of the Lost Cause and Civil War History*. The literature on the Lost Cause and Civil War memory is vast. For some of the most important works on the subject, see C. Wilson, *Baptized in Blood*; Foster, *Ghosts of the Confederacy*; Blight, *Race and Reunion*; Cox, *Dixie's Daughters*; Janney, *Burying the Dead but Not the Past*; Connelly and Bellows, *God and General Longstreet*; and Savage, *Standing Soldiers*. On the recent debates over Confederate iconography in particular, see Clinton, *Confederate Statues and Memorialization*. For recent studies that address Civil War memory in the West, see Hulbert, *Ghosts of Guerrilla Memory*; M. Stanley, *Loyal West*; and Waite, "'Lost Cause' Goes West."

83. *San Francisco Examiner*, April 21, 1869.

84. *San Francisco Examiner*, July 23, 1867. The comment draws on sentiments expressed by Robert E. Lee in his last message to his troops; *General Lee's Farewell Address to the Army of Northern Virginia*. For more tributes to the South and southerners, see *San Francisco Examiner*, July 8, 1868; January 16, 1869.

85. *San Francisco Examiner*, April 1, 1869. Similar screeds can be found in other issues of the *Examiner* throughout the postwar period. See, for instance, June 12, August 7, August 11, 1865; July 1, 1867; July 6, October 12, 1868; January 19, April 21, 1869.

86. *San Francisco Examiner*, November 23, 1868.

87. The quote comes from resolutions drafted by Washington, celebrating President Johnson's veto of the Freedmen's Bureau Bill, in *San Francisco Bulletin*, February 28, 1866.

88. *The Elevator*, July 28, 1865.

89. *San Francisco Examiner*, July 24, 1865. See also August 11, 1865.

90. *San Francisco Examiner*, January 11, 1869.

91. Jefferson Davis, *Rise and Fall of the Confederate Government*.

92. See Malone, "Democratic Party in California," appendix.

93. W. J. Davis, *History of Political Conventions in California*, 268.

94. *Alta California*, May 2, 1868 (italics in original).

95. Fourteenth Amendment to the United States Constitution, section 1.

96. Both quotations from Paddison, *American Heathens*, 22.

97. Casserly, *Issues of the Contest*, 4, 5, 8–9.

98. Outgoing Governor Frederick Low endorsed the amendment in his final message, but it was a futile effort from a lame duck politician. State of California, *Journal of the Senate during the Seventeenth Session of the Legislature, 1867–68*, 35–52. See also State of California, *Journal of the Assembly*, 17th sess. (1867/68), 52–53; and *San Francisco Bulletin*, December 14, 1868.

99. New Jersey, Ohio, and Oregon ratified the Fourteenth Amendment in the summer of 1866, only to rescind their ratifications two years later; S. Smith, *Freedom's Frontier*, 210n287; Bottoms, *Aristocracy of Color*, 71, 86.

100. Casserly, *Speech of Hon. Eugene Casserly*, 2–6. For similar remarks, see Haight, *Message of H. H. Haight*, 11.

101. Quoted in Bottoms, *Aristocracy of Color*, 88; see also *San Francisco Bulletin*, January 7 and January 17, 1870.

102. Hager, *Speech of Hon. John S. Hager*, 3–5, 11.

103. Two other free states, New Jersey and Oregon, initially rejected the amendment. They ratified it in 1871 and 1959, respectively. On the California campaign against the Fifteenth Amendment, see Berwanger, *West and Reconstruction*, 175–83; Bottoms, *Aristocracy of Color*, 87–93; and S. Smith, *Freedom's Frontier*, 210–13.

104. Paddison, *American Heathens*, 27.

105. Berwanger, *West and Reconstruction*, 180–81; *Alta California*, April 9, 1870.

106. Jo Hamilton to J. J. Rogers, April 11, 1870, in *Alta California*, April 13, 1870.

107. Bottoms, *Aristocracy of Color*, 50.

108. The full ruling is reprinted in the *Los Angeles Star*, May 7, 1870; see also *Los Angeles Daily News*, April 30, 1870; and P. Coleman, "John Ballard and the African American Community in Los Angeles," 214–17.

109. For important accounts of African Americans in the Far West, see Q. Taylor, *In Search of the Racial Frontier*; Lapp, *Blacks in Gold Rush California*; M. Campbell, *Making Black Los Angeles*; and S. Smith, "*Dred Scott* on the Pacific."

110. According to the 1860 census, there were 1,170 African Americans living in San Francisco in 1860, amounting to roughly 2 percent of the city's population. That number did not significantly increase in the following decade. Goodyear, "'Beneath the Shadow of Her Flag,'" 27.

111. *Proceedings of the First State Convention of the Colored Citizens of the State of California*.

112. See Lapp, *Blacks in Gold Rush California*; and Chandler, "Friends in Time of Need." On the progress made by the African American community of California during the war years, see the speech of Jeremiah Burke Sanderson, May 11, 1864, in Jeremiah Burke Sanderson Collection, MSS Box 2982, California State Library, Sacramento.

113. *The Elevator*, December 22, 1865; see also August 25 and October 6, 1865; and January 5 and 19, 1866. When the State Convention of Colored Citizens reconvened for the first time since the Confederate surrender in a push for black voting rights, Bell published the entire proceedings; *The Elevator*, October, 20, 27, 1865. For a brief biography of Bell and his writings, see Goodyear, "'Beneath the Shadow of Her Flag.'"

114. *The Elevator*, February 11, 1870.

115. *The Elevator*, December 15, 1865; see also March 30, 1866.

116. For more on the black response to Chinese labor and immigration, see Goodyear, "'Beneath the Shadow of Her Flag,'" 34–35; Paddison, *American Heathens*, 17, 21; and Bottoms, *Aristocracy of Color*, 8.

117. *The Elevator*, August 27, 1869; see also November 19, 1869.

118. Saxton, *Indispensable Enemy*, 72, 85; Chandler, "'Anti-Coolie Rabies,'" 38.

119. Winn's wife brought westward several family slaves in order to join her husband in California in 1849; *Jackson Mississippian*, October 26, 1849, in Ralph Bieber Collection, HEHL.

120. *Alta California*, July 21, 1870. Mayor of Sacramento, a general in the state's militia, and longtime labor movement leader, Winn is still remembered as one of California's founding fathers. For a brief biography—albeit shorn of all references to his anti-Chinese activity—see *Sacramento Daily Union*, August 27, 1883, and November 23, 1888. For more on his background and his anti-coolie organizing, see Saxton, *Indispensable Enemy*, 79.

121. *Los Angeles News*, November 17 and December 24, 1870, quoted in Zesch, "Chinese Los Angeles," 126; see also Faragher, *Eternity Street*, 440–52.

122. *Alta California*, January 19, 1869; *Sacramento Daily Union*, July 14, 1869; *Marysville Daily Appeal*, August 9, 1871.

123. Hahn, *Nation under Our Feet*, 267.

124. There is little secondary literature on this sort of activity in the Far West in the immediate postwar years. For a brief mention of California's KKK, see Paddison, *American Heathens*, 45. For a treatment of anti-Chinese violence in the 1880s, see Lew-Williams, *Chinese Must Go*. As Matthew Stanley argues, Republicans in the Middle West also drew the connection between local vigilantism and the Klan. Stanley, *Loyal West*, 124.

125. *San Jose Patriot*, April 19, 1869, reprinted in the *Alta California*, April 22, 1869. For another KKK circular received through the mail, see *Sacramento Daily Union*, May 1, 1868.

126. *Marysville Daily Appeal*, July 25, 1868.

127. *Alta California*, January 6, 1871.

128. *Sacramento Daily Union*, April 16 and May 7, 1868.

129. *Santa Cruz Times*, May 8, 1869, reprinted in *Marysville Daily Appeal*, May 13, 1869. For reports of more Klan activity around Marysville and Eureka, see *Marysville Daily Appeal*, May 19 and June 13, 1869.

130. *Marysville Daily Appeal*, March 17, 1869; *Santa Cruz Times*, May 8, 1869, reprinted in *Marysville Daily Appeal*, May 13, 1869; *Oregon State Journal*, March 20, 1869.

131. *Marysville Daily Appeal*, March 3, 1869.

132. California's Republican press rarely missed an opportunity to report on the outrages of the Klan in the former Confederacy, often linking racial violence in the South with Democratic politics in the West. See, for example, *Alta California*, April 24, April 25, May 31, September 27, 1868; *Marysville Daily Appeal*, August 12, September 24, September 26, October 9, 1868; April 29, 1871; and *Mariposa Gazette*, November 27, 1868.

133. Casserly, *Issues of the Contest*, 6. Privately, however, Casserly would fret over

the rise of the White Leagues during the 1874 campaign, writing, "[E]very 'outrage' reported from the South, gives me a chill to the very marrow—for it gives new life to Radicalism and all its atrocities." Yet note that Casserly continues to attribute the real "atrocities" to Republicans; quoted in Gillette, *Retreat from Reconstruction*, 229.

134. Quoted in G. Stanley, "Republican Party in California," 222.

135. *San Francisco Examiner*, January 19, 1869.

136. W. J. Davis, *History of Political Conventions in California*, 298–99. For more on the Democratic opposition to these acts, see *Marysville Daily Appeal*, April 15, April 16, July 22, July 28, 1871; and *Alta California*, August 17, 1871. On the continuing rebellion in the South and the federal response, see Downs, *After Appomattox*. On several occasions, Chinese immigrants attempted to make use of the KKK Act in California's courtrooms; see *Marysville Daily Appeal*, May 11, 1871.

137. For a firsthand account of the massacre, see Newmark, *Sixty Years in Southern California*, 432–35. For scholarly treatments, see Zesch, *Chinatown War*; Zesch, "Chinese Los Angeles," 137–44; Torres-Rouff, *Before L.A.*, 181–85; and Faragher, *Eternity Street*, 459–80.

138. Griswold del Castillo, *Los Angeles Barrio*, 106; Spitzzeri, "Judge Lynch in Session," 85–86, 114–17. See also Gonzalez-Day, *Lynching in the West*; and Carrigan and Webb, *Forgotten Dead*.

139. Farragher, *Eternity Street*, 263.

140. Torres-Rouff, *Before L.A.*, 194.

141. Historians are beginning to trace some of the similarities between racial violence in the South and the West, although the focus of this comparative work remains primarily on black, Hispano, and Indian victims rather than on Chinese workers. For an overview of the scholarship on lynching, see Pfeifer, "At the Hands of Parties Unknown?" For important works on the history of collective violence beyond the South, see Gonzalez-Day, *Lynching in the West*; Carrigan and Webb, "'Muerto por Unos Desconocidos'"; Carrigan and Webb, *Forgotten Dead*; Pfeifer, *Rough Justice*; Pfeifer, *Roots of Rough Justice*; Pfeifer, *Lynching beyond Dixie*; and Campney, *This Is Not Dixie*.

142. S. Smith, *Freedom's Frontier*, chap. 7; S. Smith, "Emancipating Peons," 60–70.

143. Gyory, *Closing the Gate*; Aarim-Heriot, *Chinese Immigrants*, chap. 11; Paddison, *American Heathens*, 46–49. Beth Lew-Williams refers to the 1882 law as a "Restriction Act," with the policy of exclusion only achieved by 1888; Lew-Williams, *Chinese Must Go*, 91–136, 169–234. On Chinese legal resistance to exclusion, see Salyer, *Laws Harsh as Tigers*.

Epilogue

1. M. King, "Address at the Conclusion of the Selma to Montgomery March."

2. Branch, *At Canaan's Edge*, chap. 13.

3. On the United Daughters of the Confederacy, see Cox, *Dixie's Daughters*. On monuments and Civil War memory, see Savage, *Standing Soldiers*; and Domby, *False Cause*.

4. L. Gordon, *Second Coming of the KKK*.

5. On the history of the Jefferson Davis Highway, see Kevin Waite, "The Largest Confederate Monument in American Can't Be Taken Down," *Washington Post*, August 22, 2017, from which this section has been partially adapted.

6. For the history of Confederate memorials in California, see Waite, "'Lost Cause' Goes West." See also Mike Moffitt, "Are All the Monuments to White Supremacy in California Gone Yet?," *SFGate*, April 7, 2019; and Kevin Waite, "California's Forgotten Confederate History," *New Republic*, August 19, 2019. The Southern Poverty Law Center has compiled a useful map and statistics on Confederate markers across the country, although it misses several in California: https://www.splcenter.org/20190201/whose-heritage-public-symbols-confederacy. For Civil War memory in California from a primarily Unionist perspective, see Deverell, "After Antietam," 175–89.

7. *United Daughters of the Confederacy Patriot Ancestor Album*, 23–24.

8. In addition to numerous homes within the former slave states, there was also one in Ardmore, Oklahoma, part of Confederate-held Indian Territory for much of the war. For more on these Confederate soldiers' homes, see R. Williams, *My Old Confederate Home*; and Rosenburg, *Living Monuments*.

9. *Los Angeles Times*, April 20, 1936; Moretti, *Dixie Manor Days*, 9–44.

10. Kevin Waite, "The Struggle over Slavery Was Not Confined to the South, L.A. Has a Confederate Memorial Problem Too," *Los Angeles Times*, August 4, 2017.

11. "Landmark Cemetery in Los Angeles Removes Confederate Monument," *Wall Street Journal*, August 16, 2017; "Confederate Plaque in San Diego Has a History of Controversy, Repeated Removals," *San Diego Union-Tribune*, August 16, 2017; "Confederate Monument Defaced Last Month Has Been Removed from Santa Ana Cemetery," *Orange County Register*, August 1, 2019; "Confederate Monument Removed from Santa Ana Cemetery after Being Vandalized," KTLA 5, August 2, 2019.

12. Indeed, the passage of Utah's and New Mexico's slave codes and California's Archy Lee decision coincided with Britain's attempts to offset the economic fallout from emancipation by importing indentured Asian laborers across its global empire.

13. For a particularly useful assessment of Frederick Jackson Turner's place in American historiography and a reprinting of his frontier thesis, see Turner, *Rereading Frederick Jackson Turner*. On Jefferson, see McCoy, *Elusive Republic*; Onuf, *Jefferson's Empire*; and Ronda, *Thomas Jefferson and the Changing West*.

14. The literature on western mythology is vast. Through his many works, Kevin Starr was an elegiac chronicler of the California dream. A good place to start is Starr, *Americans and the California Dream*. See also S. Smith, *Freedom's Frontier*, introduction. On the history of forgetting in Los Angeles, see Deverell, *Whitewashed Adobe*. On the romantic repurposing of California's Spanish era, see P. Young (née Kropp), *California Vieja*.

15. "The future always looks good in the golden land," Joan Didion wrote of Californians' historical amnesia, "because no one remembers the past." In the South, according to Nathanial Rich, "no one can forget it." Didion, "Some Dreamers of the Golden Dream," 4; Nathaniel Rich, foreword to Didion, *South and West*, xiv.

BIBLIOGRAPHY

Archival Sources

Bancroft Library, University of California, Berkeley
  Hubert Howe Bancroft, "Personal Observations during a Tour through the
    Line of Missions of Upper California," MSS, typescript, ca. 1870
  Washington Bartlett, "Statement of Washington Bartlett a Pioneer of 1849 for
    Bancroft Library," MSS, 1877
  E. O. Crosby, "Statement of Events in California as related by Judge E. O.
    Crosby for Bancroft Library," MSS, 1878
  John Currey, "Incidents in California, Statement by Judge John Currey for
    Bancroft Library," MSS, 1878
  Jefferson Davis Correspondence, T. W. Norris Collection
  John G. Downey Correspondence
  Robert R. Givens Letters to Family, 1849–59
  William M. Gwin Papers
  William M. Gwin, "Memoirs on the History of the United States, Mexico, and
    California of Ex Senator Wm. M. Gwin, Dictated by Himself for Bancroft
    Library," MSS, 1878
  Henry H. Haight Papers
  Benjamin Hayes Scrapbooks
  Hitchcock Family Papers
  Annis Merrill, "Statement of Recollection on Early Days of San Francisco after
    the American Occupation for Bancroft Library," MSS, 1878
  Letters of Sylvester Mowry to Edward Bicknell
  John Augustus Sutter, Personal Reminiscences, MSS
Boston Athenaeum, Boston, MA
  Pro-Union Civil War Sheet Music Collection
  Thomas Greaves Cary, "A Short History of the Conquest of Alta California," MSS
Boston Public Library, Boston, MA
  Samuel May Papers
California Historical Society, San Francisco
  Papers of Milton S. Latham
California State Library, Sacramento
  "Biography of the First Cal. Legislature," 1850, MSS
  Thomas Gilman Papers
  Jeremiah Burke Sanderson Collection
  Slavery Era Insurance Documents
Henry E. Huntington Library, San Marino, CA
  Ralph Bieber Collection (uncataloged)

Joseph Lancaster Brent Papers
William McKendree Gwin Papers
Henry H. Haight Papers
William Alexander Leidesdorff Collection
Los Angeles Probate Court Records
James Mandeville Papers
Jefferson Martenet Correspondence, 1837–92
George McKinley Murrell Correspondence
William G. Ritch Collection
Lucy Smith Crittenden Thornton Papers, 1856–69
Billington Crum Whiting Papers, 1839–1948
Historical Society of Pennsylvania, Philadelphia
William Bigler Papers, 1836–1880
Joel Poinsett Papers in Gilpin Family Papers
Library of Congress, Washington, DC
William McKendree Gwin, "Memoirs on the History of the United States,
    Mexico, and California, 1850–1860," photostat MSS
Robert Todd Lincoln Collection of the Papers of Abraham Lincoln
Papers of Thomas Jefferson
Massachusetts Historical Society, Boston
Thomas Greaves Cary Papers
Civil War Patriotic Covers
Curtis Family Papers
Theodore Parker Papers
John Bachelder Peirce Papers, 1839–81
Warren-Clarke Family Papers
    George Brown Diary, typescript, 23 February–28 June 1850
National Archives, Washington, DC
Case Files of the US Commissioner
Southern Historical Collection, Wilson Library, University of North Carolina at
    Chapel Hill
William G. Dickson Papers
George Phifer Erwin Papers
Thomas Jefferson Green Papers
Nims, Rankin, and Spratt Family Papers
Parks and McElrath Family Papers, Thomas Parks Collection
Nicholas Washington Woodfin Papers
Transy Library Special Collections and Archives, Transylvania University,
    Lexington, KY
Jefferson Davis Papers
Virginia Historical Society, Richmond
John Y. Mason Letterbooks, September 1856–July 1857
Edmund Randolph Papers
Richmond, Fredericksburg and Potomac Railroad Records, 1833–1909
Thom Family Papers
Robert Lee Traylor Papers

Government Documents

FEDERAL DOCUMENTS

Bingham, John A. "Bill and Report of John A. Bingham, and Vote on Its Passage, Repealing the Territorial New Mexican Laws Establishing Slavery and Authorizing Employers to Whip 'White Persons' and others in their Employment, and Denying Them Redress in the C Courts." Washington: Republican Executive Congressional Committee, 1860.

Brown, A. V. Postmaster-General's Report of 1859. US Senate, Executive Documents, 36th Congress, 1st session, no. 2 (serial no. 1025).

Buchanan, James. "Proclamation—Rebellion in the Territory of Utah." Online by Gerhard Peters and John T. Woolley, The American Presidency Project, https://www.presidency.ucsb.edu.

Congressional Globe. 1843–61.

Constitution of the Confederate States of America. Milledgeville: Boughton, Nisbet and Barnes, 1861.

Davis, Jefferson. Report of the Secretary of War on the Several Pacific Railroad Expeditions. Washington: A. O. P. Nicholson, 1855.

De Bow, J. D. B. Statistical View of the United States, Embracing Its Territory, Population—White, Free Colored, and Slave—Moral and Social Condition, Industry Property, and Revenue; the Detailed Statistics of Cities, Towns, and Counties; Being a Compendium of the Seventh Census. Washington, DC: Beverley Tucker, 1854.

Doolittle, James R. Condition of the Indian Tribes: Report of the Special Committee Appointed under Joint Resolution of March 3, 1865. Washington, DC: Government Printing Office, 1867.

Dred Scott v. Sandford, 60 US 393 (argued 1856; decided 1857).

Execution of Colonel Crabb and Associates. Message from the President of the United States, Communicating Official Information and Correspondence in Relation to the Execution of Colonel Crabb and His Associates. February 16, 1858, House Executive Doc. No. 64, 35th Congress, 1st Session.

Historical Statistics of the United States, 1789–1945: A Supplement to the Statistical Abstract of the United States. Washington, DC: Government Printing Office, 1949.

Johnson, Andrew. "Executive Order, June 9, 1865." Executive Order Online by Gerhard Peters and John T. Woolley, The American Presidency Project, https://www.presidency.ucsb.edu.

King, T. Butler. "Steam Navigation with China and the Sandwich Islands." Report No. 596, May 4, 1848, House of Representatives, 30th Congress, 1st Session, pp. 1–17.

Miller, David Hunter, ed. Treaties and Other International Acts of the United States of America. 8 vols. Washington, DC: Government Printing Office, 1931–48.

Register of Officers and Agents, Civil, Military, and Naval, in the Service of the United States. Washington: Alfred Hunter, 1856.

"Slavery in the Territory of New Mexico." Report 508, May 10, 1860, House Executive Documents, Volume 1069, 36th Congress, 1st Session.

Statutes at Large, Treaties, and Proclamations of the United States of America.
    Vol. 12. Boston: Little Brown, 1863.
Treaty of Wangxia, May 18, 1844, available through USC US-China Institute.
    https://china.usc.edu/treaty-wangxia-treaty-wang-hsia-may-18-1844.
US Government Documents. House Resolution 64, 36th Congress, 1st Session.
Walker, Francis A. *A Compendium of the Ninth Census (June 1, 1870), Compiled*
    Pursuant to a Concurrent Resolution of Congress, and under the Direction of the
    Secretary of the Interior. Washington, DC: Government Printing Office, 1872.
The War of the Rebellion: A Compilation of the Official Records of the Union and
    Confederate Armies. 128 vols. Washington, DC: Government Printing Office,
    1880–1901.

STATE AND TERRITORIAL DOCUMENTS

Acts, Resolutions, and Memorials of the Legislative Assembly of the Territory of
    Utah. Salt Lake City: Henry McEwan, 1866.
Acts, Resolutions and Memorials, Passed at the Several Annual Sessions of the Leg-
    islative Assembly of the Territory of Utah. Salt Lake City: Joseph Cain, 1855.
Communication of Governor Latham to the President of the United States in Rela-
    tion to the Division of the State of California. Sacramento: C. T. Botts, 1860.
The Constitution and Schedule of the Provisional Government of the Territory of
    Arizona, and the Proceedings of the Convention Held at Tucson. Tucson:
    J. Howard Wells, 1860.
Constitution of the State of California. San Francisco: Alta California, 1849.
Garrison, George Pierce, ed. *Diplomatic Correspondence of the Republic of Texas.*
    2 vols. Washington, DC: Government Printing Office, 1907–8.
In re Perkins, 2 Cal. 424 (October 1, 1852).
Journal of the Legislature of Texas. 34th Congress, 2nd session.
Laws of the Territory of New Mexico. Passed by the Legislative Assembly, Session
    of 1858–59. Santa Fe: A. De Marle, 1859.
Report of the Senate Committee on Elections, in the Contested Election Case.
    Ramirez vs. Hamilton. Sacramento: O. M. Clayes, 1864.
State of California. *Appendix to the Journal of the Assembly.* 1849/50–70.
State of California. *Appendix to the Journal of the Senate.* 1849/50–70.
State of California. *Journal of the Assembly.* 1849/50–70.
State of California. *Journal of the Senate.* 1849/50–70.
Statutes of California. San Jose, 1850.
Statutes of California. San Jose, 1852.
Statutes of California. San Jose, 1854.
Statutes of California. San Jose, 1858.
Statutes of California. San Jose, 1859.
Stovall v. Archy, a Slave. Case Files of the US Commissioner, Record Group 21,
    Records of the District Courts of the United States, 1685–2009.
"Transactions of the California State Agricultural Society during the Year 1872."
    Journal of the Legislature of the State of California, 1874. Appendix: Reports,
    3:310–22.

Newspapers and Periodicals

NEWSPAPERS

Alexandria Gazette
Alta California
Anglo-African Magazine
Arkansas State Gazette
Arkansas Whig
British Banner (London)
Broad Ax (Salt Lake City)
Brownlow's Knoxville Whig and Independent Journal
Charleston Courier
Charleston Mercury
Clarksville Jeffersonian
Columbus (GA) Daily Enquirer
Daily Confederation (Montgomery, AL)
Daily Democratic State Journal (Sacramento)
Daily Globe (Toronto)
Daily Missouri Republican
Daily Republican Banner and Nashville Whig
Daily True Delta (New Orleans)
Dallas Herald
Democratic Telegraph and Texas Register (Houston)
Deseret News (Salt Lake City)
The Elevator (San Francisco)
The Emancipator
Frederick Douglass' Paper
Fredericksburg News
Fresno Expositor
Georgia Telegraph (Macon)
Jackson Mississippian
The Liberator
Los Angeles Daily News
Los Angeles Herald
Los Angeles Journal
Los Angeles Southern News
Los Angeles Star
Los Angeles Times
Mariposa Gazette
Marysville (CA) Daily Appeal
Memphis Daily Appeal

Merced (CA) Argus
Mesilla (AZ) Times
The Mississippian (Jackson)
Mississippi Free Trader
Missouri Register (Boonville)
Nashville Daily Gazette
National Anti-Slavery Standard
New Orleans Bee
New Orleans Daily Picayune
New Republic
New York Herald
New York Times
New York Daily Times
New York Daily Tribune
North Star
Ohio State Journal (Columbus)
Orange County Register
Oregon State Journal
Pacific Appeal (San Francisco)
Pacific Rural Press (San Francisco)
Philadelphia Public Ledger
Provincial Freeman (Canada West)
Red Bluff (CA) Independent
Richmond Enquirer
Richmond Republican
Richmond Whig
Sacramento Daily Union
Sacramento Transcript
San Antonio Ledger
San Antonio Ledger and Texan
San Diego Union-Tribune
San Francisco Bulletin
San Francisco Examiner
San Joaquin Republican (Stockton, CA)
San Jose Patriot
Santa Fe Gazette
Savannah Daily Advertiser
SFGate
Sonora Democrat
Sonora Union Democrat
Southern Intelligencer (Austin, TX)
Southern Patriot (Charleston)

St. Louis Republican   Vicksburg Weekly Sentinel
Stockton Argus   Wall Street Journal
Stockton Independent   Washington Post
Texas State Gazette (Austin)   Washington States
Trinity Advocate (Palestine, TX)   Zion's Herald and Wesleyan Journal

PERIODICALS

American Railroad Journal   Latter Day Saints' Messenger and
Annual Publications of the Historical   Advocate
   Society of Southern California   Latter-Day Saints' Millennial Star
The Constitution   The Seer (Washington, DC)
De Bow's Review   Southern Cultivator
The Evening and the Morning Star   Southern Literary Messenger
   (Independence, MO)   Southern Planter
Harper's Weekly   Southern Quarterly Review
Harper's Magazine   Western Journal of Agriculture,
National Era   Manufactures, Mechanic Arts,
New Republic   Internal Improvement, Commerce,
Overland Monthly   and General Literature

Published Primary Sources

Abdy, Edward S. *Journal of a Residence and Tour in the United States of North America*. 2 vols. London: John Murray, 1835.

Abel, Annie Heloise, ed. *The Official Correspondence of James S. Calhoun*. Washington, DC: Government Printing Office, 1915.

Aspinwall, William H., et al. "Panama Rail-Road Company with a Chart Prepared by Lt. M. F. Maury." New York[?], 1849[?].

Ayres, James J. *Gold and Sunshine: Reminiscences of Early California*. Boston: Gorham Press, 1922.

Baker, Edward D. *Oration of Colonel Edward D. Baker over the Dead Body of David C. Broderick, a Senator of the United States, 18th September, 1859*. N.p., n.d.

Barrows, Henry Dwight. "Joseph Lancaster Brent." *Annual Publication of the Historical Society of Southern California and of the Pioneers of Los Angeles County, 1903*. Vol. 6. Los Angeles: George Rice and Son, 1904.

———. "Memorial Sketch of Dr. John S. Griffin." *Publications of the Historical Society of Southern California, 1897–1899*. Vol. 4. Los Angeles, n.d.

Basler, Roy P. ed. *The Collected Works of Abraham Lincoln*. 8 vols. New Brunswick: Rutgers University Press, 1953.

Bell, Horace. *On the Old West Coast: Being Further Reminiscences of a Ranger*. Edited by Lanier Bartlett. New York: Grosset and Dunlap, 1930.

———. *Reminiscences of a Ranger; or Early Times in Southern California*. Los Angeles: Yarnell, Caystille and Mathes, 1881.

Benton, Thomas Hart. *Discourse of Mr. Benton, of Missouri, before the Boston Mercantile Library Association on the Physical Geography of the Country between* the States of Missouri and California, with a View to Show Its Adaptation to Settlement, and to the Construction of a Railroad. Washington: J. T. and Lem. Towers, 1854.

Blassingame, John W., ed. Frederick Douglass Papers. Vol. 4. New Haven: Yale University Press, 1991.

Booth, A. E. Proceedings of the Second Annual Convention of Colored Citizens of the State of California, Held in the City of Sacramento. December 9–13, 1856. Sacramento: J. H. Udell and W. Randall, 1856.

Bowles, Samuel. Across the Continent. Springfield, MA: Samuel Bowles and Company, 1869.

Brent, Joseph Lancaster. Memoirs of the War between the States. N.p.: Nanine B. Sloo, 1940.

Brown, John. Autobiography of Pioneer John Brown. Salt Lake City: Stevens and Wallis, 1941.

Browne, J. Ross. Report of the Debates in the Convention of California on the Formation of the State Constitution, in September and October, 1849. Washington: John T. Towers, 1850.

Burbank, Caleb. Speech of Judge Burbank, in the Senate of California, February 7th, 1861, on the Union Resolutions. Sacramento: J. Anthony and Co., 1861.

Burch, John C. Speech of Hon. John C. Burch, Delivered at Weaverville, California, before a Mass Meeting of the Democracy and Compromise Union Men of Trinity County, May 25, 1861. Sacramento, 1861.

Captain of Volunteers. Alta California: Embracing Notices of the Climate, Soil, and Agricultural Products of Northern Mexico and the Pacific Seaboard; also a History of the Military and Naval Operations of the U.S. Government against Northern Mexico, in the Years 1846 and 1847, and the Opinion of the Hon. James Buchanan on the Wilmot Proviso. Philadelphia: H. Packer and Co., 1847.

Carr, John. Pioneer Days in California. Eureka, CA: Times Publishing Company, 1891.

Casserly, Eugene. The Issue in California. Letter of Eugene Casserly to T. T. Davenport, August 27th, 1861. San Francisco: Charles F. Robbins, 1861.

———. The Issues of the Contest. Speech of Hon. Eugene Casserly, in San Francisco, August 19, 1868. San Francisco: Independent Dispatch Print, 1868.

———. Speech of Hon. Eugene Casserly, on the Fifteenth Amendment, and the Labor Question, Delivered in San Francisco, California, July 28, 1869. San Francisco, 1869.

Chaney, William A., ed. "A Louisiana Planter in the Gold Rush." Louisiana History 3 (Spring 1962): 133–44.

"Citizen." Letters to the Hon. Wm. M. Gwin. San Francisco, 1854.

Cleveland, Henry, ed. Alexander H. Stephens in Public and Private with Letters and Speeches before, during, and since the War. Philadelphia, 1886.

Cluskey, Michael W., ed. Buchanan and Breckinridge. The Democratic Hand-Book. Washington: R. A. Waters, 1856.

Cody, William F. The Life of Hon. William F. Cody, Known as Buffalo Bill. 1879. Reprint, Lincoln: University of Nebraska Press, 2011.

Cole, Cornelius. *Memoirs of Cornelius Cole*. New York: McLoughlin Brothers, 1908.

Coleman, Evan J. "Senator Gwin's Plan for the Colonization of Sonora, Postscript." *Overland Monthly*, August 1891, 203–13.

Connelly, Henry. *The First Annual Message of Governor Connelly, Delivered before the Legislative Assembly of the Territory of New Mexico, December 4th, 1861*. Santa Fe: Santa Fe Gazette, 1861.

———. *Proclamation by the Governor*. N.p., September 9, 1861.

Cooke, Philip St. George. *The Conquest of New Mexico and California*. New York: G. P. Putnam's Sons, 1878.

Cozzens, Samuel Woodworth. *The Marvellous Country; Or, Three Years in Arizona and New Mexico*. 2nd ed. London: Sampson Low, Marston, Low, and Searle, 1875.

Cralle, Richard R., ed. *Speeches of John C. Calhoun, Delivered in the House of Representatives and in the Senate of the United States*. New York: D. Appleton, 1853.

Creuzbaur, Robert. *Route from the Gulf of Mexico and the Lower Mississippi Valley to California and the Pacific Ocean, Illustrated by a General Map and Sectional Maps: with Directions to Travellers*. Austin, TX: H. Long and Brother, 1849.

Crist, Lynda Lasswell, et al., eds. *The Papers of Jefferson Davis*. 14 vols. Baton Rouge: Louisiana State University Press, 1971–2015.

Crosby, Elisha Oscar. *Memoirs of Elisha Oscar Crosby: Reminiscences of California and Guatemala from 1849 to 1864*. Edited by Charles Albro Barker. San Marino, CA: Huntington Library, 1945.

Davis, Jefferson. *The Rise and Fall of the Confederate Government*. 2 vols. New York: D. Appleton and Company, 1881.

Davis, W. W. H. *El Gringo; Or, New Mexico and Her People*. New York: Harper and Brothers, 1857.

De Bow, J. D. B. *The Industrial Resources, Etc., of the Southern and Western States*. 3 vols. New Orleans: De Bow's Review, 1853.

Delano, Alonzo. *Life on the Plains and among the Diggings; Being Scenes and Adventures of an Overland Journey to California*. Auburn, NY: Miller, Orton and Mulligan, 1854.

Dickens, Charles. *American Notes for General Circulation*. 2 vols. 4th ed. London: Chapman and Hall, 1842.

Douglas, Stephen A. *Letter of Judge Douglas in Reply to the Speech of Dr. Gwin at Grass Valley, Cal*. N.p., n.d. Bancroft Library, University of California, Berkeley.

Dwinelle, John W. *A Funeral Oration upon David C. Broderick, Late Senator from California, Delivered at the Chapel of the New York University, on Sunday Evening, Nov. 20th, 1859*. Rochester: Benton and Andrews, 1859.

Eaton, Edward Byrom. *California and the Union*. London: Heardly and Co., 1863.

Edgerton, Henry. *Speech of Hon. Henry Edgerton of Napa, on the Resolutions upon the State of the Union, Delivered in the Senate of the State of California, Thursday, February 14th, 1861, in Reply to Hon. H. I. Thornton*. Sacramento, 1861. Benjamin Hayes Scrapbooks, Bancroft Library, University of California, Berkeley.

Emerson, Ralph Waldo. "Address on the Anniversary of the Emancipation of the Negroes in the British West Indies." In *The Works of Ralph Waldo Emerson*, edited by George Sampson, 11:125–26. London: George Bell and Sons, 1905.

Faust, Drew Gilpin, ed. *The Ideology of Slavery: Proslavery Thought in the Ante-bellum South, 1830–1860.* Baton Rouge: Louisiana State University Press, 1981.

Feller, Daniel, ed. *The Papers of Andrew Jackson Digital Edition.* Charlottesville: University of Virginia Press, 2015–. https://rotunda.upress.virginia.edu /founders/JKSN.

Field, Stephen J. *Personal Reminiscences of Early Days in California, with Other Sketches.* N.p: Stephen J. Field, 1893.

Figgis, John Neville, and Reginald Vere Laurence, eds. *Selections from the Cor-respondence of the First Lord Acton.* Vol. 1. London: Longmans, Green, and Company, 1917.

Fitzhugh, George. *Cannibals All! Or, Slaves without Masters.* Richmond: A. Morris, 1857.

Foote, Henry. *Casket of Reminiscences.* Washington, DC: Chronicle Publishing Company, 1874.

Ford, Paul Leicester, ed. *The Works of Thomas Jefferson in Twelve Volumes.* Federal ed. http://www.loc.gov/resource/mtj1.027_0841_0844.

Freehling, William W., and Craig M. Simpson, eds. *Secession Debated: Georgia's Showdown in 1860.* New York: Oxford University Press, 1992.

General Lee's Farewell Address to the Army of Northern Virginia, April 10, 1865. Petersburg, Va., 1865.

Gilpin, William. *The Central Gold Region: The Grain Pastoral, and Gold Regions of North America with Some New Views of Its Physical Geography; and Observations on the Pacific Railroad.* Philadelphia: Sower, Barnes and Co., 1860.

Goodman, Jessie H., ed. *Overland in 1849: From Missouri to California by the Platte River and the Salt Lake Trail, an Account from the Letters of G. C. Pearson.* Los Angeles: Cole Holmquist Press, 1961.

Gorham, George C. *Speech Delivered by George C. Gorham of San Francisco, Union Nominee for Governor, at Platt's Hall, San Francisco, July 10, 1867.* San Francisco: Union State Central Committee, 1867.

Grant, Ulysses S. *Personal Memoirs of U. S. Grant.* 2 vols. New York: Charles L. Webster and Co., 1885–86.

Graves, Jackson Alpheus. *My Seventy Years in California, 1857–1927.* Los Angeles: Times Mirror Press, 1927.

Gray, A[ndrew] B[elcher]. *Southern Pacific Railroad. Survey of a Route for the Southern Pacific R.R., on the 32nd Parallel.* Cincinnati: Wrightson, 1856.

Greeley, Horace. *An Overland Journey from New York to San Francisco, in the Summer of 1859.* New York: M. Saxton, Barker, 1860.

Green, Thomas J[efferson]. *Journal of the Texian Expedition against Mier.* New York: Harper and Brothers, 1845.

———. *Letter from General Thomas J. Green, of California, to Hon. Robert J. Walker, upon the Subject of a Pacific Railroad.* New York: Sibells and Maigne, 1853.

———. *Reply of Gen Thomas J. Green to the Speech of General Sam Houston, in the Senate of the United States, August 1, 1854.* N.p., 1854.

Gregg, Josiah. *Commerce of the Prairies.* 2 vols. 2nd ed. New York: J. and H. G. Langley, 1845.

Griffin, John S. *A Doctor Comes to California: The Diary of John S. Griffin, Assistant*

Surgeon with Kearny's Dragoons, 1846–1847. Edited by George Walcott Ames Jr. San Francisco: California Historical Society, 1943.

——. *Los Angeles in 1849: A Letter from John S. Griffin, M.D. to Col. J. D. Stevenson, March 11, 1849.* Los Angeles: privately printed, 1949.

Gulick, Charles Adams, Jr., ed. *The Papers of Mirabeau Buonaparte Lamar.* 2 vols. Austin: A. C. Baldwin and Son, 1922.

Gwin, William M. *An Address of Hon. W. M. Gwin to the People of the State of California, on the Senatorial Election of 1857.* San Francisco: Daily National, 1859.

Hager, John S. *Speech of Hon. John S. Hager, of San Francisco, in the Senate of California, January 28th, 1870, on Senator Hager's Joint Resolution to Reject the Fifteenth Amendment to the Constitution of the United States.* N.p., n.d. Bancroft Library, University of California, Berkeley.

Haight, Henry H. *Inaugural Address of H. H. Haight.* New York: Douglas Taylor's Democratic Book and Job Printing Office, 1868.

——. *Message of H. H. Haight, Governor of the State of California, Transmitting the Proposed Fifteenth Amendment to the Federal Constitution.* Sacramento: D. W. Gelwicks, 1870.

——. *Speech of H. H. Haight, Esq. Democratic Candidate for Governor, Delivered at the Great Democratic Mass Meeting at Union Hall, July 9, 1867.* N.p., n.d. Bancroft Library, University of California, Berkeley.

Halstead, Murat. *A History of the National Political Conventions of the Current Presidential Campaign.* Columbus, Ohio: Follet, Foster and Company, 1860.

Harpending, Ashbury. *The Great Diamond Hoax and Other Stirring Incidents in the Life of Ashbury Harpending.* Edited by James H. Wilkins. San Francisco: James H. Barry, 1913.

Harte, Bret. *Bret Harte's California: Letters to the "Springfield Republican" and "Christian Register," 1866–67.* Edited by Gary Scharnhorst. Albuquerque: University of New Mexico Press, 1990.

——. *San Francisco in 1866: Being Letters to the "Springfield Republican."* Edited by George R. Stewart and Edwin S. Fussell. San Francisco: Book Club of California, 1951.

Haskins, C[harles] W[arren]. *The Argonauts of California, being the Reminiscences of Scenes and Incidents That Occurred in California in Early Mining Days.* New York: Fords, Howard and Hulbert, 1890.

Hastings, Lansford W. *Emigrants Guide to Oregon and California.* 1845. Reprint, Princeton: Princeton University Press, 1932.

Hawes, Horace. *His Reply to the Republican County Convention, and Views on the Eight Hour Agitation, Mechanics' Lien Law, Pueblo Lands, Congressional Policy of Reconstruction, and Other Political Questions.* San Francisco: Towne and Bacon, n.d.

Hayes, Benjamin. *Pioneer Notes from the Diaries of Judge Benjamin Hayes, 1849–1875.* Edited by Marjorie Tisdale Wolcott. Los Angeles: Marjorie Tilsdale Wolcott, 1929.

Helper, Hinton Rowan. *The Land of Gold: Reality versus Fiction.* Baltimore: Henry Taylor, 1855.

Hicks, George Armstrong. "George Armstrong Hicks: A Life among the Poor of Utah." In *Playing with Shadows: Voices of Dissent in the Mormon West*, edited by Polly Aird, Jeff Nichols, and Will Bagley, 61–210. Norman, OK: Arthur H. Clark, 2011.

Inman, Henry. *The Old Santa Fe Trail*. New York: Macmillan, 1897.

Jacob, Udney Hay. *An Extract from a Manuscript, Entitled the Peace Maker*. Nauvoo, IL: Joseph Smith, 1842.

Jameson, J. Franklin, ed. *Correspondence of John C. Calhoun*. Washington, DC: Government Printing Office, 1900.

Johnson, Robert Underwood, and Clarence Clough Buel, eds. *Battles and Leaders of the Civil War*. 4 vols. Edison, NJ: Castle, 1995.

Jones, Daniel W. *Forty Years among the Indians*. Salt Lake City: Juvenile Instructor Office, 1890.

Journal of the Proceedings of the South-Western Convention, Began and Held at the City of Memphis, on the 12th November, 1845. Memphis, 1845.

Judah, Theodore D. *A Practical Plan for Building the Pacific Railroad*. Washington, DC: Henry Polkinhorn, 1857.

Kewen, E. J. C. *Speech of Col. E. J. C. Kewen, at the American Mass Meeting Orleans Hotel, Sacramento, August 8, 1855*. N.p., n.d. Benjamin Hayes Scrapbooks, Bancroft Library, University of California, Berkeley.

———. *State of the Union. Speech of Hon. E. J. C. Kewen, on the State of the Union; Delivered before the Democracy of Sacramento in Assembly Hall, April 27, 1863*. N.p., n.d. Huntington Library, San Marino, CA.

Kidwell, Zedekiah. *Report on the Impracticability of Building a Railroad from the Mississippi River to the Pacific Ocean*. Washington: Cornelius Wendell, 1856.

King, Martin Luther, Jr. "Address at the Conclusion of the Selma to Montgomery March." March 25, 1965. Martin Luther King, Jr. Papers, King Center for Nonviolent Social Change, Atlanta.

[King, T. Butler]. *First Annual Report to the Board of Directors of the Southern Pacific Railroad Company Chartered by the State of Texas*. New York: American Railroad Journal Office, 1856.

Latham, Milton S. *Remarks of Hon. Milton S. Latham, of California, upon Slavery in the States and Territories, and the Doctrine of an "Irrepressible Conflict" between "Labor States" and "Capital States," Delivered in the Senate of the United States, April 16, 1860*. Washington, DC: Lemuel Towers, 1860.

Low, Frederick F. *Inaugural Address of Fred'k F. Low, Governor of the State of California at the Fifteenth Session of the Legislature*. Sacramento: O. M. Clayes, 1863.

———. *Some Reflections of an Early California Governor Contained in a Short Dictated Memoir by Frederick F. Low, Ninth Governor of California, and Notes from an Interview between Governor and Hubert Howe Bancroft in 1883*. Sacramento: Sacramento Book Collectors Club, 1959.

Mann, Horace. *Horace Mann's Letters on the Extension of Slavery into California and New Mexico; and on the Duty of Congress to Provide the Trial by Jury for Alleged Fugitive Slaves*. Washington: Buell and Blanchard, 1850.

Marston, Anna Lee, ed. *Records of a California Family: Journals and Letters of Lewis C. Gunn and Elizabeth LeBreton Gunn.* San Diego: n.p., 1928.

Maury, Matthew Fontaine. *Captain Maury's Letters on American Affairs.* Baltimore, 1862.

———. *Commercial Conventions, Direct Trade—A Chance for the South.* N.p., 1852[?], Library Company of Philadelphia.

———. *A New Theoretical and Practical Treatise on Navigation.* Philadelphia: E. C. and J. Biddle, 1845.

———. *The Physical Geography of the Sea.* 2nd ed. New York: Harper and Brothers, 1855.

Melville, Herman. *Moby Dick.* New ed. Boston: St. Botolph Society, 1892.

Memphis Convention Corresponding Committee. *Circular to the Citizens of the United States;* together with "Steam Navigation to China," Matthew Fontaine Maury to T. Butler King, January 10, 1848. Memphis, 1849.

Mial, Charles S. *The Proposed Slave Empire: Its Antecedents, Constitution, and Policy.* London: Elliot Stock, 1863.

Mitchell, O. P. *The Olive Branch.* Marysville: California Express Job Office, 1862.

Moore, Frank, ed. *The Rebellion Record: A Diary of American Events, with Documents, Narratives, Illustrative Incidents, Poetry, Etc.* 11 vols. New York: G. P. Putnam, 1861–68.

Mowry, Sylvester. *The Geography and Resources of Arizona and Sonora: An Address before the American Geographical and Statistical Society.* Washington: Henry Polkinhorn, 1859.

———. *Memoir of the Proposed Territory of Arizona.* Washington: Henry Polkinhorn, 1857.

Newmark, Harris. *Sixty Years in Southern California, 1853–1913.* 4th ed. Los Angeles: Zeitlin and Ver Brugge, 1970.

Northup, Solomon. *Twelve Years a Slave.* Cincinnati: Henry W. Derby, 1853.

Oberg, Barbara, ed. *The Papers of Thomas Jefferson.* Vol. 35. Princeton: Princeton University Press, 2009.

Otero, Miguel Antonio. *An Abolition Attack upon New Mexico, and a Reply by Hon. M. A. Otero.* Santa Fe: Santa Fe Gazette, 1861.

Parker, Elizabeth. *The Sandwich Islands as They Are, Not as They Should Be.* San Francisco: Burgess, Gilbert and Still, 1852.

Parkhurst, John G. *Official Proceedings of the Democratic National Convention, Held in 1860, at Charleston and Baltimore.* Cleveland: Nevins' Print, 1860.

Peebles, Cornelius Glen. *Exposé of the Atlantic and Pacific Railroad Company.* New York: Astor House, 1854.

Pettis, George H. *Frontier Service during the Rebellion; or, a History of Company K, First Infantry, California Volunteers.* Providence: The Society, 1885.

Pfanz, Donald C., ed. *The Letters of General Richard S. Ewell: Stonewall's Successor.* Knoxville: University of Tennessee Press, 2012.

Phelps, John S. *A Letter from Hon. John S. Phelps to Citizens of Arkansas in Relation to a Pacific Railroad.* St. Louis: George Knapp and Co., 1858.

Polk, James K. *Polk: The Diary of a President, 1845–1849.* Edited by Allan Nevins. London: Longmans, Green and Co., 1952.

Pollard, Edward A. *The Lost Cause: A New Southern History of the War of the Confederates*. New York: E. B. Treat, 1866.

[———]. *The Southern Spy. Letters on the Policy and Inauguration of the Lincoln War. Written Anonymously in Washington and Elsewhere*. Richmond: West and Johnston, 1862.

Pratt, Parley P. *History of the Late Persecution Inflicted by the State of Missouri Upon the Mormons*. New York: Oswego County Democrat, 1840.

Proceedings of the First State Convention of the Colored Citizens of the State of California. Sacramento: Democratic State Journal Print, 1855.

Proceedings of the Friends of a Rail-Road to San Francisco, at their Public Meeting, Held at the U.S. Hotel, in Boston, April 19, 1849. Boston: Dutton and Wentworth, 1849.

Pumpelly, Raphael. *Across America and Asia. Notes of a Five Years Journey around the World and of Residence in Arizona, Japan and China*. New York: Leypoldt and Holt, 1870.

Read, Georgia Willis, and Ruth Gaines, eds. *Gold Rush: The Journals, Drawings, and Other Papers of J. Goldsborough Bruff: Captain, Washington City and California Mining Association, April 2, 1849–July 20, 1851*. New York: Columbia University Press, 1949.

"Recollections of Slavery by a Runway Slave." Serialized in *The Emancipator* in five parts, August 23, September 13, September 20, October 11, and October 18, 1838.

Redpath, James. *The Roving Editor: Or, Talks with Slaves in the South States*. New York: A. B. Burdick, 1859.

Richardson, James D., ed. *A Compilation of the Messages and Papers of the Presidents, 1789- 1908*. Vol. 4. Washington: Bureau of National Literature and Art, 1908.

Rowland, Dunbar, ed. *Jefferson Davis, Constitutionalist: His Letters, Papers and Speeches*. 10 vols. Jackson: Mississippi Department of Archives and History, 1923.

Ruxton, George F. *Adventures in Mexico and the Rocky Mountains*. London: John Murray, 1847.

Scott, Charles L. *Address of the Hon. Charles L. Scott, of California, to his Constituents on the Constitutional Right of Secession*. February 2, 1861. N.p., n.d. Benjamin Hayes Scrapbooks, Bancroft Library, University of California, Berkeley.

Selections from the Letters and Speeches of the Hon. James H. Hammond, of South Carolina. New York: John F. Trow, 1866.

Sherman, Edwin A. "Sherman Was There: The Recollections of Major Edwin A. Sherman." Edited by Allen B. Sherman. *California Historical Society Quarterly* 23 (September 1944): 259–81; 23 (December 1944): 349–77.

Smith, Gerrit. *Keep Government within Its Limits: Speech of Gerrit Smith, on the Pacific Railroad*. Washington, DC: Buell and Blanchard, 1854.

Smith, Hugh N. *Address of Hugh N. Smith, of New Mexico, to the People of That Territory*. Washington, 1850.

Smith, Joseph. *General Smith's Views of the Powers and Policy of the Government of the United States*. Pontiac, MI.: Jackson Print, 1844.

Stanly, Edward. *Speech of the Hon. Edward Stanly, Delivered at Sacramento, July 17th, 1857, at a Public Meeting Held in the Forest Theater*. N.p., n.d. Bancroft Library, University of California, Berkeley.

[Starr, Frederick]. *Letters for the People on the Present Crisis*. New York, 1853.

Stratton, R. B. *Captivity of the Oatman Girls: Being an Interesting Narrative of Life among the Apache and Mohave Indians*. 3rd ed. New York: Carlton and Porter, 1859.

Stringfellow, Thornton. *A Brief Examination of Scripture Testimony on the Institution of Slavery*. Washington, DC: Congressional Globe Office, 1850.

Strong, John L. "Cotton Experiments in California." *Overland Monthly* 6, no. 4 (April 1871): 326–35.

———. "Labor in Cotton Culture." *Overland Monthly* 13, no. 1 (July 1874): 18–25.

Stroyer, Jacob. *My Life in the South: New and Enlarged Edition*. Salem: Salem Observer, 1885.

Swallow, G. C. *Geological Report of the Country along the Line of the South-Western Branch of the Pacific, State of Missouri, to Which Is Prefixed a Memoir of the Pacific Railroad*. St. Louis: George Knapp and Co., 1859.

Taylor, E. H., et al. "California Freedom Papers." *Journal of Negro History* 3 (January 1918): 45–54.

Teel, T. T. "Sibley's New Mexican Campaign—Its Objects and the Causes of Its Failure." In *Battles and Leaders of the Civil War*, vol. 2, edited by Robert Underwood Johnson and Clarence Clough Buel, 700. Edison, NJ: Castle, 1995.

Thompson, Waddy. *Recollections of Mexico*. New York: Wiley and Putnam, 1846.

Thoreau, Henry David. *Walden*. 2 vols. Boston: Houghton Milton, 1854, 1897.

Thornton, Harry Inness, Jr. *Speech of Hon. Harry I. Thornton, Jr. on the Resolutions upon the State of the Union, Delivered in the Senate of the State of California, at the Twelfth Session of the Legislature, February 8th, 1861*. Sacramento, 1861.

Thwaites, Reuben Gold, ed. *Original Journals of the Lewis and Clark Expedition, 1804–1806*. 8 vols. New York: Dodd, Mead, 1904–5.

Tilford, Frank. *Speech of Hon. Frank Tilford, in the Senate of California, March 13, 1856, upon the Resolution of the Assembly, Concerning the Result of the Recent Election for Speaker in the U.S. House of Representatives*. Sacramento: B. B. Redding, 1856.

Tocqueville, Alexis de. *Democracy in America*. 2nd ed. Translated by Henry Reeve. 2 vols. New York: George Adlard, 1838.

Trescot, William Henry. *A Few Thoughts on the Foreign Policy of the United States*. Charleston: John Russell, 1849.

———. "Our Foreign Policy." *Southern Literary Messenger* 16, no. 1 (January 1850): 1–6.

———. *The Position and Course of the South*. Charleston: Walker and James, 1850.

Trezevant, J. T., et al. "Letter to 'Sir,' Memphis, Tennessee, March 1, 1849." Memphis[?], 1849, Library Company of Philadelphia.

The Tribune Almanac and Political Register for 1868. New York, 1868.

Turner, Frederick Jackson. *Rereading Frederick Jackson Turner: "The Significance of the Frontier in American History" and Other Essays*. Commentary by John Mack Faragher. New Haven: Yale University Press, 1998.

Twain, Mark. *Roughing It*. 1871. Reprint, New York: Harper and Brothers, 1899.

United Daughters of the Confederacy Patriot Ancestor Album. Paducah, KY: Turner, 1999.

Walker, Robert J., T. Butler King, and F. M. Dimond. *Circular to the Stockholders of the Atlantic and Pacific Railroad Company*. New York: George F. Nesbitt and Co., 1855.

Weller, John B. *Speech of John B. Weller, Delivered in Sacramento, at a Mass Meeting of the Democracy, Held on Saturday Night, July 25th, 1857*. Sacramento: James Anthony and Co., 1857.

——. *Speech of Mr. Weller, of California, in the Senate, February 13, 1854, on the Nebraska and Kansas Bill*. Benjamin Hayes Scrapbooks, Bancroft Library, University of California, Berkeley.

Whitney, Asa. *A Project for a Railroad to the Pacific*. New York: George W. Wood, 1849.

Wilson, Clyde Norman, William Edwin Hemphill, and Shirley Bright Cook, eds. *The Papers of John C. Calhoun*. 28 vols. Columbia: University of South Carolina Press, 1959–2003.

Wilson, John P., ed. *When the Texans Came: Missing Records from the Civil War in the Southwest, 1861–1862*. Albuquerque: University of New Mexico Press, 2001.

Wise, Barton Haxall. *The Life of Henry A. Wise of Virginia, 1806–1876*. New York: Macmillan, 1899.

Wise, Henry Augustus. *Los Gringos: Or, An Inside View of Mexico and California, with Wanderings in Peru, Chili, and Polynesia*. New York: Baker and Scribner, 1849.

Wise, Henry A. *Seven Decades of the Union*. Philadelphia: J. B. Lippincott and Co., 1872.

——. *Territorial Government, and the Admission of New States into the Union: A Historical and Constitutional Treatise*. Richmond[?], 1859, Virginia Historical Society.

Wrottesley, John. *Lord Wrottesley's Speech in the House of Lords, on 26th April, 1853, on Lieut. Maury's Plan for Improving Navigation with Some Remarks upon the Advantages Arising from the Pursuit of Abstract Science*. London: James Ridgway, 1853.

Young, Brigham. "Human Intelligence and Freedom—National Administrative Movements, &c." *Journal of Discourses* 8 (February 10, 1861).

Secondary Sources

Aarim-Heriot, Najia. *Chinese Immigrants, African Americans, and Racial Anxiety in the United States, 1848–82*. Urbana: University of Illinois Press, 2003.

Adams, Kevin. "War in the West." In *Cambridge History of the American Civil War*. Vol 1, edited by Aaron Sheehan-Dean, 554–75. New York: Cambridge University Press, 2019.

Agnew, Brad. "Our Doom as a Nation Is Sealed: The Five Nations in the Civil War." In *The Civil War and Reconstruction in Indian Territory*, edited by Bradley R. Clampitt, 64–87. Lincoln: University of Nebraska Press, 2015.

Alvord, Clarence Walworth, and Lee Bidgood. *The First Explorations of the Trans-Allegheny Region by the Virginians, 1650–1674*. Cleveland: Arthur H. Clark, 1912.

Angel, Myron. *History of San Luis Obispo County, California: With Illustrations and Biographical Sketches of Its Prominent Men and Pioneers*. Oakland: Thompson and West, 1883.

Archer, Seth. *Sharks upon the Land: Colonialism, Indigenous Health, and Culture in Hawai'i, 1778–1855*. Cambridge: Cambridge University Press, 2018.

Arenson, Adam. *The Great Heart of the Republic: St. Louis and the Cultural Civil War*. Cambridge, MA: Harvard University Press, 2011.

———. Introduction to *Civil War Wests: Testing the Limits of the United States*, edited by Adam Arenson and Andrew R. Graybill, 1–12. Oakland: University of California Press, 2015.

Arenson, Adam, and Andrew R. Graybill, eds. *Civil War Wests: Testing the Limits of the United States*. Oakland: University of California Press, 2015.

Arrington, Leonard J. "The Mormon Cotton Mission in Southern Utah." *Pacific Historical Review* 25, no. 3 (August 1956): 221–38.

Ayers, Edward L. *In the Presence of Mine Enemies: War in the Heart of America, 1859–1863*. New York: W. W. Norton, 2003.

Bagley, Will. Blood of the Prophets: Brigham Young and the Massacre at Mountain Meadows. Norman: University of Oklahoma Press, 2002.

Bakken, Gordon Morris. "The Courts, the Legal Profession, and the Development of Law in Early California." In *Taming the Elephant: Politics, Government, and Law in Pioneer California*, edited by John F. Burns and Richard J. Orsi, 74–95. Berkeley: University of California Press, 2003.

Ball, Durwood. *Army Regulars on the Western Frontier, 1848–1861*. Norman: University of Oklahoma Press, 2001.

Balogh, Brian. *A Government Out of Sight: The Mystery of National Authority in Nineteenth- Century America*. New York: Cambridge University Press, 2009.

Bancroft, Hubert Howe. *History of Arizona and New Mexico, 1530–1888: The Works of Hubert Howe Bancroft*. Vol. 17. San Francisco: The History Company, 1889.

———. *History of California*. 7 vols. San Francisco: The History Company, 1884–90.

Baptist, Edward E. *The Half Has Never Been Told: Slavery and the Making of American Capitalism*. New York: Basic Books, 2014.

Barnes, L. Diane, Brian Schoen, and Frank Towers, eds. *The Old South's Modern Worlds: Slavery, Region, and Nation in the Age of Progress*. Oxford: Oxford University Press, 2011.

Barr, Juliana. "Geographies of Power: Mapping Indian Borders in the 'Borderlands' of the Early Southwest." *William and Mary Quarterly* 68, no. 1 (January 2011): 5–46.

Baumgartner, Alice. *South to Freedom: Runaway Slaves to Mexico and the Road to Civil War*. New York: Basic Books, 2021.

Beale, Howard K. *The Critical Year: A Study of Andrew Johnson and Reconstruction*. New York: Harcourt, Brace, 1930.

Beasley, Delilah L. *The Negro Trail Blazers of California*. Los Angeles: Times Mirror, 1919.

——. "Slavery in California." *Journal of Negro History* 3 (January 1918): 33–44.

Beckert, Sven. *Empire of Cotton: A Global History.* New York: Knopf, 2014.

——. *The Monied Metropolis: New York City and the Consolidation of the American Bourgeoisie, 1850–1896.* Cambridge: Cambridge University Press, 2001.

——. "Slavery and Capitalism." *Chronicle of Higher Education*, December 12, 2014.

Beckert, Sven, and Seth Rockman, eds. *Slavery's Capitalism: A New History of American Economic Development.* Philadelphia: University of Pennsylvania Press, 2016.

Beller, Jack. "Negro Slaves in Utah." *Utah Historical Quarterly* 2 (October 1929): 122–26.

Belohlavek, John. "Race Progress and Destiny: Caleb Cushing and the Quest for American Empire." In *Manifest Destiny and Empire: American Antebellum Expansionism*, edited by Robert Walter Johannsen, 21–47. Arlington: University of Texas at Arlington Press, 1997.

Bemis, Samuel Flagg. *A Diplomatic History of the United States.* New York: Henry Holt, 1950.

Bender, Thomas, ed. *The Antislavery Debate: Capitalism and Abolitionism as a Problem in Historical Interpretation.* Berkeley: University of California Press, 1992.

Benedict, Michael Les. *A Compromise of Principle: Congressional Republicans and Reconstruction, 1863–1869.* New York: W. W. Norton, 1974.

——. "The Rout of Radicalism: Republicans and the Elections of 1867." *Civil War History* 18, no 4 (December 1972): 334–44.

Bensel, Richard Franklin. *Yankee Leviathan: The Origins of Central State Authority in America, 1859–1877.* New York: Cambridge University Press, 1991.

Berlin, Ira. *Many Thousands Gone: The First Two Centuries of Slavery in North America.* Cambridge, Mass.: Harvard University Press, 1998.

Bernard, Richard M., and Bradley R. Rice, eds. *Sunbelt Cities: Politics and Growth since World War II.* Austin: University of Texas Press, 1984.

Berwanger, Eugene H. *The Frontier against Slavery: Western Anti-Negro Prejudice and the Slavery Extension Controversy.* Urbana: University of Illinois Press, 1967.

——. *The West and Reconstruction.* Urbana: University of Illinois Press, 1981.

Bieber, Ralph, ed. *Southern Trails to California in 1849.* Glendale, CA: Arthur H. Clark, 1937.

Bigler, David L. and Will Bagley. *The Mormon Rebellion: America's First Civil War, 1857-1858.* Norman: University of Oklahoma Press, 2011.

Binkley, William Campbell. *The Expansionist Movement in Texas, 1836–1850.* Berkeley: University of California Press, 1925.

Bishop, M. Guy. "Politics, Land, Apostasy: The Last Days of the San Bernardino Mormon Colony, 1855–1857." *Pacific Historian* 30 (1986): 18–30.

Blackhawk, Ned. *Violence over the Land: Indians and Empires in the Early American West.* Cambridge, MA: Harvard University Press, 2006.

Blair, William A. *With Malice toward Some: Treason and Loyalty in the Civil War Era.* Chapel Hill: University of North Carolina Press, 2014.

Blevins, Cameron. *Gossamer Network: The U.S. Post and State Power in the American West*. Oxford: Oxford University Press, forthcoming.

Blight, David W. *Race and Reunion: The Civil War in American Memory*. Cambridge, MA: Belknap, 2001.

Blyth, Lance R. "Kit Carson and the War for the Southwest: Separation and Survival along the Rio Grande, 1862–1868." In *Civil War Wests: Testing the Limits of the United States*, edited by Adam Arenson and Andrew R. Graybill, 53–70. Oakland: University of California Press, 2015.

Boessenecker, John. *Badge and Buckshot: Lawlessness in Old California*. Norman: University of Oklahoma Press, 1988.

Bonner, Robert E. *Mastering America: Southern Slaveholders and the Crisis of American Nationhood*. Cambridge: Cambridge University Press, 2009.

———. "The Salt Water Civil War: Thalassological Approaches, Ocean-Centered Opportunities." *Journal of the Civil War Era* 6, no. 2 (June 2016): 243–67.

Bottoms, D. Michael. *An Aristocracy of Color: Race and Reconstruction in California and the West, 1850–1890*. Norman: University of Oklahoma Press, 2013.

Boyd, Eva Jolene. *Noble Brutes: Camels on the American Frontier*. Plano: Republic of Texas Press, 1995.

Branch, Taylor. *At Canaan's Edge: America in the King Years, 1965–1968*. New York: Simon and Schuster, 2007.

Brands, W. H. *Andrew Jackson: His Life and Times*. New York: Doubleday, 2005.

Brauer, Kinley J. "The United States and British Imperial Expansion, 1815-1860." *Diplomatic History* 12, no. 1 (Winter 1988): 19-37.

Bringhurst, Newell G. "The Mormons and Slavery: A Closer Look." *Pacific Historical Review* 50, no. 3 (August 1981): 329–38.

———. *Saints, Slaves, and Blacks: The Changing Place of Black People within Mormonism*. 2nd ed. Salt Lake City: Greg Kofford Books, 2018.

Brooks, Corey M. *Liberty Power: Antislavery Third Parties and the Transformation of American Politics*. Chicago: University of Chicago Press, 2016.

Brooks, James F. *Captives and Cousins: Slavery, Kinship and Community in the Southwest Borderlands*. Chapel Hill: University of North Carolina Press, 2002.

Brooks, Juanita. "The Cotton Mission." *Utah Historical Quarterly* 29 (July 1961): 201–21.

———. *Mountain Meadows Massacre*. Norman: University of Oklahoma Press, 1950.

Brown, Kathleen M. *Good Wives, Nasty Wenches, and Anxious Patriarchs: Gender, Race, and Power in Colonial Virginia*. Chapel Hill: University of North Carolina Press, 1996.

Brown, Walter L. *A Life of Albert Pike*. Fayetteville: University of Arkansas Press, 1997.

Burbank, Jane, and Frederick Cooper. *Empires in World History: Power and the Politics of Difference*. Princeton: Princeton University Press, 2010.

Burke, Diane Mutti. "Scattered People: The Long History of Forced Eviction in the Kansas- Missouri Borderlands." In *Civil War Wests: Testing the Limits of the United States*, edited by Adam Arenson and Andrew R. Graybill, 71–94. Oakland: University of California Press, 2015.

Bush, Lester E. "Mormonism's Negro Doctrine: An Historical Overview."
    Dialogue: A Journal of Mormon Thought 8, no. 1 (1973): 229–71.
Bushman, Richard Lyman. *Joseph Smith: Rough Stone Rolling.* New York: Vintage,
    2005.
Campbell, Marne L. *Making Black Los Angeles: Class, Gender, and Community,
    1850–1917.* Chapel Hill: University of North Carolina Press, 2016.
Campney, Brent M. S. *This Is Not Dixie: Racist Violence in Kansas, 1861–1927.*
    Champaign: University of Illinois Press, 2015.
Carpenter, Jesse T. *The South as a Conscious Minority, 1789–1861: A Study in Politi-
    cal Thought.* 1930. Reprint, Columbia: University of South Carolina Press, 1990.
Carrigan, William D., and Clive Webb. *Forgotten Dead: Mob Violence against Mex-
    icans in the United States, 1848–1928.* New York: Oxford University Press, 2013.
———. "'Muerto por Unos Desconocidos (Killed by Persons Unknown)': Mob Vio-
    lence against African Americans and Mexican Americans." In *Beyond Black
    and White: Race, Ethnicity, and Gender in the U.S. South and Southwest,* edited
    by Stephanie Cole and Allison Parker, 35–74. College Station: Texas A&M
    University Press, 2004.
Carter, John Denton. "Abraham Lincoln and the California Patronage." *American
    Historical Review* 48, no. 3 (April 1943): 495–506.
Carter, Kate B. *The Negro Pioneer.* Salt Lake City: Utah Printing Company, 1965.
Caughey, John Walton. "Don Benito Wilson: An Average Southern Californian."
    Huntington Library Quarterly 2 (April 1939): 285–300.
Chaffin, Tom. *Fatal Glory: Narciso Lopez and the First Clandestine U.S. War
    against Cuba.* Charlottesville: University of Virginia Press,1996.
Chandler, Robert J. "'Anti-Coolie Rabies': The Chinese Issue in California Politics
    in the 1860s." *Pacific Historian* 28 (1984): 29–42.
———. "Friends in Time of Need: Republicans and Black Civil Rights in Cali-
    fornia during the Civil War Era." *Arizona and the West* 24 (Winter 1982):
    319–40.
———. "An Uncertain Influence: The Role of the Federal Government in Califor-
    nia, 1846–1880." In *Taming the Elephant: Politics, Government, and Law in Pio-
    neer California,* edited by John F. Burns and Richard J. Orsi, 224–71. Berkeley:
    University of California Press, 2003.
———, ed. *California and the Civil War, 1861–1865.* Berkeley: Okeanos Press, 1992.
Chaplin, Joyce. *An Anxious Pursuit: Agricultural Innovation and Modernity in the
    Lower South.* Chapel Hill: University of North Carolina Press, 1996.
Christensen, James B. "Negro Slavery in the Utah Territory." *Phylon Quarterly* 18
    (3rd quarter, 1957): 298–305.
Clampitt, Bradley R., ed. *The Civil War and Reconstruction in Indian Territory.*
    Lincoln: University of Nebraska Press, 2015.
Clendenen, Clarence C. "A Confederate Spy in California: A Curious Incident of
    the Civil War." *Southern California Quarterly* 45 (September 1963): 219–34.
———. "Dan Showalter—California Secessionist." *California Historical Society
    Quarterly* 40 (December 1961): 309–25.
Clinton, Catherine, ed. *Confederate Statues and Memorialization.* Athens:
    University of Georgia Press, 2019.

Coleman, Patty R. "John Ballard and the African American Community in Los Angeles, 1850-1905." *Southern California Quarterly* 94 (Summer 2012): 193–229.

Coleman, Ronald G. "Blacks in Utah History: An Unknown Legacy." In *The Peoples of Utah*, edited by Helen Z. Papanikolas, 115–40. Salt Lake City: Utah State Historical Society, 1976.

Colton, Roy C. *The Civil War in the Western Territories: Arizona, Colorado, New Mexico, and Utah*. Norman: University of Oklahoma Press, 1984.

Connelly, Thomas L. "The American Camel Experiment: A Reappraisal." *Southwestern Historical Quarterly* 69 (April 1966): 442–62.

Connelly, Thomas L., and Barbara L. Bellows. *God and General Longstreet: The Lost Cause and the Southern Mind*. Baton Rouge: Louisiana State University Press, 1995.

Cooper, William J., Jr. *Jefferson Davis, American*. New York: Vintage, 2001.

———. *The South and the Politics of Slavery, 1828–1856*. Baton Rouge: Louisiana State University Press, 1978.

Cotterill, Robert S. "Early Agitation for a Pacific Railroad, 1845–1850." *Mississippi Valley Historical Review* 5 (March 1919): 396–414.

———. "Southern Railroads and Western Trade, 1840–1850." *Mississippi Valley Historical Review* 3 (March 1917): 427–41.

Cowsert, Zac. "Should Indian Territory Be Considered a Border State?" *Civil Discourse: A Blog of the Long Civil War Era*, June 20, 2016. http://www.civil discourse-historyblog.com/blog/2016/6/13/should-indian-territory-be-a -border-state.

Cox, Karen L. *Dixie's Daughters: The United Daughters of the Confederacy and the Preservation of Confederate Culture*. Gainesville: University Press of Florida, 2003.

Crapol, Edward P. "Coming to Terms with Empire: The Historiography of Late-Nineteenth-Century American Foreign Relations." *Diplomatic History* 16, no. 4 (1992): 573–97.

———. *John Tyler: The Accidental President*. Chapel Hill: University of North Carolina Press, 2012.

Crofts, Daniel W. *Lincoln and the Politics of Slavery: The Other Thirteenth Amendment and the Struggle to Save the Union*. Chapel Hill: University of North Carolina Press, 2016.

Cumings, Bruce. *Dominion from Sea to Sea: Pacific Ascendancy and American Power*. New Haven: Yale University Press, 2009.

Cunningham, Sean P. *American Politics in the Postwar Sunbelt: Conservative Growth in a Battleground Region*. New York: Cambridge University Press, 2014.

Cutrer, Thomas W. *Theater of a Separate War: The Civil War West of the Mississippi River, 1861–1865*. Chapel Hill: University of North Carolina Press, 2017.

Daly, John Patrick. *When Slavery Was Called Freedom: Evangelicalism, Proslavery, and the Causes of the Civil War*. Lexington: University of Kentucky Press, 2002.

Davis, David Brion. *The Slave Power Conspiracy and the Paranoid Style*. Baton Rouge: Louisiana State University Press, 1969.

Davis, John P. *The Union Pacific Railway: A Study in Railway Politics, History and Economics*. Chicago: S. C. Griggs, 1894.

Davis, William C. *Jefferson Davis: The Man and His Hour*. New York: HarperCollins, 1991.

Davis, Winfield J. *History of Political Conventions in California, 1849–1892*. Sacramento: California State Library, 1893.

DeFelice, Jim. *West Like Lightning: The Brief, Legendary Ride of the Pony Express*. New York: William Morrow, 2018.

DeLay, Brian. *War of a Thousand Deserts: Indian Raids and the U.S.-Mexican War*. New Haven: Yale University Press, 2008.

Demaratus, DeEtta. *The Force of a Feather: The Search for the Lost Story of Slavery and Freedom*. Salt Lake City: University of Utah Press, 2002.

Dennett, Tyler. *Americans in Eastern Asia: A Critical Study of the Policy of the United States with Reference to China, Japan and Korea in the 19th Century*. New York: Macmillan, 1922.

Derry, Linda. "Camels in Cahawba." *Alabama Heritage* 112 (Spring 2014): 28–35.

Deverell, William. "After Antietam: Memory and Memorabilia in the Far West." In *Empire and Liberty: The Civil War and the West*, edited by Virginia Scharff, 175–89. Berkeley: University of California Press, 2015.

———. "Convalescence and California: The Civil War Comes West." *Southern California Quarterly* 90 (Spring 2008): 1–26.

———. "Redemptive California? Re-thinking the Post–Civil War." *Rethinking History* 11, no. 1 (March 2007): 61–78.

———. "Thoughts from the Farther West: Mormons, California, and the Civil War." *Journal of Mormon History* 34 (Spring 2008): 1–19.

———. *Whitewashed Adobe: The Rise of Los Angeles and the Remaking of Its Mexican Past*. Berkeley: University of California Press, 2004.

Dew, Charles B. *Apostles of Disunion: Southern Secession Commissioners and the Causes of the Civil War*. Charlottesville: University of Virginia Press, 2002.

———. *Bond of Iron: Master and Slave at Buffalo Forge*. New York: W. W. Norton, 1995.

Didion, Joan. "John Wayne: A Love Song." In *Slouching towards Bethlehem*, 29–41. 1968. Reprint, New York: Farrar, Straus and Giroux, 2008.

———. "Some Dreamers of the Golden Dream." In *Slouching towards Bethlehem*, 3–28.

———. South and West: From a Notebook. London: 4th Estate, 2017.

Dobbin, Frank. *Forging Industrial Policy: The United States, Britain, and France in the Railway Age*. Cambridge: Cambridge University Press, 1997.

Dochuk, Darren. *From Bible Belt to Sunbelt: Plain-Folk Religion, Grassroots Politics, and the Rise of Evangelical Conservatism*. New York: Norton, 2011.

Domby, Adam H. *The False Cause: Fraud, Fabrication, and White Supremacy in Confederate Memory*. Charlottesville: University of Virginia Press, 2020.

Donahue, William. "The Caleb Cushing Mission." *Modern Asian Studies* 16, no. 2 (1982): 193–216.

Downey, Tom. *Planting a Capitalist South: Masters, Merchants, and Manufactures in the Southern Interior, 1790–1860*. Baton Rouge: Louisiana State University Press, 2006.

Downs, Gregory P. *After Appomattox: Military Occupation and the Ends of War.* Cambridge, MA: Harvard University Press, 2015.

———. "The Mexicanization of American Politics: The United States' Transnational Path from Civil War to Stabilization." *American Historical Review* 117, no. 2 (April 2012): 387–409.

Downs, Gregory P., and Kate Masur, eds. *The World the Civil War Made.* Chapel Hill: University of North Carolina Press, 2015.

Edling, Max. *Hercules in the Cradle: War, Money, and the American State, 1783–1867.* Chicago: University of Chicago Press, 2014.

Eelman, Bruce. *Entrepreneurs in the Southern Upcountry: Commercial Culture in Spartanburg, South Carolina, 1845–1880.* Athens: University of Georgia Press, 2010.

Egerton, Douglas R. "Rethinking Atlantic Historiography in a Postcolonial World: The Civil War in a Global Perspective." *Journal of the Civil War Era* 1, no. 1 (March 2011): 79–95.

Ellison, Joseph W. *California and the Nation, 1850–1869.* Berkeley: University of California Press, 1927.

———. "Designs for a Pacific Republic, 1843–62." *Oregon Historical Quarterly* 31, no. 4 (December 1930): 319–42.

Ellison, William Henry. "The Movement for State Division in California 1849–1860." *Southwestern Historical Quarterly* 17 (1914): 111–24.

Ely, Glen Sample. *The Texas Frontier and the Butterfield Overland Mail, 1858–1861.* Norman: University of Oklahoma Press, 2016.

Ericson, David F. *Slavery in the American Republic.* Lawrence: University Press of Kansas, 2011.

Fairbank, John King. "'American China Policy' to 1898: A Misconception." *Pacific Historical Review* 39, no. 4 (1970): 409–20.

———. *The United States and China.* 4th ed. Cambridge, MA: American Foreign Policy Library, 1983.

Faragher, John Mack. *Eternity Street: Violence and Justice in Frontier Los Angeles.* New York: W. W. Norton, 2016.

Faulk, Odie B. *Destiny Road: The Gila Trail and the Opening of the Southwest.* New York: Oxford University Press, 1973.

———. *The U.S. Camel Corps: An Army Experiment.* New York: Oxford University Press, 1976.

Fehrenbacher, Don E. *The Dred Scott Case: Its Significance in American Law and Politics.* New York: Oxford University Press, 1978.

———. *The Slaveholding Republic: An Account of the United States Government's Relations to Slavery.* Completed and edited by Ward M. McAfee. New York: Oxford University Press, 2001.

Feifer, George. *Breaking Open Japan: Commodore Perry, Lord Abe, and American Imperialism in 1853.* New York: Smithsonian Books, 2006.

Ferrier, Warren William. *Origin and Development of the University of California.* Berkeley: Sather Gate Book Shop, 1930.

Field, Kendra, and Daniel Lynch. "'Master of Ceremonies': The World of Peter Biggs in Civil War–Era Los Angeles." *Western Historical Quarterly* 47 (Winter 2016): 379–406.

Finch, L. Boyd. "Arizona in Exile: Confederate Schemes to Recapture the Far Southwest." *Journal of Arizona History* 33 (Spring 1992): 57–84.

———. *Confederate Pathway to the Pacific: Major Sherod Hunter and Arizona Territory, C.S.A.* Tucson: Arizona Historical Society, 1996.

———. "William Claude Jones: The Charming Rogue Who Named Arizona." *Journal of Arizona History* 31 (Winter 1990): 405–24.

Finkelman, Paul. "The Law of Slavery and Freedom in California, 1848–1860." *California Western Law Review* 17 (1981): 437–64.

Fitzpatrick, Michael F. "Jubal Early and the Californians." *Civil War Times Illustrated* 37, no. 2 (May 1998): 50–61.

Fogel, Robert William, and Stanley L. Engerman. *Time on the Cross: The Economics of American Negro Slavery.* New York: W. W. Norton, 1974.

Foner, Eric. *Free Soil, Free Labor, Free Men: The Ideology of the Republican Party before the Civil War.* New York: Oxford University Press, 1970.

———. *Reconstruction: America's Unfinished Revolution, 1863–1877.* New York: Harper and Row, 1988.

Ford, Lacey K., Jr. *Origins of Southern Radicalism: The South Carolina Upcountry, 1800–1860.* Oxford: Oxford University Press, 1988.

Foster, Gaines M. *Ghosts of the Confederacy: Defeat, the Lost Cause, and the Emergence of the New South.* New York: Oxford University Press, 1988.

Fowler, Harlan D. *Camels to California.* Stanford: Stanford University Press, 1950.

———. *Three Caravans to Yuma: The Untold Story of Bactrian Camels in Western America.* Glendale, CA: Arthur H. Clark, 1980.

Francaviglia, Richard V., and Jimmy L. Bryan. "'Are We Chimerical in This Opinion?' Visions of a Pacific Railroad and Westward Expansion before 1845." *Pacific Historical Review* 71, no. 2 (April 2002): 179–202.

Frazier, Donald S. *Blood and Treasure: Confederate Empire in the Southwest.* College State: Texas A&M University Press, 1995.

Freehling, William W. *The Road to Disunion: Secessionists at Bay, 1776–1854.* New York: Oxford University Press, 1990.

———. *The Road to Disunion: Secessionists Triumphant, 1854–1861.* New York: Oxford University Press, 2008.

———. *The South vs. the South: How Anti-Confederate Southerners Shaped the Course of the Civil War.* New York: Oxford University Press, 2002.

Freeman, Joanne. *The Field of Blood: Congressional Violence and the Road to Civil War.* New York: Picador, 2018.

Fry, Joseph A. "Imperialism, American Style, 1890–1916." In *American Foreign Relations Reconsidered, 1890–1993*, edited by Gordon Martel, 52–70. New York: Routledge, 1994.

Fuller, John D. P. "The Slavery Question and the Movement to Acquire Mexico, 1846–1848." *Mississippi Valley Historical Review* 21 (June 1934): 31–48.

Gallagher, Gary W. "How the West Wasn't Won." *Civil War Monitor* 9 (Spring 2019): 34–41, 75–76.

Gallagher, Gary, and Alan T. Nolan, eds. *The Myth of the Lost Cause and Civil War History.* Bloomington: Indiana University Press, 2000.

Gallagher, Winifred. *How the Post Office Created America*. New York: Penguin, 2016.

Gambill, Edward L. *Conservative Ordeal: Northern Democrats and Reconstruction, 1865–1868*. Ames: Iowa State University Press, 1981.

Ganaway, Loomis Morton. *New Mexico and the Sectional Controversy, 1846–1861*. 1944. Reprint, Philadelphia: Porcupine Press, 1976.

Garber, Paul Neff. *The Gadsden Treaty*. Philadelphia: University of Pennsylvania, 1923.

Genovese, Eugene D. *The Political Economy of Slavery: Studies in the Economy and Society of the Slave South*. New York: Pantheon Books, 1965.

———. *Roll, Jordan, Roll: The World the Slaves Made*. New York: Vintage, 1976.

Gerstle, Gary. "A State Both Strong and Weak." *American Historical Review* 115, no. 3 (June 2010): 779–85.

Gilbert, Benjamin Franklin. "The Confederate Minority in California." *California Historical Society Quarterly* 20 (June 1941): 154–70.

Gillette, William. *Retreat from Reconstruction, 1869–1879*. Baton Rouge: Louisiana State University Press, 1979.

Gobat, Michael. *Empire by Invitation: William Walker and Manifest Destiny in Central America*. Cambridge, MA: Harvard University Press, 2018.

Goetzmann, William H. *Army Exploration in the American West, 1803–1863*. New Haven: Yale University Press, 1959.

Goldfield, David. "Searching for the Sunbelt." *OAH Magazine of History* 18 (October 2003): 3- 4.

———. "Writing the Sunbelt." *OAH Magazine of History* 18 (October 2003): 5–10.

Gonzales, Phillip B. *Política: Nuevomexicanos and American Political Incorporation, 1821– 1910*. Lincoln: University of Nebraska Press, 2016.

Gonzalez-Day, Ken. *Lynching in the West, 1850–1935*. Durham: Duke University Press, 2006.

Goodyear, Frank H. "'Beneath the Shadow of Her Flag': Philip A. Bell's *The Elevator* and the Struggle for Enfranchisement, 1865–1870." *California History* 78, no. 1 (Spring 1999): 26–39.

Gordon, Linda. *The Second Coming of the KKK: The Ku Klux Klan of the 1920s and the American Political Tradition*. New York: Liveright, 2017.

Gordon, Sarah Barringer. *The Mormon Question: Polygamy and Constitutional Conflict in Nineteenth-Century America*. Chapel Hill: University of North Carolina Press, 2002.

Gordon, Sarah Barringer, and Jan Shipps. "Fatal Convergence in the Kingdom of God: The Mountain Meadows Massacre in American History." *Journal of the Early Republic* 37 (Summer 2017): 307–47.

Graebner, Norman A. *Empire on the Pacific: A Study in American Continental Expansion*. 1955. Reprint, Claremont, CA: Regina Books, 1983.

Greenberg, Amy S. *Manifest Manhood and the Antebellum American Empire*. New York: Cambridge University Press, 2005.

———. *A Wicked War: Polk, Clay, Lincoln, and the 1846 U.S. Invasion of Mexico*. New York: Vintage, 2012.

Greenly, Albert H. "Camels in America." *The Papers of the Bibliographical Society of America* 46 (Winter 1952): 336–55.

Griswold del Castillo, Richard. *The Los Angeles Barrio, 1850–1890: A Social History.* Berkeley: University of California Press, 1982.

Guelzo, Allen C. *Fateful Lightning: A New History of the Civil War and Reconstruction.* Oxford: Oxford University Press, 2012.

Guinn, James M. "How California Escaped State Division." *Annual Publication of the Historical Society of Southern California,* (1905): 223–32.

Guterl, Matthew Pratt. *American Mediterranean: Southern Slaveholders in the Age of Emancipation.* Cambridge, MA: Harvard University Press, 2008.

———. "Slavery and Capitalism: A Review Essay." *Journal of Southern History* 81 (May 2015): 405–19.

Gyory, Andrew. *Closing the Gate: Race Politics, and the Chinese Exclusion Act.* Chapel Hill: University of North Carolina Press, 1998.

Hackel, Steve W. *Children of Coyote, Missionaries of Saint Francis: Indian-Spanish Relations in Colonial California, 1769–1850.* Chapel Hill: University of North Carolina Press, 2005.

Hafen, LeRoy R. *The Overland Mail.* Norman: University of Oklahoma Press, 2004. First published 1926 by Arthur H. Clarke.

Hafen, P. Jane. "The Being and Place of a Native American Mormon." In *New Genesis: A Mormon Reader on Land and Community,* edited by Terry Tempest Williams, William B. Smart, and Gibbs M. Smith, 35–41. Layton, Utah: Gibbs Smith, 1998.

Hahn, Steven. "Capitalists All!" *Reviews in American History* 11 (June 1983): 219–25.

———. *A Nation under Our Feet: Black Political Struggles in the Rural South from Slavery to the Great Migration.* Cambridge, MA: Belknap, 2003.

———. *A Nation without Borders: The United States and Its World, 1830–1910.* New York: Viking, 2016.

———. *The Political Worlds of Slavery and Freedom.* Cambridge, MA: Harvard University Press, 2009.

———. *The Roots of Southern Populism: Yeoman Farmers and the Transformation of the Georgia Upcountry, 1850–1890.* New York: Oxford University Press, 1983.

———. "Slave Emancipation, Indian Peoples and the Projects of a New American Nation- State." *Journal of the Civil War Era* 3, no. 3 (September 2013): 307–30.

Hall, Martin Hardwick. "Colonel James Reily's Diplomatic Missions to Chihuahua and Sonora." *New Mexico Historical Review* 31, no. 3 (July 1956): 232–42.

———. "The Mesilla Times: A Journal of Confederate Arizona." *Arizona and the West* 5 (Winter 1963): 337–51.

———. *Sibley's New Mexico Campaign.* Austin: University of Texas Press, 1960.

Hämäläinen, Pekka. *The Comanche Empire.* New Haven: Yale University Press, 2008.

———. "Reconstructing the Great Plains: The Long Struggle for Sovereignty and Dominance in the Heart of the Continent." *Journal of the Civil War Era* 6, no. 4 (December 2016): 481–509.

Hammond, John Craig. "The 'High-Road to a Slave Empire': Conflict and the
    Growth and Expansion of Slavery on the North American Continent." In *The
    World of the Revolutionary American Republic: Land, Labor, and the Conflict for
    a Continent*, edited by Andrew Shankman, 346–69. New York: Routledge,
    2014.
———. "Slavery, Sovereignty, and Empires: North American Borderlands and
    the American Civil War, 1660–1860." *Journal of the Civil War Era* 4, no. 2
    (June 2014): 264–98.
Hardy, B. Carmon. "Lords of Creation: Polygamy, the Abrahamic Household, and
    Mormon Patriarchy." *Journal of Mormon History* 20, no. 1 (Spring 1994): 119–52.
Hardy, William E. "South of the Border: Ulysses S. Grant and the French Inter-
    vention." *Civil War History* 54, no. 1 (2008): 63–83.
Harlow, Luke E. *Religion, Race, and the Making of Confederate Kentucky, 1830–
    1880*. Cambridge: Cambridge University Press, 2014.
Hart, Charles Desmond. "Why Lincoln Said 'No': Congressional Attitudes on
    Slavery Expansion, 1860–1861." *Social Science Quarterly* 49 (December 1986):
    732–41.
Hart, John Mason. *Empire and Revolution: The Americans in Mexico since the Civil
    War*. Berkeley: University of California Press, 2002.
———. *Revolutionary Mexico: The Coming and Process of the Mexican Revolution*.
    Berkeley: University of California Press, 1987.
Haynes, Stephen R. *Noah's Curse: The Biblical Justification of American Slavery*.
    New York: Oxford University Press, 2002.
Heizer, Robert F. "Indian Servitude in California." In *Handbook of North Ameri-
    can Indians*, vol. 4, *History of Indian-White Relations*, edited by Wilcomb E.
    Washburn, 414–16. Washington, DC: Smithsonian, 1988.
Hernandez, Kelly Lytle. *City of Inmates: Conquest, Rebellion, and the Rise of
    Human Caging in Los Angeles, 1771–1965*. Chapel Hill: University of North Caro-
    lina Press, 2017.
Herring, George. *From Colony to Superpower: American Foreign Relations since
    1776*. New York: Oxford University Press, 2008.
Heyrman, Christine Leigh. *Southern Cross: The Beginnings of the Bible Belt*.
    Chapel Hill: University of North Carolina Press, 1997.
Hietala, Thomas R. *Manifest Design: American Exceptionalism and Empire*.
    Ithaca: Cornell University Press, 2003.
Hill, Marvin S. "The Rise of Mormonism in the Burned-Over District: Another
    View." *New York History* 61 (October 1980): 411–30.
Hittell, Theodore H. *History of California*. 4 vols. San Francisco: N. J. Stone, 1885–
    1897.
Hodder, Frank Heywood. "The Railroad Background of the Kansas-Nebraska
    Act." *Mississippi Valley Historical Review* 12 (June 1925): 3–22.
Holt, Michael F. *The Fate of Their Country: Politicians, Slavery Extension, and the
    Coming of the Civil War*. New York: Hill and Wang, 2005.
———. *The Political Crisis of the 1850s*. Rev. ed. New York: W. W. Norton, 1983.
Hopkins, A. G. *American Empire: A Global History*. Princeton: Princeton Univer-
    sity Press, 2018.

Horne, Gerald. *The Deepest South: The United States, Brazil, and the African Slave Trade*. New York: New York University Press, 2007.

Howe, Daniel Walker. *What Hath God Wrought: The Transformation of America, 1815–1848*. Oxford: Oxford University Press, 2007.

Hulbert, Matthew Christopher. *The Ghosts of Guerrilla Memory: How Civil War Bushwhackers Became Gunslingers in the American West*. Athens: University of Georgia Press, 2016.

Hull, Dorothy. "The Movement in Oregon for the Establishment of a Pacific Coast Republic." *Oregon Historical Quarterly* 17 (September 1916): 177–200.

Hunt, Aurora. *The Army of the Pacific: Its Operations in California, Texas, Arizona, New Mexico, Utah, Nevada, Oregon, Washington, Plains Region, Mexico, etc., 1860–1866*. Glendale, CA: Arthur H. Clark, 1951.

Hunt, Rockwell D. "History of the California State Division Controversy." *Annual Publication of the Historical Society of Southern California* 13 (1924): 37–53.

Hurtado, Albert. *Indian Survival on the California Frontier*. New Haven: Yale University Press, 1988.

Huston, James L. *Calculating the Value of the Union: Slavery, Property Rights, and the Economic Origins of the Civil War*. Chapel Hill: University of North Carolina Press, 2003.

Igler, David. *The Great Ocean: Pacific Worlds from Captain Cook to the Gold Rush*. New York: Oxford University Press, 2013.

Inscoe, John C. *Mountain Masters: Slavery and the Sectional Crisis in Western North Carolina*. Knoxville: University of Tennessee Press, 1989.

Inskeep, Steve. *Imperfect Union: How Jessie and John Frémont Mapped the West, Invented Celebrity, and Helped Cause the Civil War*. New York: Penguin, 2020.

Isenberg, Andrew C., and Thomas Richards Jr. "Alternative Wests: Rethinking Manifest Destiny." *Pacific Historical Review* 86, no. 1 (2017): 4–17.

Jacoby, Karl. *Shadows at Dawn: An Apache Massacre and the Violence of History*. New York: Penguin, 2008.

Janney, Caroline. *Burying the Dead but Not the Past: Ladies' Memorial Associations and the Lost Cause*. Chapel Hill: University of North Carolina Press, 2008.

Jarnagin, Laura. *A Confluence of Transatlantic Networks: Elites, Capitalism, and Confederate Migration to Brazil*. Tuscaloosa: University of Alabama Press, 2008.

Jewell, James Robbins. "Thwarting Southern Schemes and British Bluster in the Pacific Northwest." In *Civil War Wests: Testing the Limits of the United States*, edited by Adam Arenson and Andrew R. Graybill, 15–32. Oakland: University of California Press, 2015.

John, Richard R. *Spreading the News: The American Postal System from Franklin to Morse*. Cambridge, MA: Harvard University Press, 1995.

Johnson, Benjamin Heber. "Reconstructing North America: Louis Riel, Juan Cortina, and Borderlands in the Age of National Consolidation." In *Remaking North American Sovereignty*, edited by Jewel Spangler and Frank Towers, 200–19. New York: Fordham University Press, 2020.

Johnson, David Alan. *Founding the Far West: California, Oregon, and Nevada, 1840–1890*. Berkeley: University of California Press, 1992.

Johnson, Susan Lee. *Roaring Camp: The Social World of the California Gold Rush.* New York: W. W. Norton, 2000.

Johnson, Walter. "The Pedestal and the Veil: Rethinking the Capitalism/Slavery Question." *Journal of the Early Republic* 24 (Summer 2004): 299–308.

———. *River of Dark Dreams: Slavery and Empire in the Cotton Kingdom.* Cambridge, MA: Harvard University Press, 2013.

———. *Soul by Soul: Life inside the Antebellum Slave Market.* Cambridge, MA: Harvard University Press, 1999.

Jones, Sondra. "'Redeeming' the Indian: The Enslavement of Indian Children in New Mexico and Utah." *Utah Historical Quarterly* 67 (Summer 1999): 220–41.

———. *The Trial of Don Pedro Leon Lujan: The Attack against Indian Slavery and Mexican Traders in Utah.* Salt Lake City: University of Utah Press, 2000.

Josephy, Alvin M., Jr. *The Civil War in the American West.* New York: Vintage, 1991.

Jung, Moon-Ho. *Coolies and Cane: Race, Labor, and Sugar in the Age of Emancipation.* Baltimore: Johns Hopkins University Press, 2009.

Kagan, Robert. *Dangerous Nation: America and the World, 1600–1898.* New York: Vintage, 2006.

Karp, Matthew J. "Slavery and American Sea Power: The Navalist Impulse in the Antebellum South." *Journal of Southern History* 77 (May 2011): 283–324.

———. *This Vast Southern Empire: Slaveholders at the Helm of American Foreign Policy.* Cambridge, MA: Harvard University Press, 2016.

———. "The World the Slaveholders Craved: Proslavery Internationalism in the 1850s." In *The World of the Revolutionary American Republic: Land, Labor, and the Conflict for a Continent*, edited by Andrew Shankman. New York: Routledge, 2014.

Keehn, David C. *Knights of the Golden Circle: Secret Empire, Southern Secession, Civil War.* Baton Rouge: Louisiana State University Press, 2013.

Keliher, Macabe. "Anglo-American Rivalry and the Origins of U.S. China Policy." *Diplomatic History* 31, no. 2 (April 2007): 227–57.

Kellogg, Deren Early. "Lincoln's New Mexico Patronage: Saving the Far Southwest for the Union." *New Mexico Historical Review* 75, no. 4 (2000): 511–33.

Kelman, Ari. *For Liberty and Empire: How the Civil War Bled into the Indian Wars.* New York: Basic Books, forthcoming.

———. *A Misplaced Massacre: Struggling over the Memory of Sand Creek.* Cambridge, MA: Harvard University Press, 2013.

Kiser, William S. *The Borderlands of Slavery: The Struggle over Captivity and Peonage in the American Southwest.* Philadelphia: Penn Press, 2017.

———. *Coast to Coast Empire: Manifest Destiny in the Nineteenth-Century New Mexico Borderlands.* Norman: University of Oklahoma Press, 2018.

———. *Turmoil on the Rio Grande: History of the Mesilla Valley, 1846–1865.* College Station: Texas A&M University Press, 2011.

Knight, Alan. "Debt Bondage in Latin America." In *Slavery: And Other Forms of Unfree Labor*, edited by Leonie Archer, 102–17. New York: Routledge, 2013.

Kohler, Charmaine Lay. *Southern Grace: A Story of the Mississippi Saints.* Boise, ID: Beagle Creek Press, 1995.

Kornweibel, Theodore, Jr. "Railroads and Slavery." *Railroad History* 189 (Fall/Winter 2003): 34-59.

Kramer, Paul A. *The Blood of Government: Race, Empire, the United States, and the Philippines.* Chapel Hill: University of North Carolina Press, 2006.

Krauthamer, Barbara. *Black Slaves, Indian Masters: Slavery, Emancipation, and Citizenship in the Native American South.* Chapel Hill: University of North Carolina Press, 2015.

Kreitner, Richard. *Break It Up: Secession, Division, and the Secret History of America's Imperfect Union.* New York: Little, Brown, 2020.

Krick, Robert E. L. *Staff Officers in Gray: A Biographical Register of the Staff Officers in the Army of Northern Virginia.* Chapel Hill: University of North Carolina Press, 2003.

Kupperman, Karen Ordahl. *The Jamestown Project.* Cambridge, MA: Harvard University Press, 2007.

Kvach, John F. *De Bow's Review: The Antebellum Vision of a New South.* Lexington: University Press of Kentucky, 2013.

LaFeber, Walter. *The New Empire: An Interpretation of American Expansion, 1860–1898.* 1963. Reprint, Ithaca: Cornell University Press, 1998.

Lamar, Howard R. *The Far Southwest, 1846–1912: A Territorial History.* 1966. Reprint, Albuquerque: University of New Mexico Press, 2000.

———. "From Bondage to Contract: Ethnic Labor in the American West, 1600–1890." In *The Countryside in the Age of Capitalist Transformation: Essays in the Social History of Rural America,* edited by Steven Hahn and Jonathan Prude, 293–323. Chapel Hill: University of North Carolina Press, 1985.

Lapp, Rudolph M. *Archy Lee: A California Fugitive Slave Case.* Berkeley: Heyday, 1969.

———. *Blacks in Gold Rush California.* New Haven: Yale University Press, 1977.

Larson, Andrew. *I Was Called to "Dixie": The Virgin River Basin: Unique Experiences on Mormon Pioneering.* St. George, Utah: Dixie College Foundation, 1992.

Larson, John Lauritz. *Internal Improvement: National Public Works and the Promise of Popular Government in the Early Untied States.* Chapel Hill: University of North Carolina Press, 2001.

Lassiter, Matthew D. *The Silent Majority: Suburban Politics in the Sunbelt South.* Princeton: Princeton University Press, 2007.

Lassiter, Matthew D., and Joseph Crespino, eds. *The Myth of Southern Exceptionalism.* New York: Oxford University Press, 2009.

Lavender, David. *The American Heritage History of the Great West.* New York: American Heritage, 1965.

Levine, Bruce. *The Fall of the House of Dixie: The Civil War and the Social Revolution that Transformed the South.* New York: Random House, 2012.

———. *Half Slave and Half Free: The Roots of Civil War.* New York: Hill and Wang, 1992.

Lew-Williams, Beth. *The Chinese Must Go: Violence, Exclusion, and the Making of the Alien in America.* Cambridge, MA: Harvard University Press, 2018.

Licht, Walter. *Industrializing America: The Nineteenth Century.* Baltimore: Johns Hopkins University Press, 1995.

Limerick, Patricia Nelson, Clyde Milner II, and Charles E. Rankin, eds. *Trails: Toward a New Western History.* Lawrence: University Press of Kansas, 1991.

Lindsay, Brendan C. *Murder State: California's Native American Genocide, 1846–1873.* Lincoln: University of Nebraska Press, 2015.

Long, E. B. *The Saints and the Union: Utah Territory during the Civil War.* Urbana: University of Illinois Press, 1981.

Lyman, Edward Leo. "The Rise and Decline of Mormon San Bernardino." *Southern California Quarterly* 65 (Winter 1983): 321–39.

———. *San Bernardino: The Rise and Fall of a California Community.* Salt Lake City: Signature Books, 1996.

Lynch, Daniel. "On the Edge of Empires, Republics, and Identities: De la Guerra's Sword of the War and the California Native Cavalry." In *Empire and Liberty: The Civil War and the West,* edited by Virginia Scharff, 105–21. Berkeley: University of California Press, 2015.

Lythgoe, Dennis L. "Negro Slavery and Mormon Doctrine." *Western Humanities Review* 21 (Fall 1967): 327–38.

———. "Negro Slavery in Utah." *Utah Historical Quarterly* 39 (Winter 1971): 40–54.

MacKinnon, William P. "Loose in the Stacks: A Half Century with the Utah War and Its Legacy." *Dialogue: A Journal of Mormon Thought* 40, no. 1 (Spring 2007): 43–81.

Madley, Benjamin. *An American Genocide: The United States and the California Indian Catastrophe.* New Haven: Yale University Press, 2016.

Magliari, Michael. "Free Soil, Unfree Labor: Cave Johnson Couts and the Binding of Indian Workers in California, 1850–1867." *Pacific Historical Review* 73, no. 3 (August 2004): 349–90.

———. "Free State Slavery: Bound Indian Labor and Slave Trafficking in California's Sacramento Valley, 1850–1864." *Pacific Historical Review* 81, no. 2 (2012): 155–92.

Maizlish, Stephen E. *A Strife of Tongues: The Compromise of 1850 and the Ideological Foundations of the American Civil War.* Charlottesville: University of Virginia Press, 2018.

Majewski, John. *Modernizing a Slave Economy: The Economic Vision of the Confederate Nation.* Chapel Hill: University of North Carolina Press, 2009.

Majewski, John, and Todd W. Wahlstrom. "Geography as Power: The Political Economy of Matthew Fontaine Maury." *Virginia Magazine of History and Biography* 120, no. 4 (2012): 340–71.

Mancall, Peter C. *Fatal Journey: The Final Expedition of Henry Hudson.* New York: Basic Books, 2009.

Mapp, Paul W. *The Elusive West and the Contest for Empire, 1713–1763.* Chapel Hill: University of North Carolina Press, 2011.

Marrs, Aaron W. *Railroads in the Old South: Pursuing Progress in a Slave Society.* Baltimore: Johns Hopkins University Press, 2009.

Martin, Bonnie, and James F. Brooks, eds. *Linking the Histories of Slavery: North America and Its Borderlands.* Santa Fe: School for Advanced Research, 2015.

Marx, Leo. *The Machine in the Garden: Technology and the Pastoral Ideal in America.* Oxford: Oxford University Press, 1964.

Masich, Andrew E. *The Civil War in Arizona: The Story of the California Volunteers, 1861- 1865*. Norman: University of Oklahoma Press, 2006.

———. *Civil War in the Southwest Borderlands, 1861–1867*. Norman: University of Oklahoma Press, 2017.

Matthews, Glenna. *The Golden State in the Civil War: Thomas Starr King, the Republican Party, and the Birth of Modern California*. Cambridge: Cambridge University Press, 2012.

Mauss, Armand L. *All Abraham's Children: Changing Mormon Conceptions of Race and Lineage*. Urbana: University of Illinois Press, 2003.

Maxwell, John Gary. *The Civil War Years in Utah: The Kingdom of God and the Territory That Did Not Fight*. Norman: University of Oklahoma Press, 2016.

May, Robert E. "The Irony of Confederate Diplomacy: Visions of Empire, the Monroe Doctrine, and the Quest for Nationhood." *Journal of Southern History* 83 (February 2017): 69–106.

———. *John A. Quitman: Old South Crusader*. Baton Rouge: Louisiana State University Press, 1995.

———. *Manifest Destiny's Underworld: Filibustering in Antebellum America*. Chapel Hill: University of North Carolina Press, 2004.

———. *Slavery, Race, and Conquest in the Tropics: Lincoln, Douglas, and the Future of Latin America*. Cambridge: Cambridge University Press, 2013.

———. *The Southern Dream of a Caribbean Empire*. 1973. Reprint, Gainesville: University Press of Florida, 2002.

McAfee, Ward M. "California's House Divided." *Civil War History* 33, no. 2 (1987): 115–30.

McCaslin, Richard B. "Bitter Legacy: The Battle Front." In *The Civil War and Reconstruction in Indian Territory*, edited by Bradley R. Clampitt, 19–37. Lincoln: University of Nebraska Press, 2015.

McCormick, Thomas J. *The China Market: America's Quest for Informal Empire, 1893–1901*. Chicago: University of Chicago Press, 1967.

McCoy, Drew R. *The Elusive Republic: Political Economy in Jeffersonian America*. Chapel Hill: University of North Carolina Press, 1980.

McCurdy, Charles W. "Prelude to Civil War: A Snapshot of the California Supreme Court at Work in 1858." *California Supreme Court Historical Society Yearbook* 1 (1994): 33–54.

McCurry, Stephanie. *Confederate Reckoning: Power and Politics in the Civil War South*. Cambridge, MA: Harvard University Press, 2010.

———. *Masters of Small Worlds: Yeoman Households, Gender Relations, and the Political Culture of the Antebellum South Carolina Low Country*. New York: Oxford University Press, 1995.

McGinty, Brian. *Archy Lee's Struggle for Freedom: The True Story of California Gold, the Nation's Tragic March Toward Civil War, and a Young Black Man's Fight for Liberty*. Guilford, CT.: Lyons, 2020.

McGrath, Roger. "A Violent Birth: Disorder, Crime and Law Enforcement, 1849–1890." In *Taming the Elephant: Politics, Government, and Law in Pioneer California*, edited by John F. Burns and Richard J. Orsi, 27–73. Berkeley: University of California Press, 2003.

McPherson, Hallie M. "The Plan of William McKendree Gwin for a Colony in North Mexico, 1863–1865." *Pacific Historical Review* 2, no. 4 (December 1933): 357–86.

McPherson, James. *Battle Cry of Freedom*. New York: Ballantine, 1989.

———. *Embattled Rebel: Jefferson Davis as Commander in Chief*. New York: Penguin, 2014.

Meacham, Jon. *American Lion: Andrew Jackson in the White House*. New York: Random House, 2008.

Meinig, D. W. *Continental America, 1800–1867*. Vol. 2 of *The Shaping of America*. New Haven, CT: Yale University Press, 1993.

Miles, Tiya. "The Long Arm of the South?" *Western Historical Quarterly* 43 (Fall 2012): 274–81.

———. *Ties That Bind: The Story of an Afro-Cherokee Family in Slavery and Freedom*. Berkeley: University of California Press, 2006.

Monroy, Douglas. *Thrown among Strangers: The Making of Mexican Culture in Frontier California*. Berkeley: University of California Press, 1990.

Montoya, Maria E. "The Not-So-Free Labor in the American Southwest." In *Empire and Liberty: The Civil War and the West*, edited by Virginia Scharff, 159–74. Berkeley: University of California Press, 2015.

Moody, Ralph. *Stagecoach West*. New York: Thomas Y. Crowell, 1967.

Moore, Shirley Ann Wilson. *Sweet Freedom's Plains: African Americans on the Overland Trails, 1841–1869*. Norman: University of Oklahoma Press, 2016.

———. "'We Feel the Want of Protection': The Politics of Law and Race in California, 1848–1878." In *Taming the Elephant: Politics, Government, and Law in Pioneer California*, edited by John F. Burns and Richard J. Orsi, 96–125. Berkeley: University of California Press, 2003.

Mora, Anthony. *Border Dilemmas: Racial and National Uncertainties in New Mexico, 1848–1912*. Durham: Duke University Press, 2011.

Moretti, Connie Walton. *Dixie Manor Days: The Confederate Veterans Who Lived There and the UDC Members Who Made It Possible*. Redondo Beach, CA: Mulberry Bush Publishing, 2004.

Morrison, Michael A. *Slavery and the American West: The Eclipse of Manifest Destiny and the Coming of the Civil War*. Chapel Hill: University of North Carolina Press, 1997.

Morrison, Samuel Eliot. "Boston Traders in the Hawaiian Islands, 1789–1823." *Proceedings of the Massachusetts Historical Society* 54 (October 1920): 9–47.

Mueller, Max Perry. *Race and the Making of the Mormon People*. Chapel Hill: University of North Carolina Press, 2017.

Murphy, Lawrence. "Antislavery in the Southwest: William G. Kephart's Mission to New Mexico, 1850–1853." *Southwestern Studies* 54 (1978): 1–56.

Murray, Keith. "Movement for Statehood in Washington." *Pacific Northwest Quarterly* 32 (October 1914): 349–84.

Nelson, Megan Kate. "The Civil War from Apache Pass." *Journal of the Civil War Era* 6, no. 4 (December 2016): 510–35.

———. "Death in the Distance: Confederate Manifest Destiny and the Campaign for New Mexico, 1861–1862." In *Civil War Wests: Testing the Limits of the United*

States, edited by Adam Arenson and Andrew R. Graybill, 33–52. Oakland: University of California Press, 2015.

———. *The Three-Cornered War: The Union, the Confederacy, and Native Peoples in the Fight for the West.* New York: Scribner, 2020.

Nelson, Scott Reynolds. *Iron Confederacies: Southern Railways, Klan Violence, and Reconstruction.* Chapel Hill: University of North Carolina Press, 1999.

———. *A Nation of Deadbeats: An Uncommon History of America's Financial Disasters.* New York: Alfred A. Knopf, 2012.

Newell, Quincy. *Your Sister in the Gospel: The Life of Jane Manning James, a Nineteenth-Century Black Mormon.* New York: Oxford University Press, 2019.

Nichols, James David. "The Line of Liberty: Runaway Slaves and Fugitive Peons in the Texas-Mexico Borderlands." *Western Historical Quarterly* 44, no. 4 (Winter 2013): 413–33.

Nickerson, Michelle, and Darren Dochuk, eds. *Sunbelt Rising: The Politics of Space, Place, and Region.* Philadelphia: University of Pennsylvania Press, 2014.

Niven, John. *John C. Calhoun and the Price of Union.* Baton Rouge: Louisiana State University Press, 1988.

Nokes, R. Gregory. *The Troubled Life of Peter Burnett: Oregon Pioneer and First Governor of California.* Corvallis: Oregon State University Press, 2018.

Novak, William J. "The Myth of the 'Weak' American State." *American Historical Review* 113, no. 3 (June 2008): 752–72.

Nugent, Walter. *Habits of Empire: A History of American Expansion.* New York: Vintage, 2008.

Oakes, James. "Capitalism and Slavery and the Civil War." *International Labor and Working- Class History* 89 (Spring 2016): 195–220.

———. *Freedom National: The Destruction of Slavery in the United States, 1861–1865.* New York: W. W. Norton, 2013.

———. *The Ruling Race: A History of American Slaveholders.* New York: Norton, 1982.

O'Brien, Michael. *Conjectures of Order: Intellectual Life and the American South.* 2 vols. Chapel Hill: University of North Carolina Press, 2010.

Okihiro, Gary. *Island Worlds: A History of Hawaii and the United States.* Berkeley: University of California Press, 2008.

Onuf, Peter S. *Jefferson's Empire: The Language of American Nationhood.* Charlottesville: University Press of Virginia, 2000.

Paddison, Joshua. *American Heathens: Religion, Race, and Reconstruction in California.* San Marino: University of California Press and the Huntington Library, 2012.

Paludan, Phillip Shaw. "War Is the Health of the Party: Republicans in the American Civil War." In *The Birth of the Grand Old Party: The Republicans' First Generation,* edited by Robert F. Engs and Randall M. Miller, 60–80. Philadelphia: University of Pennsylvania Press, 2002.

Paolino, E. N. *Foundations of the American Empire: William Henry Seward and United States Foreign Policy.* Ithaca: Cornell University Press, 1973.

Parish, John C. "A Project for a California Slave Colony in 1851." *Huntington Library Bulletin* 8 (October 1935): 171–75.

Park, Benjamin E. *Kingdom of Nauvoo: The Rise and Fall of a Religious Empire on the American Frontier.* New York: Liveright, 2020.

Park, Joseph F. "The Apaches in Mexican-Indian Relations, 1848–1861: A Footnote to the Gadsden Treaty." *Arizona and the West* 3 (Summer 1961): 129–46.

Parrish, William E. "The Mississippi Saints." *Historian* 50, no. 4 (August 1988): 489–506.

Pascoe, Peggy. *What Comes Naturally: Miscegenation Law and the Making of Race in America.* New York: Oxford University Press, 2009.

Peck, Gunther. *Reinventing Free Labor: Padrones and Immigrant Workers in the North American West, 1880–1930.* Cambridge: Cambridge University Press, 2000.

Perrine, Fred S. "Uncle Sam's Camel Corps." *New Mexico Historical Review* 1, no. 4 (October 1926): 434–44.

Pfeifer, Michael J. "At the Hands of Parties Unknown? The State of the Field of Lynching Scholarship." *Journal of American History* 101, no. 3 (December 2014): 832–46.

———. *The Roots of Rough Justice: Origins of American Lynching.* Urbana: University of Illinois Press, 2011.

———. *Rough Justice: Lynching and American Society, 1874–1947.* Urbana: University of Illinois Press, 2006.

———, ed. *Lynching beyond Dixie: American Mob Violence outside the South.* Urbana: University of Illinois Press, 2013.

Phillips, Christopher. *The Rivers Ran Backward: The Civil War and the Remaking of the American Middle Border.* New York: Oxford University Press, 2016.

Phillips, George Harwood. "Indians in Los Angeles, 1781–1875: Economic Integration, Social Disintegration." *Pacific Historical Review* 49, no. 3 (August 1980): 427–51.

Phillips, Ulrich B. "The Central Theme of Southern History." *American Historical Review* 34, no. 1 (October 1928): 30–43.

———. *A History of Transportation in the Eastern Cotton Belt to 1860.* 1908. Reprint, Columbia: University of South Carolina Press, 2011.

Pitt, Leonard. *The Decline of the Californios: A Social History of the Spanish-Speaking Californians, 1846–1890.* Berkeley: University of California Press, 1971.

Platt, Stephen R. *Autumn in the Heavenly Kingdom: China, the West, and the Epic Story of the Taiping Civil War.* New York: Vintage, 2012.

Pletcher, David M. *The Diplomacy of Involvement: American Economic Expansion across the Pacific, 1784–1900.* Columbia: University of Missouri Press, 2001.

Poll, Richard D., and William P. MacKinnon. "Causes of the Utah War Reconsidered." *Journal of Mormon History* 20 (Fall 1994): 16–44.

Pope, James Gray. "Contract, Race, and Freedom of Labor in the Constitutional Law of 'Involuntary Servitude.'" *Yale Law Journal* 119, no. 7 (May 2010): 1474–1567.

Potter, David M. *The Impending Crisis, 1848–1861.* Completed and edited by Don E. Fehrenbacher. New York: Harper and Row, 1976.

Powell, William S., ed. *Dictionary of North Carolina Biography.* Chapel Hill: University of North Carolina Press, 1986.

Proudman, Mark F. "Words for Scholars: The Semantics of Imperialism." *Journal of the Historical Society* 8, no. 3 (September 2008): 395–433.

Quigley, Paul. *Shifting Grounds: Nationalism and the American South, 1848–1865.* New York: Oxford University Press, 2011.

Quinn, Arthur. *The Rivals: William Gwin, David Broderick, and the Birth of California.* New York: Crown, 1994.

Reeve, W. Paul. *Religion of a Different Color: Race and the Mormon Struggle for Whiteness.* Oxford: Oxford University Press, 2015.

Reeve, W. Paul, Christopher Rich, and Lajean Caruth. *"Enough to Cause the Angels in Heaven to Blush": Race, Servitude, and Priesthood among the Mormons.* Forthcoming.

Reiter, Tonya. "Redd Slave Histories: Family, Race, and Sex in Pioneer Utah." *Utah Historical Quarterly* 85, no. 2 (Spring 2017): 108–26.

Reséndez, Andrés. *Changing National Identities at the Frontier: Texas and New Mexico, 1800- 1850.* New York: Cambridge University Press, 2004.

———. *The Other Slavery: The Uncovered Story of Indian Enslavement in America.* New York: Houghton Mifflin Harcourt, 2016.

Rich, Christopher B., Jr. "The True Policy for Utah: Servitude, Slavery, and 'An Act in Relation to Service.'" *Utah Historical Quarterly* 80 (Winter 2012): 54–74.

Richards, Leonard. *The California Gold Rush and the Coming of the Civil War.* New York: Vintage, 2007.

———. *The Slave Power: The Free North and Southern Domination, 1780–1860.* Baton Rouge: Louisiana State University Press, 2000.

Richards, Thomas, Jr. *Breakaway Americas: The Unmanifest Future of the Jacksonian United States.* Baltimore: Johns Hopkins University Press, 2020.

———. "'Farewell to America': The Expatriation Politics of Overland Migration, 1841–1846." *Pacific Historical Review* 86, no. 1 (2017): 114–52.

Richardson, Heather Cox. *How the South Won the Civil War: Oligarchy, Democracy, and the Continuing Fight for the Soul of America.* New York: Oxford University Press, 2020.

———. *West from Appomattox: The Reconstruction of America after the Civil War.* New Haven: Yale University Press, 2007.

Richter, Daniel K. *Facing East from Indian Country: A Native History of Early America.* Cambridge, MA: Harvard University Press, 2001.

Riddleberger, Patrick W. *1866: The Critical Year Revisited.* Carbondale: Southern Illinois University Press, 1979.

Rippy, J. Fred. "The Negotiation of the Gadsden Treaty." *Southwestern Historical Quarterly* 27 (July 1923): 1–26.

Roberson, Jere W. "To Build a Pacific Railroad: Congress, Texas, and the Charleston Convention of 1854." *Southwestern Historical Quarterly* 78 (October 1974): 117–39.

———. "The South and the Pacific Railroad, 1845–1855." *Western Historical Quarterly* 5 (April 1974): 163–86.

Robinson, John W. "A California Copperhead: Henry Hamilton and the Los Angeles Star." *Arizona and the West* 23 (Fall 1981): 213–30.

———. "Colonel Edward J. C. Kewen: Los Angeles' Fire-Eating Orator of the Civil War Era." *Southern California Quarterly* 61 (Summer 1979): 159–81.

———. *Los Angeles in Civil War Days, 1860–1865*. New ed. Norman: University of Oklahoma Press, 2013.

Rockman, Seth. "What Makes the History of Capitalism Newsworthy?" *Journal of the Early Republic* 32 (Fall 2014): 439–66.

Ronda, James P., ed. *Thomas Jefferson and the Changing West: From Conquest to Conservation*. Albuquerque: University of New Mexico Press, 1997.

Rosenburg, R. B. *Living Monuments: Confederate Soldiers' Homes in the New South*. Chapel Hill: University of North Carolina Press, 1993.

Rosenthal, Caitlin. *Accounting for Slavery: Masters and Management*. Cambridge, MA: Harvard University Press, 2018.

Rothman, Adam. *Slave Country: American Expansion and the Origins of the Deep South*. Cambridge, MA: Harvard University Press, 2005.

———. "The 'Slave Power' in the United States, 1783–1865." In *Ruling America: A History of Wealth and Power in a Democracy*, edited by Steve Fraser and Gary Gerstle, 64–91. Cambridge, MA: Harvard University Press, 2005.

Rowland, Donald E. *John Rowland and William Workman: Southern California Pioneers of 1841*. Spokane: Arthur Clark, 1999.

Roy, William G. *Socializing Capital: The Rise of the Large Industrial Corporation in America*. Princeton: Princeton University Press, 1997.

Rugemer, Edward B. *The Problem of Emancipation: The Caribbean Roots of the American Civil War*. Baton Rouge: Louisiana State University Press, 2008.

Russel, Robert R. "Constitutional Doctrines with Regard to Slavery in Territories." *Journal of Southern History* 32 (November 1966): 466–86.

———. *Improvement of Communication with the Pacific Coast as an Issue in American Politics, 1783–1864*. Cedar Rapids: Torch Press, 1948.

Sainlaude, Stève. *France and the American Civil War*. Chapel Hill: University of North Carolina Press, 2019.

Salyer, Lucy E. *Laws Harsh as Tigers: Chinese Immigrants and the Shaping of Modern Immigration Law*. Chapel Hill: University of North Carolina Press, 1995.

Saunt, Claudio. *Unworthy Republic: The Dispossession of Native Americans and the Road to Indian Territory*. New York: W. W. Norton, 2020.

Savage, Kirk. *Standing Soldiers, Kneeling Slaves: Race, War, and Monument in Nineteenth- Century America*. New ed. Princeton: Princeton University Press, 2018.

Saxton, Alexander. *The Indispensable Enemy: Labor and the Anti-Chinese Movement in California*. Berkeley: University of California Press, 1971.

Scharff, Virginia, ed. *Empire and Liberty: The Civil War and the West*. Berkeley: University of California Press, 2015.

Schermerhorn, Calvin. *The Business of Slavery and the Rise of American Capitalism, 1815–1860*. New Haven: Yale University Press, 2015.

Schlesinger, Arthur Meier. "The State Rights Fetish." In *New Viewpoints in American History*. New ed., 220–44. New York: Macmillan, 1961.

Schmidt, Louis Bernard. "Manifest Opportunity and the Gadsden Purchase." *Arizona and the West* 3 (Autumn 1961): 245–64.

Schoen, Brian. *The Fragile Fabric of Union: Cotton, Federal Politics, and the Global Origins of the Civil War.* Baltimore: Johns Hopkins University Press, 2009.

Schroeder, John H. *Shaping a Maritime Empire: The Commercial and Diplomatic Role of the American Navy, 1829–1861.* Westport, CT: Greenwood Press, 1985.

Schulman, Bruce J. *From Cotton Belt to Sunbelt: Federal Policy, Economic Development, and the Transformation of the South, 1938–1980.* Durham: Duke University Press, 1994.

Schulten, Susan. "The Civil War and the Origins of the Colorado Territory." *Western Historical Quarterly* 44 (Spring 2013): 21–46.

Seeley, John Robert. *The Expansion of England: Two Courses of Lectures.* New ed. Cambridge: Cambridge University Press, 2010.

Sellers, Charles Grier, Jr. *James K. Polk, Continentalist: 1843–1848.* Princeton: Princeton University Press, 1966.

———. *Market Revolution: Jacksonian America, 1815–1846.* New York: Oxford University Press, 1991.

———. "Who Were the Southern Whigs?" *American Historical Review* 59, no. 2 (January 1954): 335–46.

Sexton, Jay. *The Monroe Doctrine: Empire and Nation in Nineteenth-Century America.* New York: Farrar, Straus and Giroux, 2011.

———. "William H. Seward in the World." *Journal of the Civil War Era* 4, no. 3 (September 2014): 398–430.

Shelden, Rachel A. *Washington Brotherhood: Politics, Social Life, and the Coming of the Civil War.* Chapel Hill: University of North Carolina Press, 2013.

Shelden, Rachel. "The Politics of Continuity and Change in the Long Civil War Era." *Civil War History* 65, no. 4 (December 2019): 319–41.

Shipps, Jan. *Mormonism: The Story of a New Religious Tradition.* Urbana: University of Illinois Press, 1985.

Shuck, Oscar Tully, ed. *History of the Bench and Bar of California.* Los Angeles: Commercial Printing House, 1901.

Simpson, Craig M. *A Good Southerner: The Life of Henry A. Wise of Virginia.* Chapel Hill: University of North Carolina Press, 2001.

Sinha, Manisha. *The Counterrevolution of Slavery: Politics and Ideology in Antebellum South Carolina.* Chapel Hill: University of North Carolina Press, 2000.

Skowronek, Stephen. *Building a New American State: The Expansion of National Administrative Capacities, 1877–1920.* Cambridge: Cambridge University Press, 1982.

Smith, Adam I. P. *The Stormy Present: Conservatism and the Problem of Slavery in Northern Politics, 1846–1865.* Chapel Hill: University of North Carolina Press, 2017.

Smith, Henry Nash. *Virgin Land: The American West as Symbol and Myth.* New ed. Cambridge, MA: Harvard University Press, 1970.

Smith, Mark. *Debating Slavery: Economy and Society in the Antebellum American South.* Cambridge: Cambridge University Press, 1998.

———. *Mastered by the Clock: Time, Slavery, and Freedom in the American South.*
Chapel Hill: University of North Carolina Press, 1997.

Smith, Stacey L. "Beyond North and South: Putting the West in the Civil War and
Reconstruction." *Journal of the Civil War Era* 6, no. 4 (December 2016): 566–91.

———. "*Dred Scott* on the Pacific: African Americans, Citizenship, and Subject-
hood in the North American West." *Southern California Quarterly* 100 (Spring
2018): 44–68.

———. "Emancipating Peons, Excluding Coolies: Reconstructing Coercion in the
American West." In *The World the Civil War Made*, edited by Gregory P. Downs
and Kate Masur, 46–74. Chapel Hill: University of North Carolina Press, 2015.

———. *Freedom's Frontier: California and the Struggle over Unfree Labor, Emancipation, and Reconstruction.* Chapel Hill: University of North Carolina Press,
2013.

———. "Remaking Slavery in a Free State: Masters and Slaves in Gold Rush California." *Pacific Historical Review* 80, no. 1 (February 2011): 28–63.

Smith, Wallace. *Garden of the Sun: A History of the San Joaquin Valley, 1772–1939.*
2nd ed. Fresno, CA: Linden, 2004.

Snyder, Christina. *Slavery in Indian Country: The Changing Face of Captivity in
Early America.* Cambridge, MA: Harvard University Press, 2010.

Spence, Jonathan D. *God's Chinese Son: The Taiping Heavenly Kingdom of Hong
Xiuquan.* New York: W. W. Norton, 1996.

Spitzzeri, Paul R. "Judge Lynch in Session: Popular Justice in Los Angeles,
1850–1875." *Southern California Quarterly* 87 (Summer 2005): 83–122.

Stanley, Amy Dru. *From Bondage to Contract: Wage Labor, Marriage, and the
Market in the Age of Slave Emancipation.* Cambridge: Cambridge University
Press, 1998.

Stanley, Gerald. "The Politics of the Antebellum Far West: The Impact of the
Slavery and Race Issues in California." *Journal of the West* 16 (1977): 19–25.

———. "'The Whim and Caprice of a Majority in a Petty State': The 1867 Election
in California." *Pacific Historian* 24 (1980): 443–55.

———. "Senator William Gwin: Moderate or Racist?" *California Historical Society
Quarterly* 50 (September 1971): 243–55.

Stanley, Matthew E. *The Loyal West: Civil War and Reunion in Middle America.*
Urbana: University of Illinois Press, 2017.

Starr, Kevin. *Americans and the California Dream, 1850–1915.* Oxford: Oxford
University Press, 1973.

Stegmaier, Mark J. "A Law That Would Make Caligula Blush? New Mexico Territory's Unique Slave Code, 1859–1861." *New Mexico Historical Review* 87, no. 2
(Spring 2012): 209–42.

Stiles, T. J. *The First Tycoon: The Epic Life of Cornelius Vanderbilt.* New York:
Alfred A. Knopf, 2009.

St. John, Rachel. *Line in the Sand: A History of the Western U.S.-Mexico Border.*
Princeton: Princeton University Press, 2011.

———. "The Unpredictable America of William Gwin: Expansion, Secession, and
the Unstable Borders of Nineteenth-Century North America." *Journal of the
Civil War Era* 6, no. 1 (March 2016): 56–84.

Summers, Mark Wahlgren. *The Ordeal of the Reunion: A New History of Recon-struction*. Chapel Hill: University of North Carolina Press, 2014.

Sunseri, Alvin R. *Seeds of Discord: New Mexico in the Aftermath of the American Conquest, 1846–1861*. Chicago: Nelson-Hall, 1979.

Taylor, Quintard. *In Search of the Racial Frontier: African Americans in the American West*. New York: W. W. Norton, 1998.

Teitelman, Emma. "The Properties of Capitalism: Industrial Enclosures in the South and West after the American Civil War." *Journal of American History* 106, no. 4 (March 2020): 879–900.

Teng, Yuan Chung. "American China-Trade, American-Chinese Relations and the Taiping Rebellion, 1853–1858." *Journal of Asian History* 3, no. 2 (1969): 93–117.

Thiriot, Amy Tanner. *Slavery in Zion: A Documentary and Genealogical History of Black Lives and Black Servitude in Utah Territory, 1847–1862*. Salt Lake City: University of Utah Press, forthcoming.

Thomas, Benjamin, ed. "A Threatened Invasion of California." *California Historical Society Quarterly* 13 (March 1934): 38–42.

Thomas, Emory. *The Confederate Nation, 1861–1865*. New York: Harper and Row, 1979.

Thomas, Lately. *Between Two Empires: The Life Story of California's First Senator, William McKendree Gwin*. Boston: Houghton Mifflin, 1969.

Thomas, William G. *The Iron Way: Railroads, the Civil War, and the Making of Modern America*. New Haven: Yale University Press, 2011.

Torget, Andrew J. *Seeds of Empire: Cotton, Slavery, and the Transformation of the Texas Borderlands, 1800–1850*. Chapel Hill: University of North Carolina Press, 2015.

Torres-Rouff, David Samuel. *Before L.A.: Race Space, and Municipal Power in Los Angeles, 1781–1894*. New Haven: Yale University Press, 2013.

Towers, Frank. "Partisans, New History, and Modernization: The Historiography of the Civil War's Causes, 1861–2011." *Journal of the Civil War Era* 1, no. 2 (June 2011): 237–64.

———. *The Urban South and the Coming of the Civil War*. Charlottesville: University of Virginia Press, 2004.

Truett, Samuel. *Fugitive Landscapes: The Forgotten History of the U.S.-Mexico Borderlands*. New Haven: Yale University Press, 2008.

———. "The Ghosts of Frontiers Past: Making and Unmaking Space in the Borderlands." *Journal of the Southwest* 46, no. 2 (Summer 2004): 309–50.

Utley, Robert M. *Frontiersmen in Blue: The United States Army and the Indian, 1848–1865*. Lincoln: University of Nebraska Press, 1967.

Van Hoak, Stephen P. "And Who Shall Have the Children? The Indian Slave Trade in the Southern Great Basin, 1800–1865." *Nevada Historical Society Quarterly* 41, no. 1 (Spring 1998): 3–25.

Varon, Elizabeth R. *Disunion! The Coming of the American Civil War, 1789–1859*. Chapel Hill: University of North Carolina Press, 2008.

Venit-Shelton, Tamara. "'A More Loyal, Union Loving People Can Nowhere Be Found': Squatters' Rights, Secession Anxiety, and the 1861 'Settlers' War' in San Jose." *Western Historical Quarterly* 41 (Winter 2010): 473–94.

———. *A Squatter's Republic: Land and the Politics of Monopoly in California, 1850–1900*. Berkeley: University of California Press, 2013.

Waite, Kevin, "Jefferson Davis and Proslavery Visions of Empire in the Far West." *Journal of the Civil War Era* 6, no. 4 (December 2016): 536–65.

———. "The 'Lost Cause' Goes West: Confederate Culture and Civil War Memory in California." *California History* 97, no. 1 (February 2020): 33–49.

———. "War in Indian Country." In *Cambridge History of the American Civil War*, edited by Aaron Sheehan-Dean, 1:576–600. New York: Cambridge University Press, 2019.

———. "The West and Reconstruction after the American Civil War." In *The Oxford Handbook on Reconstruction*, edited by Andrew L. Slap. New York: Oxford University Press, 2021.

Waldie, D. J. "'We Have Been and Are Yet Secessionist'—Los Angeles When the Civil War Began." *Lost LA*, KCET, July 10, 2017. https://www.kcet.org/shows/lost-la/we-have-been-and-are- yet-secessionist-los-angeles-when-the-civil-war-began#_edn33.

Waldrep, Christopher. *Roots of Disorder: Race and Criminal Justice in the American South, 1817–80*. Urbana: University of Illinois Press, 1998.

Walters, Helen B. "Confederates in Southern California." *Historical Society of Southern California Quarterly* 35 (March 1953): 41–54.

Warde, Mary Jane. *When the Wolf Came: The Civil War and the Indian Territory*. Fayetteville: University of Arkansas Press, 2013.

Warren, Louis. *Buffalo Bill's America: William Cody and the Wild West Show*. New York: Vintage, 2006.

Watford, W. H. "Confederate Western Ambitions." *Southwestern Historical Quarterly* 44 (October 1940): 161–87.

———. "The Far-Western Wing of the Rebellion, 1861–1865." *California Historical Society Quarterly* 34 (June 1955): 125–48.

Weber, Devra. *Dark Sweat, White Gold: California Farm Workers, Cotton, and the New Deal*. Berkeley: University of California Press, 1994.

Weber, Jennifer L. *Copperheads: The Rise and Fall of Lincoln's Opponents in the North*. New York: Oxford University Press, 2008.

Weeks, William Earl. *Building the Continental Empire: American Expansion from Revolution to the Civil War*. Chicago: Ivan R. Dee, 1996.

West, Elliott. *The Contested Plains: Indians, Goldseekers, and the Rush to Colorado*. Lawrence: University Press of Kansas, 1998.

———. *Creating the West, 1848–1880*. Lincoln: University of Nebraska Press, 2021.

———. "The Future of Reconstruction Studies: Reconstruction in the West." *Journal of the Civil War Era* 7, no. 1 (March 2017): 14.

———. *The Last Indian War: The Nez Perce Story*. Oxford: Oxford University Press, 2009.

———. "Reconstructing Race." *Western Historical Quarterly* 34, no. 1 (Spring 2003): 6–26.

White, Richard. *"It's Your Misfortune and None of My Own": A New History of the American West*. Norman: University of Oklahoma Press, 1991.

———. *Railroaded: The Transcontinentals and the Making of Modern America.* New York: W. W. Norton, 2011.

———. *The Republic for Which It Stands: The United States during Reconstruction and the Gilded Age, 1865–1896.* New York: Oxford University Press, 2017.

Williams, David A. "California Democrats of 1860: Division, Disruption, Defeat." *Southern California Quarterly* 55 (Fall 1973): 239–52.

Williams, Eric. *Capitalism and Slavery.* 1944. Reprint, Chapel Hill: University of North Carolina Press, 1994.

Williams, John Hoyt. *A Great and Shining Road: The Epic Story of the Transcontinental Railroad.* Lincoln: University of Nebraska Press, 1988.

Williams, Rusty. *My Old Confederate Home: A Respectable Place for Civil War Veterans.* Lexington: University Press of Kentucky, 2010.

Williams, William Appleman. *Empire as a Way of Life: An Essay on the Causes and Character of America's Past Predicament along with a Few Thoughts about an Alternative.* Oxford: Oxford University Press, 1980.

———. *The Roots of the Modern American Empire: A Study of the Growth and Shaping of Social Consciousness in a Marketplace Society.* New York: Random House, 1969.

———. *The Tragedy of American Diplomacy.* 1959. Reprint, New York: W. W. Norton, 2009.

Wilson, Charles Reagan. *Baptized in Blood: The Religion of the Lost Cause, 1865–1920.* Athens: University of Georgia Press, 1980.

Wilson, John Albert. *History of Los Angeles County, California, with Illustrations Descriptive of Its Scenery, Residences, Fine Blacks and Manufactories.* Oakland: Thompson and West, 1880.

Winfrey, Dorman H. "The Butterfield Overland Mail Trail." In *Along the Early Trails of the Southwest*, 32–44. Austin: Pemberton Press, 1969.

Woods, Michael E. "Antebellum Camel Capers and the Global Slave Power." In *Animal Histories of the Civil War Era*, edited by Earl J. Hess. Baton Rouge: Louisiana State University Press, forthcoming.

———. *Arguing until Doomsday: Stephen Douglas, Jefferson Davis, and the Struggle for American Democracy.* Chapel Hill: University of North Carolina Press, 2020.

———. *Bleeding Kansas: Slavery, Sectionalism, and Civil War on the Missouri-Kansas Border.* New York: Routledge, 2016.

———. "The Compromise of 1850 and the Search for a Usable Past." *Journal of the Civil War Era* 9, no. 3 (September 2019): 438–56.

———. "The Dark Underbelly of Jefferson Davis's Camels." *Muster: The Blog of the Journal of the Civil War Era*, November 21, 2017. https://journalofthecivilwar era.org/2017/11/dark-underbelly-jefferson-daviss-camels/.

Woodward, Walter Carleton. *The Rise and Early History of Political Parties in Oregon, 1843–1868.* Portland: J. K. Gill, 1914.

Woolsey, Ronald C. "Disunion or Dissent? A New Look at an Old Problem in Southern California Attitudes toward the Civil War." *Southern California Quarterly* 66 (Fall 1984): 185–205.

———. *Migrants West: Toward the Southern California Frontier.* Sebastopol, CA: Grizzly Bear Publishing, 1996.

——. "The Politics of a Lost Cause: 'Seceshers' and Democrats in Southern California during the Civil War." *California History* 69, no. 4 (Winter 1990/1991): 372–83.

Wright, Doris Marion. "The Making of Cosmopolitan California: An Analysis of Immigration, 1848–1870." *California Historical Society Quarterly* 19 (December 1940): 323–43.

Wright, Gavin. *Slavery and American Economic Development.* Baton Rouge: Louisiana State University Press, 2006.

Wunder, John R., and Joann M. Ross, eds. *The Nebraska-Kansas Act of 1854.* Lincoln: University of Nebraska Press, 2008.

Wyatt-Brown, Bertram. *Southern Honor: Ethics and Behavior in the Old South.* New York: Oxford University Press, 1982.

Yanochik, Mark A., Mark Thornton, and Bradley T. Ewing. "Railroad Construction and Antebellum Slave Prices." *Social Science Quarterly* 84 (September 2003): 723–37.

Yokota, Kariann Akemi. "Transatlantic and Transpacific Connections in Early American History." *Pacific Historical Review* 83, no. 2 (May 2014): 204–19.

Young, Elliott. *Alien Nation: Chinese Migration in the Americas from the Coolie Era through World War II.* Chapel Hill: University of North Carolina Press, 2014.

Young, Phoebe S. K (née Kropp). *California Vieja: Culture and Memory in a Modern American Place.* Berkeley: University of California Press, 2006.

Zesch, Scott. *The Chinatown War: Chinese Los Angeles and the Massacre of 1871.* New York: Oxford University Press, 2012.

——. "Chinese Los Angeles in 1870–71: The Makings of a Massacre." *Southern California Quarterly* 90 (Summer 2008): 109–58.

Unpublished Material

Bloss, Roy. "Senator Defiled." Unpublished manuscript. Bancroft Library, University of California, Berkeley, 1973.

Brettle, Adrian. "The Fortunes of War: Confederate Expansionist Ambitions during the American Civil War." PhD diss., University of Virginia, 2014.

Campbell, Joseph. "The Abode of Chivalry: Rebels, Rowdies, and Ricos in Secessionist Southern California." Undergraduate thesis, Durham University, 2019.

Castro, Robert F. "Liberty Like Thunder: Law, History, and the Emancipatory Politics of Reconstruction America." PhD diss., University of Michigan, 2003.

Cotterill, Robert Spencer. "Improvement of Transportation in the Mississippi Valley, 1845–1850." PhD diss., University of Wisconsin, 1919.

Dunning, David Michael. "The Southern Perception of the Trans-Mississippi West, 1845–1853." PhD diss., University of Illinois at Urbana-Champaign, 1995.

Fraga, Sean. "Ocean Fever: Water, Trade, and the Terraqueous Pacific Northwest." PhD diss., Princeton University, 2019.

Freeman, Ron. "James Madison Flake." Unpublished paper, 2011.

Hart, Charles Ralph Desmond. "Congressmen and the Expansion of Slavery into the Territories: A Study in Attitudes, 1846–1861." PhD diss., University of Washington, 1965.

Kitchen, Richard D. "Mormon-Indian Relations in Deseret: Intermarriage and Indenture, 1847- 1877." PhD diss., Arizona State University, 2002.

Lewis, Albert Lucian. "Los Angeles in the Civil War Decades, 1850–1868." PhD diss., University of Southern California, 1970.

Lutzweiler, James. "The Fierce 1845–1861 Sectional Competition for the Footprint of the First Transcontinental Railroad." Unpublished manuscript, 2011, in author's possession.

Lynch, Daniel Brendan. "Southern California Chivalry: The Convergence of Southerners and Californios in the Far Southwest, 1846–1866." PhD diss., University of California, Los Angeles, 2015.

Maggard, Alicia. "One Nation under Steam: Technopolitics, Steam Navigation, and the Rise of American Industrial Power." PhD diss., Brown University, 2019.

Malone, Thomas E. "The Democratic Party in California, 1865–1868." MA thesis, Stanford University, 1949.

McGrath, A. Hope. "An Army of Working-Men: Military Labor and the Construction of American Empire, 1865–1915." PhD diss., University of Pennsylvania, 2016.

McPherson, Hallie M. "William McKendree Gwin, Expansionist." PhD diss., University of California, Berkeley, 1931.

Norwood, Dael. "Trading in Liberty: The Politics of the American China Trade, c. 1784–1862." PhD diss., Princeton University, 2012.

Pena, Manuel. "The Implications of Slavery and Cotton on Sino-American Commercial Relations." Undergraduate thesis, Durham University, 2019.

Powell, Etta Olive. "Southern Influences in California Politics before 1864." MA thesis, University of California, Berkeley, 1929.

Rael-Gálvez, Estèven. "Identifying Captivity and Capturing Identity: Narratives of American Indian Slavery, Colorado and New Mexico, 1776–1934." PhD diss., University of Michigan, 2002.

Rappel-Kroyzer, Or. "The California Democratic Party on the Eve of the Civil War—Anatomy of Failure." MA thesis, Tel Aviv University, 2019.

Rodriguez, Sarah. "'Children of the Great Mexican Family': Anglo-American Immigration to Texas and the Making of the American Empire, 1820–1861." PhD diss., University of Pennsylvania, 2015.

Stanley, Gerald. "The Republican Party in California, 1856–1868." PhD diss., University of Arizona, 1973.

Teitelman, Emma. "Governing the Peripheries: The Social Reconstruction of the South and West after the American Civil War." PhD diss., University of Pennsylvania, 2018.

Thompson, William F. "The Political Career of Milton Slocum Latham of California." PhD diss., Stanford University, 1952.

Wallace, Clare. "Cameron Erskine Thom." Municipal Reference Library Records, Los Angeles, 1938.

INDEX

abolitionism: in Arizona, 153, 155; in California, 36, 37–38, 93, 95, 98–102, 113–14, 116–18, 122, 271n29; Frederick Douglass on, 213; Milton S. Latham on, 289n69; and Lost Cause, 225; in Mexico, 32, 45, 103, 138; and Mormons, 126–27; in New Mexico, 135; in North, 16; southern opposition to, 17, 124. *See also* antislavery activists

Accessory Transit Company, 68

Adams, John Quincy, 115

African Americans: advancement of, 208; in *Birth of a Nation*, 240; California limiting rights of, 94, 95, 97, 98–99, 101, 113, 118, 122, 221, 228, 237; California reinstating rights of, 202, 209, 229; California's attempts to ban immigration, 44–45, 94, 95, 109, 118, 219; civil rights campaigns of, 229–36, 239; Democratic Party exploiting anxieties of white voters, 8; emigration to British Columbia, 118–19, 277nn128–129; as free black labor, 213; freedom in Mexico, 253n35; and Lost Cause, 225–26; as Mormons, 129, 281n30; in Republican Party of California, 113–14, 302n60; suffrage of, 216, 218, 219–20, 223, 226–27, 228, 230; and voter registration, 228; in West, 93, 94, 212

Alabama, 241

Alabama (Confederate ship), 241

Alcatraz Island, 198, 200

Alexandria Gazette, 81, 153

Alta California, 176, 198, 232

American exceptionalism, 246

American Railroad Journal, 48

Anti-Chinese Convention, 231

antislavery activists: of California, 97, 99, 100–101, 116, 120, 121, 272n47; collective purpose of, 7; on debt peonage, 146; of Kansas, 153; on Mormons, 129; of New Mexico, 135–36, 140; on Slave Power, 125, 279n5; on slavery in West, 6, 10, 271n29; violence toward, 2, 99, 113

Apaches: and Butterfield Overland Mail Road, 83, 175; Chiricahua band of, 84, 152, 175, 193–94; Chokonen band of, 175, 194; Confederate attempts to exterminate, 194–95; Confederate enslavement of, 194, 195; Mescalero Apaches, 215; raids in northern Mexico, 84, 142, 206; raids in Southwest, 176–77, 194; relations with US military, 175; during secession crisis, 173; and transcontinental transportation projects, 64, 83; US forces fighting, 202

Apachería, 83, 175

Arapaho people, 195

Ardmore, Oklahoma, 307n8

Arizona: Apache raids in, 194; Chiricahua Apaches in, 152; Confederate Arizona, 168, 169, 171, 172, 173, 175–76, 181, 183, 190–91, 206, 208, 292n12, 294n56; Confederate invasions of, 8, 177, 190, 241; Confederate monuments in, 241; Confederate threat neutralized in, 201, 208; cotton cultivation in, 139, 153, 154; and Crittenden Compromise, 162; in Desert South, 10; Doña Ana County, 152; enslaved African Americans in, 151, 154, 246; Hispanos of, 153, 290n79; Jefferson Davis Highway in, 241; legalized slavery in, 163, 250n8; martial law in, 208; militia of, 168; mining in, 151, 153, 181, 190, 246, 283n78; Native American laborers in, 154; and New Mexico's slave code, 152, 154, 168; proslavery agenda embraced in, 3, 151–55; secessionist movement in, 7, 149, 167, 177, 191, 201, 275n92, 290n79; secession of, 167–68, 169, 173, 176, 245; separatist movements in, 2, 3, 7, 149–51, 155, 164; southern allegiances in, 88, 140, 149, 151; southernization of, 151–55; territorial constitution of, 154; territorial movement of, 152, 167, 245; and transcontinental railroad, 50, 153, 154; Union forces in, 175–76, 294n56; Unionists of, 190; and US-Mexico War, 26; white southern migrants in, 4, 151–54. *See also* Mesilla, Arizona; Tucson, Arizona

Arkansas, 62, 168, 241

Arlington, Virginia, 240

Armistead, Lewis, 184